PRINCIPLES OF AMERICAN

LAW ENFORCEMENT

AND

CRIMINAL JUSTICE

(Third Printing)

Principles of American Law Enforcement and Criminal Justice

By

WILLIAM J. BOPP, M.A.

*Assistant Professor of
Criminal Justice and Director
of the Criminal Justice Program,
Florida Atlantic University
Boca Raton, Florida
Formerly
Dade County (Florida) Public Safety Department
Oakland (California) Police Department*

and

DONALD O. SCHULTZ, M.P.A.

*Instructor in Police Science
Broward Community College
Fort Lauderdale, Florida
Formerly
Orange (California) Police Department*

CHARLES C THOMAS • PUBLISHER
Springfield • Illinois • U.S.A.

Published and Distributed Throughout the World by

CHARLES C THOMAS ● PUBLISHER

BANNERSTONE HOUSE

301-327 East Lawrence Avenue, Springfield, Illinois, U.S.A.

©*1972, by* CHARLES C THOMAS ● PUBLISHER

ISBN 0-398-02236-4

Library of Congress Catalog Card Number: 78-180804

First Printing, 1972
Second Printing, 1974
Third Printing, 1975

With THOMAS BOOKS *careful attention is given to all details of manufacturing and design. It is the Publisher's desire to present books that are satisfactory as to their physical qualities and artistic possibilities and appropriate for their particular use.* THOMAS BOOKS *will be true to those laws of quality that assure a good name and good will*

Printed in the United States of America

00-2

Dedicated to the Patrolmen

PREFACE

This book introduces students to law enforcement and criminal justice studies. The major emphasis herein is on law enforcement, for the police element is by far the dominant criminal justice component, if for no other reasons than sheer volume of work, gross manpower employed, and college student majors. There is probably more information here than can or should be presented in an introductory course, but we feel that a great mass of material should be contained in a basic text in order to allow individual professors to make the decision about what should be emphasized to their students, rather than the authors.

The book was written with the student in mind, in language that can easily be understood and related to field work. No greater compliment could be paid to the work than to label it a *practical undertaking*. It has been our belief that other introductory texts place too much emphasis on subjective values, while presupposing an academic sophistication that most beginning students simply to not possess.

The book is a three-part undertaking. Part I is a rather substantial chronology of policing in this country, beginning with the pre-American experience (which is not as contradictory as it sounds, considering that foreign law enforcement served as a foundation for our system) and ending with the events of the past decade. We feel that a large dose of pertinent history is indispensable to the overall intellectual development of law enforcement students in their march toward professional status. Unlike other texts, a full historical experience is presented, again to allow professors to determine the extent of classroom coverage and the areas to be emphasized. All introductory books contain some police history, but too often "Peelian reform" merits more space than the whole history of American policing. Strangely absent, even in those books that devote a full chapter to our history, is any coverage of law enforcement during the past century. It is as if an entire hundred-year period has been expunged from the records. Perhaps the prevailing academic view holds that a substantive historical undertaking is unnecessary in an introductory text. Obviously, we do not agree! Part I has been reprinted as a separate book, entitled *A Short History of American Law Enforcement,* underscoring the importance that we and the publisher attach to the subject.

There is a widely held belief that of all the issues facing criminal justice agencies—the police, the courts, and correctional institutions—none is more critical than the problem of isolation. Criminal justice agencies are not only isolated from each other but from the communities they have sworn to serve. Consequently, there is a need to look upon criminal justice agencies not as a group of institutions engaged in semirelated activities, but as functional components in a system that most surely will break down without interagency cooperation, meaningful interaction, constant communication, and a mutual understanding of the philosophies and roles of each component. Part II studies the recognized components of criminal justice and the phenomenon of crime, nonpunitive community involvement in the system, and criminal justice education, to which a full chapter is devoted. Although professors constantly decry the "isolationist impulse" of related agencies, few community organizations are as isolated as institutions of higher learning, especially universities. To end the interagency isolation, academia must first end its isolation, a problem that will be overcome when professors begin regarding their departments as criminal justice components, rather than merely extraneous elements.

Part III spans the wide spectrum of policing, emphasizing municipal law enforcement, but not to the exclusion of county, state, and Federal enforcement. The study covers the police service today—both structure and process. The section introduces law enforcement students to (1) the broad field of law enforcement, (2) coursework encountered in college curricula, and (3) the various field and administrative assignments that policemen may expect to receive during their careers.

The Appendix again points up our emphasis on practicality. Contained therein are a library guide and a brief discourse on writing research papers, along with other material.

The upcoming decades will be a time of great challenge for

persons seeking careers in criminal justice agencies; but it will also be a time of substantial personal enrichment, though not great financial rewards, for the field does not offer that. We hope that students will fondly recall this book as the first step in a long, successful, rewarding career in criminal justice.

William J. Bopp
Donald O. Schultz

ACKNOWLEDGMENTS

Particular gratitude is expressed to the several hundred police departments who at our request forwarded their histories, their annual reports, photographs, and material on contemporary programs. We are especially indebted to the four score criminal justice professors who assisted us in our work by responding to queries on what they would like to see in an introductory text. Many of their suggestions are contained in this book.

Colleagues to whom we owe a great deal for their timely assistance are Leon McKim, Central Piedmont Community College; Frank P. Alberico, Joliet Junior College; Wesley Brown, Jr., Northern Arizona University; C. Pershing Bell, Meramec Community College; Fred R. DeFrancesch, Loyola University of New Orleans; Frank E. Collier, San Antonio College. Lander C. Hamilton, Northern Virginia Community College; and Bernard C. Brown, University of Louisville.

Our thanks go to the American Bar Association, which kindly allowed us to reprint in the Appendix a glossary of legal terms compiled by the ABA, and for furnishing us with a booklet entitled *Law and Courts in the News,* on which we leaned heavily while writing Chapter 15. We are also grateful to the United States Chamber of Commerce for permitting us to use in Chapter 20 material on citizen-related criminal justice programs contained in *Marshalling Citizen Power Against Crime,* a Chamber publication.

Sincere appreciation is extended to the library staff at Florida Technological University for assisting us in our research, and to Judy Reed and Dale Crowe for correcting and typing the manuscript.

Space limitations constrain us from listing all the people who assisted us in our work. This we regret! But two very special contributors must be acknowledged. Only those who have published a book will understand the deep debt of gratitude we owe to Sharon Bopp and Pat Schultz, without whose patience and understanding this book would not have been written.

CONTENTS

PART I

A HISTORY OF AMERICAN LAW ENFORCEMENT

PART II

THE CRIMINAL JUSTICE SYSTEM

Chapter

PART III

ELEMENTS OF LAW ENFORCEMENT

PRINCIPLES OF AMERICAN

LAW ENFORCEMENT

AND

CRIMINAL JUSTICE

PART I

A HISTORY OF AMERICAN

LAW ENFORCEMENT

Upper part of the pillar upon which the legendary Code of Hammurabi was inscribed.

Chapter 1

BACKGROUNDS AND BEGINNINGS (TO 1607)

The history of American law enforcement is fairly short, if dated from the first enduring English settlement in the early seventeenth century. Since then, only some three centuries and threescore years have passed—a period that can be spanned by the overlapping lives of five or six men. But of course the American story actually begins many centuries before the New World was colonized. Accordingly, it will do well to review briefly certain early foreign developments.

THE EARLY EXPERIENCE

Since ancient times man has tried to develop methods of dealing with individuals who committed acts deemed harmful to their communities. The basic concept of law enforcement can be traced back to the dawn of history, where tribal customs embodied the idea of mutual protection through law and order. In essence, the people were the first police, and no other kind was necessary. Intertribal crime was often handled through retaliatory measures (branding, torture, disfigurement) initiated by the aggrieved party—assuming he had survived—or his family. This early type of enforcement led to the idea of *kin police,* whereby the responsibility for obtaining justice rested with a victim's family.[1]

Mesopotamia (Iraq), in a far-reaching innovation, promulgated a succession of legal codes, of which the most famous was the *Code of Hammurabi,* named after the King of Babylon (1947 B.C.–1905 B.C.). The code, engraved on a pillar of stone, specified laws governing the conduct of the King's subjects. It contained provisions on crimes of sex and personal violence, a law against sorcery, and a scale of penalties for violations of each

---

[1]A. C. Germann, Frank D. Day, and Robert R. J. Gallati, *Introduction To Law Enforcement and Criminal Justice* (Springfield: Charles C Thomas, Publisher, 1970), p. 39.

5

provision. The *Code of Hammurabi* was comprised of some 4,000 lines of writing which were preceded by a poetic prologue of one long sentence that ended with the lofty phrase: "Law and justice I establish in the land and promote the welfare of the people." The code shows a certain systematic order. Beginning with accusation of murder and sorcery, it passes through all grades of social and domestic life, ending with a scale of wages for all classes of workmen, even the lowliest. The three essential features of the code may be clearly defined. First, it was based on individual responsibility under the law. Hence, if a free man destroyed the eye of another, his eye would be destroyed. The second essential feature of the code was the belief in the sanctity of the oath before God, and the third was the absolute necessity of written evidence in all legal matters.

The early Greek city states saw some developments in the dual areas of law and enforcement. In 593 B.C. Solon was elected chief magistrate of Athens, whereupon he initiated a series of fundamental reforms, including the prohibition of slavery for indebtedness, the division of the population into classes based on property, and the granting of full citizenship to even the lowest classes. By this time the law of the land was being *written.* The administration of justice was the responsibility of the Heliaea, juries chosen by lot from among 6,000 representatives of the Athenian tribes. Aggrieved parties took their claims to the Heliasts, who voted in secret ballot for conviction or acquittal. The law specified that in no case would a trial last more than one day.[2]

The most significant innovations, however, were made by the Romans. The development of law is perhaps the greatest of Roman achievements and one that probably best survived into modern times. According to tradition, the legal affairs of ancient Rome were in the hands of patrician magistrates who had succeeded the kings. In the fifth Century B.C. the people demanded the publication of the laws and the abolition of patrician privileges. In response to public pressure, a committee of ten distinguished citizens compiled a code based on Roman customs, and in 451 B.C. it was set up on ten bronze or wooden tablets in the

[2]Wallace K. Ferguson and Geofrey Bruun, *Ancient Times To 1520,* 4th ed. (Boston: Houghton Mifflin Company, 1969), pp. 28-29.

Forum. Two more tablets were added a year later. These twelve tablets formed the basis of Roman civil law. The opening passage of the code placed the responsibility for enforcement of the law in the hands of individual citizens and in the courts:[3]

> If a man is summoned to court and does not go, let witnesses be called and then let the plaintiff seize him. If he resists or runs away, let the plaintiff lay hands on him. If he is ill or aged, let the plaintiff provide an animal to carry him.

During the time of the Roman Empire the sources of law developed and changed in various ways. The most important enactments were *leges* (legislation), which were rules laid down by the emperor, or pronouncements of the assembly. Decrees passed by a majority vote of the Senate were called *senatus consulta.* It was also customary for consuls, magistrates, and governors to issue edicts on taking office, giving their interpretation of the law and the action they would take or permit in various circumstances. In 27 B.C. a military police unit, The Praetorian Guard, was created to maintain security at the emperor's palace. The emperor later created the first nonmilitary police force by forming the Vigiles of Rome, a group of a thousand or so men whose job it was to keep peace in the city and to fight fires. The edicts of individual Roman magistrates were exhibited in the Forum and, although each one only affected the issuing magistrate, it became usual for other magistrates to adopt most of a predecessor's edicts. In 130 A.D. the emperor instructed jurists to codify this praetorian law into permanent law under the title *Edictum Perpetuum.*[4]

ANGLO-SAXON CONTRIBUTIONS

In 500 A.D., when the Germanic tribes (Anglo-Saxons) from central Europe invaded England, they brought with them a tribal police system which was strange to a land which for four hundred years had been subject to Roman influence. Germanic law, unlike that of the Romans, was not a result of governmental legislation, but was made up of customs of the tribe and was generally unwritten. There was no studied effort to sift through the facts of a case as had been done in Roman courts. Instead, an appeal was

---

[3]John Liversidge, *Britain in the Roman Empire* (New York: Frederick Praeger, Publisher, 1968), p. 295.

[4]*Ibid.*, pp. 295-296.

made to the gods to decide the issue. The burden of proof was on the accused to clear himself, this being done in one of three ways:[5]

> **By compurgation.** The defendant would try to exonerate himself by taking a solemn oath that he did not commit the offense in question. Friends or relatives were often hired as "oath helpers" to aid the accused. The defendant and his "witnesses" were made to recite an exact oath, and if the slightest slip was made in reciting the words, the adjudication was "guilty."
>
> **Trial by ordeal.** In cases where the oath was judged to be insufficient to prove innocence, the accused had to clear himself by undergoing a painful ordeal, such as thrusting his hand into a pot of boiling water to retrieve a small object, or carrying a red-hot poker in his hand for twenty paces. Upon completion of the ordeal, the injured hand was wrapped for three days and if after that time it appeared to be healing properly, then the defendant was found innocent.
>
> **Trial by combat.** In some cases a formal duel was arranged between the defendant and his accuser. Trial by combat was usually reserved for the more affluent, who had their champions fight for them. If a defendant's champion was killed, then the accused was adjudged guilty and he paid a fine.

Eventually, however, the barbaric culture of the Anglo-Saxons fused with the more civilized Latin culture to create a medieval system of law enforcement which was, in many ways, unique. In time, two important principles emerged. First was the conception that wherever the king was present, wrongdoing was particularly serious. No unlawfulness should disturb the king's peace lest the perpetrator "be made to make twofold compensation." Gradually the idea of the special nature of the king's peace was to grow until one need but commit an offense anywhere in the realm to *disturb the peace* of the king. The second conception was that all the king's subjects in some way belonged to him. The king was entitled to special compensation if a free man was killed or injured, for he enjoyed the king's protection. The free man, or *churl,* was the prototype of the yeoman, the free farmer who—within the law and subject only to his duty to his king—was master of his own fate. Much of Anglo-Saxon society was founded on this basis. The practice of trying violators of the law in the name of the Crown is

---

[5]*Supra* note 2, p. 99.

still alive in England today. It has been passed on to America where men are tried by the state in lieu of individual plaintiffs.[6]

THE CAPITULARIES OF CHARLEMAGNE

In the eighth century A.D., Charlemagne founded an empire in France which was based on two forces: one material—military supremacy; the other moral—religion. A collection of legislative acts or customs, the *Capitularies of Charlemagne,* were passed in 785 A.D. They were the combined work of people and king, providing penalties for crimes and articulating procedures to be followed by government.in its dealings with the citizenry. Enforcement of the acts rested with feudal lords who ruled geographical entities known as *contes* (counties). In 875 A.D. marshals, forerunners of today's French *gendarmerie,* were created by the king to maintain security.[7]

ENGLISH INNOVATIONS

During the reign of Alfred the Great (871 A.D.-900 A.D.) England was divided into geographical districts known as shires. A shire was roughly equivalent to a county. Local governing units were also more clearly defined. An area in which ten families lived was called a tithing. Ten tithings were known as a hundred. As population burgeoned, hundreds became parishes. Over the years a number of significant law enforcement institutions were created in England, some of which have remained relatively intact to this day. The following innovations deserve attention.

The Tithingman

From each tithing a man was chosen to insure that the members of his group obeyed the law. Each person in the tithing was required to give his pledge or surety for the good conduct of himself and other members of the tithing. The system was primarily one of social control and if one member of the group committed a crime, the whole community acted as prosecutors.

---

[6]Beram Saklatvala, *The Origins of the English People* (New York: Taplinger Publishing Company, 1969), pp. 87-91.

[7]Lucien Romier, *A History of France* (New York: St. Martins Press, 1966), pp. 59-63.

The duties of the tithingman were to raise the hue and cry and to run through the streets informing all that a crime had been committed. This sytem of mutual responsibility was called the mutual pledge system.

The Shire-Reeve

In order to maintain law and order in the shires, the king appointed a reeve (judge) to act in his behalf. The shire-reeve acted as magistrate and chief law enforcement officer in the county. The term *shire-reeve* was modified over the years until it became *sheriff.* To keep peace within his jurisdiction, the shire-reeve often traveled by horseback to each hundred to hold court and to investigate allegations of wrongdoing.

The Parish Constable System

As the hundreds grew in size, parishes were created. With this development, the first real law enforcement officer, the constable, was appointed by local noblemen to police the rural parishes and to maintain the weapons and equipment of each hundred. The parish constable was appointed for a one-year term of service.

The Watch and Ward System

During the reign of Edward I (1272-1307), the first official police agencies were created in England's burgeoning towns. Groups of men were appointed by town guilds to patrol the streets at night, to maintain a fire watch, and to arrest those who committed crimes. They were known as the *watch and ward.*

Justice of the Peace

In 1326 Edward II created the office of justice of the peace to supplement the mutual pledge system. At first, noblemen were appointed to the position, their primary job being to assist the sheriff in maintaining order in the county. In time, however, the peace justice assumed the role of chief county magistrate in addition to his police function. Because of their noble birth, justices of the peace began to assert leadership over constables. By the end of the fourteenth century the constable served the justice by inquiring into criminal offenses, serving summonses, executing warrants, and taking charge of prisoners. This "essentially set the pattern for the next 500 years. The Justice remained the superior, the constable the inferior, conservator of the peace until the second quarter of the nineteenth century."[8]

CONCLUSION[9]

Meanwhile, over the years, the local pledge system continued to decline. Community support languished. And with considerable reason. What was everybody's business became nobody's duty, and citizens who were bound by law to take their turn at police work gradually evaded personal police service by paying others to do the work for them. In theory constables were appointed annually, but in fact their work was done by deputies or substitutes who so acted year after year, being paid to do so by the constables. These early paid police officers did not rank high in popular estimation as indicated in contemporary references. They were usually ill-paid and ignorant men, often too old to be in any sense efficient. But, as the local pledge system was declining, innovations were cropping up in the emerging cities of the seventeenth and eighteenth centuries. Those first law enforcement officers were increasingly assisted by a paid night-watch force. Although these nominally were responsible for guarding the cities against thieves and vandals, apparently they were not effective. Reportedly they did little more than roam the streets at night, periodically calling out the condition of the weather, the hour, and the fact that "all was well."

[8]Reprinted from The President's Commission on Law Enforcement and Administration of Justice, *Task Force Report: The Police* (Washington: U. S. Government Printing Office, 1967), pp. 3-4.

[9]*Ibid.*, p. 4.

An artist's conception of a public execution in early London.

Chapter 2

IN COLONIAL AMERICA (1608-1783)

Puritanism, which dominated the intellectual life of colonial New England for nearly a century after its founding, has been a major force in shaping the American mind. Puritan ideology rested on the assumption that government was necessary because of the sinfulness of man, hence it was essential that government enforce conformity to law—God's law as the Puritans interpreted it. The Puritans established their government on a religious and a civil foundation. They felt that government should be based on the consent of the governed; however, the Puritans defined liberty as the freedom to do what was "just and right." They accepted the existence of a fundamental law that transcended the importance of any human law or edict. In Puritanism, the fundamental law was to be found in the Scriptures. On the idea of a "Bible commonwealth," John Cotton, an early Puritan leader, stated:[1]

> It is very suitable to God's all-sufficient wisdom, and to the fullness and perfection of Holy Scriptures, not only to prescribe perfect rules for the right ordering of a private man's soul to everlasting blessedness with himself, but also for the right ordering of a man's family, yea, of the commonwealth too, so far as both of them are subordinate to spiritual ends...

To the Puritans their system left no room for the toleration of "outside" ideas. Activistic, moralistic, even rationalistic, Puritanism developed in different directions on American shores. And, according to leading scholars one of its paths led to political intolerance and the suppression of dissent; another led to a comparatively high intellectual and literary level.[2]

In time, however, the theocracy established by the Puritans began to crumble, partly as a result of internal tensions and partly

---

[1]From Cotton's letter to Lord Saye in 1630, reprinted in Gerald N. Grob and Robert N. Beck, Eds., *American Ideas,* Vol. I (New York: The Free Press, 1963), p. 43.

[2]*Ibid.,* pp. 5-6.

because of environmental factors. Yet, even after the passing of Puritanism, their ideas lingered on, and these ideas can be seen even today in the promulgation of laws and in their enforcement. Prohibition, for example, was a natural outgrowth of Puritan thought. For better and for worse the mark of the Puritan mind has been indelibly stamped on the American scene, and the unfolding history of law enforcement bears that imprint.

THE EARLY EXPERIENCE

When in the seventeenth century settlers began migrating to the New World, they brought with them the systems of law enforcement, admittedly imperfect, that they had known in Europe. Yet, although the basic structure of the institutions and ideas remained intact for a time, the physical and eventually the cultural environment of America forced modifications in even the most revered and deeply entrenched customs.

Jamestown and Dale's Laws

The earliest settlers to America's eastern shore were decimated not only by the harsh environment of their strange new surroundings, but by internal descension and petty jealousies. To use the phrase of a later day, the colony suffered from "too many chiefs, and not enough Indians." Practically one half of Jamestown's early settlers were gentlemen accustomed to taking orders from no one, "ten times more fit to spoil a commonwealth than to maintain one."[3] As a result, only thirty-eight of the original one hundred forty-four settlers survived the first year. Jamestown seemed headed for a disastrous fate; however, the arrival of the legendary John Smith saved the day. Smith forced everyone to work, under threat of banishment to the wilderness for slackers. In 1609 a "great fleet" left London bound for Jamestown carrying six hundred men, women, and children. Arriving in time for the severe American winter, the "unbridled multitude" entered into a "starving time" in which people died by the scores. The pioneers of Jamestown survived because of an almost superhuman will to do so and because of a system of law and enforcement initiated by two

---

[3]David Hawke, *The Colonial Experience* (New York: The Bobbs-Merrill Company, Inc. 1966), p. 91.

early leaders, Thomas Gates and Thomas Dale. The law, often referred to as Dale's Laws, but formally titled *Laws Divine, Moral and Martial,* was a mixture of civil and martial law. The legal code was strict as was the enforcement of it. The severity of punishment for seemingly minor infractions emphasized the degree to which the settlers were expected to conform to established procedure. The law was enforced *to the letter!* When in 1612 several colonists attempted to escape from Virginia in stolen boats, the governor had them shot, hanged, and broken on the wheel, according to their degree of involvement. This system was in direct conflict with the English system of justice which the settlers had known, a system which had emphasized human liberty and personal freedom. *Dale's Laws* represented a severe and repressive set of measures, yet, one must keep in mind that the code was promulgated in response to a need, an important element in the total American experience. Had these early laws not been so severe and so rigidly enforced, the whole colony should surely have perished. According to a noted historian:[4]

> If these laws had not been so strictly executed, I see not how the utter subversion of the colony should have been prevented. And for all their harshness, they did give the settlers a government of laws. . .

The Chesapeake Sheriff

The impetus for settling Maryland came mainly from gentlemen adventurers who dreamed of reproducing in the New World the England they had known. The old English hundred was resurrected as the key local unit. Although the earliest Maryland settlement was considered a military outpost, by 1632 the office of sheriff had been substituted for the provost marshal, the chief military law officer. The *Chesapeake sheriff* resembled closely the English sheriff, with only minor modifications. He was the ranking police and financial officer of each county. He served warrants and made arrests. He collected taxes, ministers' dues, and fees owed the governor; and he received ten percent of all he took in. At first the sheriff was chosen by the county court from among three men recommended by the governor; but by 1645 he was picked from among eight members of the county court, with the post rotating

---

[4]*Ibid.,* p. 97.

annually to a new member. The position served as a financial reward for magistrates, who otherwise went unpaid.

The Monthly Courts

As the Chesapeake colonies patterned their local governing units after the English model, each county was assigned its own monthly court, staffed by court commissioners, or justices of the peace as they would later be called. The judges, appointed by the governor, were supposed to travel their districts and dispense justice. Officers of the court included sheriffs, constables, clerks, and coroners.

New Netherlands' Schout Fiscal

When the Dutch West India Company settled New Netherlands (New York), it created the office of *schout fiscal* (sheriff-attorney). Like many of the offices in colonial times, the schout fiscal fulfilled a multitude of assignments. In New Netherlands he was attorney general and sheriff. In this double capacity he saw that all placards, ordinances, military regulations, and commands of the states general (governor) and the company were executed and obeyed. In addition, the schout acted as a check on the excesses of other appointed officials. The first schout fiscal, Hendrick Van Dyck, evidently felt the press of his many duties, as he was dismissed for drunkenness.[5]

The Military Police

The use of the military in policing civilian communities has a long history in America. In fact, many towns were initially policed by militia units for considerable periods of time. Fort Pontchartrain (Detroit), for example, labored under martial law for the first hundred years of its existence. Law enforcement in New Orleans was handled by the military for eighty-five years before a formal police constabulary was founded. In Cincinnati, soldiers from nearby Fort Washington provided police protection for years. The story was the same in hundreds of other communities.

---

[5] Herbert L. Osgood, *The American Colonies in the Seventeenth Century* (Gloucester: Peter Smith, 1957), pp. 105-106.

Sometimes, citizen police and the militia worked side by side in bringing law and order to early towns. Even after formal police departments were established, each state chose to retain its militia. The use of militia as a police force is deeply entrenched in the American experience. Throughout history, incidents of collective crime and violence have brought requests from local officials that the militia be dispatched to aid or replace besieged local police units. The habit of relying on the militia to perform needed public safety functions started early in the country and has persisted to this day.

TOWARD AN AMERICAN SYSTEM OF LAW ENFORCEMENT

A system of American law enforcement was being formed long before the Revolution as colonial administrators adopted and adapted the usages of their European systems to the peculiar jurisdictional scheme and altered social circumstances prevailing in the New World. Cultures met and blended, as did law enforcement methods. The result was a brand of enforcement which resembled Old World institutions but which, in rather substantial ways, was unique. As the early settlements grew in size the problems created by this growth prompted a movement toward comprehensive laws and firm, often rigid, law enforcement. America, even in the seventeenth century, was gaining a reputation for lawlessness, wanton violence, and hedonism, a reputation not entirely unearned, although the English conception of the New World as a hotbed of criminal activity was greatly exaggerated. Yet crime existed and violence occurred regularly enough to be of concern to colonial leaders. It will do well to briefly examine the systems of pre-Revolutionary law enforcement in two early colonial towns: Boston and New York.

The Boston Watch

On April 12, 1631, the Boston Court ordered that "watches" be set up at sunset, thereby founding the first night watch in America. The watch consisted of six men and an officer and took on the characteristics of a military guard. In 1634 the position of constable was created, with William Chesebrough assuming the post. On February 27, 1636, a town watch was created that differed from the early watch in that it was staffed by citizens—

not soldiers—who were appointed by the town government. The town watch, except for a brief time during the Revolution, was to persist in one form or another for almost two hundred years. It was not until 1712, however, that Boston voted to pay watchmen for their toil. Boston's early laws were numerous and the punishment for violations was often extreme. Some examples:

1639. Edward Palmer, a carpenter, was commissioned to build stocks (a device in which criminals were set for punishment) for the City of Boston. When finished, he presented his bill to city officials, who thought it to be exorbitant and proceeded to fine him five pounds and lock him in his own device.

1649. Margaret Jones was hanged for witchcraft when it was reported that "a little child was seen to run from her."

1650. The wearing of "great boots" and other such extravagant articles of dress was forbidden unless the wearer was worth two hundred pounds. That same year, Oliver Holmes was whipped "for being a Baptist."

In 1652, in response to a series of accidental fires, the watch was supplied with bells to sound the alarm. Their tour of duty was modified to a seven-hour shift—ten P.M. to five A.M. In 1701 the watch was directed to patrol silently—without bells—from "ten o'clock till broad daylight." In 1735 watchmen were "ordered to cry the time of night and state of the weather, in a moderate tone, as they walk their rounds after twelve o'clock." Few significant changes in the structure of Boston law enforcement occurred until after the Revolution.[6]

Changes in New York

As the population of New Netherlands burgeoned, the Dutch government established a burgher watch in 1643 to assist the schout fiscal in enforcing the few laws that had been promulgated. In an effort to motivate citizens to obey the law, a gibbet, or whipping post, was installed on the waterfront, on which violators were spread-eagled, beaten, and displayed for all to see.

In 1652 the flourishing settlement on Manhattan Island was incorporated and named Nieuw Amsterdam (New York City).

[6]Edward H. Savage, *Police Records and Recollections* (Boston: John P. Dale & Company, 1873), pp. 5-26.

That same year a *rattel wacht* (rattle watch) was formed, made up of citizens equipped with rattles for summoning assistance. The watch was a sentinel-type organization assigned to fixed posts. In 1658 the first police force worthy of the name was established when eight *paid* watchmen were appointed to replace the citizen volunteers.

When in 1664 the British took over Nieuw Amsterdam, the Dutch and English cultures blended and the police force underwent minor modification. The police of the city, now known as New York, were placed under the command of a high constable, Obe Hendrick by name. Law enforcement remained relatively static for the next several decades. In 1693 the first uniformed officer was appointed, as the mayor, Isaac De Reimer, selected a twelve-man watch to secure the city, which now numbered five thousand. The first precinct station, called a watch house, was constructed in 1731, the same year a stage line was initiated from Boston to New York.

CRIMINAL JUSTICE IN THE COLONIES

To be accused of a crime in colonial America, regardless of the nature of the offense, was a traumatic experience even for the innocent. For the burden of proof rested not with the accuser, but with the accused. Accounts of crime in newspapers and history books indicate that accusation was tantamount to conviction, if not in a court of law then in the court of public opinion, and conviction always meant punishment of some sort, punishment that was often physically painful. Early laws banned not only traditional antisocial behavior—murder, rape, robbery, theft, etc.—but "offensive behavior," such as gossiping, name calling, mockery, and taunting. Colonial courtrooms overflowed with complainants anxious to file charges of libel or petty slander against neighbors, debtors, or even members of their own families. More often than not a whispered slander led to a trial, a conviction, and public punishment, all in the same day. Punishment was purposely harsh, as colonial officials wished to deter future crime. The rate of recidivism must have been low, for few people could survive more than one or two brushes with colonial criminal justice. In each community certain devices were installed for use by the courts in punishing offenders. Some of the more common

The end result of criminal justice in Colonial America often meant punishment by simple, yet effective, devices. *(Courtesy of Patterson Smith Publishing Corp.)*

apparatuses used were the following:[7]

The Bilboes. This device consisted of a long iron bar with two shackles, not unlike handcuffs, into which an offender's legs were locked. The bar prevented the prisoner from moving. It was not unusual for an offender to be sentenced to two days in the bilboes for "swearynge."

The Ducking Stool. The ducking stool was an armchair fastened to the end of two beams and and placed at the edge of a pond or river. Offenders were strapped into the chair and plunged into the water as often as the sentence directed. Dunking was the most ignoble form of early punishment; it was usually reserved for gossiping housewives and drunken sailors.

The Stocks. In New England the first public building erected in a new community was a meeting house; however, before even it was built, a pair of stocks was installed. Stocks were simply low wooden benches with leg-holes, in which prisoners were secured. It was the duty of citizens to pass by the unfortunate prisoner and reproach him for his sins.

The Pillory. The pillory, or "stretch-neck" as it was called, was an upright hinged board with a hole in which a person's head was set fast. During the early use of the device, prisoners' ears were nailed to either side of the head-hole and they were made to stand in an upright position for hours. A farmer who plowed his field on a holy day, and was caught, could expect to spend his next work day in the pillory.

The Brank. The brank, or "scolds bridle," was an iron cage of great weight which covered the entire head. Often a flat tongue of iron was placed in the prisoner's mouth to prevent conversation. The brank was an English invention which did not achieve popularity in the New World. It was generally reserved for "paupers, blasphemers, and insubordinate wives."

LYNCH LAW

In backwoods areas, where no formal criminal justice systems existed, citizens were often tempted to take the law into their own

---

[7]Alice Morse Earle, *Curious Punishments of Bygone Days* (Montclair, New Jersey: Patterson Smith Publishing Corp. Originally published in 1896, reprinted in 1969).

hands. Most resisted the temptation, but some did not. Where the power of the civil government had not been fully established, persons would band together to mete out "justice" to those individuals who had transgressed on the peace, safety, or property of another. This private administration of justice was termed *lynching* or *lynch law* after its American originator, who many believe was Charles Lynch, a Virginia farmer who at the time of the Revolution headed a small band of men who tracked down and punished desperadoes, outlaws, wayward Indians, and British sympathizers.

Lynching was not an American phenomenon. It had been used in medieval Germany, in Spain, and even in seventeenth-century England. But the frequency with which Americans used it, together with the incredibly long period of time it persisted in certain sections of the country—notably the West and the Southeast—gave it a distinctly American flavor. As time went on, lynchings began to take the form of hangings as America's burgeoning population and its ever expanding frontier created the need for some type of law enforcement, formal or otherwise. If lynching proved anything, it was that there was a dramatic need for formal, professional law enforcement systems which negated the need for extralegal collective citizen violence.

DEVELOPMENTS IN ENGLAND

By the end of the seventeenth century, the English parish-constable system began to break down, partly because of the crush of population—London alone had approximately 500,000 inhabitants—and partly because of an alarmingly high crime rate. A system of night watchmen had been established in the reign of Charles II; however, watchmen were generally old and feeble citizens who "paraded the streets at night with a lantern, loudly proclaiming their presence by shouting the hours and announcing the state of the weather."[8]

Deputy-constables were found to be little more than professional criminals who worked, for a price, in close cooperation with thieves, vice-purveyors, and lawbreakers of every variety.

---

[8]Charles Reith, *A Short History of the British Police* (London: Oxford University Press, 1948), pp. 5-6.

London's growing trade and industry added to the problem by attracting to the city drifters and rogues from the countryside. Seeing the need for reform, King George in 1737 initiated action to allow city councils to levy taxes to pay nightwatchmen. Thus, *for the first time, tax money was used to pay police salaries.*

In 1748 novelist Henry Fielding was appointed magistrate for Westminster and Middlesex, thanks in no small measure to influential friends who hoped to relieve him of long-standing poverty. Fielding, however tainted his appointment, was a smashing success at his job. He initiated the idea that citizens should band together to *prevent crime,* rather than resisting it individually or waiting for authority to repress it. This concept was to be developed into "the new science of preventive police."* Fielding organized a small group of volunteers to police the crime-ridden Bow Street neighborhood. Remarkably, crime was checked. The volunteer patrols, made up of male householders, were eventually paid for their services and, in time, became the Bow Street Runners and Patrols. A mobile group who moved swiftly to the scenes of crimes to begin immediate investigations, the Bow Street Runners were the first police detective units.

*A term coined by Scottish social reformer Patrick Colquhoun, who founded the Thames River Police.

Sir Robert Peel, British Home Secretary, who in 1829 submitted to Parliament the Metropolitan Police Bill, a legislative enactment of enormous importance in the evolution of law enforcement.

Chapter 3

LAW ENFORCEMENT IN THE
POST-REVOLUTION PERIOD (1784-1829)

T he American Revolution rudely interrupted the trend toward formal civilian law enforcement as troops—either English or American, depending on which was the occupying force—took over the public safety duties previously performed by civilians. In most cases the conflict resulted in the suspension of jury trials and the replacement of civil magistrates by military tribunals. The military primarily concerned itself with defense against external attack and, as a consequence, petty crimes were often ignored and vice was allowed to flourish Protection against internal disorder was of little concern to the Army, and only cursory attention was paid to citizens' demands for police protection. Furthermore, the military itself contributed to the crime problem, wartime soldiers being a rather raucous lot. After the Revolution, however, civilian governmental control was resumed and life in America approached a state of near normalcy. On September 9, 1787, a court in Boston passed the following sentences: "One burglar to be hung; five female thieves to be whipped; four males thieves whipped; two big thieves to sit on the gallows; one counterfeiter to stand in pillory and have the right ear cut off. . ."[1]

Indeed things *were* returning to normal.

Although the end of the Revolution returned law enforcement to civilian control, it also aggravated the crime problem. Many upper-class Loyalists had left the country during the English evacuation and, as a result, an important component of social control was removed from communities badly in need of a stabilizing influence. Furthermore, the economic life of the young nation had suffered greatly during the war, prompting crimes

[1]Edward H. Savage, *Police Records and Recollections* (Boston: John P. Dale and Company, 1873), p. 41.

against persons to rise dramatically. Thieves and desperadoes had little trouble evading capture as war-damaged areas, of which most communities had their share, were converted into sanctuaries for rogues. Each community had a name for these shanty towns—in New York City it was Canvas Town. Civil policemen were reluctant to enter these areas unless accompanied by the militia. Not surprisingly, crime and vice thrived.

Toward the end of the eighteenth century law enforcement in the cities was still a rather haphazard undertaking as watchmen walked their rounds shouting out useless information while crimes were perpetrated within plain view. Some communities attempted to deal with the rising incidents of crime and violence by enlarging their police forces and creating specialized crime units; however, although some minor modifications were made in the system of policing, few major structural changes occurred in the post-Revolution period. In 1785 Boston appointed Captain John Ballard, William Billings, and Christopher Clarke as inspectors of police—the first in America.[2] By the end of the eighteenth century the responsibility for policing New York City was divided among five classes of police officers, none of whom wore uniforms:[3]

The Mayor. The mayor was the city's chief law enforcement officer who supervised the overall police operation and took charge at fires, riots, and major breaches of the peace.

The High Constable. The constable was the mayor's chief assistant. Under law he was required to enforce all state laws and city ordinances. One of the earliest high constables was Jacob Hays, a highly respected officer who had a talent for dealing single-handedly with large mobs without resorting to force.

Constables. By the close of the eighteenth century, New York City had sixteen constables. Constables executed arrest warrants, quelled riots, and maintained order. They were elected annually and worked on commission. The more arrests made by a constable, the higher his remuneration.

Marshals. The city's forty marshals were appointed by the

[2]*Ibid.*

[3]James F. Richardson, *The New York Police* (New York: Oxford University Press, 1970), pp. 16-19.

mayor and held office at his pleasure. Marshals had basically the same responsibilities as constables, their primary duty being to "bring criminals to justice." Marshals were also paid according to the revenue they generated.

      Watchmen. Watchmen patrolled the city during the hours of darkness. They did not possess police powers and could arrest only if a crime was committed in their physical presence. Watchmen were compensated on a per diem basis. By the turn of the century there were seventy-two watchmen, a figure that increased sevenfold within twenty years.

In 1789 Congress created the first federal enforcement officer in the person of the United States marshal.[4] That same year Congress provided for a Supreme Court of six members by passing the Judiciary Act of 1789, a move which was not to have its full impact on law enforcement for over 150 years.[5] In 1829 the Postal Act was passed and police powers were conferred on a federal agency. Postal inspectors were later appointed to enforce the postal laws.[6]

In 1801 Boston became the first United States city to require by statute the maintenance of a permanent night watch. Boston had little trouble finding applicants for the job because of the generous pay: fifty cents per night. On March 10, 1807, the first police districts were established. On June 16, 1823, Boston appointed its first marshal, James Pollard, a Harvard graduate and a practicing attorney.[7]

Young America was growing by leaps and bounds and communities which had previously relied on the militia for police protection soon found it necessary to create civil police forces. In 1797 Providence hired twelve night watchmen to assume the job formerly held by volunteers and the militia. The men wore no

[4]John L. Sullivan, *Introduction to Police Science* (New York: McGraw-Hill, Inc., 1966), p. 150.

[5]Richard T. Current, T. Harry Williams, and Frank Freidel, *American History: A Survey* (New York: Alfred A. Knopf, 1964), p. 131.

[6]*Supra* note 4, p. 150.

[7]Roger Lane, *Policing the City—Boston: 1822-1885* (Cambridge: Harvard University Press, 1967), p. 11.

uniforms, save a cloak, and carried a curved staff as a weapon and for identification purposes. In 1801 the first civilian police officers were appointed in Detroit. Three years later a mobile patrol and a night watch were created. In 1802 Cincinnati, with a population of 800 persons, was incorporated as a town. It had been an unincorporated frontier community since 1788, under the protection of soldiers. Provision was made for the yearly election of a marshal, but in 1803 a disastrous fire prompted the city council to provide for a night watch. All male citizens over the age of twenty-one years were required to serve in rotation without pay. Each night twelve men reported to the watch house where they chose an "officer of the night" who divided them into two classes of six men each to patrol the streets. They were equipped with a rattle for summoning aid, and a lantern. In 1803 the military police passed out of existence in New Orleans and a municipal force was commissioned. Mayor Etienne De Bore appointed a committee of city councilmen to inspect prisons and formulate rules and regulations regarding the police function. Having adopted the regulations in special session, the mayor and his council appointed twenty-five men to carry out the duties of a "police force." A year later the "patrol militia," a civilian patrol unit, was established and in 1806 the *Garde de ville* (city watch) was created. Later that year, however, the grand jury arraigned the force as "inefficient" and it was disbanded. In 1818 money was appropriated to pay watchmen for their services and a professional force consisting of a captain and six watchmen was hired.

The post-Revolutionary War period saw great strides in the improvement of the country's transportation system. Roads and waterways began connecting all parts of the country. In 1807 Robert Fulton's famous steamboat voyage from New York to Albany created a new chapter in communication. Between 1789 and 1810 the total tonnage of American vessels engaged in overseas traffic rose from 125,000 to 1,000,000. In 1818 the turnpike era was well underway as most major cities were connected by new or rebuilt roadways.[8] Great industrial and port cities were emerging and American law enforcement, which was using seventeenth-century police methods to deal with nineteenth-century

[8]*Supra* note 5, pp. 172-173.

problems, was in no position to meet the challenge of crime created by the changes in the nation's social life. Crime and its effects were becoming a way of life to city dwellers. To compound citizens' worry over crime and violence, the American press of the era seemed to devote an inordinate amount of space to crime news, especially sensational street crimes. Fisher Ames, a noted writer of the era, lamented: [9]

> Some of the shocking articles in the paper raise simple, and very simple, wonder; some terrour; and some horror and disgust. Now what institution is there in these endless wonders?...do they not shock tender minds and addle shallow brains? They make a thousand old maids, and eight thousand booby boys afraid to go to bed" alone...yet there seems to be a rivalship among printers, who shall have the most wonders, and the strangest and most wonderful crimes.

Yet the propensity of the press to gather and print eye-witness accounts of crime notwithstanding, the rate of serious crimes did seem to be rising alarmingly. When in 1812 America again went to war with England, selective mob action created concern among the people for their safety.

DEVELOPMENTS IN ENGLAND

English police reformers were busily at work in early nine-teenth-century England, although they often met with resistance from a suspicious citizenry and politicians and merchants interested in the financial exploitation of crime. Patrick Colquohoun, magistrate, author, and noted police scholar, published books and pamphlets in which he propounded the principle of *preventing* crime and disorder, an idea he readily acknowledged was inspired by Henry Fielding's Bow Street Runners.[10] Colquohoun's attempts to implement the idea failed because of his inability to overcome much of the prejudice which existed against any formal police unit. He died in 1820, a bitter and defeated man.

Yet, even though Colquohoun's plan met with failure, it was clear that something had to be done to bring law and order to

---

[9]Frank Luther Mott, *The News in America* (Cambridge: Harvard University Press, 1952), p. 50.

[10]Charles Reith, *A New Study of Police History* (London: Oliver and Boyd, 1956), p. 27.

England. Highwaymen and thieves openly pursued their calling, even boasting of successful exploits in inns and eating places. People dared not walk the streets of London after dark unless they were armed. The houses of citizens resembled armed fortresses. In 1822 Sir Robert Peel took office as Home Secretary and attempted to persuade Parliament of the need for a professional police department. Like Colquohoun, he was rebuffed. Peel, however, was not a man to surrender easily. It took him seven years to muster enough political strength to pass his proposal. In 1829 Peel submitted the Metropolitan Police Bill to Parliament, which after much heated debate, passed it, thus enacting the most significant piece of police legislation in history. On September 29, 1829, formal policing began in London as 1,000 men in six divisions began patrolling the streets.

Peelian reform, as it was popularly called, did not meet with the immediate approval of the citizens of London. In fact, many condemned the plan as dangerous and provocative. But, eventually, Peelian reform received widespread acceptance, and the policemen, who were at first sneeringly referred to as "blue devils," became known affectionately as "bobbies" after Peel. The basic tenets of *Peelian reform* were as follows:[11]

1. The police must be stable, efficient, and organized along military lines.
2. The police must be under government control.
3. The absence of crime will best prove the efficiency of police.
4. The distribution of crime news is essential.
5. The deployment of police strength both by time and area is essential.
6. No quality is more indispensable to a policeman than a perfect command of temper; a quiet, determined manner has more effect than violent action.
7. Good appearance commands respect.
8. The securing and training of proper persons is at the root of efficiency.
9. Public security demands that every police officer be given a number.
10. Police headquarters should be centrally located and easily accessible to the people.

[11] A.C. Germann, Frank D. Day, and Robert R.J. Gallati, *Introduction to Law Enforcement and Criminal Justice* (Springfield: Charles C Thomas, Publisher, 1970), p. 54.

11. Policemen should be hired on a probationary basis.
12. Police records are necessary to the correct distribution of police strength.

The first commissioners of police were Colonel Charles Rowan and Richard Mayne. The new police "office" was in a house at 4 Whitehall Place, the rear of which opened onto a courtyard known as Scotland Yard, a name derived from the fact that it had formerly been the residence of ambassadors from the kings of Scotland.

Although Peelian reform had no immediate effect on the United States, it was to later serve as a model for all police departments desirous of creating a professional police force. Peelian reform marked the birth of modern policing. Its impact is still felt in this country and abroad.

CONCLUSION

America was moving forward as a center of commerce and trade. Cities were evolving and the social dislocation caused by structural changes in the fabric of the new nation created predictable police problems. Although England experienced many of the same problems, its solution—the Metropolitan Police Force—could not be used to the same effect in America. In England the people were used to centralized governmental control; however, Americans had a healthy suspicion of a strong central government, and to even suggest a single unified police force might have led to another revolution. As a result, the country's law enforcement agencies muddled through the period, fragmented and decentralized. There was a lag between the general progress of the country and the ability of the police to cope with the everyday problems created by that progress. The lag threatened to become a chasm in the coming era, a period in which many of the internal national conflicts which had been submerged came bursting to the surface.

Edward H. Savage, Boston Chief of Police (1870-1878), an exceptionally able and humane man, was the first great American police administrator.

Chapter 4

THE GROWTH OF URBAN POLICE SYSTEMS
(1830-1865)

As American towns burgeoned in population during the first third of the nineteenth century, the "traditional police"— sheriffs, constables, marshals, night watchmen, citizen volunteers— were unable to cope with the increasing crime and tumult caused by economic depressions, political upheavals, and a country in transition. Governments' initial response to widespread crime and violence was to increase in numbers the watch and ward; however, it was soon clear to even the most backward public officials that what was needed was a complete restructuring of the system of town law enforcement. The antiquated watch-and-ward system was simply inadequate to handle the problems of the day. When large-scale rioting began plaguing urban areas, it became obvious that towns would have to create a new class of permanent professional police officers to meet the challenge. Reform in the police system came first in communities which experienced extreme criminal violence and rioting.[1] In the face of such difficulties, police machinery went utterly to pieces.

CRIME, RIOTS, AND A NEW POLICE

Although crime and violence existed in colonial America, it was tolerated by citizens because it usually consisted of petty vice, drunken assaults, and aimless brawls which were dangerous largely to the participants and not to honest citizens. In fact, small riots were often looked on as sporting events. As the press of population began to become a factor in towns, this early tolerance eroded when the scope and intensity of antisocial behavior exploded into crime waves, routs, tumultuous assemblies, and

[1]The National Commission on the Causes and Prevention of Violence, *Violence in America* (New York: Signet Books, 1969), p. 56.

dangerous riots.

The nineteenth century saw the beginning of what, unhappily, has become an American tragedy, not to mention a challenge for the nation's lawmen: the bizarre murder case. Tinged with overtones of sex, the phenomenon of grisly homicides made their ugly mark on the national scene. With the pyrotechnic entry of the penny press, the normal pressure on the police to solve gruesome murders became even greater as the fledgling newspaper industry sensationalized every case to the horrified delight of a fascinated public. Three cases typified the era's homicidal fare: [2]

The Robinson-Jewett Case. In Philadelphia in 1836 a prostitute, Helen Jewett, was found brutally murdered in her room. A young clerk by the name of Robinson was arrested and charged with the crime by a police force which had been pressured by the press into a premature arrest. Robinson was tried, but during the course of his trial, evidence was presented that exonerated the defendant, thereby prompting editorial barbs at the police, the court, and the jury.

The Webster Case. In 1849 the dismembered parts of Dr. George Parkman's body were found in the laboratory of a Harvard chemistry professor named John W. Webster, a creditor of Parkman's. Webster was tried and convicted of murder and sentenced to die on the gallows. At his execution a mob of persons rioted when they were unable to get a better view of the hanging. Two hundred and fifty people were admitted as witnesses, many of whom were policemen.

The Sickles Case. In 1859 Daniel E. Sickles shot and killed Phillip Barton Key, United States Attorney for the District of Columbia, for seducing his wife. Sickles, a member of the United States House of Representatives, was arrested and tried for the murder. The newspapers gave the trial front page treatment. Sickles, an obviously guilty man, was acquitted by a jury which granted that special leniency was reserved for outraged husbands who strike down rival lovers.

Publicized crimes of the day, coupled with extreme collective violence, indicated to citizens that cities needed to be secured, and public officials moved to secure them by implementing urban police systems.

---

[2]John Lofton, *Justice and the Press* (Boston: Beacon Press, 1966), pp. 74-75.

Philanthrophy and the Police: The Philadelphia Story

Philadelphia's problems with crime, violence, and vice were not unique, but the impetus for creating a day police force in that city was. In 1833 Stephen Girard, a wealthy philanthropist, died and bequeathed a large sum of money to the city of Philadelphia for the financing of a "competent police." The intent of the generous but peculiar bequest was as follows:[3]

> To enable the corporation of the City of Philadelphia to provide more effectually than they now do for the security and property of the persons and property of the inhabitants of the said city by a competent police, including a sufficient number of watchmen really suited to the purpose; and to this end I recommend a division of the city into watch districts of four parts, each under a proper head; and that at least two watchmen shall in each round or station patrol together.

The will either stimulated or shamed the city into action and later that year an ordinance was passed providing for a day force of twenty-four policemen as well as 120 night watchmen. Girard's simple but innovative recommendations were followed, and some equally precedent-setting ideas of the mayor were incorporated into the ordinance, which centralized control of the new force in a single head known as a captain, who was appointed by the mayor. Vacancies in higher ranks were to be filled by promoting those who "have distinguished themselves by diligence, integrity, and skill in an inferior grade," thus lessening political influences over the force. The new force proved successful; though within two years, partly because of politics and partly because of economics, the ordinance was repealed and the previous system was resurrected.[4]

It became clear almost immediately that the old way of policing the city was inadequate. The defects in the system were dramatically underscored when, in 1838, Negro rioting exploded in Philadelphia. Scores were killed and historic Pennsylvania Hall was burned. In 1842 riots again broke out and hundreds of churches, meeting places, and homes were burned. In 1848 Philadelphia reestablished an independent day force, consisting of thirty-four

[3]Raymond B. Fosdick, *American Police Systems* (New York: The Century Co., 1921), pp. 63-64.

[4]*Ibid.*, p. 69.

policemen. The old night watch remained in its original form. Six years later, in 1854, the day and night forces were consolidated and placed under a marshal, popularly elected every two years.

Boston's Police: Problems and Opportunities

Boston's time of tumult began on August 11, 1834, when a hostile crowd, led by a gang known as the Boston Truckmen, routed nuns from Mount Benedict Convent and burned the structure to the ground.[5] A second major disturbance occurred when the controversial editor, William Lloyd Garrison, was assaulted in the office of *The Liberator* by a crowd infuriated by his anti-slavery writings.[6] On June 11, 1837, the Broad Street Riot occurred when volunteer firemen engaged in a bloody clash with an Irish funeral procession. The conflict was a result of the smoldering resentment toward immigrants, and it marked the first time in Boston's history that the militia had to be called out to quell a disturbance.[7] On April 15, 1838, the General Court of Massachusetts passed a bill creating a permanent day police force to supplement its night watch. By June, nine policemen "with all but the civil powers of constables," were assigned to "whatever duties the council might require."[8] The new police worked so well that in 1839 the elated mayor of Boston, Samuel A. Eliot, declared that "the public peace has been uninterrupted during the past year, and. . .the reputation of the city has suffered no such blow as was inflicted on it in previous years."[9] Although the new police were working well, the city experienced trouble in finding a competent marshal to run the force. Finally, the sixth marshal in a decade, Francis Tukey, was appointed in 1846. Marshal Tukey, only thirty-two years old, was one of America's first legendary law enforcement officers. Taking control of the police department, which had now grown to thirty-eight, Tukey created a competent

---

[5]James McKellar Bugbee, "Boston Under the Mayors: 1822-1880," *The Memorial History of Boston,* Ed. Justin Winsor (Boston: 1881), Vol. III, Ch. II, pp. 238-240.

[6]Roger Lane, *Policing the City—Boston: 1822-1885* (Cambridge: Harvard University Press, 1967), pp. 31-32.

[7]*Supra* note 5, pp. 243-246.

[8]*Supra* note 6, p. 37.

[9]*Ibid.,* p. 39.

and efficient force and built a reputation for himself as a "tough cop." When he expanded his night police force to twenty-two, it captured more criminals than the entire rival body of over two hundred night watchmen. It also served to antagonize much of the public and the city's politicians. Marshal Tukey initiated a *show up,* a weekly roundup of rogues and cutthroats who were paraded before the entire police force. In 1853 Tukey was charged with malfeasance in office and replaced, thus ending an unforgettable era in the history of Boston law enforcement. The years that followed saw a dramatic transformation of police operations: police divisions were created and eight precinct stations were opened and staffed; the city created the country's first detective division in 1851 and followed it by organizing the first harbor patrol in 1853. On May 19, 1855, the separate Boston watch and police were reorganized into the Boston Police Department. The Civil War years were marked by urban disruptions, including a major draft riot, which severely tested the mettle of the new Boston Police Department, and a major police scandal that rocked the very foundation of the department. The Boston Police Department not only survived but grew and prospered. When in 1870 Boston's aldermen fired their chief of police, the entire command structure of the police department—to its everlasting credit—nominated one of its own as a replacement. The board followed the recommendation and Edward Hartwell Savage, an impeccably honest and humane man, was appointed. Many men were to become distinguished, reform-minded American police administrators in the upcoming decades; Savage, however, was the first. Chief Savage remained in office for eight years, during which he was to effect substantial internal reforms. The crime rate was significantly lowered. Incidents of public drunkenness and affray were lessened. Officers' pay was raised, manpower was deployed on a more equitable basis, and the chief became a moral force for community change. Under Chief Savage's administration "there were no dramatic incidents, scandals, or investigations. . . The principle of law enforcement was accepted, while the pacification of the city was measured by declining rates of intemperance and of homicide, and by the passing of riot as a normal form of political expression."[10]

[10]*Supra* note 6, p. 178.

New York's Model Police

By 1844 the population of New York City had risen to 550,000, while the police force numbered 1,000. The force consisted of three distinct components: the police proper, known as Harper's Police, after the mayor; the municipal police; and the night watch, who were compensated at the rate of one dollar and twenty-five cents per night. Recognizing the difficulties involved in maintaining three separate police units, the New York legislature abolished its night watch and implemented a combined day and night police force. Thus, New York City became the first American community to create a unified police department. The force was fashioned after Sir Robert Peel's bobbies, the London Metropolitan Police Department. The next year, eight-pointed copper stars were issued to officers for purposes of identification. New York City's first Chief of Police was also appointed that year. All was not rosy for New York law enforcement, however. The composition of the police force was predominately Irish, provoking deep antagonisms in the community. In 1855 Chief of Police Matsell was accused of "Irishizing" his force, a charge he denied. The city's face was rapidly changing and vicious gang fights became commonplace. In 1851 jealousy between the followers of two popular stage actors erupted into the Astor Place Riots, in which scores of people were killed. Gangs such as The Bowery Boys and The Dead Rabbits terrorized citizens, with little interference from the police. New York's melting pot had not yet reached a boil, and racial and ethnic tensions were at fever pitch.

The Idea Spreads

Other communities soon followed the lead of Philadelphia, Boston, and New York in establishing urban police forces. In 1842 Cincinnati appointed a paid day police force of two men to supplement its night watch. By 1855 the day force had grown to one hundred men, three of whom were detectives. The following year uniforms of a sort were issued to each man. In 1859 Detroit inaugerated a merchant's police to patrol the downtown commercial area. By 1866 the force was enlarged to fifty-one men, and a detective bureau was formed. Two years later a sanitary unit was created to assist the Board of Health.

THE CONTROVERSY OVER UNIFORMS

Police in the middle nineteenth century were characterized by their ragtag dress and undisciplined appearance. It was not unusual for officers on the same police force to be dressed in an entirely different fashion. The summer uniform in most cities consisted of white duck suits, except for those officers who did not own a suit, in which case it was short-sleeved shirt, color unspecified, and baggy trousers. In 1853 J. W. Gerard, a noted journalist of the time, wrote a description of the New York Police:

> If you want one suddenly by night or by day, where will you look for him?. . .look at their style of dress, some with hats, some with caps, some with coats like Joseph's of old, parti-colored. If they were mustered together they would look like Falstaff's Regiment.

In response to increasing criticism of police slovenliness, officials in major cities began to provide their forces with uniforms, thereby igniting another controversy among citizens and policemen as well. Many policemen fought the adoption of uniforms vigorously, maintaining, at least privately, that the job was dangerous enough without advertising that one was an officer. Furthermore, uniforms would hinder many extracurricular

Police uniforms in the pre-Civil War era resembled gentlemen's livery, as illustrated above by the policemen of the City of Boston. From left to right: captain, patrolman, deputy chief, chief, lieutenant, and patrolman.

activities such as drinking and sleeping on duty. Citizen opposition to police uniforms was as emotional as officers' resistance was pragmatic. The basis of opposition was an American suspicion of all forms of militarism. Some writers blasted the idea as being "un-American" and "un-democratic"; "an imitation of royalty." Community leaders sneered at the "poppinjays" governments would create with the new livery. Statutes proposing uniformed police forces were consistently voted down by legislators who feared antagonizing the citizenry and angering policemen. Some police departments were persuaded to adopt regulation caps, though the headgear was often stuffed into a handy pocket when an officer patrolled his beat. Even attempts to force policemen to wear badges met with bitter opposition. It was not until 1861 that

Detroit's "Flying Squad" sped to the scene of crimes in progress and tumultuous assemblies, relying on its trusty two-horsepower vehicle. During the Civil War the controversy over police uniforms was resolved as policemen adopted uniforms strikingly similar to Union Army livery. *(Courtesy of the Detroit Police Department)*

uniforms received the full approval of American citizens. In that year the Civil War erased any stigma attached to a uniform.[11]

POLICE PERSONNEL: A CRISIS OF CONFIDENCE

Conditions in American cities during the era cried out for the strong hand of a well-organized police. But, with few exceptions, it was a cry unanswered, as most forces overlooked the most fundamental kind of reform: the need for competent line personnel. Journalists often complained that the police "inspired no respect." Newspaper stories abounded with tales of policemen actually fleeing from the scene of trouble. Gangs set upon and beat patrolmen for sport. Adding to the negative police image was the insistence of some officers to place themselves above the law they had sworn to enforce. In 1852 the New York Board of Aldermen released a report which documented the areas of police misconduct. The Board charged that:

> Assaulting superior officers, refusing to go on patrol, releasing prisoners from the custody of other policemen, drunkenness, extorting money from prisoners—these were offenses of daily occurrence, committed often with impunity under the protection of a political overlord.

To say, as did one Presidential commission, that "the police mission in the mid-1800s precluded any brilliance," was an understatement. But what could young America expect? Officers were badly paid, untrained, and ill-equipped. They often labored under the domineering influence of corrupt politicians in communities that were seemingly oblivious to their plight. It was little wonder that the quality of personnel attracted to the police craft was generally low. Yet, with all the negative aspects of the dangerous and dirty task, a dedicated group of young men still chose to pursue careers as policemen. And this has become a recurring historical phenomenon. No matter how many corrupting influences infiltrated a police department, regardless of how many officers went bad, there was always a group in that department, sometimes a small one, which resisted the temptations and remained impeccably honest and fair-minded in the face of tremendous obstacles.

[11]Howard O. Sprogle, *The Philadelphia Police: Past and Present* (Philadelphia: 1887), p. 123.

EARLY METHODS OF POLICE ADMINISTRATION

In colonial days, police executives were chosen in a rather haphazard fashion: some were popularly elected for varying terms of office; others were appointed by mayors, councilmen, or governors; still others simply assumed posts no one else wanted. But as the country grew in size and the problems of policing became more pronounced, citizens and public officials began to realize that new methods were needed to oversee city police operations. The very creation of an executive head—a marshal or chief—was a dramatic step forward; but it was only *one* step. Complicating the search for a method was the "spoils system," a phenomenon that made even the best methods suspect in the eyes of the public. Police departments in cities were often totally in the hands of the politicians in power. Early negative reaction to this system of political domination resulted in the establishment of partisan administrative boards to run police departments.

Partisan Administrative Boards

In the middle nineteenth century, many city governments lodged the power to oversee police operations in the hands of administrative boards staffed by judges, politicians, businessmen, and private citizens.[12] The plan was hailed by many as an impressive reform in police management and hundreds of towns and cities experimented with the concept, including New York City, Cincinnati, New Orleans, and Omaha. But the system of multiple control soon proved faulty. The boards, whether appointed or elected, were partisan in nature, meaning that they still reflected the views of the political party in power. Accordingly, "both police management and police protection continued to flounder in political uncertainty, intrigue, partisanship, and corruption."[13] Police corruption became a national issue, and state legislatures, dominated by rural politicians who used any opportunity to stifle urban political bosses, were quick to strike by enacting statutes

[12]International City Managers' Association, *Municipal Police Administration,* 5th ed. (Washington: International City Managers' Association, 1961), p. 43.

[13]*Ibid.*

which swept away local control of the police, substituting in its place a system of state control.

State Control of the Police

Like many police reforms, the system of state control began in New York City when in 1857 the state legislature ruled that New York City was too corrupt to govern itself and seized control of the New York Police Department, arousing bitter resentment from politicians and citizens who held mass meetings, engaged in violent demonstrations, and even instituted court suits to protest the action. The legislature passed the Metropolitan Police Bill which was modeled after Sir Robert Peel's London Metropolitan Police Bill of 1829. The police force was to be regulated by a board appointed by the governor. When the state tried to implement the new law, New York City's mayor, Fernando Wood, defiantly formed a police force loyal to him. For a time two complete sets of policemen patrolled the streets of New York City. Clashes were

A police riot. For a time in 1857 two separate and distinct police forces patrolled the City of New York: one was controlled by the city; the other was a state-appointed force named the Metropolitan Police but popularly referred to as "the Mets." A series of clashes occurred between the two rival forces *(depicted above)*, but in the end the state force prevailed as the Mets won the series. *(Courtesy of the Patterson Smith Publishing Corp.)*

frequent and, in one bizzare incident, hundreds of club-swinging policemen from both forces engaged in a pitched battle on a main thoroughfare.[14] The state-appointed police, or the Mets as they were called, finally won out and assumed full police control of the city, a power wielded by them for thirteen years. State control spread quickly and the plan was adopted by Baltimore in 1860, St. Louis and Chicago in 1861, Kansas City in 1862, Detroit in 1865, and Cleveland in 1866. State control was doomed to fail, however, as it was not uniformly applied within states which adopted enacting legislation. Furthermore, citizens and politicians in cities were not going to stand idly by and pay taxes to support police departments over which they had no control. Some state police boards were maintained for only a year or two, while others persisted for decades.

THE EFFECT OF THE CIVIL WAR AND RECONSTRUCTION ON POLICE OPERATIONS

The Civil War and the period of reconstruction that followed had a devastating impact on many police departments, especially those in the South. The continuity of local government was shattered, police reform was retarded, and stormy politics and social upheaval became the order of the day. In a number of cases, civil policing was suspended and the Army filled the enforcement gap. In those cases where civil authorities retained the authority to police their communities, law enforcement officers were often ousted for political reasons. During the reconstruction of the South, men who had allied themselves with the Confederacy, as most had, were generally disenjoined from participating in government. The result of this bitter experience was to be felt for many years in the South as Southern law enforcement fell far behind law enforcement in other sections of the country. Texas' experience in this regard is somewhat typical.

Texas seceded from the Union in 1861 and joined the Confederacy. While very little war action was conducted on Texas soil, a group called Terry's Texas Rangers, led by Colonel Benjamin

---

[14]George W. Walling, *Recollections of a New York Chief of Police* (New York: 1887), Ch. 4.

Terry and made up of many Texas Rangers and former members, managed to involve itself in innumerable military encounters. During the post-Civil War period, the Texas Rangers were reorganized under the direction of Reconstructionist Governor E.J. Davis and charged with the enforcement of unpopular "carpetbagger" laws. The force quickly fell into disrepute among Texans and it was years before it retained the trust and confidence of the citizenry.

When New Orleans was captured in 1861, civil government was disbanded, martial law was established, and the military, under a provost marshal, took over the duties of policing the city. Following the war, attempts were made to establish a professional police force, but it was 1898 before one was created.

The Southern states were not alone in experiencing problems caused by the Civil War. Northern states, too, experienced difficulties, some of which were created by the Federal provision that permitted draftees to buy their way out of the Union Army by paying three hundred dollars to the government. Laboring men, reasoning correctly that it was a rich man's law, displayed their

Resisting the draft during the Civil War. In 1863 the bloodiest riot in history occurred when mobs protesting President Lincoln's draft call roamed New York City, burning, looting, and lynching. In three days 1,200 were killed and 8,000 were wounded. *(Courtesy of Patterson Smith Publishing Corp.)*

displeasure with the provision by staging a series of draft riots, the most notable of which occurred in New York City in 1863.

CONCLUSION

The creation of urban American police systems was a necessary and desirable occurrence. Like many other governmental innovations however, it was a concept that was late in coming and one that was fraught with problems. In rapidly industrializing societies there has almost always been a gap between what government accomplished and what was actually needed by citizens. The case of law enforcement was no exception. America was reaching the crossroads of an era, one in which the old ideas and methods of a basically rural country would rapidly change to those of a more dynamic, urban society. Law enforcement was about to enter an era of chaos and confusion, a period of high crime, social crises, and militancy. The police were ill-equipped to handle the challenge, so certain basic innovations would be undertaken to professionalize law enforcement. Yet, even though America's police had come under rather scathing criticism from journalists, public officials, and professors, and stories abounded about their inefficiency and incompetence, there existed a bond between the general community and policemen. Police officers, with all their faults, were still viewed by most citizens as public servants who fulfilled a critical function and who deserved respect because of the very nature of their job. There were, in fact, few community relations problems because the community looked on their police departments as social service agencies. And the police responded by lodging indigents in jail overnight, by providing daily free meals to the needy, who could be seen each night lining up in the rear of precinct houses as patrolmen ladled out soup; by using horse-drawn paddy wagons as ambulances, by delivering Christmas food baskets to the underprivileged, and by providing similar social services. The police, however, were to lose this bond with the community, for as police departments became larger, better equipped, and more professional, they also became isolated and aloof from the citizens they had sworm to serve. Social services performed by early municipal forces were eventually turned over to *ad hoc* agencies so that the police could get on with the business of policing. This problem—to professionalize the police without losing public respect—has been a recurring historical dilemma and one that has persisted to this day.

In 1861 President Abraham Lincoln's life was saved by Allan Pinkerton *(pictured above walking behind Lincoln)*, who learned of an assassination plot and warned the President.

Chapter 5

POLICING THE OLD WEST (1848-1890)

The treacherous environment of the Old West created special problems in law enforcement, especially in light of the fact that formal policing was not always available to those who needed it most. In some cases the absence of policemen prompted citizens to band together in groups to protect their lives and property from those who would take advantage of the vulnerability of scattered settlements. All too often, these groups went too far in enforcing the law and maintaining order and the result was a form of collective citizen lawlessness which terrorized the very people they sought to protect. When law enforcement officers were available—generally in raucous cattle towns, mining camps, and port cities—they often were little better than their adversaries. In truth, many sheriffs and marshals had been desperadoes prior to their entry into police ranks. The West was fraught with danger, and the early pioneers—be they homesteaders, cattlemen, miners, or entrepreneurs—had to provide for their safety. They could not concern themselves with the legal niceties that Easterners took for granted. If law enforcement was often harsh and brutal, it was in response to a harsh and brutal environment. The name of the game was survival, and extreme measures were needed to insure that survival. There were four general types of Western law enforcement: extralegal citizen police, formal police, legal citizen police. and para-police. Some communities had police systems which combined several of the above groupings, while others suspended formal policing during times of crisis so that extralegal but more effective methods could be employed.

EXTRALEGAL CITIZEN POLICE

From the earliest times, the American West was the home of two contrasting personalities—the honest settler and the outlaw. Both sought a home and a profitable existence, but each pursued it in a decidedly different manner. In the absence of formal law enforcement and criminal justice systems, citizens found it necessary to band together to provide a defense against those who would plunder, steal, and kill. Vigilance committees, groups of organized citizen volunteers which patrolled towns to guard against "evil," sprang up across the West. Although vigilante methods were used in all Western states, they were first employed in California where the lure of gold attracted a human mess which threatened to legitimize murder as a form of social expression. Of all California communities, law and order seemed to have been scarcest in early San Francisco.

From the gold rush days to the dawning of the twentieth century, citizens in San Francisco consistently found it necessary to form vigilance committees. Between 1849 and 1854 it was estimated that California experienced 4,200 murders, almost half of which occurred in San Francisco.[1] In 1851 San Francisco's first vigilance committee was organized "for the protection of the lives and property of the citizens and residents of the city. . . ." A constitution was framed and regular meetings were held to plan strategy. The committee's first official act was to capture, try, and hang, in full view of the citizenry, a suspected burglar, John Jenkins, who earned the dubious honor of being the key figure in the first public execution in America. Three more executions within ninety days convinced the lawless that San Francisco was no longer a safe haven for them, and a measure of order was brought to the city. Several other committees were formed over the years, the most famous being the Committee of Public Safety, formed in 1877, and headed by William T. Coleman, a businessman. The most dramatic achievement of the organization was to muster 3,000 citizens to hang a gambler suspected of killing a county supervisor.[2] However, contrary to popular belief, the vigilance committees were not hysterical lynch mobs bent on violence and revenge. Most were made up of honest men who, because of circumstances not of their own making, were forced to take collective action to protect their communities. The first San

[1] Leroy R. Hafen and Carl Coke Rister, *Western America,* 2nd ed. (Englewood Cliffs, New Jersey: Prentice-Hall, Inc., 1950), pp. 441-442.

[2] N. Ray Gilmore and Gladys Gilmore, *Readings in California History* (New York: Thomas Y. Crowell Company, 1966), pp. 190-191.

Francisco vigilance committee, for example, tried ninety-one cases: forty-one defendants were subsequently released; fifteen were remanded to local law enforcement authorities; fourteen were banished; one was whipped, and only four were hanged.

Vigilance committees were created in Arizona, Montana, Colorado, and Nevada. In fact, every important mining town in the West experimented at one time or another with the idea. Although the name of the organization was different in each community—some were called committees, some were referred to as vigilantes, still others coined the term "regulators"—the function remained the same: root out and punish wrongdoers. As formal policing reached the West vigilance passed out of vogue, except on an *ad hoc* basis.

FORMAL POLICE

The coming of formal policing to the West was an immensely important phenomenon in the history of American law enforcement. The exploits (sometimes fictionalized) of legendary western lawmen so captured the imagination of the young nation that the extreme methods employed by these officers achieved a degree of legitimacy in the public eye. Although extreme police methods did not originate in the West, romanticized accounts of the police enterprise west of the Mississippi molded public opinion on what the role of a policeman—any policeman—ought to be. Thanks to the image created for lawmen by the Eastern press, the ideal policeman was viewed as one who (1) was large in stature, (2) was harsh in attitude, (3) possessed a low point of tolerance, (4) was courageous in the extreme, and (5) possessed ample firepower and the will to use it. What appeared to be most important to the public was the effectiveness of lawmen in dealing with their adversaries. Apparently there was little concern over the absence of reasonable standards of humane conduct toward criminals or suspected criminals. The swashbuckling methods of Western sheriffs and marshals served as examples for police officers in all sections of the country to emulate. The legacy of the Western lawman—extreme individual action, restricted loyalties, a belief that order must be kept at all costs, a reliance on firearms to settle disputes—can be seen to this day.

The Texas Rangers[3]

In 1823 Stephen F. Austin hired a body of ten men to protect one of Texas' early settlements from bandits and marauding Indians. The ten were ordered to "range" wide areas of the frontier and guard against unwelcome intruders. On the eve of Texas' War for Independence, the group was enlarged to twenty-five men and officially named the Texas Rangers.

When, in 1845, Texas was admitted to the union, the Rangers became the first official state police agency in America. Their primary job was to protect the state's scattered settlements from Indian incursions. The war years saw the Rangers' strength

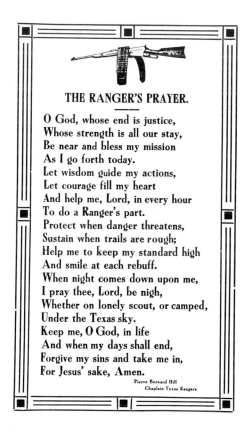

THE RANGER'S PRAYER.

O God, whose end is justice,
Whose strength is all our stay,
Be near and bless my mission
As I go forth today.
Let wisdom guide my actions,
Let courage fill my heart
And help me, Lord, in every hour
To do a Ranger's part.
Protect when danger threatens,
Sustain when trails are rough;
Help me to keep my standard high
And smile at each rebuff.
When night comes down upon me,
I pray thee, Lord, be nigh,
Whether on lonely scout, or camped,
Under the Texas sky.
Keep me, O God, in life
And when my days shall end,
Forgive my sins and take me in,
For Jesus' sake, Amen.

Pierre Bernard Hill
Chaplain Texas Rangers

---

[3]Compiled and excerpted from the following publications obtained from the State of Texas: *The Texas Ranger; The Story of the Texas Rangers; Badges With History; A Brief Sketch of Texas Ranger History;* and from Walter Prescott Webb's book, *The Story of the Texas Rangers.*

increased to that of a small army, and while they did fight in the Mexican War, their primary duty, the protection of settlements, remained the same. When in 1848 the war with Mexico ended, Rangers' duties were expanded to combat cattle thievery and outlaw activities along the Rio Grande, a task they performed with great gusto and efficiency. Texas Ranger exploits soon became legendary. When the Indian problem abated, the Rangers turned their full attention to capturing, or killing, desperadoes, who were now plaguing the state. Each Ranger captain was furnished with a list containing 3,000 names—thieves, robbers, and highwaymen all. Sometimes the methods of this early police force were questionable: on one occasion the killer of an Army major was hanged without benefit of judge or jury. But the times dictated the methods, and frontier Texas was an untamed land. The following quote by a Ranger captain describes the Rangers' policy for dealing with bandits:

> We're after bandits. If they stampede, pick you out the nearest one to you. Keep him in front of you and keep after him, get as close to him as you can before you shoot. It makes no difference in what direction he goes, stay with him until the finish. These are picked men, and they say they can cope with any Ranger or regulars. If we can overhaul them in the open country, we will teach them a lesson they will never forget.

Tactics notwithstanding, the Rangers brought a measure of law and order to Texas. Famous outlaws such as Sam Bass, King Fisher, and John Wesley Hardin had their careers terminated violently in the Lone Star State. The requirements for becoming a Ranger were simple. Applicants had to be big, tough, and unafraid of physical combat. The stock questions posed to prospective recruits were, Can you shoot? Can you ride? Can you cook? Three consecutive affirmative answers all but assured one of a job.

Policing the Towns

Town policing also gained a special place in American history. Names such as Wild Bill Hickok, Wyatt Earp, Pat Garrett, and Bat Masterson have achieved a degree of immortality, due in no small measure to the electronic and print media's efforts to chronicle the heroic exploits of Western lawmen, even if truth came off second-best in the telling. The towns in which many early policemen toiled—Dodge City, Tombstone, San Antonio, Laramie,

Cheyenne, El Paso—also gained an unremitting place in history. The law enforcement experience of Wichita, Kansas, a cowtown, was in many ways typical of other Western communities. In 1870 Wichita appointed its first formal lawman, a marshal; he lasted less than one month. Three more marshals were appointed, each leaving after several weeks on the job. It was not unexpected that men were not particularly enthusiastic about risking life and limb for seventy-five dollars a month. In 1871 Michael Meagher was appointed as Wichita city marshal. The following account of Meagher's activities is from the official records of the Wichita Police Department:

> During the early cowtown days of Wichita, the rougher elements of the city were brought under control by Meagher and his small force, supplemented by "special officers" during the cattle drive months. By the time that Wichita's most publicized lawman, Wyatt Earp, was hired as a sixty-dollar-a-month policeman in Meagher's department, the cowtown era was nearing an end in Wichita. It must be assumed from the record that Earp learned a great deal about law enforcement from Mike Meagher, who during his five years in Wichita was able to handle any situation that arose, from disarming a drunken, revolver-shooting cowboy to arresting wild and desperate men. It was from Meagher that Earp learned his technique of applying a long barrel of a six-shooter to the skull of a riotous cowboy.

From this early foundation, the Wichita police system evolved into a competent police agency. In 1897 Wichita established a significant precedent by popularly electing Sam Jones town marshal, the first Negro in history to hold that post.

LEGAL CITIZEN POLICE

Western communities that commissioned formal law enforcement officers often found it necessary to assist and support them in very practical ways. When a situation arose that could not be handled by the police, citizens were called in to supplement the force, which, more often than not, consisted of one man—a sheriff or a marshal. These "casual deputies," as they were called, acted as an enthusiastic police reserve to be pressed into duty as posses, jail guards, and replacements when the town police were away.

The ancient concepts of hue and cry and watch and ward were used in Western communities, whose citizenry viewed pragmatically the need for mutual protection and assistance. An almost family-like cooperation existed between law enforcement and the community, and Western sheriffs often resembled the tithingmen of old. Citizen involvement with the police, as much as any other factor, eventually fused the scattered early settlements and mining camps into homogeneous communities.

PARAPOLICE

Most Western towns did not have strong, effective police forces, and even those few that did could not provide all the needed public safety services. The great open spaces between towns had virtually no police protection, a factor that took on new significance with the advent of stagecoaches and the railroads. As prosperity hit the West, companies were forced to transport large quantities of gold, silver, and cash across desolate areas, many of which were infested by badmen. In order to protect their interests, mining companies, stagecoach lines, banks, railroads, shipping concerns, and merchant associations hired private guards to safeguard valuable cargo. These early parapolice officers were at first assigned to "ride shotgun" on cash and bullion shipments. However, as crime rates soared, the responsibilities of parapolicemen were expanded. Although most officers were employed directly by the companies they policed, private detective agencies were formed by men who viewed Western lawlessness, or at least the policing of it, as an exiting and lucrative way of making a living. These agencies hired themselves out to the highest bidder and, in so doing, changed the philosophy of private policing from prevention to detection and apprehension. Many of the more dynamic private police forces not only performed guard service but tracked down and arrested dangerous criminals. Of the scores of private detective agencies, none was more famous or more effective than the legendary Pinkertons.

The Pinkerton Detective Agency

The Pinkerton Detective Agency was founded by Allan Pinkerton in Chicago in 1850. Although much of its later activities were directed at the breaking of strikes in the East, a major part of its early functions included tracking down Western desperadoes, especially train robbers, a task it fulfilled rather effectively. Allan Pinkerton, who had been the City of Chicago's first detective, was a gifted man whose exploits were nationally known. He organized the secret service division of the United States Army in 1861 and was made its first chief. Later, while employed by the Wilmington and Baltimore Railroad, he saved Abraham Lincoln's life by uncovering an assassination plot directed against the President.[4] In the West, fragmented police agencies—most of which consisted of one man who was overworked and underpaid—were often powerless to act against the badmen of the day, and the Pinkertons were hired by mining companies and railroads to fill the law enforcement void. More than one train robber who had eluded a sheriff and his *ad hoc* deputies ended up in a fatal confrontation with a well-armed force of Pinkerton men. Pinkertons labored under few of the constraints that limited formal law officers: they recognized no jurisdictional boundaries; politics were of little regard to them; legal restraints were often ignored. Consequently, they enjoyed a string of successes of which few police agencies of the time—public or private—could boast. But even though the Pinkerton Detective Agency performed a valuable and necessary function, it often did so with an enthusiasm that ignored the rules of law. For example, in a raid on the suspected hideout of the notorious Jesse James, a thirty-two-pound iron bomb, wrapped in flaming, kerosene-saturated rags, was thrown into the suspected hideaway. After the explosion it was discovered that Jesse had fled earlier, but his mother and his small brother had not. The young boy was killed and his mother lost her right arm. Public opinion polarized against the Pinkertons over the incident and Jesse James was on his way to becoming a folk hero, thanks in no small measure to the ill-advised action of the famous detective agency.[5] Yet, in the Pinkertons' defense it must be said that many of their own men had fallen in battles with outlaws; some had been shot in ambush. The bitterness of the post-Civil War period led to violent and bloody clashes between Eastern detectives and Western badmen, who robbed and murdered in the name of a defeated cause (The Confederacy) and who looked on themselves as guerrillas rather than outlaws. The Pinkertons employed methods of questionable morality, but they did a job which, in its way, helped bring a semblance of order to the West.

[4] Paul B. Weston and Kenneth M. Wells, *Criminal Investigation* (Englewood Cliffs, New Jersey: Prentice-Hall, Inc., 1970), pp. 9-11.

[5] Carl W. Breihan, *Jesse James* (New York: Frederick Fell, Inc., 1953), pp. 118-120.

CONCLUSION

The early Western lawmen—be they citizens, policemen, or parapolicemen—have gained a place in this country's history.

A motley crew of misdemeanants en route to the local lockup. *(Courtesy of the Kansas City Police Department)*

Authors have portrayed these pioneers as either heroes or villains. They were, in fact, average men who were pressed into service to fight a battle against crime and violence. Some used excessive force in fulfilling their responsibilities and many were drawn toward law enforcement careers for all the wrong reasons. But in the main, Western citizens received better police protection than they paid for and infinitely better protection than they deserved. For less than one-hundred dollars a month sheriffs and marshals risked their lives nightly. Casual deputies, virtually unpaid, often pursued and arrested professional killers. Parapolicemen with no special training hunted down some of the most notorious desperadoes in the West. The price of policing the West was high, however, as untold numbers of officers forfeited their lives in defense of their communities.

August Vollmer, Chief of Police, Berkeley, California (1905-1932). This picture was taken about the time of his retirement June 30, 1932. Most of the time, after becoming Chief, Vollmer wore a business suit, but on special occasions, such as reviewing his officers, he did wear a uniform. *(Courtesy of Alfred E. Parker, Catalina Island, California)*

Chapter 6

LAW ENFORCEMENT IN THE GILDED AGE
(1866-1919)

T he late nineteenth century seemed to be characterized by corruption, materialism, and an indifference to many old American ideas and values. Mark Twain was so disenchanted with the era that he sardonically termed it "the Gilded Age," a name that has struck.[1] The simple and genial philosophies that the country had known for years—romantic, optimistic, heavily religious, individualistic in nature—were to be subjected to the new order, a social, economic, and industrial revolution. Whether the changes that this revolution created were desirable is a question best left for others to answer. America, for good or ill, was changing and it presented an enormous problem for law enforcement officials.

Between 1860 and 1910, America's urban population increased sevenfold. Cities with more than 50,000 inhabitants increased from 16 to 109. The population of New York City jumped from one million to over three million. As might be expected, crime rose astronomically over this period. American society was becoming more dynamic, more complex, increasingly impersonal, and of utmost importance, more mobile; yet the police had no state extradition laws, no criminal records or crime statistics, and no system of interdepartmental communications. Fragmented police departments were still using rural methods to police an increasingly urban society. Realizing that they were fighting a losing battle against crime and violence, some forward-thinking police executives decided to band together in a professional association that would work to solve their problems.

---

[1]Richard N. Current, T. Harry Williams, and Frank Freidel, *American History: A Survey* (New York: Alfred A. Knopf, Inc., 1964), p. 561.

A NATIONAL POLICE CHIEFS' ASSOCIATION[2]

Early in 1871 St. Louis Police Chief James McDonough proposed that "a convention of the heads of police forces of every
city in the union be held to inaugurate and adopt a code of rules
and regulations whereby the whole detective force of the country
can act in unison for the prevention and detection of crime."
Later that year, 112 police officials met in convention to discuss
the increase in crime, the apparent breakdown in the morals of
young people, alcoholism, and other related topics, including the
subject of a uniform crime-reporting system. No clear-cut
decisions were made at the meeting, although one thing became
clear: a permanent association of police chiefs was needed. However, it was not until twenty-two years later that real progress was
made in that direction. In 1893 Chief William S. Seavey of Omaha
proposed a meeting of police executives in Chicago. Fifty-one
chiefs of police attended to discuss "matters of mutual interest."
The primary topic was the desirability of mutual cooperation to
suppress crime and apprehend criminals. The five-day meeting was
so successful that it was decided that a permanent organization
should be immediately formed. Objectives were defined, a constitution was drafted, and the National Chiefs of Police Union was
born. In 1902 the group decided to change its name to the International Association of Chiefs of Police (IACP), a name which it
still bears. The first major contribution of the IACP was the establishment of a central clearing house for criminal identification
records. The clearing house was later converted to a fingerprint
repository. Cities desiring to make use of the repository were
assessed between ten and one hundred dollars per annum,
depending on their size. Over the years, the IACP was to evolve
into one of the most innovative institutions in law enforcement
and one that worked, often against tremendous odds, to professionalize the American police service. Later chapters chronicle
the IACP's total contribution to policing.

THE SEARCH FOR AN IDEAL SYSTEM OF
POLICE ADMINISTRATION
The Decline of State Control

Toward the end of the nineteenth century, the system of state

[2]Excerpted from "IACP," *The Police Chief,* September 1969, pp. 37-39.

control of municipal police departments began to decline, partly because of its lack of success—it did not end corruption, it simply changed the corruptors—and partly because local political bosses could not ply their evil trade without controlling police operations, so they went about restoring the needed control. The decline of state control over police forces actually began in 1868 when the Democratic party, at a convention in Cleveland, sounded the cry for home rule, a not unexpected maneuver considering that Democratic machinery ran most urban areas. The precedent for ending state domination was established in New York City by one of America's classic figures of corruption, Boss Tweed.

William Marcy Tweed, mayor of New York City, was a man who thought big. Tweed's Ring, as his political machine was called, set out to rob the city of some 200 million dollars. The state-controlled police force was a hindrance to Boss Tweed, so he swept it aside and set out to fulfill his master plan of graft and corruption. So extensive became his largesse that almost the entire system of criminal justice was purported to be either on his payroll or afraid to defy him.[3] Said the *New York Times.*[4]

> Our independent police department, which has given us a disciplined and uniformed force in place of a vagabond band of ragamuffins, will yield obedience to that power which demands free rum and votes and gives us police justices who set free fully one-half of all the villains the police properly arrest.

By analyzing Tweed's massive financial empire, the *New York Times* was able to present front page evidence of millions of dollars in graft, thus forcing city policemen into action. One by one Tweed's Ring was arrested until the Boss himself was tried and convicted. Tweed went to jail, where he stayed until his death. The end of state control was a desirable occurrence; but all too often the system that replaced it was one of corrupt political domination, as in New York City. Boss Tweed in many ways typified the cross that honest urban policemen and administrators were forced to bear in the Gilded Age. Three more systems of police administration were to be tried before a workable principle was found: the bipartisan board, the commission government plan, and unified administrative leadership.

[3]John Lofton, *Justice and the Press* (Boston: Beacon Press, 1966), pp. 78-79.

[4]Raymond B. Fosdick, *American Police Systems* (New York: The Century Co., 1920), pp. 94-95.

Birth and Death of the Bipartisan
Administrative Board

The idea behind the bipartisan administrative board, which was in vogue for a short time toward the end of the century, was that politics could never be eliminated from the management of police departments. So a board made up of representatives of both political parties offered the most impartial administrative system. The reasoning was that one partisan administrator could watch another, thus eliminating corrupting influences. The bipartisan principle proved to be unsuccessful in its aim to lessen the influence of politics by taking the police department out of the hands of a single party; in actuality, political influence was simply compounded by turning it over to both parties, which often formed an unholy alliance to thwart aggressive law enforcement. The largest city to try the short-lived concept was Philadelphia.

Enter and Exit the Commission-Government Plan

The next major innovation in police administration came at the turn of the century with the creation of commission government in a number of cities. The concept embodied the integration of legislative and executive powers in a small commission elected at large by popular vote. One member of the commission was designated to be commissioner of public safety, his authority encompassing police and fire operations, the enforcement of building codes, and health and welfare services. The International City Managers' Association termed the concept "amateur supervision by a popularly-elected, transient police administrator. . . complicated by the demands of other important municipal services.[5] Although some communities still use the plan, it fell into disrepute early in the game and many cities which adopted it turned to other methods.

Single Executive Control

After years of trial and error a system of single executive control emerged as the most reasonable and efficient method of operating a police agency. In this system, one man—in theory a professional—was directly appointed by a city's ruling body (or

[5]International City Managers' Association, *Municipal Police Administration,* fifth edition (Washington: International City Managers' Association, 1961), p. 44.

elected by the community) to run the police department. Unified administrative leadership, even today the best proven method of administering police operations, dramatically pointed up the folly of multiple control.

The Search for a Method

In groping for a workable method of administering police operations, major cities went through truly agonizing searches for an "ideal system." Experiment after experiment was tried, but most proved unworkable. Each time a scandal occurred in a police department, public outrage dictated a change in the police organizational setup. The experience in Cincinnati illustrates the unhappy wanderings of a city in search of a method:[6]

1859—Board of four commissioners appointed by mayor, police judge, and city auditor.

1860—Board abolished; Chief of police appointed by the mayor.

1873—Board of four commissioners popularly elected.

1874—Control by mayor reestablished.

1877—Board of of five commissioners appointed by governor.

1880—Control of mayor reestablished.

1885—Board of three commissioners appointed by local board of public works.

1886—Board of four commissioners appointed by governor.

1902—Board of four commissioners appointed by mayor and council. . . .

By way of summary, six major methods of controlling police operations were attempted by municipal and state governments in the nineteenth and early twentieth centuries:

1. Popular elections.
2. Partisan administrative Boards.
3. State control.
4. Bipartisan administrative boards.
5. Commission-government plans.
6. Single executive control.

All, save the last method, proved in varying ways unsuccessful.

THE CORRUPTION ISSUE

Police corruption in the post-Civil War era was conspicuous. It

[6]*Supra* note 4, p. 112.

was a time of big city political bosses, and policemen often had to either cooperate with grafting politicians, ignore obvious violations of the law, or seek other employment. Much police corruption was of the minor variety. The story of a Boston police detective, George S. Chapman, was typical. Chapman, on an assignment to watch for a congregation of pickpockets in Hartford in 1867, was himself arrested for pickpocketing.[7] However, in a disturbing number of cases it was the system of law enforcement and government that was corrupt, and officers were simply swept up in a tide which they could neither control nor resist.

The San Francisco "System"[8]

In many ways the story of San Francisco at the turn of the century was illustrative of the malaise that gripped a number of the country's major cities. Corruption pervaded every component of local government, including, of course, the police department. It was the type of corruption that began at the top of the governmental structure—with the mayor, the board of supervisors, and the police commission—and spread down the pyramid until even the beat patrolmen were effected by it. Under the San Francisco "system" certain favored individuals were given immunity to the law in return for a fee, usually a substantial one, to the right person—the mayor's "representative." Gamblers were allowed to ply their trade, and certain other classes of vice flourished openly. As a result, a virtual reign of terror prevailed. Street robberies were a daily occurrence. Merchants were robbed in broad daylight. Honest citizens were afraid to walk the streets at night. Although street crimes were prevalent, the most substantial criminal income was made in city hall. For example, the mayor decided that it was a good idea to extract large sums of money from the city's "French Restaurants." In San Francisco, the term "French Restaurant" meant any establishment which contained a public restaurant on the ground floor and private supper bedrooms on the second floor. Not unexpectedly these places did a good deal of

[7]Roger Lane, *Policing the City—Boston 1822-1885* (Cambridge: Harvard University Press, 1967), p. 146.

[8]A full account of the San Francisco "system" may be found in Franklin Hichborn's *The System* (Montclair, New Jersey: Patterson Smith Publishing Corp. Originally published in 1915; reprinted in 1969.)

business. The mayor, in collusion with the police commission and the police chief, revoked the liquor license of a French Restaurant known as Tortoni's. All other French Restaurants in the city were notified that when their licenses expired they would not be renewed because of trumped up violations of the city code. The police commission had arbitrary power to revoke licenses. Without a liquor license, which had to be renewed every three months, the restaurants could not remain in business. One of the police commissioners would not agree to the mayor's plan, so he was summarily dismissed and replaced by a more cooperative commissioner. As everything appeared darkest to the French Restaurant Association, an attorney magically appeared on the scene guaranteeing the proprietors that he, for a fee, could get their licenses renewed. The Association signed a contract with the attorney—the mayor's man—for a fat fee and they were never again bothered.

Just as crime and violence threatened to revive San Francisco's committees of vigilance, the district attorney, an honest public official, assisted by a small group of policemen, initiated a probe which ended with the arrest and indictment of the mayor and the chief of police, the resignation of sixteen San Francisco supervisors, and the shocking exposé of the "system" to the rest of the state and the nation. The later trials, known as The San Francisco Graft Prosecution, were marred by extreme violence. On one occasion a witness' home was dynamited. On another an assistant district attorney was shot down as he stood in his courtroom. However, in the end, the corruptors were imprisoned for their crimes and a virtual revolution in city government ended the San Francisco "system."

THE PENDLETON ACT: AN END TO THE SPOILS ERA

Police corruption in the Gilded Age was a complex phenomenon. To allege that it was caused by one or two social, economic, or political factors is to perpetrate an inaccuracy, for it was a multifaceted problem. The police were badly trained, poorly equipped, overworked, underpaid, and politically dominated, to mention but a few of the early wrongs. In simplest terms the environment of the era made it exceedingly difficult to be an honest policeman. In 1883 the Federal Government, reacting to the assassination of President James Garfield by a frustrated office-seeker, passed the Pendleton Act, thus ending seventy-five years of the "spoils system," at least at some governmental levels.

The Pendleton Act of 1883 was a civil service law which "classified" a limited number of Federal jobs so that applicants would have to be chosen by competitive written examinations. To administer the Act, a bipartisan civil service commission was established. Initially only 14,000 of 100,000 positions were placed on the classified list, but within a half-century a majority of Federal employees were under civil service.

Although the Pendleton Act did not apply to municipal government, it did set a precedent for civil service coverage. The Federal Government's success with the system motivated many communities to adopt it. The enactment of civil service regulations in many cities eliminated one causative element of police corruption, but only one.

THE ADVANCE OF TECHNOLOGY: A TWO-EDGED SWORD

The years following the Civil War saw a flood of inventions and technological innovations. In the entire history of the United States to 1860 only 36,000 patents had been issued, but from 1860 to 1890 there were 440,000! Police departments did not rush to take advantage of technological achievements, although a few law enforcement agencies did employ some of the new-fangled devices. In 1867 the first call boxes were installed for use by patrolmen in selected urban areas. By 1878 police in the District of Columbia had installed telephones in precincts, the first police agency in the country to use the device on a regular basis. In 1880 the Chicago Police Department was first to use a combined telephone and telegraph call box system. Chicago in 1884 established the country's first criminal identification bureau. The New York Police Department, emulating the private shipping industry, in 1908 became the first police department to install wireless telegraph on its patrol boats. Probably the most grisly use of technology occurred in 1891 when New York became the first state to electrocute a man for murder.

The advent of technology also had a negative impact on law enforcement, partly because of social pressures—society became increasingly impersonal, dynamic, and complex—and partly

During the late 1800s a novel communication system was developed in Chicago by the Gamewell Telephone and Telegraph System. Boxes equipped with telephones were installed at various places throughout a city so that patrolmen and citizens could immediately communicate with police headquarters. This, the Gamewell System, was the forerunner of today's modern call boxes. *(Courtesy of the New Haven Police Department)*

because criminals often seemed to make better use of the new achievements than did the police. Burglars replaced gunpowder with nitroglycerin. Safes were entered and locks picked with burglarly devices of enormous complexity. The development of systems of transportation made it easy for criminals of all types to achieve a degree of mobility previously denied them. The police, on the other hand, were virtually trapped within arbitrarily set political boundaries—city limits, county lines, state lines.

The old and the new of another era. On the left, a Bertillion operator measures a suspect's body for identification purposes; while on the right, a fingerprint technician illustrates the identification method that replaced the Bertillion system. *(Courtesy of the Chicago Police Department)*

The science of criminal investigation began to emerge in the post-Civil War period, spurred on by the advance of technology and the growing sophistication of criminals. The new science was truly an international phenomenon as scientists from scores of countries invented new concepts and improved existing ones. In 1883 Alphonse Bertillion, a youthful employee in the identification division of the Prefecture of Police in Paris, conducted a survey of his files which indicated that no two people had the

same physical measurements. As a result of the survey, Bertillion developed the first system of criminal identification. Responding to criticism from Paris policemen that they could not stop and measure each suspect they encountered, Bertillion created a system of visual identification which concentrated on the characteristics of a person's head. The size and shape of a man's head was categorized along with descriptions of certain facial features until a portrait of him emerged. Positive identification of a suspect could then be made from photographs. This system was called portrait parlé. In 1892 a method called fingerprints began to replace portrait parlé as a system of personal identification. The concept was not new; the Chinese had experimented with it over one thousand years before. However, an English scientist named Francis Galton offered conclusive proof of the uniqueness of individual fingerprints. The discovery that no two fingerprints were alike furnished police agencies with a criminal identification method of revolutionary proportions. Nine years later Sir Richard Henry developed a system for classifying fingerprints which allowed clerks to have speedy access to print files. In 1910 an American, Albert Gross, developed a system of authenticating questioned documents and for the first time American courts accepted as admissable scientific evidence in this area.

LABOR MILITANCY AND THE POLICE

The Gilded Age saw the rise of "big business." As business became big, consolidated, and national in its scope, it was inevitable that labor would attempt to follow suit and create an organization that would match the power of capital. Laboring men, not unexpectedly, wanted a bigger piece of the action. Thwarting their efforts, however, were unresponsive management and a hostile, antiunion public. During the early years of trade unionism, disputes between labor and management consistently deteriorated into extreme collective violence. All too often poorly trained, ill-equipped, and outnumbered police departments found themselves thrust into these controversies. In a number of cases labor violence was confronted and suppressed by management without police help, there being no formal law enforcement in some turbulent areas. A few of the more dramatic manifestations involved extremist groups like the Molly Maguires (1870s); but most violent and bloody occurrences simply involved the police or para-policemen and angry working men. Typical were the Haymarket Affair (1886), the Carnegie Steel Strike (1892), and the Great Strikes of 1917-1919.

The Molly Maguires[9]

The Molly Maguires was a secret society whose members ter-

---

[9]Walter J. Coleman, *Labor Disturbances in Pennsylvania, 1850-1880* (New York: Arno Press, 1936, reprinted 1970).

rorized the eastern Pennsylvania coal fields in the early 1870s. The Mollies were of the ancient order of the Hibernians, a group that had revolted against their landlords in Ireland and who now rebelled against English mine owners in America. The Molly Maguires intimidated coal operators with such direct methods as murder. There being no effective formal police forces in the eastern Pennslyvania region at the time, the Philadelphia and Reading Railroad—owner of most of the mines—set out to engage parapolice help. The indomitable Pinkertons were contacted and they agreed to send one of their most capable investigators, Detective James McParlan, to infiltrate the Mollies. McParlan worked his way into the organization and became a Molly leader. As a result of his undercover exploits, authorities were able to arrest, convict, and execute many Mollies, thereby curtailing their reign of tyranny.

On May 4, 1886, an anarchist threw a bomb into a formation of Chicago policemen in Haymarket Square. Eight officers were killed and sixty-seven others were wounded in one of the blackest moments in police history. *(Courtesy of the Chicago Police Department)*

The Haymarket Affair[10]

On May 4, 1886, in the midst of a strike at the McCormick Harvester Company in Chicago, a group of anarchists—European radicals who wanted to destroy "class government" by terroristic tactics—called a meeting in Haymarket Square to protest "police harassment" of strikers. During the meeting the Chicago police appeared and ordered the protestors to disperse. Suddenly a bomb was thrown into the phalanx of policemen by an unknown assailant. When the smoke had cleared, eight policemen has been killed and sixty-seven others had been wounded. Chicago officials rounded up eight anarchists and charged them with the murders of the officers on the grounds that they had incited the individual who had thrown the bomb (he was never captured). In a trial heavy with emotion and vituperation, all were convicted and four were condemned to death. The Haymarket Affair polarized public opinion against labor, which was widely thought to be dominated by anarchists and radicals, and it set the tone for future police-labor confrontations.

The Carnegie Steel Strike[11]

When in 1892 the management of Pennsylvania's Carnegie Steel Company announced that a small group of workers would have to take cuts in salary, trouble followed. Workers shut down the plant and gathered to protest management's action. Management promptly hired three hundred Pinkerton guards to reopen the plant. The Pinkerton Detective Agency was now more a strike-breaking firm than an investigating body. The Pinkertons marched on the plant where they were met by strikers armed with guns, dynamite, clubs, and knives. In the battle that ensued, three guards and ten strikers were killed and hundreds of participants were injured. At the battle's end the Pinkertons surrendered and were unceremoniously escorted from the scene. Management and local police officials petitioned the state for assistance, whereupon some eight thousand National Guard troops were sent to preserve order. They did, but not before an anarchist tried, unsuccessfully, to assassinate a Carnegie executive.

[10]*Supra* note 1, pp. 509-510.

[11]*Ibid.*, p. 511.

The Great Strikes of 1917-1919

Labor militancy reached its peak in the 1917-1919 period when a wave of strikes spread across the country involving at one time or another more than five million workers, ranging from longshoremen to Metropolitan Opera stars. Time after time, policemen and parapolice firms—notably the Pinkerton Agency—were called upon to man the barricades against strikers. Time and time again blood was spilled by the police and by their adversaries. In many instances troops had to be called out as militant activity went beyond the bounds of reason. However, the police were by no means immune to labor militancy within their own ranks. In 1919 no less than thirty-three police departments had been granted charters from the American Federation of Labor (AFL). By far the most famous case of police-labor militancy occurred in Boston in 1919.

The Boston Police Strike

In 1919 the lot of Boston's policemen was indeed unhappy. In fact, the conditions under which patrolmen labored were scandalous. Policemen were entitled to but one full day off every fifteen days, and even then were required to obtain written permission from superiors to go beyond the city limits of Boston. Officers, depending on their assignments, worked between seventy-three and ninety-eight hours weekly. The little off-duty time they received was often spent on standby duty in the back rooms of precinct stations. Precincts were old and vermin-ridden and the rickety bunk beds provided for standby officers had to be shared by two men. Although promotional examinations were given by the department, it was perfectly legal for police administrators to ignore top scorers and promote political cronies. In addition to their regular duties, officers were made to fulfill "miscellaneous services" such as delivering unpaid tax bills. For this, patrolmen were paid $1,300 per annum—about twenty-five cents an hour, half of what war-workers made, and considerably less than streetcar motormen earned.[12] In August, 1919, the Boston Social Club, the patrolmen's fraternal organization, petitioned the American Federation of Labor for a union charter, which was granted. Police Commissioner Edwin U. Curtis, out-

[12]*The Boston Globe*, September 9, 1919, p. 12.

The Boston Police Strike of 1919 stunned the nation and brought a quick response from government. On the left is former Superintendent of Police William Pierce, who mobilized a volunteer police force to replace striking officers. On the right, Boston Police Station Number 1 stands vacant in the wake of the strike.

raged at the action, issued an order forbidding union membership; however, the officers, led by the president of their union, Patrolman John F. McInnes, defied the order and refused to disband. Curtis brought McInnes and eighteen other leaders up on departmental charges, tried and convicted them but delayed sentencing in deference to Mayor Andrew J. Peters, who had appointed a committee of thirty-four citizens to try and seek a solution to the problem. The Committee of Thirty-four, as it was called, was headed by James J. Storrow, a dedicated civic leader. The committee came up with a solution to which all the parties, except

Curtis, agreed. The main issue in the settlement involved leniency for the nineteen officers: the patrolmen demanded it; the mayor urged it; and Storrow and his committee recommended it. Whereupon Commissioner Curtis suspended the nineteen. On September 9, 1,117 of Boston's 1,544 policemen went on strike to protest the suspensions.[13] It should be noted that the political atmosphere at the time was not conducive to the settling of disputes. The mayor was a Democrat; the Commissioner, a former mayor, was Republican. They had both attended school in New England at competitive institutions. Compounding the problem was the fact that the power to appoint the police commissioner rested not with the mayor but with Governor Calvin Coolidge, a lifelong Republican. Commissioner Curtis failed to mobilize a replacement force for the strikers on the first night of the walkout, leaving the city virtually unprotected. Some historians feel that Curtis' initial

[13]Claude M. Foess, *Calvin Coolidge* (Boston: Little, Brown and Co., 1940), pp. 203-218.

inaction was due to his refusal to believe his men would strike, while others allege that the Commissioner did so to polarize public opinion against the patrolmen. Crime and violence—mostly minor—erupted and troops were dispatched to Boston. A volunteer police force was also organized. Extreme physical force was used by the troops in restoring order: groups of people were indiscriminately fired into; machine guns were turned on a crowd which refused to disperse; gamblers fleeing crap games were fired upon, and on at least one occasion soldiers on horseback with drawn sabers swept Scollay Square clean of people by employing a classic cavalry charge. Throughout the critical stages of the strike, the Governor refused to act or even comment on the affair. Only after civil and military authorities appeared to have the situation under control and public opinion had clearly been mobilized against striking officers did Governor Coolidge release a statement. Stated Coolidge: "There is no right to strike against the public safety by anybody, any time, anywhere!"[14] When the smoke had cleared, the 1,117 strikers were fired, a new police force was hired, and Coolidge, who had become a national hero because of his belated remark, was on the road to the Presidency, an office he was ill-equipped to assume. Boston's action in firing the striking patrolmen set a precedent for dealing with rebellious policemen which lasted for nearly a half-century.[15]

The Organization of Police Rank and File

Although the general phenomenon of labor militancy had an impact on the internal workings of police departments, the Boston Police Strike was an extreme example of that impact. Few police departments of the day even threatened to strike, much less engage in it. But the country's working men were unionizing and it was only natural that policemen, most of whom came from laboring backgrounds, would organize too. Some affiliated with unions but most banded together in fraternal groups, social clubs, and benevolent associations. While these organizations performed a social role, they also provided the collective strength officers

[14]*Ibid.*, pp. 219-233.

[15]Elmer D. Graper, *American Police Administration* (New York: The Macmillian Co., 1921), p. 318.

needed to press economic issues. They were not unions, but many fulfilled a number of union-like functions. New York City led in the establishment of police rank-and-file organizations with the founding of the Patrolmen's Benevolent Association (PBA) in 1894. Many police forces followed suit and soon these types of groups abounded. Probably the most significant occurrence in this

An early paddy wagon ready for patrol duty—except for buttoning up that blouse! *(Courtesy of the Chicago Police Department)*

area came in 1915, when two Pittsburgh patrolmen, Martin L. Toole and Delbert H Nagle, founded the Fraternal Order of Police (FOP). The FOP soon became a national organization, the primary strength of which centered in the industrial cities of the Northeast. What the labor union was to the worker, the FOP and like organizations became to the policeman. However, the FOP was different from a union in two major respects: (1) it prohibited striking and (2) it enrolled everyone from patrolman to chief. Fifty years after its inception, the FOP was to become one of the largest and most powerful organizations of its type in America.

THE STATE POLICE

The changing American social scene, now unalterably modified by technology and the predictable events caused by a nation in transition, forced state governments to seek new ways in which to meet the challenges of the era. In 1893 Charles and Frank Duryea built and operated the first gasoline-powered automobile in the United States. Less than twenty-five years later there were nearly five million automobiles on the roads.[16] That, coupled with the inadequacy of the state militia, rural police agencies, and para-police organizations to cope with labor disorders, led state legislatures to consider creating state police agencies.

A number of early state police experiments had been undertaken by some states. In 1835 the Texas Rangers were formed; in 1865 Massachusetts appointed a handful of state constables to suppress commercialized vice, the country's first general state police force; in 1901 the Arizona Rangers were established; while in 1903 Connecticut formed a small state patrol force. In 1905 New Mexico created a mounted patrol to police its borders.[17] But these were small agencies with sharply limited functions and by 1905 it was obvious that a new approach was needed. In that year Pennsylvania, in a sharp break with tradition, created a State Constabulary.

The Pennsylvania State Police Department was as unique from other police forces as night was from day. Other law enforcement agencies had evolved through centuries of painfully gradual development. But, as one police scholar put it, the Pennsylvania force "was not evolved...it was made."[18] Traditional concepts of police organization and administration were totally ignored. Recognized and accepted police practices were shunned. The Pennsylvania State Police Force was a revolutionary concept and one that signaled the beginning of a new era in law enforcement administration.

The Pennsylvania State Constabulary was commanded by a superintendent of police, who was responsible only to the governor, an important administrative breakthrough. From its inception, it operated as a mounted and uniformed force assigned to patrol the entire state, not just selected areas. It did this by systematically creating troop headquarters and substations in even the most remote areas of the state. Pennsylvania had created a true

[16]*Supra* note 1, p. 589.

[17]Bruce Smith, *The State Police* (New York: The Macmillian Co., 1925), pp. 34-39.

[18]*Ibid.*, p. 39.

Members of the Pennsylvania State Police in 1906, a year after their founding. President Theodore Roosevelt *(pictured above)* was an enthusiastic backer of the force from the beginning, and he once stated, "I feel so strongly about them that the mere fact that a man is honorably discharged from this Force would make me at once, and without hesitation, employ him for any purpose needing courage, prowess, good judgment, loyalty, and entire trust-worthiness." *(Courtesy of the Pennsylvania State Police)*

state police organization. "Both in its scheme of organization, and in its policy of continuous patrol, this organization represented a distinct departure from earlier state practice."[19]

For the next dozen years there was little extension of the state police concept. No new state police forces were formed and existing forces seemed content to expand gradually and adopt the procedures of other state organizations that seemed to be working. In many cases Pennsylvania's Constabulary served as a model. However, in response to emerging traffic problems, labor disorders, and civil turmoil, other states eventually followed the lead of the pioneers.

In 1917 civil unrest prompted New York to establish a state police, modeled after Pennsylvania's idea. That same year, the Colorado Rangers were established. The Michigan State Police was organized in 1917. West Virginia set up a Department of Public Safety. In 1919 New Jersey, Maryland, and Delaware followed

[19]*Ibid.*, p. 40.

suit.[20] By 1920 two distinct types of state forces had evolved: (1) those which had general law enforcement duties and (2) those whose primary responsibility was motor vehicle control. The fledgling state police movement was to meet great resistance from many quarters. Three of the early forces—those in Colorado, Arizona, and New Mexico—were disbanded because of politics. Laboring men often despised the state police, which they believed was established to break strikes. The American Civil Liberties Union was to later initiate court suits to test the legality and constitutionality of many forces. But state police forces survived this early controversy and, in time, received popular public acceptance as a necessary and desirable institution.

THE RISE OF FEDERAL ENFORCEMENT AGENCIES

Federal law enforcement agencies were created in a rather haphazard fashion by a United States Congress responding to the emergence of selected problems. Most were set up on an *ad hoc* basis, that is their jurisdiction was generally limited to specific crimes or classes of crimes. It was well into the twentieth century before any type of coordinated effort was undertaken to unify fragmented Federal police agencies. Some of the early developments in this area represented a response to crises, rather than the thoughtful and studied implementation of a needed investigative component.

In 1861 Congress appropriated money to "investigate crimes against the United States"; seven years later the Internal Revenue Service appointed twenty-five "detectives." Although Congress passed a bill in 1842 to combat counterfeiting, it was 1865 before the Secret Service was assigned to investigate violations of it. Expanded duties of the Service were to include protection of the President and Vice-President and their immediate families. On June 22, 1870, the United States Attorney General appointed a handful of detectives to investigate the importation of women from Europe for immoral purposes. In 1886 the United States Customs Service organized the Border Patrol. By the first decade of the twentieth century, it became apparent that the Federal Government needed a professional staff of full-time general

---

[20]*Ibid.,* pp. 41-45.

investigators to handle the rising volume of lawlessness, mostly of the white-collar variety, against the Government. Accordingly, in 1908 President Theodore Roosevelt organized the Bureau of Investigation to serve as the investigative branch of the Department of Justice. The Bureau, forerunner of the FBI, was small in number and not noted for its brilliance, at least in the early days.

THE ADVENT OF WOMEN POLICE

The dawning of the twentieth century saw a good deal of police reform, much of it well accepted by a public tired of inefficient policing, corruption, and a spiraling crime rate. However, some of the early innovations were, to say the least, controversial. One of the most radical new ideas involved the employment of women as police officers.

Although women had been employed as police matrons since 1845, the first actual appointment of a woman to perform police duties came in 1893, when Mrs. Marie Owens, a policeman's widow, was hired by the Chicago Police Department as a "patrolman," a position she held for thirty years.[21] In 1905 Mrs. Lola Baldwin was officially appointed to do "protective work" with young girls at Oregon's Lewis and Clark Centennial Exposition.[22] In 1910 the Los Angeles Police Department appointed the first full-time paid "policewoman" when it hired Mrs. Alice Stebbins Wells. Mrs. Wells was a rather imaginative woman. Prior to her appointment she had conducted a crime survey that concluded, not coincidentally, that there was a crying need for women in police work. Armed with this information, she persuaded a hundred prominent citizens to sign a petition to the mayor demanding that he add her to the police force. Mrs. Wells kept the petition secret so that the antifeminist press would not editorially condemn her and her concept. The mayor, a practical man who interpreted the petition as a mandate from a substantial number of civic leaders, hired Mrs. Wells.

[21] Chloe Owings, *Women Police* (Montclair, New Jersey: Patterson Smith Publishing Corp. Originally published in 1925, reprinted in 1969), pp. 99-100.

[22] Edward Eldefonso, Alan Coffey, and Richard C. Grace, *Principles of Law Enforcement* (New York: John Wiley & Sons, Inc., 1968), p. 121.

Soon other communities followed Los Angeles' example. By 1915 twenty-five cities had policewomen "paid from police appropriations." Chicago, with twenty-one, had the largest number.[23] Policewomen in Chicago had the following duties:[24]

1. The return of runaway girls to their homes.
2. The warning of young girls.
3. The suppression of dance hall evils.
4. The suppression of petty gambling in stores frequented by children.
5. The suppression of the sale of liquor to minors.
6. Service at railroad depots.
7. The conducting of investigations and the securing of evidence.

In 1915 policewomen earned between $800 and $1,200 per annum, substantially less than policemen. By the summer of that year, the International Association of Policewomen was organized in Baltimore. The objectives of the organization were threefold:[25]

1. To gather information as to the progress of policewomen's work and to furnish authentic data in response to inquiries from individuals and communities wishing to establish this work.
2. To maintain such a standard of character and efficiency as will attract to the work the highest type of women.
3. To advance general service to the community.

Incredibly, policewomen were striving for professionalism nearly four decades before most of their male counterparts progressed beyond the talking stage. In 1918 the Welfare Bureau of the New York City Police Department was placed under the direction of Mrs. Ellen O'Grady, who was given the rank of deputy police commissioner. Mrs. O'Grady was the first woman to be appointed to an executive position on an American police department. During the first six months of her command, Mrs. O'Grady's

[23]U. S. Census Bureau, *General Statistics of Cities* (1915), p. 18.

[24]*Supra* note 16, p. 228.

[25]*Ibid.*, pp. 232-233.

bureau handled 6,709 investigations.[26]

In 1919 Indianapolis created a Bureau of Policewomen. The Bureau handled over 5,000 cases in its first year of operation and won an enthusiastic commendation from its chief of police. That year, policewomen in Dayton, Ohio, persuaded city officials to establish and finance a Policewomen's House for misdemeanants and destitute females. A similar project was successfully undertaken in Seattle. By 1920 the International Association of Policewomen was encouraging policewomen and policewoman candidates to seek college-level training.

From 1910 to 1920 policewomen made substantial gains: pay began to improve; working conditions were bearable; they gained a measure of acceptance from their male colleagues; and of utmost importance, they rendered a needed service to the community. Over the years, the role of the policewoman was expanded to include a wide spectrum of police duties. Police honor roles contain the names of women who made outstanding contributions to their profession; some even made the ultimate sacrifice by forfeiting their lives to protect the community they had sworn to serve.

THE EMERGENCE OF AMERICAN POLICE LITERATURE

The post-Civil War period saw the emergence of police literature, an important intellectual development in the evolution of any craft, but especially important to an occupational group attempting to attain higher status in the eyes of the public, as many law enforcement agencies were trying to do. Foreign police scholars—especially those in England and France—began writing books on the subject of police administration, history, and reform before the close of the eighteenth century. By the third decade of the nineteenth century, a significant number of scholarly works had been produced by European authors, including Patrick Colquhoun and John Wade. But American law enforcement experienced an understandable lag in this area and it was late in the nineteenth century before a significant number of police books began appearing on the scene. However, when law enforcement literature began to appear, it did so in great profusion. Some of the most critically acclaimed works included *Police Records*

[26]*Semi-Annual Report of the Police Commissioner, New York City,* July 1, 1918, p. 27.

and Recollections (1873) by Edward H. Savage, a 240-year history of the Boston Police Department; Augustine Costello's *Our Police Protectors* (1885), a history of the New York Police Department from colonial times to the post-Civil War period; *The Philadelphia Police: Past and Present* (1887) by George W. Walling; George A. Tappan's *A 20th Century Souvenir: the Officers and Men of the Boston Police* (1901); Louis N. Robinson's *History and Organization of Criminal Statistics of the United States* (1911); *On the Enforcement of Law in Cities* (1913) by Brand Whitlock and *European Police Systems* (1915) by Raymond B. Fosdick.

Police scholars in the Gilded Age, admittedly a small group, provided the cornerstone for an American police literature. Slowly, almost painfully, it evolved until, in less than a century, it began to motivate a movement toward police professionalization and to provide a medium for education, self-examination, and reform.

PIONEERS IN POLICE TRAINING

Although the most dramatic innovations in police training programs occurred in later eras, the foundation for those later developments was laid in the first two decades of the twentieth century by pioneering departments and individuals. The movement toward police training was motivated in no small measure by Raymond B. Fosdick, who, in his book *European Police Systems,* compared the efficiency of European and United States police forces, with the American police coming off decidedly second best.[27]

The first formal training school for policemen was established in Berkeley in 1908. The following year the New York City Police Department established a police academy, an outgrowth of its School of Pistol Practice which had been in operation since 1895.[28] Detroit established a training school for officers in 1911, while Philadelphia followed suit two years later. New York expanded the scope of its training to include detectives, also in

[27]V. A. Leonard, *Police Organization and Management* (Brooklyn: The Foundation Press, 1951), pp. 136-137.

[28]Allen Z. Gammage, *Police Training in the United States* (Springfield: Charles C Thomas, Publisher, 1963), p. 6.

1911.[29] In 1916 the University of California at Berkeley created the first training school for policemen in a university. Two years later the chief of police in Berkeley persuaded university officials to offer liberal arts courses for policemen, while the police department would teach technical police subjects. In 1918 the first school for policewomen was created at the University of California at Los Angeles.[30] California had clearly established itself as an early leader in the field of police training, a lead it has never relinquished.

DEVELOPMENTS IN MUNICIPAL POLICING

Although the "big three" police departments—Boston, Philadelphia, and New York—led the way in implementing meaningful police reforms, they were joined by other emerging communities in instituting reforms and adopting new ideas. Just two years after Alexander Graham Bell invented the telephone, the Cincinnati Police Department installed a telephone exchange to serve the entire department, the first police agency in the country to completely replace the telegraph with the telephone. In 1881 Cincinnati organized a patrol wagon service, the second of its kind in the country. The department was reorganized in 1886: a detective unit was established; mounted policemen on horseback replaced foot patrolmen on outlying beats; an annual departmental inspection was inaugurated; a police library was placed in the headquarters building, and a system of awards was initiated to reward meritorious service in the ranks. By the second decade of the twentieth century, Cincinnati had created a traffic squad, replaced its horse patrol with automobiles and motorcycles, and established a criminal identification bureau.

In 1901 the Fitchburg, Massachusetts, Police Department was reorganized: a civil service system was implemented; patrol wagon service commenced; and the reserve police force, created five years earlier, was expanded. The department, following the lead of others, was organized along semimilitary lines. The following year a police ambulance service was initiated. In 1908 fifty-seven call

---

[29]*Supra* note 16, pp. 111-116.

[30]*Supra* note 29, pp. 60-62.

boxes and red lights were installed throughout the city. Several years later the city commissioned its first motorcycle detail.

One of the earliest police motorcycles, an Excelsior Autocycle, was used by the Detroit Police Department in 1915. Pedal to get rolling, then belt drive took over. *(Courtesy of the Detroit Police Department)*

The Flint, Michigan, Police Department appointed its first chief of police in 1890, replacing the earlier marshal system. Ten years later its first police station was built. In 1912 serious police reform began in Flint: the force was expanded to forty-four men; the department began furnishing uniforms and nightsticks to its officers, and the pay of policemen was doubled.

The Detroit Police Department established a juvenile unit in 1877, augmenting it with a truancy squad six years later. In 1897 bicycle patrolmen were added to the force. The Scorcher Cops, as they were known, were assigned almost exclusively to the apprehension of speeding bicycle riders, of which Detroit had its share. With the advent of the automobile, Detroit soon established itself as a leader in traffic safety innovations. Some of the Detroit Police

The world's first police car was a Detroit Police Model T Ford with home-made antenna. *(Courtesy of the Detroit Police Department)*

traffic safety firsts included: creation of the first "school safety patrol," installation of the first stop sign and the first automatic traffic signal light, formation of the first traffic school for violators, and the first use of pedestrian control by loudspeaker.

In 1895 uniforms were issued for the first time to officers in the Los Angeles Police Department. They were accompanied with an order from the chief of police to "keep your coats buttoned, stars pinned over left breast on outside of coat, and hold your clubs firmly," a bit of good advice for those early policemen. During the next ten years the Central Police Station was built, a police alarm system was installed, a bicycle squad was organized to patrol residential areas, and a new substation was opened. In the years immediately preceding World War I, a fingerprint repository was initiated and juvenile and identification bureaus were formed.

In 1905 *August Vollmer* was elected town marshal of Berkeley, a new California city. When the office of marshal was eliminated and replaced by the position of chief of police, Vollmer was appointed to the post, an appointment he held until 1932. Chief Vollmer was a gifted administrator who brought professional law

A traffic semaphore in the 1920s, operated by a Detroit patrolman. The Detroit Department was an early leader in developing and utilizing traffic safety devices. *(Courtesy of the Detroit Police Department)*

enforcement to Berkeley at a time when it was little more than a dream in other departments. Vollmer was instrumental in creating the first training school for policemen in Berkeley, and it was largely through his efforts that the University of California initiated its early criminology program. Police departments from across the country emulated Berkeley innovations, and the department served as a model for many agencies desiring internal reform. August Vollmer was to become the patriarch of California law enforcement and one of the most significant figures in the history of American policing. The Vollmer philosophy of municipal law enforcement consisted of twelve elements. Considering the stage of development of the American police, they were no less significant than the twelve tenets of Peelian reform:

1. The public is entitled to police service as efficient as budget and manpower permit.
2. Courtesy is of paramount importance in all public and private contacts with citizens.
3. Police personnel of the highest intelligence, good education, unquestioned integrity, and with a personal history demonstrating an ability to work in harmony with others

are necessary to effectively discharge the police responsibility.

4. Comprehensive, basic, advanced, and specialized training on a continuing basis is essential.

5. Broad responsibility should be assigned to the beat officer.

>   Crime prevention through effective patrol.
>
>   Investigation of all offenses.
>
>   Traffic law enforcement.
>
>   Juvenile duties.
>
>   Public relations expert.
>
>   Report writer.
>
>   Thoroughly competent witness.
>
>   A generalist rather than a specialist.

6. Superior supervision of personnel and effective leadership.

7. Good public relations in the broadest sense.

8. Cooperation with the press and news media.

9. Exemplary official and personal conduct.

10. Prompt investigation and disposition of personnel complaints.

11. Adherence to the law enforcement code of ethics.

12. Protection of individual rights while providing for the security of persons and property.

THE VOLSTEAD ACT: LEGALLY ENFORCED ABSTINENCE

The attempts by certain groups to force—through legislative enactment by executive decree, or through moral suasion—communities to abstain from imbibing alcoholic beverages has been a recurring phenomenon in America, harking all the way back to colonial days. Many early groups spoke of "temperance" rather than outright "prohibition," choosing to persuade not legislate. It was not that those early groups did not want restrictive legislation; legislation was simply a politically impossible maneuver, so the old temperance societies chose preachment and promise of everlasting damnation to servants of "demon rum." But as the clamor against overindulgence grew, fragmented temperance organizations unified, became more militant, and a fullblown national movement evolved, one which abandoned the idea of temperance by persuasion and demanded abstinence by law.

The first great wave of prohibition began in 1846. Within ten years, thirteen states had adopted laws prohibiting the manufacture, sale, or consumption of most types of alcoholic beverages. By 1863, however, the wave receded as the number of prohibition states had shrunk to five, four of which were southern states which were to later secede from the union.[31]

Undismayed, the movement, made up of such groups as the Prohibition Party, the Women's Christian Temperance Union (WCTU), and the International Order of Good Templars (IOGT), enlisted the aid of church groups and social service agencies, and there was "a siege against the saloons."[32] By the 1880s another wave of prohibition arrived, again to be short-lived. By 1913 the prohibition movement was battle-scarred, but unbowed. Few observers gave it an even outside chance for success, but an unexpected factor was suddenly introduced into American life: World War I.

The war accomplished three things for prohibitionists: (1) it centralized authority in Washington, thus giving the national government sweeping new powers to enact drastic legislation; (2) it stressed the importance of saving food, making it appear unpatriotic to "pour hundreds of millions of bushels of grain annually into the breweries," and (3) it outlawed all things German. As most brewers were German, it was an easy task for prohibitionists to denounce them not only as enemies of temperance but as enemies of peace and the American way.[33] As the Anti-Saloon League of New York stated:[34]

> The liquor traffic aids those forces in our country whose loyalty is called into question at this hour. The liquor traffic is the strong financial supporter of the German-American Alliance. The purpose of this Alliance is to secure German solidarity for the promotion of German ideals. . . .

With a new prestige gained through the war measures, disciples of prohibition pressed hard for their goal. In October, 1919, after

---

[31]Charles Merz, *A Dry Decade* (Seattle: University of Washington Press, 1969), p. 3.

[32]Norman H. Clarke, *The Dry Years: Prohibition and Social Change in Washington* (Seattle: University of Washington Press, 1965), p. 29.

[33]*The New York Times,* June 18, 1917, p. 1.

[34]*Supra* note 32, p. 27.

years of trying, their efforts bore fruit when Congress passed, over President Wilson's veto, the drastic Volstead Act, which was later to be the Prohibition (Eighteenth) Amendment. The Act prohibited all liquor containing more than one half of one percent of alcohol. Prohibition had come.

CONCLUSION

American law enforcement was entering a period of crisis. A law had been passed which significant numbers of people had not the slightest intention of obeying. Thrust into the untenable position of enforcing an unenforceable law, policemen were given the choice of exerting strong control over the country's drinking habits, or looking the other way as the public engaged in a socially acceptable vice. Some police departments followed the former course, others the latter. Too many police officials and politicians looked on prohibition as a way to give the public what it wanted—full access to speakeasies—while lining their pockets with payoff money received from illicit bars. Prohibition set the cause of police professionalization back decades. It has been said that prohibition was a "minus sum" game which produced no winners, only losers. But there was a winner created by legally enforced abstinence. In the late 1880s, the Italian population in many large American cities was terrorized by a group of foreign-born extortioners and racketeers. Prohibition was to convert these small time criminals into a powerful criminal syndicate whose evil influence was to spread across the country. The group was the Sicilian Society known as the Mafia.[35]

---

[35] Frank Shay, *Judge Lynch: His First Hundred Years* (Montclair, New Jersey: Patterson Smith Publishing Corp. Originally published in 1938, reprinted in 1969), p. 161.

In 1924 an unknown young attorney, John Edgar Hoover, was appointed Director of the troubled Federal Bureau of Investigation. Under Hoover's leadership, the FBI was to emerge as one of the most respected police agencies in the world. *(Courtesy of the FBI)*

Chapter 7

POLICING PROHIBITION (1920-1929)

Prohibition, "the noble experiment that failed," should have worked. It had almost everything going for it, including a dry Constitution, a dry Congress, dry state legislatures, and support from a majority of the public. But it did not work because its supporters failed to take one factor into account: human frailty. There were individuals and groups who, for a price, worked diligently to fill the need created by this frailty. Whiskey literally poured across the border from Canada. It came in cars, in trucks, and in buses; it flowed through in planes and in boats; it gushed into cities by railroad car, in briefcases, in coat pockets, and in a hundred and one other ways. Whiskey that was not smuggled into the country was manufactured here in the thousands of unlawful stills that had popped up across the land. Bootlegging—the manufacture, sale, or transportation of illegal alcohol—became a big business, too big to remain disorganized. Gangs of all kinds and descriptions arose to form syndicates to capitalize on the demand for the illegal commodity.

Policing prohibition, even under the best of circumstances, would have been difficult. But the circumstances were far from ideal. The nation's police forces were generally badly paid, ill-trained, and poorly equipped. Many worked under the heavy hand of domineering politicians who had entered into collusive relationships with gangsters to thwart, rather than suppress, liquor law violations. Those agencies that honestly tried to enforce prohibition, including the Federal Government, did so in a rather swashbuckling and self-defeating manner. Prohibition inaugurated the most extensive effort ever undertaken to legally change the social habits of an entire nation. Consequently, it would have been reasonable to expect that the enforcement of such a unique enterprise would have been launched carefully, with specially selected and trained police forces whose enforcement efforts would be tempered toward enlisting public support and aid. No such course of action was followed. Thousands of small consumers were arrested while large dealers pursued their business with little interference, thus antagonizing the very people whose support the police vitally needed. There was much effort to accomplish by force what could be accomplished only by suasion. There was no recognizable pattern of enforcement. Some communities moved vigorously to enforce all violations of the new law, while others proceeded on a more selective course. Some agencies concentrated on arresting consumers, while others focused their efforts on producers and suppliers. Still others took a permissive attitude toward the entire law, overlooking all violations, both major and minor. This latter attitude was generally motivated by economics, not altruism.

On the Federal level, three agencies were charged with the enforcement of prohibition: The Bureau of Internal Revenue, the Customs Bureau, and the United States Coast Guard. The supervision of these agencies was placed in the hands of an Assistant Secretary of the Treasury. Five persons held that office between 1920 and 1925, and for a period of five months the office was vacant. Federal enforcement agents were appointed without the protection of civil service, a situation which lent itself to corruption. Agents in the field were supervised by state directors, forty-eight in all. From 1921 to 1925, 184 men were in and out of

This armored car was a familiar sight in Detroit during prohibition as it sallied forth to meet the enemy—bootleggers. *(Courtesy of the Detroit Police Department)*

those forty-eight positions.[1] It was little wonder that the Federal Government experienced little success in policing prohibition.

THE NEW CRIME SITUATION

Prohibition had an accelerating influence on crime. New classes of crime and criminality were created and some traditional crimes took on new significance because of the intensity and frequency with which they were increasingly being committed. Adding to the crime problem was the automobile, which was becoming a weapon (e.g. gangland slayings), an accomplice (e.g. bank robberies), and a victim (e.g. auto thefts). Police, spread thin because of prohibition, were almost helpless to do anything about the rapidly rising crime rate. The trend of crime was upward and the newness of it all baffled even the experts.

Organized Crime

The demand for a particular product—intoxicating liquor—coupled with the failure of society to provide lawful means for satisfying the demand created crime organizations of mammoth proportions. Underworld empires based on beer and liquor flourished. The open flaunting of the law by millions of otherwise honest citizens even gave the new crime lords an aura of respectability. Bootleggers were often looked upon as professional men in the same social class as physicians, attorneys, and bankers. Gangs arose to organize the early fragmented liquor trade, and before long even the smallest operators owed allegiance to some type of organization. Gangs were usually classified in three ways:[2]

The Neighborhood Play Group. Neighborhood play groups, or social clubs, had existed in large cities well before prohibition. They held neighborhood dances; sponsored picnics, clambakes, and bank concerts; gave parties, and built clubhouses for fraternal activities. In some neighborhoods everyone who was anyone was a member of the neighborhood

---

[1]The National Commission on Law Observance and Enforcement, *Preliminary Report on Prohibition*, Vol. 1 (Washington: U.S. Government Printing Office, 1931), p. 13.

[2]The Illinois Association for Criminal Justice, *The Illinois Crime Survey* (Montclair, New Jersey: Patterson Smith Publishing Corp. Originally published in 1929, reprinted in 1968), pp. 1001-1015.

social club. When the Volstead Act was passed, many formerly legitimate groups turned their activities to the illicit liquor trade, not for profit but for their own use, a main function of clubs being to allow members to drink in a congenial atmosphere. Later, however, the lure of big money motivated a large number of neighborhood play groups to enter the illegal trade for a profit. Social clubs were actually converted into organized criminal gangs within short periods of time. The transformation of a Chicago amateur baseball team called the Ragen Colts was in many ways typical of the evil metamorphosis that changed legal community organizations into extralegal crime syndicates. The Colts was a rather good baseball team at the turn of the century. Later it became an athletic club which sponsored neighborhood sporting events of all kinds, along with annual picnics and minstrel shows. Gradually, as politicians and prospective office holders sought out its leaders for help in seeking public office, the club assumed a more political stance. When prohibition came, the activities of the Colts were predictable. They entered the illegal beer business, hired themselves out as strongarm men and actually gunned down rivals in the beer business. From baseball team to mob in less than twenty years.

The Ethnic Gang. Even before prohibition small-time criminal gangs had existed in large cities. These gangs differed from neighborhood play groups in that they were formed for the business administration of crime. Most had an ethnic flavor. Early gangs engaged in terror tactics—bombings, assaults, and threats of violence—in order to extort money from frightened merchants. Extortion letters often contained the mark of the Black Hand, the symbol of a secret Sicilian society. Prohibition created a fertile ground for these ethnic gangs, and small mobs were converted into massive crime syndicates which gripped cities in an iron fist. The Al Capone Gang was probably the best example of an ethnic gang which, through a combination of skill and brutality, arose to control the vice of one of the nation's largest cities, Chicago. Before Capone went to jail for income tax evasion in 1931, it was charged that he had more than 1,000 gunmen on his payroll.

The Professional Gang. Professional gangs had basically the same goals as ethnic gangs; however, they were generally feudal groups whose members were of many nationalities. Chicago's Dion O'banion Gang was a professional organization which recruited its members from the ranks of skilled criminal craftsmen: safe-crackers, armed robbers, and successful burglars. O'banion took over and organized the vice of a section of Chicago. He was not destined to survive, though. Internal problems and the competition from the Capone Gang were to prematurely end his business enterprise and his life.

The emergence of a *professional* class of criminals led to intergang rivalries that stunned the country and focused the attention of the world on American lawlessness. Bloody gang wars were waged on the streets of cities; policemen were shot down as they walked their beats, and the blasts of bombs and the burst of machine gun fire became familiar city sounds. In Chicago a total of 257 gangland murders occurred between 1923 and 1929. During 1926 and 1927 Cook County, Illinois, had 130 gang murders, none of which was solved.[3] Public patience with the gangster era ended when in 1929 one group of hoodlums, purported to be from Al Capone's gang, machine gunned to death seven hoodlums of a rival mob in a garage on Chicago's North Side. This, the Saint Valentine's Day Massacre, prompted some thirty retaliatory gang murders that year and polarized citizen opinion against gangsterism.[4]

Auto Theft

The problem of auto theft was created the day the automobile was invented. Although cars were stolen from the time they first hit the nation's streets, the development of speedy, streamlined autos, mass-produced in great numbers, caused a virtual wave of auto thefts. In 1918 the nation's twenty-eight largest cities reported about 27,000 auto thefts. Within ten years, this number had increased to nearly 100,000.[5] Few crimes pointed up the

[3]The Citizens' Police Committee, *Chicago Police Problems* (Montclair, New Jersey: Patterson Smith Publishing Corp. Originally published in 1931, reprinted in 1969), pp. 3-4.

[4]John Lofton, *Justice and the Press* (Boston: Beacon Press, 1966), pp. 100-101.

[5]August Vollmer, *The Police and Modern Society* (Berkeley: University of California Press, 1936), p. 59.

growing helplessness of the local police better than auto theft. Thieves' operations were not limited to specifically defined political boundaries, although the police were virtual prisoners within their jurisdictions, with little coordination or cooperation between departments. Furthermore, auto theft was a relatively new crime and law enforcement agencies had little experience with the phenomenon. Municipal and state governments passed laws against automobile thefts; however, they soon discovered that cars were stolen for varying reasons. Consequently, by the mid-1920s, multiple laws dealing with auto thefts were passed which dealt not only with the actual theft but also with the intent of the thief. The three most prevalent forms of auto theft were the following:

Joy Riding. Whereby a vehicle was used without the consent of its owner, but with no intent to permanently deprive him of his car. This offense was committed primarily by young people in need of transportation.

Auto Theft. The crime of auto theft generally referred to a professional offense committed by one who had the intention of altering and reselling the car or stripping it of parts. Expert theft rings shipped cars all over the world. Some thieves even purchased automobile dealerships as an outlet for their stolen stock.

Auto Theft as a Crime Tool. Possibly the most dangerous type of theft was perpetrated by those criminals in need of a fast getaway car to use during armed robberies. Some robbers hatched elaborate plots to stash stolen getaway cars at different locations, baffling pursuing peace officers.

Kidnapping

Kidnapping for ransom was not an invention of the 1920s. The earliest recorded kidnapping had occurred in Philadelphia in 1874 when four-year-old Charley Ross was abducted and held for ransom.[6] But like so many other crimes, the incidents of kidnapping peaked during the twenties and early thirties. Again, like other crimes, it was successful, at least at first, because of the inability of the police to cope with it. Kidnappings in the pro-

---

[6]George A. Walling, *Recollections of a New York Chief of Police* (Montclair, New Jersey: Patterson Smith Publishing Corp. Originally published in 1890, reprinted in 1969).

hibition era aroused public concern because of the consistency with which the victims were killed. The most sensational case occurred in 1924 when Nathan Leopold and Richard Loeb, two wealthy youths, kidnapped and killed fourteen-year-old Bobby Franks for no apparent reason. The Leopold-Loeb case was front-page news for months. If one positive thing came from the case, it was that it galvanized public opinion against such acts, thus motivating new laws and modern methods of communication to combat the problem. Eight years after the Leopold-Loeb case, the infant son of flyer Charles A. Lindbergh was kidnapped and killed, prompting additional legislative action in this area.

Armed Robbery

Many police administrators of the day blamed the alarming increase in armed robberies during the 1920s on the ready availability of high-powered guns and automobiles. The old "slugger" who pursued his calling with a lead pipe or blackjack was replaced by the masked holdup man wielding a submachine gun and driving a black Packard Sedan. By 1925 America was experiencing 125,000 holdups a year. Due to the lucrative nature of the crime, former pickpockets, burglars, and forgers armed themselves and changed occupations. No gas station, mail truck, bank, bar, restaurant, or store was safe from the new breed of "stickup man." Everything from Fort Knox to the corner grocery store was a prospective target.[7]

EMPIRICAL INQUIRY INTO POLICE ACTIVITY

High crime rates, gangsterism, violent individual and collective antisocial behavior, coupled with the obvious inability of the police to effectively deal with these problems, led to considerable public concern with American law enforcement. The country was riding the crest of a crime wave of epidemic proportions and the police appeared powerless to combat it. Citizen concern prompted many communities to create *ad hoc* commissions to scrutinize the police problem—and in some cases, crime and the criminal justice system—for the purpose of recommending a remedy for the malaise. More than one-hundred surveys into crime and the break-

[7]*Supra* note 5, pp. 28-34.

down of policing were conducted during the decade. America has a tradition of empirical inquiry into police activity. That tradition began in the prohibition era.[8]

In 1920 six prominent attorneys—including Roscoe Pound and Felix Frankfurter—formed a committee under the auspices of the National Popular Government League, a private organization, to investigate the law enforcement practices of the United States Department of Justice. The committee's findings hardly instilled confidence in Federal law enforcement. According to the committee, Justice Department agents consistently made searches and arrests without warrants; inflicted corporal punishment on suspected criminals; planted agent provocateurs in radical political organizations; compelled, through terror tactics, persons to be witnesses against themselves, and propagandized against radical groups in order to enlist public support for the department's harassment activities.[9]

In 1912 the Cleveland Bar Association requested the Cleveland Foundation to conduct a massive survey of the city's criminal justice system—the police, the criminal courts, the bar, and correctional institutions. The Foundation undertook the task and found waste, inefficiency, duplication of effort, some corruption, overburdened courts, crowded jail facilities, and a generally poor quality of police manpower. The Foundation's findings were not just an indictment of law enforcement in Cleveland, but a critique of the general system of American policing:[10]

> Police machinery in the United States has not kept pace with modern demands. It has developed no effective technique to master the burden which modern social and industrial conditions impose. Clinging to old traditions, bound by old practices which business and industry long ago discarded, employing a personnel poorly adapted to its purpose, it grinds away on its perfunctory task without self criticism, without imagination, and with little initiative.

[8]Delmar Karlen, *Anglo-American Criminal Justice* (New York: Oxford University Press, 1967), pp. 98-99.

[9]National Popular Government League, *Report Upon the Illegal Practices of the U.S. Department of Justice* (New York: Arno Press. Originally published in 1920, reprinted in 1969).

[10]The Cleveland Foundation, *Criminal Justice in Cleveland* (Montclair, New Jersey: Patterson Smith Publishing Corp. Originally published in 1926, reprinted in 1969), p. 5.

In 1926 a group of civic organizations formed the Illinois Association for Criminal Justice. After its inception, a study was conducted of organized crime in the state, the police, and the machinery of justice. With regard to the police, the Association reached the following conclusion:[11]

> The fundamental cause of the demoralization of the police. . .is corrupt political influence, the departments being dominated and controlled for years by such influence. Until the condition is removed, there is little hope for any substantial betterment.

In 1928 a special Grand Jury was convened in Chicago to investigate crime in Cook County. What it uncovered was the tip of an iceberg of graft and corruption. A three-cornered alliance between politicians, the police, and gangsters was exposed. The Grand Jury declared that the Chicago Police Department was "rotten to the core," a bit of an overstatement but one which reflected the depth to which the department had fallen in the eyes of the citizenry.[12]

In 1929 President Herbert Hoover announced the appointment of the National Commission on Law Observance and Enforcement, consisting of eleven members, with former United States Attorney General George W. Wickersham as chairman. The Commission was to take two years to complete its work; however, it fulfilled its task well and in 1931 the most comprehensive criminal justice survey in the country's history was handed to the President. It is discussed in the following chapter.

IN RESPONSE TO CRITICISM

The police establishment was stung by the barrage of criticism which had been leveled at it from the survey commissions. Some police officials tried to defend themselves and their departments against charges of corruption and inefficiency, but most commissions had done their work well and indictments were painstakingly documented. While the criticism did not motivate a revolution in law enforcement, certain substantial reforms and modifications were undertaken by police agencies desirous of upgrading themselves.

[11]*Supra* note 3, p. 372.

[12]*Supra* note 3, p. 3.

In the private sector the National Automobile Theft Bureau was created by the insurance industry to maintain a national clearing house for stolen car information. The Bureau, headquartered in New York City, was staffed with highly trained investigators whose job it was to track down large auto-theft rings. A federal law prohibiting the interstate transportation of stolen cars gave the Bureau and the police a needed tool to combat the illegal business.

In 1924 the Justice Department appointed a young attorney, John Edgar Hoover, to direct the Federal Bureau of Investigation. Hoover completely reorganized the FBI, divorcing it from politics and starting it on the road toward professionalization. Within eleven years, Director Hoover had established an identification division as a national clearing house for criminal fingerprint records, formed a technical laboratory to aid in the investigation of cases, created a training school for newly appointed special agents, and founded a national academy which offered agent training to municipal, county, and state law enforcement officers. The FBI was given expanded jurisdiction by a Congress which began passing new laws at an unprecedented rate. The FBI's additional duties led to an increasingly hazardous situation for agents, who in 1934 were empowered to carry firearms.

The enforcement of prohibition also underwent some modification. A Prohibition Bureau was organized within the Treasury Department, and during President Herbert Hoover's administration, a change in philosophy was implemented. Agents were given public relations training to motivate them to "act always as gentlemen."[13] The Bureau's emphasis was placed on detecting and capturing large liquor dealers rather than small-time consumers. A policy on the use of firearms was adopted because of previous incidents of weapon misuse by agents. Prohibition agents were ordered to abandon dramatic raids aimed at making sensational headlines and concentrate on enforcing the law in a quiet, orderly manner. In 1929 Eliot Ness was appointed head of the Prohibition Bureau. Ness was a competent and dedicated administrator whose enforcement efforts were loosely depicted in a later television show entitled "The Untouchables."

The prohibition era saw a movement toward meaningful educa-

---

[13]*The New York Times,* April 23, 1929.

tional programs for policemen, although the decade was more a period of experimentation than anything else. In 1923 the University of California at Berkeley granted the first baccalaureate degree to a student with a minor in criminology. The recipient, a Berkeley police officer, was probably the first man in the country to be awarded a college degree in a course of study which included technical police subjects. In 1925 Harvard University established the Bureau of Street Traffic Research in the Graduate School. In 1929 the University of Chicago inserted a police training program into the school's regular curriculum. The curriculum stressed courses in police administration. Although the program was short-lived, it was the first time in history that technical police training courses were integrated into a regular, undergraduate curriculum.[14]

Municipal law enforcement, the recipient of most of the criticism aimed at criminal justice agencies, was also quick to react to public disapproval. The Chicago Police Department organized "flying squads" to speed to the scene of crimes and begin immediate investigations. The city purchased a fleet of thirty-six high-powered automobiles for that purpose. A staff of 250 detectives was assigned to the state attorney's office. The department also tried to end its discriminatory liquor law arrest procedure by forming a "dress suit squad" to apprehend "exclusive society violators of the law."

In 1924 Philadelphia, in response to citizen outrage over crime conditions, appointed as Director of Public Safety a United States Marine Corps Brigadier-General, Smedley D. Butler. During his second week in office, over 2,000 people were arrested for violating the prohibition laws and more than 1,000 saloons were closed. A wholesale reorganization of the department was undertaken, and eight lieutenants were suspended for dereliction of duty. General Butler invited the city's 1,600 firemen to "pitch-in and help enforce the law."

Many police agencies paid a heavy price for professionalizing.

[14]Allen Z. Gammage, *Police Training in the United States* (Springfield: Charles C Thomas, Publisher, 1963), pp. 62-64.

Berkeley Police Sergeant "Bumpy" Lee *(left)* and Officer Ralph Proctor *(right)* survey the intersection of Bancroft Way and Telegraph Avenue. Across the street is the campus of the University of California. *(Courtesy of the Berkeley Police Department)*

Police deaths reached a new high in the decade. In Kansas City alone twenty-six officers were killed in the line of duty from 1920-1929.

During the 1920s the Los Angeles Police Department underwent broad changes: standards for personnel were elevated; the training program was lengthened and intensified; a building program resulted in badly needed precinct stations; specialized technicians, such as research chemists and ballistics experts, were hired, and a pistol range was built.

Detroit, in an effort to place policemen where they were most needed, opened and staffed seven new precinct stations. A full radio system was operationalized in patrol cars.

The New Orleans Police Department initiated a medical training program for its officers and in 1922 received a national award for being the only force in the country fully equipped to administer first aid to citizens.

In 1928 Orlando W. Wilson was appointed Chief of Police of Wichita. O. W. Wilson was to establish himself as one of the nation's most distinguished police administrators and scholars, a man whose name was to become synonymous with dedication, honesty, and enlightened leadership. Under Wilson's eleven-year reign, the Wichita Police Department experienced a total rejuvenation: officers were encouraged to seek college-level training;

entry standards were uplifted; a police academy was initiated; record-keeping procedures were reorganized; foot patrolmen, an expensive proposition, were reassigned to patrol cars for maximum manpower efficiency; a junior traffic squad, made up of school children, was organized, and principles of sound management and administration were strengthened at all levels of the department.

In 1928 Cincinnati created a centralized bureau of records, and a new system of crime classification was established in conjunction with the International Association of Chiefs of Police. The system was so successful that it was used as a model for the FBI's *Uniform Crime Reports,* thus establishing the Cincinnati Police Department as a pioneer in the field of modern police records.

CONCLUSION

The history of law enforcement in the 1920s may be viewed by the iconoclast in a totally negative context; as a history replete with police corruption, patronage, nepotism, graft, brutality, and collusive involvements with gangsters. But to assume that the most dramatic historical machinations of the era were also the most significant is to come away with a distorted appraisal of an institution upon which conflicting and often impossible demands were made. It is not historically significant that large numbers of policemen became grafters, that many command officers were corrupt, that crime became organized, and that criminals ruled cities. Under the political and social circumstances that existed in the 1920s, it would have been difficult to expect otherwise. What was truly significant about the era was that with all the pressures to sell out to the corruptors, a dedicated group of policemen bucked the tide of corruption and made substantial contributions to their craft, to their departments, to their communities, and to their country. The twenties produced both the corruptor and the corrupted, but it also produced a breed of incorruptable men and women whose accomplishments stand out for all to view.

Orlando W. Wilson, Chief of the Wichita Police Department and one of the most respected names in the history of American law enforcement.

Chapter 8

THE THIRTIES: A NEW DEAL FOR THE POLICE (1930-1939)

S oaring crime rates, rampant gangsterism, police corruption, and the open and flagrant flaunting of the law by otherwise honest citizens convinced many Americans that prohibition was simply not worth the price that the country was paying. By the end of the 1920s, Al Capone had built an empire which was grossing 60 million dollars per year, an empire which had diversified into gambling, labor unions, and laundries. When in October of 1929 the Wall Street crash plunged the nation into a depression, groups of citizens banded together in organizations to work for the repeal of the Eighteenth Amendment, reasoning that an end to prohibition would lower taxes and bring prosperity to the land. Two years later the growing movement for repeal was to receive strong backing when the Wickersham Commission completed its investigation and released its findings.

THE WICKERSHAM COMMISSION REPORTS

In 1931 the National Commission on Law Observance and Enforcement reported that prohibition was not being enforced because basically it was unenforceable. But the Commission went far beyond an analysis of prohibition. In what a newspaper of the era called "the most astonishing document ever submitted to our government by a responsible committee," the Wickersham Commission released fourteen volumes which probed deeply into the entire machinery of American criminal justice. Two of the reports directly concerned the police: *Report Number 11—Lawlessness in Law Enforcement* and *Report Number 14—The Police.* Neither was particularly complimentary. The police had been found to be using third-degree methods—physical and psychological torture—to extract confessions from suspects. Furthermore, it was reported that (1) police corruption was widespread and training was almost

107

non-existent; (2) inefficiency was the rule rather than the exception; (3) communications systems were ineffective; (4) political interference in police operations hampered honest enforcement efforts, and (5) police executives were often ill-suited to handle their jobs. The Commission cited one example of a big city mayor appointing his tailor to the position of chief of police "because he had been his tailor for twenty years and he knew he was a good tailor and so necessarily would make a good chief of police."[1] American law enforcement was not entirely without its bright lights, however, as the Commission found a number of police departments which were superior in every respect. Milwaukee was cited as a relatively "crime free" city where criminals were speedily detected, arrested, tried, and convicted. The Commission reflected that Milwaukee's success was largely due to the continuity of police command; the police department had had but two chiefs in forty-six years. The Detroit Police Department was commended for its efficient use of the police radio, an efficiency which had resulted in a phenomenal arrest rate.[2] But American policing, despite the shining accomplishments of a few agencies, was still badly in need of reform and the report on the police prepared by August Vollmer and political scientists David G. Monroe and Earle W. Garrett among others, made ten recommendations relating to the police:[3]

1. The corrupting influence of politics should be removed from the police organization.
2. The head of the department should be selected at large for competence, a leader, preferably a man of considerable police experience, and removable from office only after preferment of charges and a public hearing.
3. Patrolmen should be able to rate a "B" on the Alpha Test, be able-bodied and of good character, weigh 150 pounds, measure 5 feet 9 inches tall, and be between 21 and 31 years of age. These requirements may be disregarded by the chief for good and sufficient reasons.

---

[1] National Commission on Law Observance and Enforcement, *Report on the Police* (Montclair, New Jersey: Patterson Smith Publishing Corp. Originally published in 1931, reprinted in 1968), p. 3.

[2] *Ibid.,* p. 5.

[3] *Ibid.,* p. 140.

4. Salaries should permit decent living standards, housing should be adequate, eight hours of work, one day off weekly, annual vacation, fair sick leave with pay, just accident and death benefits when in performance of duty, reasonable pension provisions on an actuarial basis.
5. Adequate training for recruits, officers, and those already on the roll is imperative.
6. The communication system should provide for call boxes, telephones, recall system, and teletype and radio.
7. Records should be complete, adequate, but as simple as possible. They should be used to secure administrative control of investigations and of department units in the interest of efficiency.
8. A crime prevention unit should be established if circumstances warrant this action, and qualified women police should be engaged to handle juvenile delinquents' and women's cases.
9. State police forces should be established in states where rural protection of this character is required.
10. State bureaus of criminal investigation and information should be established in every state.

For the first time in history American law enforcement had a set of guidelines on which to base reform efforts and technological improvements. Over the years students of law enforcement have relied heavily on the Wickersham Commission Reports as a source of scholarly material. The positive impact of the National Commission on Law Observance and Enforcement on the police craft has been immeasurable.

THE MARCH TOWARD PROGRESS

Spurred by the Wickersham Reports, the police entered a time of real progress. Prohibition, mercifully, was repealed, thereby eliminating one problem with which the police had been grappling. Municipal police departments began to professionalize their operations, furnished by Wickersham with the model to do so and the ammunition to motivate politicians to permit internal reform and the adoption of technological innovations.

Police departments moved quickly to minimize the influence of external politics and to upgrade working conditions for sworn personnel. In 1931 the Detroit Police Department initiated a new system for the selection of personnel. Before the decade was over, a merit promotion system was to be installed. Within months after the release of the findings of the Wickersham Commission, the

Cincinnati Police Department created an improved retirement system. In 1935 the police credit union was formed, one of the first in the country. In 1931 the Tucson Police Department was placed under civil service, lessening to a great degree the political interference which had for years hampered the cause of professional law enforcement in that city.

Advanced technology made its imprint on police departments. In 1931 sophisticated systems of radio communications were established in scores of cities, including Kansas City, New Orleans, and Cincinnati. In 1934 Cincinnati created one of the most modern crime laboratories in the country, equipped with ballistics equipment, x-ray, a polygraph (first used by the Berkeley Police Department), moulage, and other equipment. In 1935 the Kansas City Police Department installed two-way radios in patrol cars, and each car was equipped with the new familiar "whip" antenna.

Police departments also began to experiment with innovative administrative techniques. Emulating business and the military, many departments for the first time initiated principles of sound management. In 1936 August Vollmer published *The Police and Modern Society,* a major work in the field of police administration and one which for years served as a classic text that police com-

During the gangster era, policemen found it necessary to adopt advanced weaponry and high-powered automobiles. *(Courtesy of the Columbus, Ohio, Police Department)*

mand officers and executives consulted in modifying the structure and function of their agencies. Typical of the new emphasis on sound administrative techniques, the state of Texas reorganized its state police by creating a Department of Public Safety to unify fragmented state law enforcement agencies, including the Texas Rangers. In New Orleans the system of dual control of police operations was eliminated and the responsibility for managing the department was lodged in a supervisor of police. In 1939 the San Antonio Police Department was completely reorganized by Chief Ray Ashworth. Chief Ashworth devised a system of organization which is virtually intact to this day.

Probably the most significant developments in law enforcement during the 1930s occurred in the dual fields of police training and education. By the end of the decade every state, with the exception of Wisconsin, had created a state police force. These early state forces led the way in implementing progressive training programs, most of which were at least three months in duration. The first state police academy was established in New York, with Pennsylvania quickly following suit. By 1934 state police schools had been established in Michigan, New Jersey, Connecticut, Oregon, Washington, and Texas.[4] The impact of these early schools cannot be overstated, for they motivated municipal departments to implement training programs of their own, although municipal training programs were to lag sadly behind their state counterparts. The state police were to take up some of the slack by permitting, on a limited basis, selected municipal policemen to attend state training academies. The FBI also had a significant influence on municipal law enforcement when in 1935 it created the National Academy for the training of local police officers. In the early thirties, Northwestern University established the Northwestern Traffic Safety Institute—a two-week traffic course, under the direction of Frank M. Kreml. In 1935 Northwestern's program—which over the years was to become one of the most distinguished of its kind—was expanded to include three courses: one for local policemen, one for state officers, and an advanced course for graduates of the basic program.[5]

[4]Allen Z. Gammage, *Police Training in the United States* (Springfield: Charles C Thomas, Publisher, 1963), pp. 10-16.

[5]*Ibid.,* p. 19.

In the field of police education, San Jose State College established the first complete police major program in the country in 1931. The following year August Vollmer was appointed Professor of Police Administration at the University of California at Berkeley, where he drafted a curriculum which, for the first time in history, allowed students to major in either the technical, legal, or social areas of policing and obtain an A.B. degree with a major in criminology. In 1935 the first police cadet program in American history was created when O. W. Wilson's Wichita Police Department agreed to hire annually fourteen University of Wichita upper-division students. The students worked part-time for the police department—for pay—while pursuing their education at the university. Graduates, who took both technical police subjects and academic courses, received an A. B. in political science. Many sought employment with the Wichita Police Department upon graduation. That same year, Michigan State College (later to become Michigan State University) established a four-year program leading to a B. S. in police administration. The program was eventually to be housed in the School of Police Administration and Public Safety. It has become one of the largest and most respected police programs in the country. Before the decade was over, more than twenty colleges and universities were to begin offering police training programs of one sort or another.[6]

THE DEPRESSION'S EFFECT ON THE POLICE

The Depression had a devastating effect on America: millions were jobless; people who had never before experienced economic problems were homeless; the economy sank lower and lower. Yet the phenomenon created few problems for the police. There were few signs of social disruption, even though communists constantly agitated for revolution with no success. In fact, outbursts of collective violence were minimal, the notable exception occurring in 1932 when World War I Veterans rioted in Washington in protest over the government's refusal to pay them a bonus for wartime service.

The Depression had a positive impact on police operations in two ways. First, during the Depression police departments were able to recruit from a population which, for the first time,

[6]*Ibid.*, pp. 64-72.

included many unemployed college graduates. People who under normal conditions would not have given a second thought to entering the police service now stood in employment lines in hopes that they could win a patrolman's appointment. New blood was infused into law enforcement agencies badly in need of such a transfusion. For years municipal departments made good use of this newly found manpower bonanza. As general economic conditions improved, however, the police job became less and less attractive and many college graduates left the service to seek more gainful employment. Little provision had been made to financially attract and keep college-educated policemen; so when the Depression's effects began to ease, wholesale resignation of college graduates were forthcoming. But some stayed on, men who found that the rewards they received from policing far transcended the material satisfactions that they could have received in business or industry. Although relatively small in number, this group of dedicated, well-educated men were to assume roles of trust and responsibility on police departments and, some decades hence, were to spearhead a movement to professionalize the nation's police.

Second, the New Deal, President Franklin Delano Roosevelt's answer to the Depression, had as one of its goals the employment of large numbers of people. Accordingly, the Works Progress Administration (WPA) was created to "help men keep their chins up and their hands in," a task it fulfilled by embarking on a massive construction program. The WPA, among other projects, built or rebuilt over 110,000 public buildings.[7] Law enforcement reaped wholesale benefits from this program. New police stations were constructed; older buildings were renovated. Special facilities, such as firing ranges, substations, jails, maintenance garages, and police academies, which would not otherwise have been built for decades, were among WPA projects.

The social problems of the Depression were national in scope, so it was only logical that the solutions for them would come from Washington. Accordingly, the Federal Government assumed sweeping new authority, passing legislation and assuming control over matters which, during other times, would have been

---

[7]Richard N. Current, T. Harry Williams, and Frank Friedel, *American History: A Survey* (New York: Alfred A. Knopf, 1964), p. 740.

thoroughly opposed by local and state governments. But this was an extraordinary time and extraordinary measures were needed. Local reliance on the Federal Government to solve social and economic problems led to a similar reliance on Washington to solve the crime problem. As a result, the FBI was thrust into a crime-fighting role which had previously been filled by municipal police departments.

THE FBI AND CONTEMPORARY DESPERADOES

The Depression saw the rise of a new kind of American outlaw—one who was in many ways similar to the lawless element that had terrorized the Old West a half-century previously, but who, by the very nature of the tools of his trade, was different and a hundred times more deadly. Instead of horses, these contemporary desperadoes drove high-powered cars. Instead of six-shooters, their basic tool was the submachine gun. In place of stage coaches and trains, they robbed armored cars and banks. Small bands of desperadoes roamed the country almost at will, holding up banks, kidnapping tellers, shooting down guards, policemen, or anyone else who stood in the way of a successful job. One of the most notorious contemporary outlaws was John Dillinger, bank robber and murderer. In September, 1931, Dillinger was arrested by local authorities and jailed in Lima, Ohio. Less than one month later Dillinger, assisted by his confederates, broke jail and killed the sheriff. After a three-month orgy of murder and robbery, he was apprehended in Arizona and lodged in Crown Point, Indiana's "escape-proof" jail. He escaped within the month, leaving the state in a stolen sheriff's car. With an estimated five thousand policemen in pursuit, Dillinger (1) stopped for a haircut in a barber shop, (2) bought getaway cars, (3) enjoyed a home-cooked dinner with his family in his home town, and (4) burglarized a police station, relieving it of arms and ammunition. Dillinger's exploits pointed up, once again, the impotence of the local police in dealing with violent interstate crimes and criminals. The Dillinger episode prompted the Federal authorities to act. The FBI was granted expanded enforcement powers and ordered to end the reign of terror of the latter-day outlaws. The FBI was remarkably efficient in doing just that. In July, 1934, John Dillinger was killed by agents as he left a theatre in Chicago. Three months later Pretty Boy Floyd was shot down in East Liverpool, Ohio. The following month Baby Face Nelson, Public Enemy Number One, was killed in a shootout with agents near Niles Center, Illinois. The FBI and J. Edgar Hoover became heroes to a nation in the throes of a depression and badly in need of heroes. The success of the FBI prompted Congress to pass a whole list of new Federal crimes, including kidnapping and robbery of banks insured by the Federal Deposit Insurance Corporation.[8]

CONCLUSION

Municipal police forces began making significant progress in the thirties. Salaries were improved, political influence was eased, new equipment was adopted, modern facilities were built, and old structures were renovated. Some police departments (e.g. Berkeley, Cincinnati, and Wichita) were true models, shining examples of what law enforcement agencies ought to be like. But a lingering problem persisted even in this era of progress. What the American police service needed more than any technical or administrative innovation was manpower—superior manpower. When the Depression forced an army of qualified personnel to seek employment on police departments, municipal governments failed to respond by significantly upgrading salaries and fringe benefits to a point where they were competitive with the private sector, and the army was whittled to a platoon by Depression's end. The decade saw the Federal Government adopt broad new powers to end the Depression. A corresponding increase in Federal powers was aimed at solving the nation's crime problem. Accordingly, the role of the FBI was expanded. Police agencies were beginning to move toward professionalization, but a dread social phenomenon was to interrupt the journey—war.

[8]William E. Leuchtenburg, *Franklin D. Roosevelt and the New Deal* (New York: Harper and Row, Publishers, Inc., 1963), p. 334.

Tracer bullets being fired from machine guns by special agents of the FBI during night firearms training. *(Courtesy of the FBI)*

Chapter 9

THE WAR YEARS AND AFTER (1940-1949)

Any substantial change in the social environment of the country has a direct effect on law enforcement. Economic crises, labor disputes, technological advancements, breakthroughs in methods of transportation and communication, new legislation, and foreign immigration all had a significant impact on the structure and function of American policing. Anything that affects the nation in a dramatic way also affects the police. When in the early 1940s the United States entered World War II, special problems—both internal and external—were created for the police.

THE POLICE GO TO WAR

During World War II the ranks of local and state police agencies were seriously depleted as tens of thousands of officers went off to war. The war may well have been law enforcement's finest hour to date. Policemen abroad distinguished themselves in battle, but they paid a heavy price. More than a few police stations contain plaques honoring the department's war dead. At home the shortage in qualified manpower created the need for extraordinary measures.

A Civilian Defense Corps was established to perform work created by the war. Air raid drills became a constant part of American life, and civilian air raid wardens were assigned to see that citizens complied with the rather strict blackout procedures that had been specified by government. Meetings and awareness lectures were also conducted by these dedicated people, who served on a volunteer basis.

Most police departments found it necessary to mobilize auxiliary police units to fill the vacancies created by the war. Auxiliary policemen were individuals who for one reason or another—advanced age, a physical infirmity, etc.—could not serve in the military. The auxiliary units were often activated by special

117

legislation which stipulated that they would be disbanded when the war ended and the troops returned home. Auxiliary officers were generally full-time policemen, with limited police training, who acted as replacements for regular officers in the service. Auxiliary policemen performed admirably during their tours of duty and some gallantly forfeited their lives in defense of their communities. Some auxiliary police units, especially those in coastal cities where an enemy attack was considered a possibility, were trained in first aid, chemical warfare, and bomb dismantling procedures in case of invasion.

Reserve (part-time) police units were established in many communities. Reserve officers, who generally worked without pay, were put to work performing routine duties—traffic direction, guard duty, clerical work, etc. Reserve officers also rode with policemen to maintain two-man patrol cars.

Most major law enforcement agencies were subjected to basically the same war-related pressures; however, one department, the Metropolitan Police Department in the District of Columbia, found itself faced with a crisis, for all the obvious reasons. Although the exigencies that the men of the Metropolitan Police Department encountered were in many ways unique, their sacrifice and dedication in the face of adversity were typical of those made by their brothers nationwide.

With the declaration of war on December 7, 1941, the call upon the services of the Metropolitan Police Department increased rapidly. Some members of the department were immediately detailed to augment the White House police force, while others were dispatched to guard embassies, power plants, bridges, and other vital installations against sabotage. The Board of Commissioners afforded the department some relief when on March 5, 1942, it permitted the hiring of fifty special policemen, who were known as defense guards. These defense guards were strategically deployed so that policemen could be relieved for patrol duty. The department was fast losing its experienced manpower to the Armed Services. No fewer than 341 had either enlisted or been drafted. Civilian augmentation of the police department began, and six thousand volunteers were processed for an auxiliary police force. The Washington Police Academy was founded to train the recruits. Citizens from every walk of life generously offered their services as clerks, instructors, even laborers. Regular police personnel, after completing their tours of duty, often came back for another eight or ten hours of work with the volunteers. Precinct captains very often worked twenty-four hours a day, and dozens of volunteers worked in the precinct stations registering more auxiliary policemen. This grand force of Washington citizens, armed with a badge, an overseas cap, a raincoat, a web belt, whistle, baton, armband, and helmet, was a great deterrent to the commission of crime, not only during blackouts, but at other times. When the war ended, the *ad hoc* bodies of civilian volunteers disbanded after long and honorable service.[1]

BLACK MARKETING

Although the rate of many classes of crimes fell during the war—in fact, the prison population even decreased for various reasons—certain war measures created added problems for the police. Every nation that has ever fought a war has had its share of citizens who made excessive profits from the sale of commodities in short supply. During earlier conflicts—the Civil War, the Spanish-American War, World War I—this activity was not generally unlawful; but with the coming of World War II drastic regulations were passed making war profiteering illegal. The Federal Government issued a list of fixed prices on selected commodities which made it unlawful to charge more than the stated price. In addition, there was rationing of certain goods. Some of the commodities affected by the war measures were meats, butter, and gasoline. The Office of Price Administration (OPA), the War Production Board, and the War Labor Board were created to regulate prices, to stabilize wages, and to regulate industrial allocation and proposal. In addition, there were hundreds of local ordinances which dealt with these issues. War profiteering occurred, though, and a term was popularized which referred to the illicit sale and purchase of commodities and goods—the black market.

The OPA organized the Enforcement Department which strenuously enforced black market ordinances. Between 1942 and 1947, there were 12,415 cases turned over to the United States

[1]Reprinted with editorial adaption from Howard V. Covell's "A Brief History of the Metropolitan Police Department," Washington: 1946, pp. 7-9.

Department of Justice for prosecution; all but 815, less than seven percent, were won by the government.[2]

The war measures also prompted other violations of the law as war profiteers stole and counterfeited ration currency, thus bringing the United States Secret Service and the FBI into cases. The competence and cunning of this new breed of counterfeiters presented an added challenge to Federal investigators who were forced to develop sophisticated new detection devices. Special lamps and chemical tests were but two of the techniques used to detect bogus or altered bills. Professional criminals, working freelance or with organized crime cartels, plagued the government and threatened the war effort.

Yet, despite fairly widespread violations of the war measures, the great mass of American citizens obeyed the law, displayed a remarkable tolerance for the rights of others, contributed to the war effort, and supported law enforcement, especially harried officers in municipal agencies.

THE FBI AND INTERNAL SECURITY

When the situation in Europe had deteriorated to the point where it was obvious that American involvement in a war was imminent, President Franklin Delano Roosevelt moved to broaden the Federal Bureau of Investigation's internal security function. The President dispatched word to the FBI and to local police agencies of the Bureau's enlarged role:[3]

> The Attorney General has been requested by me to instruct the Federal Bureau of Investigation of the Department of Justice to take charge of investigative work in matters relating to espionage, sabotage, and violations of neutrality regulations. This task must be conducted in a comprehensive and effective manner on a national scale, and all information must be carefully sifted and correlated in order to avoid confusion and irresponsibility. To this end I request all police officers, sheriffs, and other law enforcement officers in the United States promptly to turn over to the nearest representative of the Federal Bureau of Investigation any information obtained by

[2]Marshal B. Clinard, *The Black Market* (Montclair, New Jersey: Patterson Smith Publishing Corp. Originally published in 1952, reprinted in 1969), p. 239.

[3]Harry and Bonaro Overstreet, *The FBI in Our Open Society* (New York: W. W. Norton and Company, Inc., 1969), pp. 88-89.

them relative to espionage, counterespionage, subversion activities,
and violations of the neutrality laws.

The FBI opened field offices in Puerto Rico and the Canal
Zone, and in six regions of the country where large military installations were located. The Army and Navy requested the Bureau to
involve itself, in a limited way, in the security of defense plants
producing war-related items. The Bureau created an intelligence
division, along with a component for translating and decoding
messages. The FBI's internal security work during the war was
professionally carried out and amazingly successful. The image of
the FBI as a superior investigative unit was once again enhanced—
deservedly so.

THE POSTWAR PERIOD

When the war ended, former policemen returned home to
resume their careers in law enforcement. They were joined by
other· veterans, many of whom had been military policemen or
special investigators, and a cadre of mature, well-trained, disciplined young men infused new blood into the police service. If
this new breed of policemen had one shortcoming, it was that they
were relatively uneducated, at least beyond high school. But there
were no colleges on Iwo Jima, Guam, and Normandy, and furthermore, many institutions had discontinued their police programs
for the duration of the war, making it unreasonable to demand
advanced education from applicants. But the postwar period saw
movement toward expanded educational programs for policemen,
though it would be a decade before a significant number of police
programs were created.

One of the most important postwar educational trends was the
development of the junior college concept. While some sections of
the country were slow to grasp the concept, one state—
California—moved at breakneck speed in that direction, to the
everlasting benefit of law enforcement. Police science seemed to
fit perfectly into the junior college scheme of things. California
also expanded its four-year programs, and police or criminology
majors were created at Fresno State College, Los Angeles State
College, and Sacramento State College. By the end of the decade
Los Angeles had law enforcement programs at four institutions of
higher learning—a junior college, a state college, a state university,
and a private university. The Los Angeles Police Department,

about which more will be said in the following chapter, was destined to ascend to a status of leadership in many areas of police work, thanks in no small measure to the educational attainments of its personnel, 3,000 of whom were hired between 1945 and 1950. It is no coincidence that those police departments which had within commuting range specialized educational programs, and who encouraged their officers to enroll in college, rose to a position of respect in their field (e.g. Berkeley, Wichita, Los Angeles).

The postwar period saw a good deal of progress in the area of police training. Recruit and in-service training programs burgeoned as municipal law enforcement agencies converted their hastily established wartime schools for auxiliary officers into full-fledged police academies. The period 1946-1949 was termed by one police scholar as "the period of greatest activity" in the police training field.[4] In 1948 the Los Angeles Police Department became the first police agency in the country to inaugurate a system of roll call training, whereby uniformed officers were given brief periods of intensified training immediately prior to going on duty. By the end of the decade most every department of any size had a police academy. Those that did not usually sent their recruits to nearby training schools or engaged in on-the-job training. The South, which had lagged sadly behind the rest of the nation in establishing police training courses, began to catch up as New Orleans, Miami, and Augusta inaugurated training schools.

The decade also saw a movement toward adopting some of the technological achievements of an increasingly mobile society. For example, in 1948 the New York Police Department became the first major agency to employ a police helicopter for patrol purposes.

CONCLUSION

Returning World War II veterans, toughened and matured by military service, provided police departments with a source of manpower of unquestioned value. Young, dynamic, dedicated to police work, these youthful veterans were badly needed by law enforcement agencies, which for a half decade had marked time as

---

[4]Allen Z. Gammage, *Police Training in the United States* (Springfield, Illinois: Charles C Thomas, Publisher, 1963), p. 21.

far as progress was concerned. The postwar period saw some movement toward professionalization, but it was mostly a time in which many departments searched for positive direction. The sudden influx of personnel into previously poorly staffed agencies created the need for updated training programs and the nation's police departments were kept busy just selecting, processing, training, and breaking-in recruits. For the second time in two decades the FBI successfully stepped into a breach produced by an explosive social phenomenon. The FBI had earned the respect of a greatful nation. In many ways the FBI provided local law enforcement with direction, for the Bureau had dramatically illustrated what a police component could do if it was staffed by competent, well-educated personnel who were provided with advanced training and the most modern hardware, and who were allowed to ply their trade relatively free from the influence of politicians.

William H. Parker, Chief of Police, City of Los Angeles. *(Official photograph of the Los Angeles Police Department)*

Chapter 10

THE EMERGENCE OF THE CALIFORNIA POLICE (1950–1959)

THE KEFAUVER COMMITTEE'S INQUIRY

The new decade had hardly begun when a police scandal of major proportions was exposed, a scandal that shook the very foundation of the urban system of law enforcement. In 1950 an accumulation of facts motivated governmental action to investigate crime in interstate commerce. On May 10, the Senate Crime Committee was born, chaired by Senator Estes Kefauver of Tennessee. What the committee found was a web of graft, corruption, and organized crime.

The Kefauver Committee, as it became known, conducted a nationwide investigation into organized crime. Committee members went to New York City, Chicago, Cleveland, Miami, Tampa, Kansas City, St. Louis, Detroit, Philadelphia, and Las Vegas where they found that:[1]

> A nationwide crime syndicate does exist in the United States of America, despite the protestations of a strangely assorted company of criminals, self-serving politicians, plain blind fools, and others who may be honestly misguided that there is no such combine.

Witnesses by the hundreds were summoned to testify before the committee and the names of crime cartel members became household words—Joe Adonis, Frank Costello, Anthony Accardo, "Lucky" Luciano. The syndicate was found to be run by an international criminal organization called the Mafia. Nearly everywhere the committee went, it found constables, police officers, and detectives who took bribes to protect gamblers and prostitutes from prosecution. Bigger fry—sheriffs, police chiefs, and command officers—were found to be on the syndicate's payroll, too. A police captain in Chicago admitted to receiving a

---

[1] Estes Kefauver, *Crime In America* (New York: Greenwood Press, Publishers, 1968), p. 12.

$30,000 "gift" from a gambler. The Sheriff of Dade County, Florida, acknowledged that his assets had grown from $2,500 to $70,000 during his five years in office, all on a $7,500 a year salary. In addition, his wife had transported more than $25,000 out of state, presumably for safekeeping. In Tampa the Sheriff of Hillsborough County was indicted by a grand jury for taking protection money from a gambler and for neglect of duty. In Kansas City, syndicate members were shown to have a hand in police department promotions. The police commissioner of East St. Louis, Missouri, an elected public official, was found to have collected $131,425 in "political contributions" in six years on which he dutifully paid income taxes, and banked. It was discovered that the day John J. Grosch was elected to the office of criminal sheriff of Orleans Parish (New Orleans), he was given a new Cadillac limousine by "unnamed friends." Other sheriffs in Louisiana refused to answer crime commission queries about why they banked more money per year than their yearly salary. The story was the same in Detroit, New York, Las Vegas, Philadelphia, and elsewhere.

Exposures of crime and corruption had occurred before in America with only minor public outrage, but this time things were different, thanks to the youthful television industry. The committee's hearings were televised to the nation, and the myth of the sinister, cunning, shrewd criminal that had been foisted on the public by books and in films, was exploded as the flesh-and-blood criminal was exposed to be a bumbling, rather oafish individual whose command of the English language left something to be desired. Millions of viewers watched enthralled as an almost endless parade of hoodlums immortalized the phrase: "I refuse to testify on the grounds that it might tend to incriminate me."

The Kefauver proceedings had a significant impact on the American people in two respects: (1) they shattered the traditional image of the sinewy, brainy criminal, and (2) they showed how easy it was to corrupt the nation's underpaid police forces. By 1951 wholesale police reforms were being undertaken by urban communities which had suffered a televised black eye. Some reformers harkened back two decades to the reports of the Wickersham Commission as they sought to upgrade their departments. The type of corruption uncovered by both Wickersham and Kefauver had come from the top of governmental pyramids and had infected the entire structure. One answer to this problem was not simple but it was basic—end corrupt political domination of police departments. Police chief appointment procedures were updated, the operating relationship between police executives and higher authority was revised, and more independence was given to police commanders by elected public officials, who began to stand somewhat aloof from their police departments for fear of charges of tampering.

Even though corruption was widespread, not all communities that were visited by the Kefauver Committee were found to have corrupt police forces. Quite the contrary, a number of very fine police agencies actually received enthusiastic commendations from the senator from Tennessee. One of Senator Kefauver's most glowing testimonials was directed at an agency which he described as a "white spot" in the nation's pattern of crime—the Los Angeles Police Department. Led by Los Angeles, the entire state of California was to be thrust into supremacy in the police field within the short space of a decade.

THE CALIFORNIA POLICE

California had had bright spots in policing since the turn of the century. For example, the Berkeley Police Department under August Vollmer had been well thought of nationally for years, as had other departments of similar size. But, although Berkeley could offer a model for professional law enforcement, its very size prevented it from having a dramatic impact on policing in the state. It did not dominate a region because it was not a core city. But Los Angeles was a core city and when the Los Angeles police initiated serious reform, a trend was begun which rapidly spread to all areas of the state. Soon the LAPD became a world famous police organization.

One of the most significant actions in the history of American law enforcement occurred on August 9, 1950, when William H. Parker was appointed Chief of Police of the City of Los Angeles. Parker had been in the police service since 1927, working his way through the ranks to chief. During the Depression, and while still employed by the police department, he received an LL.B degree from the Los Angeles College of Law. When the Depression ended and a mass exodus of college-educated men from police ranks occurred, Parker chose to remain in the police service. Chief Parker served his country during World War II, receiving a Purple Heart for wounds received during the Normandy Invasion, along with the French Croix de Guerre with Silver Star, and the Italian Star of Solidarity.

Chief Parker recognized the absolute necessity of employing only superior personnel. He toughened up entry level procedures, and it showed. Six months after his appointment, the Los Angeles Police Department probably had the most stringent selection procedures in the country. During one patrolman's examination only 17 of 2,300 applicants passed the written examination.

Much has been said of William H. Parker, but perhaps the most accurate commentary was made by another great police administrator, O. W. Wilson:[2]

> I have watched his operations and the progress of his department with an interest stimulated by the discovery that he was making the most of his rare opportunity to modernize and professionalize police service. He immediately reorganized his department to simplify and assure his control over its operations and to facilitate the attainment of police objectives. He also adopted the best of known police procedures and urged his exceptionally qualified staff to develop new ones. . . .What Parker was doing required more courage than is possessed by most men. . . .

Not only did the Los Angeles Police Department serve as a model of what a law enforcement agency should be, but William H. Parker offered a shining example of the "new breed" American police administrator. Some of Parker's operational innovations included:

1. Formation of an internal affairs division to investigate citizen complaints of police misconduct.
2. Co-authorship of a city Board of Rights procedure guaranteeing the separation of police discipline from politics.
3. Creation of a bureau of administration, which included two new components: the intelligence and the planning and research divisions.
4. Establishment of an intensive community relations program.
5. The disbursement of a fleet of patrol helicopters.
6. Enactment of a strict firearms use policy that included

---

[2]O. W. Wilson, *Parker on Police* (Springfield: Charles C Thomas, Publisher, 1957), p. vii.

internal department review of all weapons discharges.

7. The construction of a modern police administration building. Five million dollars in savings was realized because of Chief Parker's planning.

California experienced an economic boom during the 1950s as industry, business, and commerce attracted millions of new residents to the state. A virtual technological revolution occurred. The aircraft industry centered its activities in California, along with countless electronics concerns, communications companies, and shipping interests. Salaries for workers were raised in order to attract professional talent from out of state. California constructed a massive freeway system to handle its burgeoning auto traffic. Institutions of higher learning, especially junior colleges, were opened at an unprecedented rate, and they were tuition free. The phenomenal growth caused both problems and opportunities for the California police.

In the field of higher education, some three score public institutions were opened by the end of the decade. The increased demands for police services, coupled with higher salaries and the growing complexity of the police task, led to the creation of law enforcement programs at many of these colleges. By the end of the decade, there were forty-three separate institutions which awarded degrees in law enforcement or a related subject. Thirty-five were junior colleges. Over seventy-six percent of the nation's two-year law enforcement programs were in California. Motivated by the easy access to a free quality education, California's policemen flocked to enroll in school. In 1958 Allen P. Bristow wrote that "Peace officers throughout the state are utilizing these educational opportunities to a great degree."[3] Within a decade the police in California had raised their educational level significantly and, as a whole, became the country's best educated group of municipal officers.

In the area of training, California again led the way as departments established and expanded pre-service and in-service training programs, a number of which became affiliated with the state's junior colleges. The California Highway Patrol symbolized the

[3]Allen P. Bristow, "Junior Colleges Play Important Role in Professionalization," *California Peace Officer* (Sacramento: Peace Officer's Assoc. of State of Calif., July-Aug., 1958), p. 35.

state's emphasis in this area when in 1954 it constructed a massive training academy on 224 acres of ground in Sacramento for the initial cost of $625,000. In 1959 the State of California created by legislative action the Peace Officers' Standards and Training (POST) Commission to require statewide standards for recruiting and training personnel.

At a time when other states were experiencing difficulties with corrupt elected sheriffs, California's system of county law enforcement showed remarkable stability. In many ways the stable sheriff system was typified by the Los Angeles County Sheriff's Department, a superior agency. When Sheriff Peter J. Pitchess, a former FBI agent with a law degree, was elected in 1958, he was only the second man to hold that office since 1932. Under Sheriff Pitchess' administration technological and administrative innovations were adopted and the police academy was expanded in size and in scope until it had attained a worldwide reputation for creative programs.

The story was the same in almost all sections of the state: a highly trained, well-educated, and higher-paid class of policemen that made good use of advanced technology and management techniques. It was not difficult to figure out why the police in California had made such remarkable progress. The public and government had committed themselves to the idea of honest, efficient, and professional law enforcement, free from the domineering influence of corrupt politicians.

DEVELOPMENTS IN MUNICIPAL POLICING

To allege that the only bright spot on the national law enforcement scene in the 1950s was California is to perpetrate a fraud. Admittedly, California was the first state to professionalize their police on so grand a scale—and on such a statewide level—but some states and communities were moving in that direction, and a number of police agencies in other parts of the country were striving to professionalize at breakneck speed.

Negro civil rights actions surfaced in the 1950s, led by the National Association for the Advancement of Colored People (NAACP). Most movement in that direction was conducted in court, though some strategies involved open demonstrations. Those few unlawful demonstrations that did occur were non-violent in nature. As a result some police administrators began to

A Philadelphia Police Department "motor bandit patrol car" taking a call from headquarters as it patrols its assigned area, usually a part of the city where the incidence of crime was highest. *(Courtesy of the Philadelphia Police Department)*

view their responsibilities as more than just the protection of life and property and preservation of the peace. A few forward thinking executives foresaw racial problems approaching, and they moved to improve relations between their departments and the community. In 1957 the St. Louis Police Department created the nation's first formal police-community-relations component. But law enforcement was slow to act in this area, for it was an era in which the management principles of business and industry had been adopted by chiefs of police desirous of upgrading their function, and to reassign manpower from street duty to community-relations work was considered wasteful by many police commanders. That outlook was to change drastically during the next decade.

Specialized police training programs were expanded during the decade. In 1951 Michigan State University initiated a four-week basic police course, along with a one-week command school. That same year the Southern Police Institute was established and twelve-week training courses were offered to supervisory, administrative, and command officers. The Institute was housed on the campus of the University of Louisville. In 1953 the Police Training Institute of the University of Illinois was operationalized to train the state's police officers, especially recruit officers. In 1959 the New York State legislature enacted the New York Municipal Police Training Act, making it the first state to mandate minimum training requirements for municipal policemen.

In 1950 two books were published that had a remarkable, although not immediate, effect on municipal policing: O. W. Wilson's *Police Administration* and *Municipal Police Administration,* 3rd edition, by the International City Managers' Association. Police executives nationwide utilized the principles contained in the two works to reform their agencies. Both books became giants in the field, but Wilson's remains a classic. By the middle of the decade the nation's superior police departments, now for the first time in history more than a handful, reflected the basic but innovative tenets set down by Wilson, who had battle-tested his philosophy in the field. The writings of O. W. Wilson and the ICMA have had a profound effect on the American police service.

CONCLUSION

There were a number of bright lights in law enforcement by the end of the decade and, although most of them were in California, other sections of the country were also beginning to move forward. Admittedly, though, the struggle to professionalize was a fragmented effort rather than a nationwide march. Municipal law enforcement was making considerable progress toward freeing itself from the clutches of partisan political influence, a major step toward honest, efficient policing. Things were indeed progressing well, albeit at a slower clip than many professionals liked. But storm clouds were on the horizon; and the police, as they had so many other times in their history, were about to face a trying time.

Chapter 11

PROTEST, POLITICS, AND THE STRUGGLE
TO PROFESSIONALIZE (1960-1969)

The 1960s comprised a decade in which the concept of police professionalism progressed from a regional commitment to a national movement. It was also a decade in which the police, especially municipal officers, found themselves under fire—verbally, physically, and philosophically—from critics of everything from an unpopular war to the welfare system.

During the era citizens with grievances ignored traditional avenues of redress and took to the streets to protest. Negro civil rights demonstrations escalated, but angry and impatient minority group members also engaged in tumultuous riots and civil disturbances. Student unrest exploded into reality as college students, protesting the war in Vietnam and American social conditions, engaged in violent and disruptive campus protests which often spilled over into city streets. The crime rate escalated. Narcotics addiction threatened to reach epidemic proportions. Extremist groups at both ends of the political spectrum were organized. Political assassinations occurred with depressing regularity. And in the middle, as government's most visible representatives, were the police, trying desperately to maintain some semblence of order in the face of unrestrained political passions, attempting to assume a professional stance against some of the deadliest and most provocative tactics ever used by protestors. All the while the crime rate rose astronomically.

THE CRIME PROBLEM

From 1960-1969 the population of the country rose approximately thirteen percent, while reported crimes rose 148 percent. Some of the increase could be attributed to better methods of crime reporting; however, it was clear that crime—serious crime—was increasing at an alarming rate: aggravated assault rose 102 percent; forcible rape was up 116 percent; robbery climbed 177

135

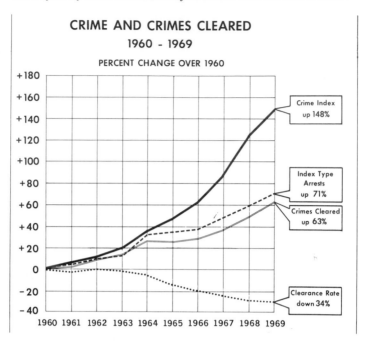

(Courtesy of the FBI's *Uniform Crime Reports)*

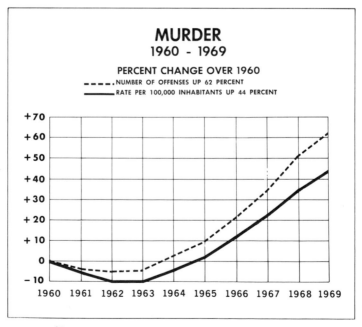

(Courtesy of the FBI's *Uniform Crime Reports)*

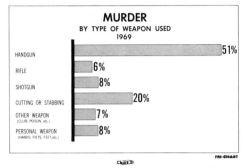

(Courtesy of the FBI's *Uniform Crime Reports*)

percent; burglary rose 117 percent, and murder went up 62 percent.[1] In addition to an upsurge in traditional crimes, other types of crimes rose significantly, and although the movement to professionalize the police was beginning to show measureable results, the decade began, as had the previous one, with a disturbing exposé of police lawlessness.

Police Corruption

In January, 1960, eight Chicago policemen were arrested for complicity in a professional burglary ring when a professional burglar with whom they had been working informed on them. The police had allowed him to ply his trade for a cut of the profits. It took four police vans to haul the contraband from the officers' homes.[2]

Citizens of Denver were stunned when later that year thirty members of their police department were key principals in a half-million-dollar burglary ring. The "Police Burglars of Denver" was front page news nationwide.[3]

Also in 1960 the New York State Investigation Commission uncovered a collusive relationship between policemen in Buffalo and vice lords. Gambling and prostitution were allowed to flourish

[1] Federal Bureau of Investigation, *Uniform Crime Reports–1969* (Washington: U. S. Government Printing Office, 1970).

[2] Ralph Lee Smith, *The Tarnished Badge* (New York: Thomas Y. Crowell Company, 1965), pp. 157-173.

[3] *Ibid.,* pp. 14-40.

while officers looked the other way and actually issued courtesy cards to racketeers, granting them membership in honorary police societies.[4]

The following year a CBS television documentary entitled "Biography of a Bookie Joint" showed Boston policemen entering and leaving with great frequency a South Boston Horse Parlor. In later public hearings, the Police Commissioner resigned.[5]

In January, 1964, twenty-three gambling-related indictments were handed down by a Marion County, Indiana, grand jury. Twenty-two of the indictments were for Indianapolis police officers, only three of whom were patrolmen.[6]

The frequency of the corruption together with the apparent widespread nature of it—the exposés pointed to a national malady rather than regional problem—once again motivated police reform. Probably the most significant upheaval occurred in Chicago, where O. W. Wilson was appointed Superintendant of Police. Significant innovations were initiated by the legendary police administrator and within a relatively brief period of time public confidence was restored in the beleaguered Chicago Police Department.

Political Assassinations

Political passions reached such fever pitch in the 1960s that the most direct and dreaded form of protest—murder—was invoked on a shocking number of occasions. Politicians, civil rights leaders, and controversial heads of extremist groups were gunned down by men whose motivation and mental stability differed in almost every case. And the incidents of political assassination were not sectional occurrences; apparently no part of the nation was immune from them. As usual, local police officials, occasionally assisted by Federal Officers, were assigned the task of investigating each offense and bringing the assailant to justice. The assassinations placed extreme pressures on the police agencies in whose jurisdiction they were perpetrated. Most handled their responsibilities

[4]*Ibid.*

[5]William J. Bopp, *The Police Rebellion* (Springfield: Charles C Thomas, Publisher, 1971) p. 173.

[6]*Supra* note 2, pp. 122-147.

in a competent and professional manner. Some, however, were not equal to the task.

In 1962 in Jackson, Mississippi, Medgar Evers, field representative of the NAACP, was gunned down in front of his home. He died a short time later. Local and state police, together with agents from the FBI, worked on the case until a white segregationist was arrested and brought to trial.

The following year President John F. Kennedy was shot and killed from ambush as he rode in a Dallas, Texas, motorcade. Several hours later the suspected assailant was captured, but not before he had killed Dallas police officer J.D. Tippet. The President's alleged assassin was also killed when he was shot in the basement garage of the police station by an enraged Dallas nightclub operator who had gained access to the scene.

Later in the decade two extremist leaders—one black and one white—were shot and killed by former followers. Malcolm X, previously a Black Muslim and leader of the Nationalistic Organization for Afro-American Unity, was felled by a hail of bullets as he addressed a group of four hundred blacks in New York City's Audubon Ballroom. George Lincoln Rockwell, founder and head of the American Nazi Party, was killed by gunfire in the parking lot of an Arlington, Virginia, shopping center. In both cases the police arrested and brought the killers to justice.

The assassinations of the Reverend Martin Luther King, Jr., in Memphis, and Senator Robert F. Kennedy in Los Angeles, stunned the nation. Their killers were arrested, brought to trial, and convicted through the use of tried and true police investigative techniques.

Mass Murders

Although no civilized society can excuse or condone political murders, most were committed by a man or men with a purpose, albeit a grisly one. One type of deadly crime during the decade was so irrational, so purposeless that the sanity of the perpetrators had to be questioned, and usually was in later court trials. The number of senseless mass murders during the decade, together with the inflammatory publicity surrounding them, terrorized communities across the land.

In Chicago Richard Speck murdered eight student nurses in their quarters. In Boston, the "Boston Strangler" plied his deadly trade as that city and the nation watched in horror. In Los Angeles, Charles Manson's "family" had its name indelibly etched on the blackest pages of American history. But "the crime of the century" occurred in Austin, Texas, on the campus of the University of Texas, on a hot afternoon in August, 1966, when Charles Whitman secreted himself in a tower 307 feet above the sprawling campus and, with a veritable arsenal of weapons at his side, shot forty-four people, thirteen fatally. Three policemen and a civilian ascended the tower where Whitman was encountered and shot to death. Although a later investigation and autopsy revealed that Whitman was suffering from a brain tumor and had been consuming Dexedrine tablets, neither the tumor nor the stimulants were believed responsible for his actions. The ultimate explanation of the conduct of the "mad man in the tower" died with Whitman.

A FUSILLADE FROM THE SUPREME COURT

During a time when police officers were waging a frontal attack on crime and violence, the United States Supreme Court, led by Chief Justice Earl Warren, released a number of court decisions that were highly critical of police action.

In *Mapp v. Ohio* (1961) the court held that the Fourth Amendment of the Constitution applies to all the states through the due process clause of the Fourteenth Amendment. In *Gideon v. Wainright* (1963) the court required that states must appoint counsel for indigent defendants in both capital and noncapital cases. The court decided in *Escobedo v. Illinois* (1964) that when the police process shifts from the investigatory to the accusatory stage, and its purpose is to elicit a confession, the subject must be allowed to consult with an attorney. In *Miranda v. Arizona* (1966) the Supreme Court held that policemen must advise suspects of certain Constitutional guarantees in order to make a confession admissible as evidence. In addition the court stated that the privilege against self-incrimination applied to police interrogations as well as to court hearings. Two later cases related to the American juvenile court system. In *Kent v. United States* (1966) the Warren Court held that a juvenile court must grant defendants a hearing prior to transferring jurisdiction to a criminal court, while in re Gault (1967) it was decided that the due process clause of the Fourteenth Amendment was applicable to state juvenile courts. It is interesting to note that of these six major landmark decisions, four were decided by a five to four vote.

As a result of these Supreme Court decisions, a clamor arose against the Warren Court, not only from within police ranks but also from the general public, though a move to impeach the Chief Justice drew little backing. Policemen became disturbed over the rulings, partly because they restricted police power and authority during time of crisis, but mostly because the police felt they were thrust into the position of having to anticipate Supreme Court action. Police actions in many of the earlier landmark cases had been considered legal and prudent by lower courts and appellate tribunals; however, the Warren Court, often by a five to four vote, negated earlier precedents and lower court rulings. What was perfectly legal one year was often ruled illegal retroactively a year or two later by the Supreme Court. Opinion polls showed that a majority of the American public felt that the "pendulum had swung too far to the left," and that court was "coddling criminals."

MILITANCY AND THE POLICE

The social atmosphere of the 1960s was strikingly similar to that which existed during earlier eras. Militancy, protest, civil unrest, and the rise of extremist groups appeared in great, and intermingled, profusion. Again, like the turmoil of a bygone period, the police were assigned to combat disorders and, in so doing, contracted a case of militancy themselves.

Racial Protest and Urban Rioting

The nonviolent Negro protest that had originated in the previous decade escalated in the sixties as moderate black leaders were able to enlist broad support for their cause. Massive demonstrations filled city streets, and in the majority of cases, demonstrations were remarkably free of violence, due in no small measure to good police handling, a talent that was learned more by field experience and sound administrative leadership than through tactical training programs. Besides massive demonstrations and lengthy protest marches, other tactics were undertaken. Sit-ins, wade-ins, voter registration drives, boycotts, and rent strikes were only a few of the devices employed by protestors. And although the police were only occasionally the targets of protest, demonstrators found that an "incident" involving local law enforcement officers could serve to more dramatically publicize their demands. In fact, Stokely Charmichael, an early leader of the Student Non-Violent Coordinating Committee (SNCC), stated that a demonstration which did not provoke a police response was unsuccessful. On a number of occasions demonstrations did provoke extreme police action, and the entire law enforcement community suffered because of the ill-advised actions of a few departments.

By mid-decade the cry for desegregation had been smothered by urban black rioting, striking first in the Watts section of Los Angeles, but spreading quickly to other cities—Tampa, Cincinnati, Atlanta, Newark, Detroit, Miami, and Chicago to mention but a few. The police, ill-trained, badly equipped, and unprepared for such disorders, were thrown into the breach. Criticized by conservatives for being too permissive, accused by liberals of overreacting, law enforcement officers tried to restore order to communities that often simultaneously made conflicting demands on them. Policemen came under attack from all quarters for their handling of racial rioting. By 1966 a new philosophy had pervaded the civil rights movement as "we shall overcome" was replaced by "black power" and "burn, baby, burn." An additional threat to the police surfaced with the rise of black nationalist groups, such as the Black Panther Party (BPP), the Republic of New Africa, the United Slaves (US), who believed in such direct action as murder and arson. Policemen became targets for snipers as black reactionaries stockpiled weapons and used them to shoot down officers

Police Killed by Felons, 1960–1969

Type of Police activity	Total	Type of assignment					
		2-man cars	1-man cars		Foot	Detective and special assignment	Off duty
			Alone	Assisted			
Total	561	164	*153	53	34	111	46
1. Responding to "disturbance" calls (family quarrels, man with gun, etc.)	107	47	17	14	9	16	4
2. Burglaries in progress or pursuing burglary suspects	53	16	21	3	1	11	1
3. Robberies in progress or pursuing robbery suspects	112	26	26	13	7	21	19
4. Attempting other arrests	157	39	49	15	9	33	12
5. Handling, transporting, custody of prisoners	36	11	10	1		13	1
6. Investigating suspicious persons and circumstances	53	13	26	1	3	8	2
7. Ambush, deranged persons (no warning-unprovoked attack)	43	12	4	6	5	9	7

*99 city police officers, 54 county and State police officers.

(Courtesy of the FBI's *Uniform Crime Reports*)

Police Killed by Felons, 1960-1969

Type of Police activity	Region				
	Total	North-eastern States	North Central States	Southern States	Western States
1. Responding to "disturbance" calls (family quarrels, man with gun, etc.)	107	20	32	39	16
2. Burglaries in progress or pursuing burglary suspects	53	4	15	20	14
3. Robberies in progress or pursuing robbery suspects	112	25	34	31	22
4. Attempting other arrests	157	17	27	90	23
5. Handling, transporting, custody of prisoners	36	4	9	21	2
6. Investigating suspicious persons and circumstances	53	5	13	21	14
7. Ambush, deranged persons (no warning—unprovoked attack)	43	9	13	14	7
Total	561	84	143	236	98

(Courtesy of the FBI's *Uniform Crime Reports*)

from ambush. Confrontations between policemen and Black Panthers consistently led to bloody consequences, which more often than not brought cries of police harassment from Panthers. At one point the police were accused of "murdering" twenty-nine Panthers, and news services, magazines, newspapers, and television networks accepted the number and the accusation as true, even though the source was a BPP attorney. After the claim had been made, accepted, and published or broadcast, the *New Yorker* magazine, in a brilliantly incisive job of investigative reporting, exposed the claim and the figure as contrived and false.

Student Unrest

In 1964 student unrest exploded into reality when a sit-in demonstration at the University of California at Berkeley turned into the largest case of mass civil disobedience in California's history as 830 police officers from a variety of agencies arrested 773 persons. Motivated by a number of causes but rallying around a common belief in the invalidity of the Vietnam War, student protest spread like wildfire from campus to campus. Names like Kent State, Columbia, Berkeley, and Jackson State became household words as peaceful protest evolved into massive acts of civil disobedience, then into riotous activity. Marches on draft boards were conducted, often deteriorating to extreme collective violence, amidst the now familiar cries of "police brutality." Radical students, many of whom were from affluent backgrounds, formed associations, such as the Students for a Democratic Society (SDS), the Progressive Labor Party (PLP), the Socialist Workers Party (SWP), or the Venceremos Brigade (VB). Although the ideology and political orientation differed among the various

Police brutality? A participant in a "peace" demonstration in Oakland, California, is about to strike a police officer from behind with a pipe concealed in a sheet of rolled newspaper.

The age of militancy. *(Courtesy of the St. Petersburg Police Department)*

organizations, their goal was the same: smash the American "system." Failing to receive widespread support, some groups and individuals went underground and engaged in isolated terroristic tactics. Explosions rocked a number of governmental buildings, and several innocent people were killed through indiscriminate acts of wanton terrorism. Violent student unrest reached its peak in 1968, when during the Democratic National Convention in Chicago, thousands of angry demonstrators clashed with police, thus bringing denunciations of the student protest movement by conservatives and bitter accusations of abusive and excessive police action by liberals. As a result of the incident, the split between liberals and the police, always present to some extent, became a chasm. Student lawlessness tended to muddy the traditional police view of criminality, for here were large groups of affluent, college-educated young people engaging in violent, disruptive acts and felonious conduct, a situation with which policemen were unfamiliar. Gone now was that rather clear-cut police image of the criminal which saw law violators as coming from economically deprived, uneducated, lower-class groupings.

The Cities' Response To Violence: Police Review Boards

American's cities, faced with growing internal strife, sought to alleviate some of the causative factors of civil insurrection by establishing extraordinary community relations programs. Many communities created imaginative programs of substance and merit, but others chose to implement superficial, stopgap devices aimed more at pacifying minority group leadership than attacking the underlying causes of their frustrations. One such device was the police review board.

The concept of the police review board, a panel of citizens established to hear public grievances against individual officers, was not new; the idea dated back to the 1930s, and the city of Philadelphia even established one in 1958. But it was not until the 1960s that the idea was operationalized to any great extent.

Proponents of review boards viewed the clashes between blacks and policemen as a deep-seated problem which had to be corrected immediately. Abrasive police-Negro relationships were not, in fact, the most pressing problem; they were a symptom of a greater dilemma, for the police as governments' most visible repre-sentatives simply manned the barricades against citizens with complaints against higher authority. For city fathers to send their officers out to hold back a demonstration of jobless men, then after the two groups had clashed to suggest that what was needed was a police review board to attack the problem was, at best, shallow thinking. Yet that is basically what happened. City officials in community after community established police review boards, thereby attacking a symptom of a multifaceted problem which went unsolved.

Police review boards had basic structural and philosophical weaknesses which doomed them to failure from the start. First, they were discriminatory. Of all the components of city government, only the police were forced to labor directly under citizen scrutiny, a situation which did not go unnoticed in the law enforcement community. Second, citizens served on boards without pay and with no special training. The result was a high personnel-turnover rate that contributed to a lack of continuity in the decision-making process. Third, the lack of sophistication of board members led to fewer sustained complaints against policemen than in the earlier systems of internal police review, giving the impression that police review panels were overly lenient, thereby alienating the people who were supposed to benefit most from the plan. Fourth, review boards, although advisory in nature, wrested from chiefs of police the responsibility for meting out internal discipline, an unhealthy situation at best. Fifth, the boards' procedures often refused to grant policemen the most basic protections of due process. Last, implementors of the review board concept failed to anticipate the depth and intensity of police resistance to it. Although the boards were attacked primarily for their administrative weaknesses, there is evidence which indicates that review boards were more a symbolic issue to police officers, who saw them as a liberal capitulation in the face of urban violence.

Police review boards were established in Rochester; York, Pennsylvania; Minneapolis, and New York City. In each city they were bitterly opposed by rank-and-file patrolmen's associations who, through referenda, lobbying, and court action, succeeded in eliminating the device from their communities. The fight over civilian review in New York City began as a typical labor-management dispute; but before it was over, it had evolved into one of the most significant events in police history, an incident which ranks in importance with the Boston Police Strike of 1919.

In 1966 Mayor John Lindsay added four civilians to the New York Police Department's Complaint Review Board, which had been manned previously by three deputy police commissioners. The move was resisted by the 25,000-member Patrolmen's Benevolent Association (PBA), which sought to force a referendum on the issue. Strangely, the PBA's plan to have the citizens of New York City vote on the idea was strenuously opposed by Mayor Lindsay, a civil libertarian, who battled, unsuccessfully, to keep the measure off the ballot. Against tremendous odds and with the state's three most influential political figures—Lindsay, Senator Jacob Javits, and Senator Robert F. Kennedy—on the other side, the "Lindsay plan" went to the electorate, which voted it out of existence by an astounding 1,313,161 to 765,468. Never in history had patrolmen waged so brazen a battle against their bosses and won.[7]

The significance of the NYPBA's victory went far beyond the city limits of New York. Patrolmen across the nation learned from the PBA's experience that they possessed political muscle which, once flexed, could bring substantial rewards. A movement toward police militancy was started in New York City, a movement that shows no sign of abating.

Police Militancy

Policemen, particularly patrolmen in urban areas, sick of unfavorable court decisions, battle-weary from policing demonstrations and riots, tired of extreme liberal criticism, but buoyed by the success of the New York Patrolmen's Benevolent Association, set out to better their economic lot by utilizing old-fashioned, not so subtle, trade union tactics. Police associations and fraternal organizations which had originally been founded for social and benevolent purposes were transformed into professional confederations whose new concern was with bread-and-butter issues. Membership in the Fraternal Order of Police (FOP) burgeoned to over 100,000. Fragmented local police organizations banded together in state and national consortia for lobbying purposes. A national police union was created, although early recruitment was spotty.

[7]*Supra* note 5, pp. 10, 133.

Almost from the occurrence of the historic event in New York City, a series of labor-management disputes developed that were settled only after extreme measures had been taken by patrolmen. In November, 1966, patrolmen in Pontiac, Michigan, called in sick, en masse, to enforce demands for a wage increase. This tactic, termed the "blue flu," was to become widespread. During the spring of 1967 patrolmen in Detroit engaged in a ticket slow-

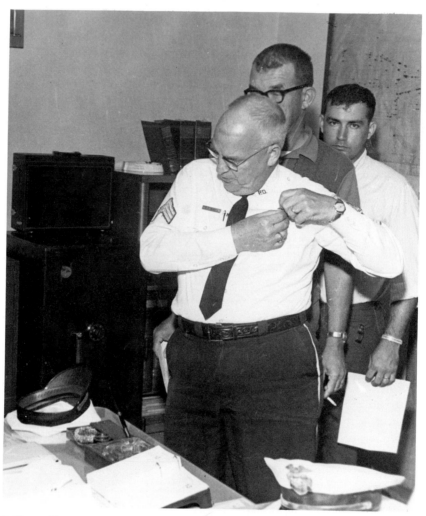

Police militancy. Members of the Plant City, Florida, Police Department line up to turn in their badges after a dispute with city officials over a pay increase.

down and sick-strike in quest of a pay raise. On July 17, 1969, the first strike of uniformed employees in the history of the State of California occurred when the Vallejo police and fire departments walked off their jobs for five days. "Job actions"—work slow-downs and stoppages; strikes; ticket blizzards (the writing of large numbers of nonrevenue-producing traffic citations), mass resignations—occurred in literally hundreds of communities, large and small, including Boston; New York; Minneapolis; Atlanta; San Diego; Plant City, Florida; Chicago Heights, Illinois; and Poplar Bluff, Missouri. Policemen began receiving generous pay increases and fringe benefits, but they were paying a heavy price for it in public support, even though the overwhelming number of police officers in the country never engaged in extreme acts. Many policemen viewed with ambivalence the actions of rebellious officers. It was obvious that trade-unionist principles were not compatible with the idea of police professionalization but it was hard to argue with success, especially when success manifested itself in such tangible ways.

Empirical Inquiry into Crime, Riots, and Police Activity

The social conditions of the decade—termed by iconoclasts the "sick sixties"—spurred official governmental inquiries into the problems of the era. Commissions were appointed, grand juries convened, committees formed, and task forces flooded com-munities to uncover the causes and preventions of various social dilemmas. Many of the commissions were *ad hoc* bodies assigned to investigate specific incidents: a riot, student unrest at a college, a lawful demonstration that had deteriorated into a tumultuous assembly, or questionable police tactics in restoring civil order. Other commissions, especially those appointed by the President of the United States, were formed to probe a general social problem: crime, civil disorder, violence, etc.

Unfortunately, by the time most commissions released their investigative results to the public, opinion on the issues in question had polarized and the findings generally pleased only those whose previously held views were reinforced. In fact, commissions, especially Presidential commissions, became an issue themselves as more often than not they recommended grandiose solutions with a price tag which the public and politicians refused to accept. In

addition to official inquiries, individual authors, generally sociologists at large urban universities, published a great mass of books
on the social ills of the country.

Policemen were often roundly criticized for their handling of
riots and demonstrations as well as for "failing to relate" to their
communities. Much of the criticism was warranted, but some of it
was shrill, unreasonable, and of questionable value. A favorite
tactic of a riot commission was to blame equally the police and
their adversaries, then warn that the only way to prevent a future
occurrence was to appropriate massive sums of money to alleviate
social miseries.

It did not take long for Presidential commissions to fall into
disrepute with the citizenry who were too upset about crime and
violence to look upon the perpetrators as victims. One
commission, however, did gain acceptance, not only from the
public and the politicians but also from the criminal justice community it had been assigned to investigate.

In the summer of 1965 President Lyndon Johnson established
the President's Commission on Law Enforcement and
Administration of Justice. The commission was chaired by
Nicholas Katzenbach. An impressive array of advisors and consultants were involved in the investigations, and in February of
1967 the commission released its general report, *The Challenge of
Crime in a Free Society,* which was soon followed by task force
reports on the police, the courts, corrections, juvenile delinquency
and youth crime, organized crime, an assessment of crime, science,
and technology, narcotics and drugs, and drunkenness.

Task Force Report: The Police contained a thoughtful analysis
of police problems and offered reasonable solutions to them. The
approach was conservative; the language was guarded, and
criticism was tempered by reason. The subjects of the report, the
nation's police, were criticized but not attacked. Missing was the
flamboyancy that had been the stock in trade of other commissions. Some of the commission's most noteworthy findings and
recommendations follow.

1. The police were isolated from the communities they had
    sworn to serve, and from other components in the criminal
    justice system. Police science and law enforcement pro-
    grams were adding to this isolation by offering courses so
    technical and vocational in nature that classes were

attended primarily by policemen.

2. City officials had all but abdicated their responsibilities for running police agencies by delegating that responsibility to police chiefs.

3. Police chiefs were often appointed because of demonstrated skill as investigators rather than for administrative competence.

4. Police executives had failed to assume their roles as major policymakers.

5. Fresh blood should be infused into police departments by creating new entry level classifications, and by allowing lateral entry. Minority recruitment should be emphasized.

6. Minimum training and educational requirements should be established for all levels of officers.

7. Formal community relations and internal investigating units should be created.

8. Fragmented local police services should be pooled or consolidated in order to eliminate waste and duplication.

The President's Crime Commission was successful primarily because it was a team effort by a staff eminently qualified to engage in the type of activity for which they were chosen. No single individual, group, or social philosophy dominated the commission. While other commissions were often referred to by the name of their chairmen (i.e. Kerner Commission, Walker Report, Eisenhower Commission), the President's Commission on Law Enforcement was consistently referred to by its designated name, not by the name of its chairman or dominant member.

THE POLICE REACT

Many police administrators throughout history have had the will to reform their departments, but without the assistance of higher governmental authorities and the application of significant amounts of money, plans could not be operationalized. However, in the sixties, especially during the last third of the decade, law enforcement began making real progress toward that long sought goal—professionalization. In the face of tremendous obstacles and under attack from without, the nation's police made astounding progress. From a craft to a profession? Not quite, but at least the goal was attainable; and what was more important, the police, including the rank-and-file, knew it. Led by the International Association of Chiefs of Police, furnished with a blueprint for reform by a Presidential Commission, and financed by a Federal anticrime package, the police moved forward with enthusiasm.

The Role of the IACP

In 1962 Quinn Tamm, formerly an assistant director with the FBI, was appointed Executive Director of the International Association of Chiefs of Police. That year the Institute for Police

In 1962 Quinn Tamm was appointed Executive Director of the International Association of Chiefs of Police. Under Tamm's leadership, the IACP has been a positive force for meaningful police reform. *(Courtesy of the IACP)*

Management was formed to help raise funds for the Association. The role of the Field Operations Division, which had been created in 1960, was expanded and teams of consultants were sent to conduct management and reorganizational studies for police departments, both large and small, in forty states. The IACP offered a source of professional advice and knowledge, plus an outside perspective of police operations, that were unavailable elsewhere. Hundreds of law enforcement agencies, including those in Baltimore, Boston, Chicago, Cincinnati, Dallas, Pittsburgh, Seattle, and Washington made use of this service, and no community to which IACP consultants were dispatched was quite the same after a survey. The Association founded a major library and research center and a Management and Research Division. Besides providing technical assistance, the IACP was a major source of professional ideas and judgment, and a moral force which helped the police grow and expand during a time of strife.

The Omnibus Crime Control and Safe Streets Act of 1968

In 1968 the Congress passed the Omnibus Crime Control and Safe Streets Act, the most comprehensive piece of crime legislation in the nation's history. Although some sections of the bill applied to Federal policing, the real significance of the measure was in its recognition that law enforcement was primarily a local function and that fragmented crime efforts had to be better financed and coordinated. The Law Enforcement Assistance Administration (LEAA) was established within the Department of Justice and those police departments which had wanted to professionalize but could not because they lacked the funds, were provided with the resources to do so. Planning grants were disbursed to states to establish state planning agencies whose task was to draw up comprehensive programs aimed at improving law enforcement and criminal justice. Regional planning councils were set up within the states. When the planning agencies were operationalized, they submitted their proposed programs to LEAA, which then funded them through block action grants. Congress also authorized the Law Enforcement Assistance Administration to make discretionary grants (action grants given to cities, states, or agencies which had programs approved). Programs spanned the full spectrum of criminal justice activities. In Florida, for example, both hardware and software programs were undertaken as money was provided for cadet programs, special crime-fighting units, burglary-robbery prevention programs, community-relations activities, halfway houses, an organized crime and racketeering strike force, training programs, and a state uniform-crime-reporting system, to mention but a few federally funded projects.

In what could become the most far-reaching and far-sighted Federal program, the Office of Academic Assistance (OAA) was formed within the Law Enforcement Assistance Administration to administer the Law Enforcement Education Program (LEEP). LEEP provided financial aid to students enrolled in colleges and universities who upon graduation pledged to seek careers in criminal justice. Loans of up to $1,800 per academic year were made available to pre-service students, while grants of up to $300 per semester were made available to in-service students working in criminal justice agencies. In LEAA's first year, 1969, its total budget was $63 million. In 1970 LEAA's budget was $268 million: $184,522,420 of which was spent for block action grants; $31,999,760 for discretionary grants; $29.9 million for planning grants, and $18 million for academic assistance.

Community Relations Programs

Municipal police departments, especially those serving urban areas, moved to implement meaningful community relations programs, some of which were funded by Federal grants, but most of which were locally sponsored and run. Permanent departmental community-relations units became popular, and their numbers burgeoned during the decade, especially in the post-1966 period. Towns and cities created programs of real and lasting significance. The Philadelphia Police Department began sponsoring "town hall" meetings to which citizens were invited to participate in an open forum. Storefront centers were opened in Oakland, New York, and dozens of other cities. The St. Louis Police Department, a leader in the field, developed more than a dozen community-based programs designed to reach every citizen in the city regardless of race, sex, age, occupation, or social class. Policemen in Dallas embarked on an experimental program to educate elementary school children about the evils of crime. The Monterey Park,

California, Police Department began dispatching beat patrolmen to meet and greet new arrivals to the community.

Police in the 1960s began a national movement to chip away at the iceberg of isolation that had been building up over the decades. The problem was acute and one that could not be solved in short order because of its long-standing existence. But progress was made as police departments showed that they had the will and the enthusiasm to attack an issue of major social importance.

Nonlethal Weapons

Police officers had come under a good deal of criticism for their use of lethal weapons in the apprehension of felons and in the handling of civil turmoil, even though official inquiry into these actions exonerated the police from blame in the overwhelming majority of cases. Groups of citizens demanded that the police adopt nonlethal weapons in addition to conventional tear gas canisters and projectiles, a cry welcomed by the police who for years had sought, with little success, the development of such weaponry. Private industry, in response to this need, engaged in crash programs aimed at producing nonlethal weapons. The police adopted these devices as fast as they could be perfected and tested for efficiency, effectiveness, and safety.

The first contemporary nonlethal weapon adopted by a significant number of police agencies was a small aerosol spray can containing a potent chemical agent that caused extreme irritation and temporary incapacitation when sprayed in an attacker's face. The device was a major breakthrough in police weaponry because it offered, for the first time, an inexpensive, portable nonlethal weapon which could be carried by individual officers for use in close contact work. The police came under some early criticism for adopting the weapon when it was alleged that eye damage could result if it was misused. However, many departments drafted strict policies limiting usage, while pointing out, rather effectively, the dangers involved in alternate apprehension devices—firearms and nightsticks. In time the vast majority of citizens accepted the device as a necessary and desirable weapon, and the black-sheathed aerosal can fastened to officers' leather gear became a familiar sight to the public.

To combat mob violence, a device called "pepper fog" was

adopted by scores of state and local agencies. The "pepper fog" was a machine that sprayed thousands of cubic feet of tear gas per minute over an area, but which could be held by one man. The weapon was battery-operated and it too became a familiar sight at the apex of police riot squad and crowd-control formations.

Although the development of chemical agents received first priority from private manufacturers and police administrators, other nonlethal weapons began appearing on the scene, albeit on an experimental basis. A tranquilizer gun that was designed to incapacitate people in much the same way that animals were temporarily disabled was tested, but a seemingly endless series of operational problems kept it from being perfected. A weapon called the "stun gun" was developed, which was a special shoulder weapon that fired a flat, circular disc of woven material, filled with bird shot—a "stun bag." The blow delivered by the projectile was heavy but nonlethal. Other devices that made an appearance during the decade included chemical dye which could be sprayed on rioters during the height of action for later identification, a slippery substance called "banana peel" which could be applied to city streets to prevent rioters from achieving personal mobility, and an electronic device which produced a loud sound that disbursed rioters without causing permanent ear damage.

Advanced Technology

Unlike other eras, the police in the 1960s showed no reluctance to adopt technological innovations and adapt them to fit their peculiar circumstances. Record-keeping functions were updated. Police cars were fitted with special accessories. Crime laboratories were opened and stocked with sophisticated equipment. Fragmented police agencies, some 40,000 strong, moved to lessen their isolation from one another by creating computer-based information systems and advanced communications centers.

At the Federal level, the FBI in 1965 began to develop its National Crime Information Center (NCIC), an operational information systems program. Operationalized in 1967, the NCIC collected information on wanted persons, stolen vehicles and stolen property, and provided police terminals to those communities and states which wanted to participate.

Local and state agencies also created information systems.

A view of the FBI National Crime Information Center located at FBI Head-quarters, Washington, D.C. Employe in foreground is operating the control typewriter, and viewed at the right is the control console for the Center. *(Courtesy of the FBI)*

Michigan founded the Law Enforcement Information Network (LEIN). The California Highway Patrol began a statewide file of stolen vehicles called Autostatis. A regional records system was conceived in the San Francisco Bay area. This system, the Police Information Network (PIN), was to become statewide in scope. Communities pioneering in establishing like systems included New York, Chicago, St. Louis, and Los Angeles.

Police agencies also built and staffed modern police com-munications centers whose primary function was to make maximum use of field units. As the decade ended there seemed to be a trend toward equipping patrolmen with miniaturized trans-ceivers so that officers could leave their cars without losing communications contact.

Police agencies followed the lead of the New York and Los Angeles Police Departments and helicopters and airplanes were pressed into service for patrol and investigative work. By the end of the decade, hundreds of police aircraft had been commissioned by municipal police departments, sheriffs departments, and state agencies.

Police Educational Programs

Prior to the establishment of the Law Enforcement Assistance Administration, the education of policemen and prospective police officers was a sometime thing which was systematically under-taken in but one state—California. Scattered communities across the country were admittedly enthusiastic about higher education for policemen, but these cities and towns were in no way indicative of the norm. At the heart of the problem was economics. Early studies indicated that because of low pay, most line officers were forced to work second jobs. To give up this extra source of income to pursue an expensive and time-consuming educational program was too much to ask of officers, who often worked rotating shifts, making a difficult idea almost impossible. In California this problem was less acute, as police salaries were significantly higher than those in the rest of the nation, the policy of departmental educational incentives was widespread, and junior colleges were tuition-free, with only a minimal charge for education at state colleges and universities. With the advent of LEEP, college education became available for the first time to officers throughout the country, and colleges and universities, in response to a felt need, began opening their doors to policemen as students for the first time.

From 1960 to 1967 the number of college programs for police increased from about 100 to 234. From 1967 to 1969 college police programs increased to 409, containing 32,000 student majors. By 1970 no less than 890 colleges had applied for and received LEEP funds. As a new decade dawned, other states, notably Florida, Georgia, Illinois, New York, Texas, and Washington, challenged California's leadership in law enforcement education.

Police Training

Law enforcement training improved during the decade, but not enough to keep abreast of the increasing complexity of the police task. Recruit training expanded greatly as eight states followed California's primacy and passed minimum standards legislation. But this expansion was a relative thing as some departments went from ten hours of recruit training to two hundred hours of training, a big statistical jump, though not nearly an acceptable one. As far as in-service training was concerned, a Ford Foundation survey found it "more a wish than a reality."

Administrative Innovations

Municipal police executives, assisted by the International Association of Chiefs of Police, the President's Commission on Law

Enforcement, and the Law Enforcement Assistance Administration, sought to upgrade the structure and function of their departments through administrative innovations. Principles of sound management were utilized to maximize efficiency. Police agencies found that increased citizen demands made it necessary to form certain specialized units. As a result, community-relations sections, internal-affairs units, staff-inspectional services, planning and research divisions, legal-advisor staffs, task force patrols, intelligence components, and security sections were created by many major departments, with even smaller agencies engaging in specialization, but to a lesser degree.

CONCLUSION

Policemen in the 1960s were subjected to extreme social pressure and some of the most deliberately provocative actions in history. They responded by effecting meaningful internal reforms. The educational level of officers was uplifted. Training was improved. Advanced technology was employed. Leadership was strengthened. A group of very able and talented police administrators arose to lead their departments toward professionalization, men who seemed destined to join the Savages, the Vollmers, the Wilsons, and the Parkers as police giants—Frank Rizzo, Philadelphia; Curtis Brostron, St. Louis; Charles R. Gain, Oakland; S. R. Schrotel, Cincinnati; E. Wilson Purdy, Dade County, Florida; Clarence Kelley, Kansas City; Thomas Reddin, Los Angeles.

The decade of the 1960s was the most fruitful one in the history of American law enforcement. It has been said that more was done to upgrade the police during these ten years than during the preceding fifty years. Possibly, but there is a good deal of progress yet to be made, especially in the areas of community relations and training. The old problem of trying to professionalize the police without isolating them from the community is yet to be answered satisfactorily. Another question that must be resolved is the issue of police militancy. If it is allowed to continue in its more extreme forms, then the movement toward professionalizaion could be slowed. But men of competence and goodwill are working long and hard on these problems, and the police are forging ahead, honestly trying to do a difficult and dangerous job under trying circumstances, and trying to win public support for their actions.

PART II

THE CRIMINAL

JUSTICE SYSTEM

(Courtesy of the *National Council on Crime and Delinquency*)

Chapter 12

THE CRIME PROBLEM

The Federal Government and each of the states have defined by statute the meaning of the word "crime." And although the various penal codes differ from state to state, the definition of crime is strikingly similar throughout the country. California's definition will serve as well as any:

> A crime. . .is an intentional act committed or omitted in violation of a law forbidding or commanding it, and to which is annexed either of the following punishments:
>   1. Death.
>   2. Imprisonment.
>   3. Fine.
>   4. Removal from (public) office.
>   5. Disqualification to hold and enjoy any office of honor, trust, or profit in this state.

Crime is a multifaceted phenomenon which does not lend itself to simple explanations or easy solutions. Reported crime in America has risen spectacularly during the past several decades. From 1960-1969 crimes of violence—murder, forcible rape, robbery, and aggravated assault—rose 130 percent. During that same period crimes, against property—burglary, larceny of fifty dollars and over, and auto theft—rose 151 percent. A portion of this rise may be explained by better reporting procedures and a growing population, but there is a good deal of evidence to indicate that crime is increasing far beyond population growth. Furthermore, experts feel that most crimes that occur are not reported to the police.

THE FBI'S UNIFORM CRIME REPORTS[1]

The medium for transmitting crime data to citizens and the police is the FBI's *Uniform Crime Reports (UCR)*. The *UCR* gives a nationwide view of crime based on police statistics made possible by the voluntary cooperation of local law enforcement agencies.

---

[1]Excerpted from the FBI's *Uniform Crime Reports*—1969 (Washington: U.S. Government Printing Office, 1970).

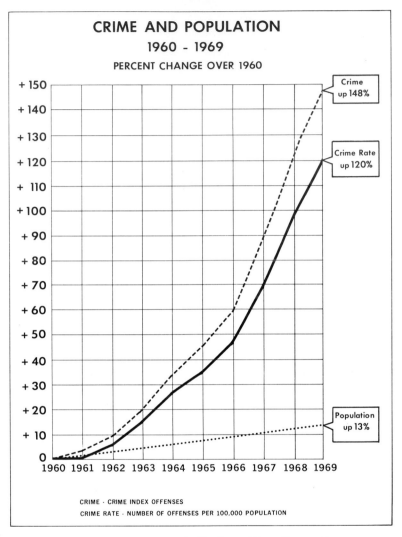

(Courtesy of the FBI's *Uniform Crime Reports*)

Police agencies representing approximately ninety-eight percent of the population furnish crime statistics to the FBI. The Uniform Crime Reporting Program, which is run by the FBI but which receives advice and assistance from the International Association of Chiefs of Police, employs seven crime classifications to establish an index to measure the trend and distribution of crime. The crimes in the FBI's crime index are the following:

    1. Murder and nonnegligent manslaughter.

2. Forcible rape.
3. Robbery.
4. Aggravated assault.
5. Burglary—breaking and entering.
6. Larceny, fifty dollars and over in value.
7. Auto theft.

These seven crimes were selected for the Crime Index because (1) they are all serious crimes, either by nature or by volume and (2) they represent the most common local crime problem. At the end of each calendar year this crime data, along with other information, is sent to the FBI by individual police agencies. The Bureau then tabulates, classifies, and interprets this great mass of information and publishes it in the *Uniform Crime Reports,* issued

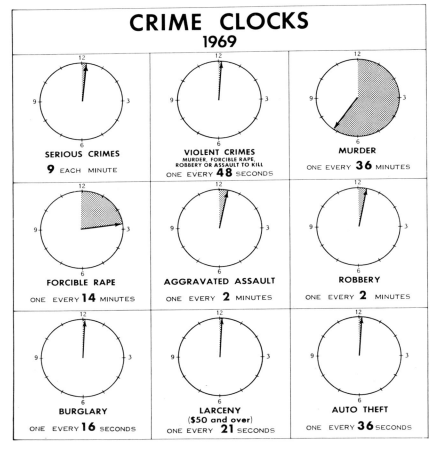

(Courtesy of the FBI's *Uniform Crime Reports*)

each summer. In addition to a summary of the yearly Crime Index, the *UCR* also contains facts on crime clearances, persons arrested and charged, careers in crime, police employe information, data on policemen killed, and crime trends. Charts and graphs are employed to illustrate crime trends over periods of months and years. Both the number of offenses and the rates per 100,000 population are charted. At the end of each decade a comprehensive ten-year summary is published. One of the FBI's most dramatic techniques for impressing the American people with the severity and frequency of crime is the crime clocks, illustrations of nine clocks showing time intervals for serious crimes.

The *Uniform Crime Reports* have come under some criticism from academics who are concerned that the publication does not give a "true picture" of the total crime problem. But the FBI has never claimed that the publication gives a "true picture." The *UCR* does present a general crime picture from which reasonable conclusions can be drawn. And although no system of this type can ever be made perfect, the Bureau is constantly modifying its procedures to provide the most professional service possible.

A CLASSIFICATION OF CRIMES

In order to study crimes, especially in a concise manner, some workable system of classification must be employed. Crimes may be broken into classes denoting their seriousness—misdemeanors and felonies; they may be typed, as does the FBI, into a crime index; or they may be classified according to the motive of perpetrators. However, although the preceding methods are appropriate to use in some circumstances, a more valid classification system, at least for this discussion, is one that deals with the patterns of crime. Accordingly, five patterns of crime will be briefly surveyed: (1) traditional crime (2) professional crime, (3) organized crime, (4) white collar crime, and (5) civil disobedience. The latter type of crime is rarely used in this context. In fact, some may argue against its inclusion in a study of crime patterns, but recent world and national events make it essential that it be included in a contemporary discussion of crime. Initially it must be stated that these five patterns of crime do not necessarily make up separate and distinct entities, for there are a great many crimes that for one reason or another fit into more than one category.

Traditional Crime

Traditional crimes are those which have been defined as criminal for long periods of time and which all reasonable people accept as evil on their face. Traditional crimes go back to tribal times—before the existence of criminal law—where even then they were branded as wrong. These crimes may be found in ancient tribal codes and in the Ten Commandments. Such crimes include murder, larceny, robbery, burglary, rape, assaults, and personal injuries.[2] They are not unlike those found in the FBI's Crime Index, although traditional crimes are much more numerous than the ones in that classification. Except in extraordinary cases perpetrators of traditional crimes invoke little public sympathy because of the long and widespread acceptance of them as wrongdoing. Defendants who plead not guilty in court to a traditional crime rarely attack the fairness or desirability of the law, for this is a useless gesture due to the heritages on which the law has been based.

Professional Crime[3]

For purposes of this study, professional crime is defined as crime committed for personal economic gain by individuals whose major source of income is from criminal pursuits and who spend the majority of their working time in illegal enterprises. There is reason to believe that professional criminals are responsible for a large proportion of all property crimes committed and probably an even larger proportion of total property loss through such crimes. As in many legitimate occupations, the success of professional criminals is measured by the amount of income earned. Some make only a modest living, while others have very high incomes, sometimes exceeding $100,000 a year. So-called run-of-the-mill professionals regularly gather at certain bars and restaurants which in effect function as criminal job placement centers. These centers tend to attract the low-status professional criminal; apparently the successful practitioner in crime does not go to the employment office.

[2]Ruth Shonle Cavan, *Criminology,* 3rd ed. (New York: Thomas Y. Crowell Co., 1962), p. 9.

[3]Adapted and reprinted from the President's Commission on Law Enforcement and Administration of Justice, *Task Force Report: Crime and Its Impact—An Assessment* (Washington: U.S. Government Printing Office, 1967), pp. 96-100.

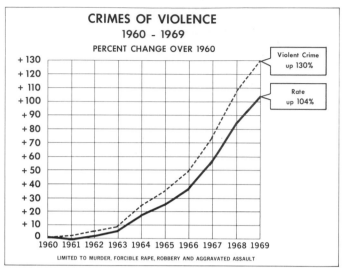

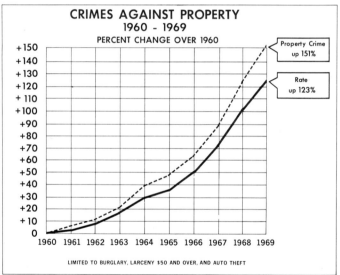

(Courtesy of the FBI's *Uniform Crime Reports*)

There is a sharp distinction between the professional and the amateur thief, which can be seen in the following three characteristics of professional crime.

Skills

The professional has a comprehensive complex of technical skills, personal contacts, and the knowledge necessary in order to make a good living at crime in comparative safety. Professional thieves have a contempt for the amateur's crude techniques, low income, and inability to avoid arrest.

Specialization

There is evidence that some individual professional criminals tend to specialize in a limited number of related rackets. Many exclude certain kinds of activities; many do not use violence.

Group Activity

Many professional criminals enjoy a sense of identity and solidarity and work within a set of well-defined norms and codes of loyalty, helpfulness, and honesty in dealing with one another. Studies reveal that the more successful a professional is, the more he is apt to conform to this pattern.

In order to be successful, professional criminals will do business with loan sharks who are relied upon for capital to finance jobs, and fences who will buy stolen merchandise. Whenever possible professionals will apply "the fix," which is a term that denotes the bribing of those who would set up impediments to the criminal's goal objective.

Organized Crime[4]

Organized crime is a society that seeks to operate outside the control of the American people and their governments. It involves thousands of criminals, working within structures as complex as those of any large corporation, subject to laws more rigidly enforced than those of legitimate governments. Its actions are not impulsive, but rather they are the result of intricate conspiracies carried on over many years and aimed at gaining control over whole fields of activity in order to amass huge profits.

The core of organized crime activity is the supplying of illegal goods and services—gambling, loan sharking, narcotics, and other forms of vice—to countless numbers of citizen customers. But organized crime is also extensively and deeply involved in legitimate business and in labor unions. Here it employs illegitimate methods—monopolization, terrorism, extortion, tax evasion—to drive out or control lawful ownership and leadership and to exact illegal profits from the public. To carry on its many activities secure from governmental interference, organized crime corrupts

[4]Adapted and reprinted from the President's Commission on Law Enforcement and Administration of Justice, *Task Force Report: Organized Crime* (Washington: U. S. Government Printing Office, 1967), pp. 1, 6-8.

public officials.

The present confederation of organized crime groups arose after Prohibition, during which Italian, German, Irish, and Jewish groups had competed with one another in racket operations. The Italian groups were successful in switching their enterprises from prostitution and bootlegging to gambling, extortion, and other illegal activities. They consolidated their power through murder and violence.

In 1950 the Senate's Special Committee to Investigate Crime in Interstate Commerce, chaired by Senator Estes Kefauver of Tennessee, declared that a nationwide syndicate known as the Mafia operated in many large cities and that the leaders of the Mafia usually controlled the most lucrative rackets in their cities. In 1957 twenty of organized crime's top leaders were convicted (later reversed on appeal) of a criminal charge arising from a meeting at Apalachin, New York. At the sentencing, the judge stated that they had sought to corrupt and infiltrate the political mainstreams of the country, that they had led double lives of crime and respectability, and that their probation reports read "like a tale of horrors."

Today the core of organized crime in the United States consists of twenty-four groups operating as criminal cartels in large cities across the nation. Their membership is exclusively men of Italian descent; they are in frequent communication with each other, and their smooth functioning is insured by a national body of overseers. To date, only the FBI has been able to document fully the national scope of these groups, and FBI intelligence indicates that the organization as a whole has changed its name from the Mafia to La Cosa Nostra.   Our Thing

Organized crime in its totality thus consists of these twenty-four groups allied with other racket enterprises to form a loose confederation operating in cities. Each of these twenty-four groups is known as a "family," with membership varying from as many as 700 men to as few as twenty. There are over 5,000 members is all. Most cities with organized crime have only one family; New York City has five. Each family can participate in the full range of activities in which organized crime is known to engage. Family organization is rationally designed with an integrated set of positions geared to maximum profits. Like any large corporation, the organization functions regardless of per-

The above apparatus chart, being worked on by two Florida Department of Law Enforcement Crime Information and Intelligence Analysts, is an example of the analysts' link-cluster technique. This technique is a method of showing interconnection between organized crime figures, criminal groups and subversive activities. *(Courtesy of the Florida Department of Law Enforcement)*

sonnel changes, and no individual—not even the leader—is indispensable. If he dies or goes to jail, business goes on.

The hierarchical structure of the families resembles that of the Mafia groups that have operated for almost a century on the Island of Sicily. Each family is ruled by one man, the boss, whose primary functions are maintaining order and maximizing profits. Subject only to the possibility of being overruled by the national advisory group, which will be discussed below, his authority on all matters relating to his family is absolute.

Beneath each boss is an underboss, the vice-president or deputy director of the family. He collects information for the boss; he relays messages to him and passes his instructions down to his own underlings. In the absence of the boss, the underboss acts for him.

On the same level as the underboss, but operating in a staff capacity, is the *consigliere,* who is a counselor, or advisor. Often an elder of the family who has partially retired from a career of crime, he gives advice to family members, including the boss and the underboss, and thereby enjoys considerable influence and power.

Below the underboss are the *caporegime* (lieutenants), some of whom serve as buffers between the top members of the family and lower echelon personnel. To maintain their isolation from the police, the leaders of the hierarchy (particularly the boss) avoid direct communication with the workers. All commands, information, complaints, and money flow back and forth through a trusted go-between. A caporegima fulfilling this buffer capacity, however, unlike the underboss, does not make decisions or assume any of the authority of his boss.

Other caporegima serve as chiefs of operating units. The number of men supervised in each unit varies with the size and activities of particular families. Often the caporegima has one or two associates who work closely with him, carrying orders, information, and money to the men who belong to his unit. From a business standpoint the caporegima is analogous to plant supervisor or sales manager.

The lowest level members of a family are the *soldati,* the soldiers or "button men" who report to the caporegime. A soldier may operate a particular illicit enterprise (e.g. a loan-sharking racket, a dice game, a lottery, a bookmaking operation, a smuggling operation) on a commission basis, or he may "own" the enterprise and pay a portion of its profit to the organization in return for the right to operate.

Beneath the soldiers in the hierarchy are large numbers of employes and commission agents who are not members of the family and who are not necessarily of Italian descent. These are the people who do most of the actual work in the various enterprises. They have no buffers or insulation from law enforcement. They take bets, drive trucks, answer telephones, sell narcotics, tend the stills, work in legitimate businesses.

The highest ruling body of the twenty-four families is the "commission." This body serves as a combination legislature, supreme court, board of directors, and arbitration board: its principal functions are judicial. Family members look to the commission as the ultimate authority on organizational and jurisdictional disputes. It is composed of the bosses of the nation's most powerful families and has authority over all twenty-four.

White Collar Crime

The term "white collar crime" was invented in 1939 by noted criminologist Edwin H. Sutherland, who defined it as "crime committed by a person of respectability and high social status in the course of his occupation."[5] No one knows for sure the extent of white collar crime; most instances are not reported, although it is pervasive in society. Some examples of white collar crime are tax cheating, false advertising, unfair labor practices, infringement of patents, fraud, and embezzlement. Obviously white collar crime is not just an individual phenomenon, but one that involves institutions—banks, brokerage firms, construction companies, political parties, labor unions, and even colleges and churches.

White collar crime is not as socially unacceptable as so-called "street crime," thus it is harmful for a variety of reasons. First, it causes severe financial losses, estimated at tens of billions of dollars each year. Second, it also may result in physical harm, especially in cases involving building code violations and Pure Food and Drug Act violations. Third, white collar crime causes serious damage to social and economic institutions by undermining public confidence in the ability of those institutions to consistently act in an ethical and a responsible manner. Fourth, it adversely affects the entire moral climate of society by eroding citizens' belief in the free enterprise system.

Civil Disobedience

Few philosophies are as controversial as civil disobedience, which may be defined as the refusal to obey certain governmental laws or demands either for the purpose of influencing legislation or governmental policy or because those laws or demands are believed to be immoral or unconstitutional. Although the concept is a complex one, its cornerstone rests on the idea that there is a fundamental law or natural law which far transcends man-made law. This belief in the existence of a fundamental law dates back thousands of years, and philosophers point out that even Jesus violated man-made laws for a purpose.

In the United States there is some justification for civil disobedience. Americans decided to form a society and establish a

---

[5] Edwin H. Sutherland and Donald R. Cressey, *Principles of Criminology,* 8th ed. (New York; J. B. Lippincott Co., 1970), p. 40.

government by contract. By the terms of this social contract government was created to protect each man's natural rights (e.g. life, liberty, property rights), while each individual promised to abide by the decisions of the majority and to surrender to society his private right to enforce the law. Provision was made in the Declaration of Independence for civil disobedience if government were to become repressive or unresponsive to citizens. Regarding this point, the Declaration of Independence reads:

> Governments are instituted among Men, deriving their just powers from the consent of the governed,—That whenever any Form of Government becomes destructive of these ends, it is the Right of the People to alter or to abolish it, and to institute new Government, laying its foundation on such principles and organizing its powers in such form, as to them shall seem most likely to effect their Safety and Happiness.

So there is justification for civil disobedience in this country. However, although some proponents and practitioners of the idea have used it wisely and have, in some cases, brought about needed social changes, there is a mounting body of evidence which indicates that civil disobedience has been invoked unwisely, too frequently, and with little justification during recent years. Persons and groups with a single grievance (e.g. stiff marijuana laws, the draft, an unfair university policy) have sought to bring down the *entire* structure of government in protest over it. Characterized by selfishness, a myopic perspective on social affairs, a predisposition to oversimplify incredibly complex issues, and an inclination to attack symbolic problems rather than real ones, these individuals and groups break reasonable laws in the name of civil disobedience prior to attempting legal and socially acceptable methods of redressing grievances. It is apparent that some proponents of the concept have failed to read the Declaration of Independence in its entirety, or they would have encountered the passage which states:

> Prudence, indeed, will dictate that Governments long established should not be changed for light and transient causes. . . . But when a long train of abuses and usurpations, pursuing invariably the same Object, evinces a design to reduce them [the people] under absolute Despotism, it is their right, it is their duty, to throw off such Government. . . .

Furthermore, many activists refuse to recognize that, like any other contract, the American social contract demands dual responsibility. In payment for the protection afforded by government, individuals are expected to give up some natural rights, even to the extent of obeying unfair laws. Too frequently a citizen will engage in an extremely violent act in order to destroy the American system but, once arrested, will demand his full share of rights and guarantees from the very system he seeks to destroy, a highly irresponsible act, but not an uncommon one.

Just as individuals have the right to resist oppressive government, so too does government have the right and duty to seek out and bring to justice individuals who would use civil disobedience as a guise in carrying out violent and disruptive acts aimed at destroying institutions for "light and transient causes."

When thousands gather to peacefully protest an injustice, government must protect them. But when those thousands engage in tumultuous action and violent activity, then government has a right to exert that force which is necessary to bring order to the scene, within the limits of the various legislative and judicial restraints.

THEORIES OF CRIME CAUSATION

Crime is a social phenomenon, and as such it has attracted scholarly attention from those attempting to better understand its root causes. Curiosity is a stimulus for study, making crime one of the most studied types of human activity in existence. The discipline most concerned with the study of crime is criminology, which may be defined as the scientific study of the causes of crime and criminal behavior, the nature of societies' reaction to the breaking of laws, and the prevention of crime. Criminologists strive to develop a body of knowledge and principles that will contribute to programs of social control. Although criminology is generally viewed as a subfield of sociology, there is no consistent definition of who a criminologist is, although sociologists, psychologists and psychiatrists, forensic chemists, penologists, and even police administrators and attorneys may be characterized as criminologists if their scholarly contributions to the discipline are substantial and consistent with the general objectives of the field. It is appropriate that an historical summary of some of the prominent schools of criminological thought be surveyed.

Schools of Criminology: An Historical Summary

The Classical School

The classical school of criminology developed in Europe during the latter part of the eighteenth century. According to this school of thought, man's behavior was ruled by the base emotions of pleasure and pain. Thus, if an act was more pleasureful than painful, the individual would probably engage in it, just as he would most certainly avoid it if it invoked more pain then pleasure. In effect, the school was founded on the rather simplistic idea of hedonistic psychology. One of the first contributors to the classical school was Cesare Beccaria, who worked to include the doctrine in penal reform. His objective was to inflict punishment uniformly for each specific violation of the law so that just enough pain would be inflicted to overbalance the pleasureable effect that the crime had on the perpetrator. By this method individuals could be reformed and crime prevented—so thought Beccaria.

The Geographic School

The geographic school, popularized during the middle nineteenth century by A. M. Guerry and Adolphe Quetelet, expounded the principle that crime was an expression of social conditions and was caused by a conflict between the law and the competing value systems present in the community. Accordingly, criminologists in this school centered their studies of crime in geographical and social areas. This was the first major criminological school that considered proverty a root cause of crime.

The Socialist School

The basis for the socialist school of thought rested on the writings of Karl Marx and Frederick Engels. According to socialist arguments, crime was bound up with the exploitation of working classes by capitalistic societies. By "exploiting" the workers, a variety of criminal responses were to be expected. Naturally, the prevention of criminality would result when the "system" was changed.

The Typological Schools

The fundamental premise behind the philosophy of the typological schools of thought was that criminals differ from non-criminals in certain verifiable ways. Cesare Lombroso, one of the giants in criminology, asserted that there were three types of criminals: (1) born criminals, (2) insane criminals, and (3) criminaloids, who were normal people who committed crimes only under unusual circumstances. Lombroso's most noted theory, that of the born criminal, was formulated after long study in which he found that most convicted criminals seemed to have certain primitive and savage characteristics, such as an asymmetrical cranium, a flattened nose, and a low sensitivity to pain. A list of such physical features that were thought to indicate criminality was articulated, and anyone who had five or more stigmata was a criminal type, although the physical anomalies were not believed a cause of crime, but simply an identification element of "born criminals." Another typological school explained criminality as a manifestation of feeblemindedness.

The Contemporary Criminologist

Over the years, the fundamental problem with schools of criminological thought (other than the fact that some theories were false on their face) was that each failed to accept as valid explanations other than their own. Today, the two main approaches, the sociological school and the psychiatric school, do recognize the existence of the others and the validity of each approach, though there is some controversy over which should be emphasized. The question of which element, "personality" or "culture," should be of prime importance in trying to explain criminality is not always answered consistently by partisan scholars. There is, however, a movement toward a multiple-factor approach which sees crime as a multifaceted phenomenon, produced by a variety of factors. Thus, no single, narrow theory is appropriate. Crime is the work of individuals who, because of a unique blend of factors, have chosen or have been chosen for antisocial behavior. The following excerpt from the President's Commission on Law Enforcement illustrates the prevalent belief in a multifaceted answer to crime:[6]

> The most natural and frequent question people ask about crime is "why?" They ask it about individual crimes and crime as a whole. In either case it is an almost impossible question to answer. Each single crime is a response to a specific situation by a person with an infinitely complicated psychological and emotional makeup who is subject to infinitely complicated external pressures.

[6]*Supra* note 3, pp. 1-2.

(Courtesy of the National Council on Crime and Delinquency)

Chapter 13

JUVENILE DELINQUENCY

NATURE AND EXTENT[1]

Juvenile delinquency is one of the nation's major unsolved problems. It is more than a headline issue, more than a matter óf public safety. It is not a single problem which calls for a single answer.

Delinquency is a tangle of profoundly interwoven problems that are inseparable from the social system in which we live. It is a chronic problem that will not yield easily to efforts of prevention and control. Neither can it be resolved by crash programs leaving underlying social causes unchanged.

Delinquency is not a new or uniquely American problem. The particular forms and varieties of youthful antisocial behavior may change with the times, but delinquency remains an intrinsic part of industrial society. Today's expanding youth population, and the increasing complexities of modern life, call for innovative long-range programs—as well as immediate action—for dealing with youth problems.

There are different ways of looking at delinquency and its manifestations. One possible approach is to suggest that societies which place a high premium on freedom, initiative, and success should hardly expect to contain all of its members in a conventional mold. According to this approach, delinquency is one form of breaking out of that mold. Another related approach is to suggest that democratic societies always have to tolerate a fairly high percentage of nonconformity among youth. However, in any approach to delinquency, while nonconformity and unconventional behavior are factors to be recognized, the protection of society comes first. Ways must be found to deal with deviant

---

[1] Reprinted with editorial adaption from the *Annual Report of Federal Activities in Juvenile Delinquency, Youth Development, and Related Fields.* U. S. Dept. of Health, Education, and Welfare, Social and Rehabilitation Service, (1971).

behavior which leads to the destruction of property; criminal acts, or violence.

Destructive behavior needs to be channeled into constructive activity in order to reverse the effects of this social blight in our future generations.

Planning for the prevention of delinquency must be based on the realistic appraisal of the problem. Resources for coping with the problem must be adequate, and feasible programs need to be undertaken. However it is approached, the problem of juvenile delinquency needs to be recognized as a fundamental challenge to our ability to make the American dream mean something in a nuclear society.

The Size of the Delinquency Problem

With the single exception of 1961 the upward trend in juvenile delinquency rates has continued.

The FBI's *Uniform Crime Reports* and The Department of Health, Education, and Welfare's *Juvenile Court Statistical Reports* show not only spiraling rates of delinquency but also increasing involvement of youth in serious crimes.

During the past decade (1960-1969) the volume of police arrests of persons under eighteen years of age for all offenses except traffic violations increased at a pace almost four times the percentage rate of increase in the national population. While the number of young people in the age group ten to seventeen increased twenty seven percent during this period, the arrest rate of persons under the age of eighteen doubled (see Table I). When only the Crime Index offenses are considered in computing this long-term trend, the rate of increase registers a startling ninety percent for the decade.

Similarly, during the same period of time, juvenile arrests for violent crimes increased 148 percent, while arrests for property offenses increased eighty-five percent. While the total youth population aged ten to seventeen constituted approximately sixteen percent of the total population of the United States in 1969, persons under eighteen years of age were involved in thirty-two percent of the Crime Index offenses which were solved.

A similar trend is indicated by *Juvenile Court Statistics*–1969, the latest year for which complete statistics are available. Nation-

TABLE I
1969 ARREST RATES FOR PERSONS UNDER AGE 18
FOR CRIME INDEX OFFENSES*

Offense Charged	Percentage of Persons Under Age 18 Arrested in 1969	Increase 1960–1969 (%)
Murder	9.4	151
Aggravated Assault	16.4	123
Forcible rape	20.1	86
Robbery	33.4	13
Burglary	53.7	72
Larceny-theft	53.1	100
Auto Theft	58.0	63

*Uniform Crime Reports–1969

ally, the volume of juvenile court cases increased 9.9 percent over the previous year. Boys' cases registered a 10.1 percent increase, girls' cases a nineteen percent increase. Delinquency, however, continues to be primarily a male problem—with four times as many males as females being referred to the juvenile courts in 1969.

Although the problem of juvenile delinquency remains concentrated primarily in the urban areas of the country, the statistics indicate a problem of considerable magnitude in the rural and suburban areas as well. According to the *1969 Uniform Crime Report:*

> Nationally, persons under 15 years of age made up 10% of the total police arrests; under 18, 26%; under 21, 39%; and under 25, 51%. In the suburban areas, the involvement of the young age groups in police arrests is again markedly higher than the national figures with the under 15 age group represented in 13%; under 18, 35%; under 21, 50%; and under 25, 63%. In the rural areas, the distributions were lower for the younger age groups, with the under 15 group being involved in 5% of the cases; under 18 in 21%; under 21 in 38%; and those under 25, 53%. When only the serious crimes are considered 22% of all arrests in 1969 were for persons under the age of 15 and almost one-half under 18 years of age.

Likewise, the 1969 Juvenile Court Statistics show that juvenile court cases increased in all areas of the country. Nationally, juvenile court cases increased 9.9 percent in that year; urban courts experienced a 9.8 percent increase, while the increase in semiurban courts was 9.2 percent and rural courts registered an 8.8 percent increase. The number of juvenile court cases handled by predominantly urban areas, however, was almost three times higher than in the rural areas. Sixty-six percent of all the cases were handled by the urban courts, twenty-eight percent by semi-urban courts, and six percent by rural courts.

Drug offenses, too, are becoming increasingly prevalent among young people, as evidenced by the statistics contained in the 1969 *Uniform Crime Report.* In 1964 twenty-three percent of the persons arrested for Narcotic Drug Law violations were under twenty-one years of age; by 1969 the percentage had jumped to fifty-five. When marijuana offenses alone are considered, twenty-seven percent of the persons arrested were under eighteen years of age, and sixty-three percent were under twenty-one.

Statistics, however, tell only part of the story. As the President's Commission on Law Enforcement and Administration of Justice pointed out in *The Challenge of Crime in a Free Society:*

> These reports (The *Uniform Crime Reports* and the *Juvenile Court Statistics*) can tell us nothing about the vast numbers of unsolved crimes or about the many cases in which delinquents are dealt with informally instead of being arrested or referred to court."

Indeed, various self-report studies indicate that approximately ninety percent of all youth commit acts for which they might be brought to the attention of juvenile courts if apprehended.

Alarming as these juvenile delinquency statistics may be, however, it is necessary to view them in perspective.

In part, these increases are the result of better statistical reporting and better record-keeping systems adopted by police departments and other official agencies. In part, they may stem from increased formal actions on the part of law enforcement agencies. In part, too, they are the product of a phenomenal increase in the youth population in recent years—a rate of increase which is significantly higher than that of the adult population. And, in part, they are the consequence of an increasing urbanization which has exacerbated conditions in which delinquency rates have traditionally been high.

Moreover, despite the increasing involvement of juveniles in Crime Index offenses, the majority of youth continue to be apprehended for "minor" crimes, and a significant number are arrested for actions which, if committed by an adult, would not be considered criminal.

In 1969 boys under eighteen years of age were most often arrested for larceny and burglary. Large numbers, however, were also apprehended for disorderly conduct, curfew and loitering violations, and running away. Similarly, while a large number of girls under eighteen were arrested for larceny, a significant proportion of both boys and girls were arrested for other violations of state and local laws which are not broken down in the *Uniform Crime Reports,* but rather are classified as "all other offenses, except traffic." This category encompasses such offenses as truancy, ungovernable behavior, and similar activities, as well as other offenses which pertain to both adults and juveniles.

Finally, the fact that a large percentage of juvenile crimes are committed in groups—the estimates range from sixty to ninety percent—may also result in "inflated" statistics which are out of proportion to the number of crimes actually committed.

Delinquency and The Inner City

Despite the rise in suburban delinquency, more often than not the world around the delinquent is the inner-city slum.

By 1980 seventy-five percent of the population of the United States will live in metropolitan areas. As has already been indicated, crime and delinquency rates are considerably higher in the more deprived centers of these metropolitan areas where slum conditions prevail.

In inner-city areas where income is low, unemployment high, housing poor, health resources inaccessible, and recreation facilities inadequate, the crime and delinquency rates are staggering.

In other words, where crime and delinquency rates are highest, one is certain to find all the other evidences of social disintegration. As the Crime Commission report made clear:

> Negroes who live in disproportionate numbers in slum neighborhoods account for a disproportionate number of arrests. Numerous studies indicate that what matters is where in the city one is growing up, not religion or nationality or race. . .For all groups, delinquency rates were highest in the center and lowest on the outskirts of the city but for Negroes, movement out of the inner-city and absorption into America's middle class have been much slower and more difficult than for any other ethnic or racial group.

One of the gravest challenges facing the nation today, then, is to be found in the interlocking problems of poverty, discrimination, and the cities.

Few things cause more concern or are more frightening and real than violent crime in our cities. The twenty-six cities with populations of 500,000 or more contribute about half the total reported major violent crimes, yet comprise only about one-fifth the total reporting population. That violent crimes in the city are committed primarily by young persons between the• ages of eighteen and twenty-four, followed by youth in the fifteen and seventeen group, is a gloomy portent for the future.

Violent crime is overwhelmingly committed by males, usually with poor education, and little or no employment skills. Violent crime rates for Negroes appear to be considerably higher than those for whites.

The urgent need to reduce violent crime among urban nonwhite youth is obvious, requiring a total effort toward changing their demoralizing conditions and life patterns; the unequal opportunity and discrimination they confront, and the overcrowding and decay of the urban ghettos in which most of them live.

Middle Class Delinquency—Suburbia

The Crime Commission report observed:

> It is likely that the official picture exaggerates the role played by social and economic conditions, since slum offenders are more likely than suburban offenders to be arrested and sent to juvenile court. In fact, recent self-report studies reveal suburban and middle class delinquency to be more significant a problem than was ever assumed.

Many suburban communities find themselves faced with a rapid population growth. This rapid growth has made it difficult for suburbs to increase the level of services needed by their residents— including resources to meet pressing problems such as delinquency.

A study of delinquency in an education-conscious and middle class suburb revealed that two thirds of the delinquents were from the least affluent families. Thus, special problems arise for poor youth in middle class communities. Failure in education in a community which emphasizes education for the college-bound puts special pressure on both parents and children.

Since current trends are toward movement from the city to the suburbs, the pattern of delinquency in middle class suburban communities is likely to become more pronounced. There is a grave need not only for more information about the quantity and quality of delinquency in suburban areas but also for the provision of services to meet the special needs of suburban delinquents and their families.

Changing Patterns of Youthful Behavior

This century has seen a period of unprecedented rapid social, industrial, ideological, and political change.

During the postwar era, the pace of change has increased still further, transforming the world in a way that no one twenty-five years ago could have anticipated. These years have brought to the more advanced nations of the world an affluence never before dreamed of. They have seen the liberation—often accompanied by violence—of the majority of the world's population from colonial rule. They have seen a time of such extraordinary scientific and technological innovation that physical, human, and social environments have been profoundly transformed.

During the 1960s Americans lived in mounting historical crisis. The symptoms were everywhere: poverty and urban deterioration in the world's richest nation, racism in a society committed to equality, civil disturbances in the streets of urban slums, campus unrest, and the growing disaffection and alienation among those from the best educated generation in history.

This rapid pace of change has produced new forms and expressions of youth revolt and protest—ranging from rejection of society and withdrawal from the community, to attempts to overthrow the "system" through violent confrontations. The shifts in youthful behavior have been so frequent and sudden that adults often have been unable to perceive, much less understand, what is happening.

Institutional Response to Youth

Youth protest and rebellion, whether it takes the form of student violence or disengagement and alienation from society, is often the response of youth to institutional systems that exclude them or that they perceive to be degrading.

Youth deeply resent the definitions, categories, and restrictions that have been assigned to them. If on the other hand, they are accepted as legitimate partners, as they were in the past when their labor was required by a less efficient society, they are more likely to participate in, and give support to, the key systems of the community.

Young people are not content to have things done for them; they want a share in shaping their destinies. They are seeking one of the most important of all human needs: to be taken seriously, to have their voices heard.

Whether adult society and youth can bridge the gap depends in large part upon the capacity of our institutions to develop procedures that will enable those who seek change to be part of the process of change. Special efforts must be made to find ways of including those who have suffered the most from exclusion and who have traditionally been labeled as deviant. Youth who have little or no hope or confidence in themselves or their situation must be convinced that they are of value and worth, not only to themselves but also to their community and its institutions.

An effort to involve youth in the community and its institutions is part and parcel of a total effort at institutional change.

Institutional change is defined for the purposes of this report as the effort to improve institutional practices, procedures, and policies in such a way so as to improve their responsiveness to youth and delinquent needs, to improve their effectiveness in combating juvenile delinquency, and to improve their abilities to provide meaningful and constructive youth roles in the carrying out of their activities.

In the modern world the family has become a focal point where a great many institutional influences meet, but the way in which families function depends on the way they are influenced by various community institutions.

Today, the family and local community can no longer exercise any strong control over the activities and content of education, industry recreation, health services, or law enforcement. It is just the other way around. This is especially true of poor families, since their functioning is almost completely dependent upon public institutions. When they need help, they have neither the resources or know-how to make independent choices among both public and private alternatives.

Many of the agencies serving the poor are unable to serve them well. Restrictive regulations, inadequate budgets, personnel shortages, and fragmentation among the public services also serve as barriers to adequate assistance. Families who are exclusively dependent upon public services that cannot provide adequate solutions to their problems are especially subject to the feelings of hopelessness and surrender that are often instrumental in promoting marital conflict and inability to assume meaningful parental roles.

The Official Response to Delinquency—Labeling and Stigma

When official agencies respond to certain behaviors by placing a youth in the delinquent category, they attach a label that seriously affects his future opportunities and conduct.

Once a youth is stamped delinquent, the police, the court, the school, and other official agencies respond to him on the basis of that label in a manner different from the way they respond to those without it. The label also becomes known to the public, which then views the youth with suspicion.

Further, the young person may begin to perceive himself as different or "bad" and act accordingly. Having a record makes it more difficult for a youngster to walk conventional paths and have equal access to the opportunities of society. Faced with this dilemma, the young person may be propelled to act out further the delinquent role he has been assigned.

Without the evidence to show that official actions by police and courts are successful in preventing further delinquency, the exercise of caution in determining which young people are to be labeled assumes overwhelming significance.

There is reason to believe, on the other hand, that the very act of official intervention has an impact directly contrary to that which it is designed to create. While the court may see its intervention as helpful and rehabilitative, prospective employers, for example, tend to view less benignly the fact that the youth "has a record."

The schools may view with suspicion the youngster who has been pronounced delinquent. Further, it is important to draw the distinction between engaging in one delinquent act and the repetitive commission of delinquent acts.

Many young people may engage in one or two delinquent acts

as a relatively normal part of their adolescence. Occasional and minor delinquency need not presage a delinquent career. To funnel such youth into the formal juvenile justice and correctional system may have the unfortunate and unnecessary consequence of contributing to the development of a career in delinquency.

Correctional Agencies

The field of youth corrections faces two serious problems: (1) funds and facilities are inadequate to the demands placed on correctional institutions by the community and (2) the validity of the techniques of present day corrections has been seriously challenged.

Even with its swing away from large institutions to smaller correctional facilities, the correctional process still segregates and labels those in its custody. It still stands at the last resort—the end of the line for those unfortunate enough to enter its jurisdiction.

The Crime Commission report stated:

> ...for the large bulk of offenders, particularly the youthful, the first, or the minor offender, institutional commitments can cause more problems than they solve. Institutions tend to isolate offenders from society, both physically and psychologically, cutting them off from schools, jobs, families, and other supportive influences and increasing the probability that the label of criminal will be indelibly impressed upon them.

In many communities, however, youth are referred to the correctional system because no treatment alternatives exist. This is true most frequently in the poorer residential areas where the lack of social welfare resources and other alternatives often require the police to send children to court; and the courts, in turn, often have no alternative but to send these children to correctional institutions.

"The Statistics on Public Institutions for Delinquent Children— 1969" (the latest year for which complete statistics are available) indicates that approximately 52,000 children and youth were living in residential correctional institutions in that year, a four percent decrease over the previous year. Of these youth the preponderant majority (43,000) were in training schools; an additional 1,500 were in forestry camps and ranches, and 3,200 were in reception and diagnostic centers.

Such institutional care is expensive. The 1969 figures show that approximately 258.2 million dollars was spent on public institutions serving delinquents in that year, at a per capita cost of $5,031.

Even more important is the fact that the traditional forms of institutionalization are relatively ineffectual in rehabilitating most delinquent youth. The recidivism rate for youth released from public and private residential institutions ranges from an estimated fifty percent to eighty percent.

The *1968 Uniform Crime Report* stated:

> The younger the age group, the higher the repeating rate, has been documented many times, as it is here. . .of the offenders under 20 released in 1963, 74% were rearrested by 1969, 72% of those 20 to 24, and 69% of the offenders 25 to 29 years. When viewed by race, the Negro rearrested rate, 71%, was higher than the white offender rate of 61%. All other races, made up primarily of Indian Americans, had a rearrest rate of 82% between 1963 and 1969. Of the 1,419 female offenders released in 1963, 47% had been rearrested for new offenses by 1969.

Correctional services for youth should be an integral part of the network of services for all youth in the community.

A giant step toward rehabilitation—learning a trade in a vocational school's print shop. *(Courtesy of the State of California Department of Corrections)*

Correctional treatment should be closely related to the other systems that exist to reintegrate its charges into the main currents of society. Youth in training schools or in a community-based facility should have available to them the same breadth of services offered to their peers on the outside.

Support must be given to the search for alternative methods of providing services to achieve this integration of correctional systems into broader services offered in the community. States and local communities must be given the opportunities and incentives to innovate and experiment with these methods and to develop correctional programs that are incorporated into the community, so that the isolation, alienation, and disassociation that often follow from traditional correctional experiences do not disconnect young offenders from society.

Finally, much of the help that probationers and parolees need can come from community institutions—help from schools in acquiring the education necessary for employment and help from employment services and vocational training facilities in finding jobs. If probation and parole officers are to mobilize community resources to deal more effectively with offenders, they must develop new work styles that reach out to community resources and relate them to the needs of their caseloads.

New approaches to rehabilitation may make possible the assignment of probation and parole officers to specific target communities to act as advocates and mobilizers of resources for problem youth living in these communities. The role of the community corrections worker might be analogous to that of the ombudsman, a spokesman for the target population in the larger community. New approaches might also make it possible for courts and correctional agencies to recruit and train both professional and nonprofessional workers to carry out these and other new roles in the community.

Juvenile Delinquency Prevention and Control Act of 1968

The Juvenile Delinquency Prevention and Control Act of 1968, as an ongoing Federal program, provides assistance in assessing the adequacy and effectiveness of existing state and local resources. It encourages the creation of new kinds of preventive services and the coordination of these endeavors with both existing community programs and resources available under other Federal legislation.

The approach to prevention and rehabilitation embraced by the Act is community-based in orientation. It fosters programs which provide services to youth in or close to their home neighborhoods, drawing on services from agencies in the community, providing opportunities for the youth to participate actively and meaningfully in community activities.

The Act provides for preventive programs which offer specialized services to predelinquent youth, but which do not label them or separate them from their peers. It stresses treatment of the offender in the community rather than in an isolated residential correctional institution as well as the development and support of community agencies which deal with youth nonjudicially.

As a corollary, the Act seeks to strengthen the services of agencies, organizations, and institutions serving delinquent youth and young people in danger of becoming delinquent by upgrading the competence of personnel working in the juvenile justice and related systems, training new personnel to enter professions in the delinquency prevention and control field, and developing new techniques and practices.

Focus on Youth Development

The national program set forth in the Juvenile Delinquency Prevention and Control Act of 1968 is based on the assumption that America's goals for its youth extend beyond curtailment of antisocial activities.

In establishing the goal of delinquency prevention, as well as rehabilitation, it seeks to maximize the potential of young people for productive participation in society and for lives of self-actualization.

This effort seeks increased commitment on the part of youth to a society which they can perceive as responsive, relevant, and just; a society in which meaningful opportunities are available to them; a society in which they have a significant share and stake.

This represents only one aspect of the Government's program in juvenile delinquency. A number of other programs are administered by other agencies within the Department of Health, Education, and Welfare, as well as in other agencies and departments.

A summer camp conducted by policemen. *(Courtesy of the Montgomery, Alabama, Police Department)*

It follows that the national program must systematically assemble and redirect many of the current approaches to addressing problems of youth. Both this effort and the task of developing new approaches rest on recognition of a basic set of factors that research and experience have proven tenable:

1. There is a web of interconnected social factors that shape youthful behavior.

2. The key institutions of our society play a most important role in the creation and prevention of antisocial behavior.

3. Many problems of youth cannot be viewed exclusively as problems of individuals, but must be regarded as reflecting problems in our major social institutions.

4. Solutions to youth problems and antisocial behavior can most readily be derived from an exploration and appraisal of the social conditions producing them rather than from excessive demands for punishment, repressive action, and undue pressures for conformity.

Rather than viewing the prevention and control of juvenile

delinquency, treatment and rehabilitation, and correctional and community services as disparate activities conducted by widely distinct personnel without mutual understanding and common ties, the program calls for the maximum possible unification of all of them. In view of what is known about the minimal essential conditions for the development of socially adequate human beings, and what has already been learned about the causes and consequences of antisocial behavior, it is no longer rational to compartmentalize either the thinking, methods, or program resources.

The new ordering of service networks and resources will enable the nation to broaden its perspectives on youth—both their problems and their place in society.

It will not only guarantee continued efforts to control delinquency and treat offenders, but it will also promote increased activity in addressing many of the conditions that produce them. By basing programs for youth on perception of antisocial behavior as more than just a problem of law enforcement, or as problems in education, family disorganization, employment, housing, and social conflict, this country is on the way toward its preventive goal.

At the same time, this nation will be taking steps toward raising the general level of opportunity for all youth, whether in slum or suburb. The Juvenile Delinquency Prevention and Control Act has put this country in possession of a national program that looks toward the future and makes possible a range of activities that provide assistance to states and communities to (1) develop programs with respect to the increasingly visible youth culture existing across the nation at this very time, (2) direct national efforts at basic changes in important institutions, (3) upgrade services in the areas where delinquency and crime rates are highest and identify and provide special services to youth who are too often neglected merely because they live in areas where delinquency and social disorganization are low, and (4) make further improvements in the services available within the juvenile justice system so that the youth passing through it will not stand in danger of continuing their delinquent careers.

In order for this national program to have maximum success, it should encourage young people themselves to assist in its implementation. There can be no greater indication of our dedication to youth than to ask them to become involved as active participants, not mere recipients, in the local and state service projects the Act makes possible.

New Administration

On June 8, 1970, the Youth Development and Delinquency Prevention Administration was created to administer the Act, replacing the Office of Juvenile Delinquency and Youth Development. This action is indicative of Departmental support for the program, and its recognition of the importance of a strong effort in the area of delinquency prevention and control. This resulted in placing it on an equal basis with the efforts of the other administrations in the social and rehabilitation service—aging, assistance payments, community services, medical services, and rehabilitation services.

Additionally, the recent decentralization of the program through the placement of full-time Associate Regional Commissioners for Youth Development and Delinquency Prevention Services in each of the ten regional offices of the Department of Health, Education, and Welfare is designed to provide for a strengthened effort through the development of closer working relationships among the Federal, state, and local levels of government. By providing a vehicle for close liaison between the administering agency and the state agencies, immediate access is afforded to the technical assistance and expertise of these specialists in the development of plans and programs.

The Youth Development and Delinquency Prevention Administration's Central Office has also undergone reorganization with the establishment of the Division of National Planning and Program Development. Its major functions include (1) assisting in the development of a national strategy for delinquency prevention, rehabilitation, and youth development, (2) overseeing the development and implementation of the program, (3) developing national guidelines and standards for the implementation of the program, and (4) coordinating field activities with other Federal programs concerned with delinquency and youth development.

Experience gained in the administration of past juvenile delinquency programs and the Juvenile Delinquency Prevention and Control Act, indicates a variety of problems, the solution to which calls for a major change in the program emphasis and direction of the Youth Development and Delinquency Prevention Administration.

1. There is little coherent national planning or established priority structure among the major programs dealing with the problems of youth development and delinquency prevention.

2. There is a strong indication that although bits and pieces of the Federal response to the problems of youth and delinquency may be achieving their discrete objectives, the whole, in terms of the overall effectiveness of Federal efforts, may be less than the sum of its parts.

3. There is a lack of effective national leadership dealing with all youth, including delinquents. The present array of programs demonstrate the lack of priorities, emphasis, and direction in the Federal Government's efforts to combat delinquency.

4. Although there is a lack of resources devoted to delinquency prevention, in many cases grantees have not made maximum use of existing resources.

5. Grantees have not sufficiently coordinated either the development or the implementation of programs with state planning agencies. One factor is that there may have been many state planning agencies which were not ready for such coordination. Because data was frequently unavailable on the extent and nature of delinquency and on gaps in existing services, action projects were not linked with the development of the state comprehensive plan and/or were not directed to the most pressing statewide delinquency problems.

6. State planning has been spasmodic and ineffective. This is due in large part to the fact that a sufficient theoretical knowledge base was lacking and only an extremely limited amount of technical assistance was forthcoming. For the same reasons, many of the projects submitted were of poor or limited quality.

7. There has been a noticeable lack of joint funding or use of

other outside resources by grantees.

8. No model systems for the prevention of delinquency or the rehabilitation of delinquent youth have been developed or implemented. Nor has there been feedback of knowledge, gained from funded research, for use in the development of such systems.

9. Severe budget constraints negate the effective implementation of Title I (grants for planning, preventive, and rehabilitative services) of the Juvenile Delinquency Prevention and Control Act of 1968.

In order to meet the shortcomings outlined above, a new national strategy is being developed and put into operation. Part of this national strategy calls for the extension and modification of the Juvenile Delinquency Prevention and Control Act of 1968 to provide for a new program emphasis and direction. It also calls for operational change in the delivery of services as well as possible changes in the present structuring of services.

THE POLICE JUVENILE UNIT

As a result of an increasing rate of youth crimes, many police agencies employ juvenile specialists to support the efforts of beat-patrol officers. Although many patrol calls relating to juvenile actions are handled completely by the uniformed officer, some require a follow-up investigation by the juvenile specialist. The juvenile officer is able to spend time counseling a potential delinquent, investigating unsafe or unfit home conditions, and other types of time-consuming activities that the patrol officer cannot perform.

Juvenile officers are also expected to visit schools and develop a close cooperation between the school system and the police department. This is an important undertaking, as many potential juvenile problems can be found through the behavior of students while attending school. Often it will be necessary to question a juvenile at school. Rapport with school officials makes this type of task routine. With years of good cooperation as a foundation,

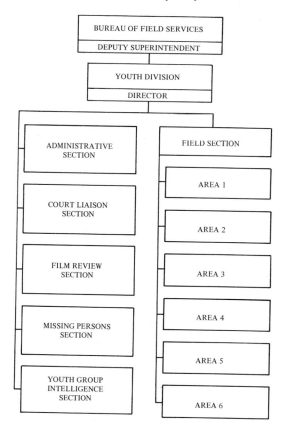

Organization chart of a police department's youth services division. (*Courtesy of the Chicago Police Department*)

school officials and police personnel are able to work together to solve a common problem.

The Police Juvenile Officer

Personnel selected to be assigned to the juvenile unit must be carefully chosen. Some of the desirable qualifications that a police administrator should look for are as follows:

1. A desire to be a juvenile officer. The officer should have a sincere dedication to be a specialist in this area.

2. Education should be considered, as the juvenile officer will

work closely with educated professionals. A minimum requirement should be a two-year college education.

3. The men chosen to serve in the juvenile unit should be public-relations minded and be able to conduct themselves well in front of a group as juvenile officers are often called upon to lecture to various civic organizations.

4. Juvenile officers should be able to communicate with todays youth. A sincere interest to help must be imparted to the juvenile victim, witness, or offender.

The juvenile division is an excellent assignment for police-women. Women are usually able to establish a good working relationship with younger boys and girls and also teen-aged girls. History reveals that women police have made a substantial contribution to American law enforcement wherever they have been assigned, but they have particularly distinguished themselves as

The police and the children—a labor of love. *(Courtesy of the Los Angeles County Sheriff's Department)*

juvenile officers. Many innovative juvenile programs, both within and outside of police departments, have been initiated by police-women.

(Courtesy of the New Haven Police Department)

Chapter 14

THE POLICE

O ver the years law enforcement has become increasingly complex. A century ago police officers communicated with one another by rapping their nightsticks on the cobblestone streets; today computerized radio systems do the job. Sophisticated hardware has replaced the crude devices of old; extended periods of training have replaced the early apprenticeship system; helicopters and automobiles have replaced fixed-post sentries and horse-drawn patrol wagons. Yet contemporary policemen have the same general objectives as did their counterparts of old: (1) to protect life and property and safeguard the individual liberties guaranteed by the Constitution and (2) to prevent crime and disorder and preserve the peace.

Policemen are given certain limited powers to pursue these objectives. Those powers are either derived from or restricted by six sources:

1. The United States Constitution.
2. Legislation of the United States Congress.
3. Legislative enactments of the various states.
4. Local and county ordinances.
5. Court decisions interpreting the constitutions and the statutes.
6. Court precedents.

THE POLICE MISSION[1]

The police mission, succinctly stated, is maintenance of social order within carefully prescribed ethical and constitutional restrictions. The mission as currently defined involves:

1. **The Prevention of Criminality.** This activity views the

---

[1]Reprinted with permission from the International City Management Association's *Municipal Police Administration,* 6th edition (Washington: The International City Management Association, 1969), pp. 3-4.

police role in constructive terms and involves taking the police into sectors of the community where criminal tendencies are bred and individuals motivated to indulge in antisocial behavior, and includes seeking to reduce causes of crime.

2. **Repression of Crime**. This activity stresses adequate patrol plus a continuing effort toward eliminating or reducing hazards as the principal means of reducing the opportunities for criminal actions.

3. **Apprehension of Offenders**. This activity views quick apprehension as the means to discourage the would be offender. The certainty of arrest and prosecution has a deterrent quality which is intended to make crime seem less worthwhile. Additionally, apprehension enables society to punish offenders, lessens the prospect of repetition by causing suspects to be incarcerated, and provides an opportunity for rehabilitation of those convicted.

4. **Recovery of Property**. This activity seeks to reduce the monetary cost of crime, as well as to restrain those who,

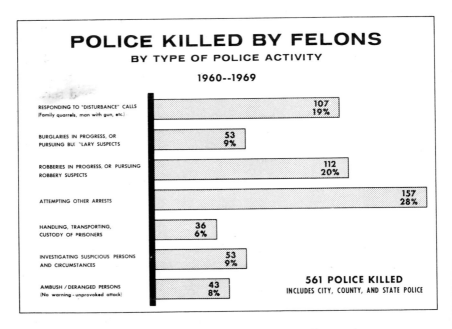

(Courtesy of the FBI's *Uniform Crime Reports*)

The evolution of the badge, Los Angeles Police Department. 1. 1869-1890; 2. 1890-1909; 3. 1909-1913; 4. 1913-1923; 5. 1923-1940; 6. 1940-. *(Courtesy of The Los Angeles Police Department)*

though not active criminals, might benefit from the gains of crime.

5. **Regulation of Noncriminal Conduct.** This aspect of the police mission involves sundry activities that are only incidentally concerned with criminal behavior, such as the enforcement of traffic and sanitary-code provisions. The main purpose is regulation, and apprehension and punishment of offenders are means of securing compliance. Other methods used to obtain compliance are education (e.g. observance of laws) and the use of warnings, either oral or written, to inform citizens of the violations without taking punitive actions.

6. **Performance of Miscellaneous Services.** This involves many service activities peripheral to basic police duties and includes, for example, the operation of detention facilities, search and rescue operations, licensing, supervising elections, staffing courts with administrative and security personnel, and even such completely extraneous things as chauffeuring officials.

While these six general responsibilities may be accepted by the police and the community-at-large as the police mission, there is often sharp disagreement on the appropriateness of specific methods and operations used to fulfill them. Various groups may staunchly defend different points of view or values and seemingly or actually work against one another; the resulting conflict may cause the police to fall short in reaching the common objective— superior law enforcement protection for the community.

THE POLICE VENTURE

Few institutions in America are more decentralized, more fragmented, and more isolated than the police. There are more than 40,000 separate law enforcement agencies in the country, employing an estimated 460,000 men and women, only about 30,000 of whom work for the Federal Government. Police departments vary in size from one, in boroughs and towns, to approximately 32,000 in New York City. Law enforcement in the United

Table 49.—Full-Time Police Department Employees,[1] December 31, 1969, Number and Rate per 1,000 Inhabitants, by Geographic Divisions and Population Groups

[1969 estimated population]

Geographic division	TOTAL (3,832 cities; population 117,815,000)	Population group					
		Group I (56 cities over 250,000; population 43,186,000)	Group II (93 cities, 100,000 to 250,000; population 13,794,000)	Group III (252 cities, 50,000 to 100,000; population 17,631,000)	Group IV (439 cities, 25,000 to 50,000; population 15,709,000)	Group V (1,085 cities, 10,000 to 25,000; population 17,373,000)	Group VI (1,907 cities under 10,000; population 10,122,000)
TOTAL: 3,832 cities; population 117,815,000:							
Number of police employees	254,984	131,723	25,293	29,029	24,662	27,154	17,123
Average number of employees per 1,000 inhabitants	2.2	3.1	1.8	1.6	1.6	1.6	1.7
Interquartile range	1.2–2.0	1.7–2.8	1.5–2.0	1.3–1.9	1.3–1.8	1.3–1.8	1.2–2.1
New England: 331 cities; population 8,493,000:							
Number of police employees	17,685	2,939	3,070	4,332	3,413	3,012	919
Average number of employees per 1,000 inhabitants	2.1	5.0	2.7	2.0	1.8	1.5	1.4
Interquartile range	1.3–1.9	(2)	2.5–2.8	1.7–2.1	1.5–2.0	1.3–1.7	.9–1.7
Middle Atlantic: 927 cities; population 26,529,000:							
Number of police employees	73,964	48,853	3,515	5,317	5,578	6,278	4,423
Average number of employees per 1,000 inhabitants	2.8	4.0	2.3	1.8	1.7	1.6	1.6
Interquartile range	1.1–2.0	3.5–4.1	1.9–2.5	1.2–2.1	1.3–2.2	1.2–1.9	.9–2.0
East North Central: 817 cities; population 25,116,000:							
Number of police employees	54,731	30,339	4,198	6,097	4,705	5,858	3,534
Average number of employees per 1,000 inhabitants	2.2	3.3	1.7	1.5	1.4	1.5	1.7
Interquartile range	1.2–1.8	2.0–2.9	1.6–1.9	1.2–1.8	1.2–1.6	1.3–1.7	1.2–1.9
West North Central: 405 cities; population 8,792,000:							
Number of police employees	14,957	6,391	1,445	1,221	1,687	2,392	1,821
Average number of employees per 1,000 inhabitants	1.7	2.4	1.5	1.3	1.2	1.4	1.5
Interquartile range	1.1–1.7	1.7–1.9	1.3–1.5	1.1–1.5	1.1–1.4	1.2–1.6	1.2–1.9
South Atlantic: 346 cities; population 12,217,000:							
Number of police employees	28,460	13,036	4,695	3,395	2,521	2,943	1,870
Average number of employees per 1,000 inhabitants	2.3	3.2	1.8	2.0	1.8	1.9	2.0
Interquartile range	1.6–2.3	1.9–2.2	1.6–1.9	1.7–2.0	1.6–1.9	1.6–2.2	1.5–2.6
East South Central: 139 cities; population 4,698,000:							
Number of police employees	8,307	3,287	1,534	760	1,083	981	662
Average number of employees per 1,000 inhabitants	1.8	1.9	1.7	2.1	1.6	1.5	1.8
Interquartile range	1.4–2.0	1.8–2.0	1.8–1.9	1.8–2.1	1.4–1.8	1.4–1.8	1.5–2.0
West South Central: 267 cities; population 11,142,000:							
Number of police employees	17,231	8,684	2,291	2,137	1,503	1,658	958
Average number of employees per 1,000 inhabitants	1.5	1.7	1.5	1.3	1.3	1.3	1.5
Interquartile range	1.1–1.7	1.4–1.8	1.3–1.4	1.1–1.5	1.1–1.4	1.1–1.5	1.1–1.9
Mountain: 190 cities; population 4,797,000:							
Number of police employees	8,177	2,661	1,443	970	1,070	885	1,148
Average number of employees per 1,000 inhabitants	1.7	2.0	1.7	1.4	1.5	1.5	1.7
Interquartile range	1.2–1.9	1.9–2.0	1.5–1.6	1.1–1.4	1.3–1.7	1.2–1.7	1.3–2.1
Pacific: 410 cities; population 16,030,000:							
Number of police employees	31,472	15,533	3,102	4,800	3,102	3,147	1,788
Average number of employees per 1,000 inhabitants	2.0	2.4	1.7	1.6	1.6	1.7	2.1
Interquartile range	1.5–2.1	2.0–2.4	1.4–1.8	1.4–1.9	1.3–1.7	1.5–1.9	1.6–2.6

Suburban Police and County Sheriff Departments

Suburban:[3] 1,953 agencies; population 44,445,000:		**Sheriffs: 1,158 agencies; population 32,716,000:**		
Number of police employees	74,040	Number of police employees		44,524
Average number of employees per 1,000 inhabitants	1.7	Average number of employees per 1,000 inhabitants		1.4
Interquartile range	1.1–1.9	Interquartile range		0.4–1.2

[1] Includes civilians.
[2] Only one city this size in geographic division.
[3] Includes suburban, city and county police agencies within metropolitan areas. Excludes core cities. Suburban cities are also included in other city groups. Population figures rounded to the nearest thousand. All rates were calculated on the population before rounding.

(Courtesy of the FBI's *Uniform Crime Reports*)

States is primarily a local function, with 39,750 agencies located in counties, cities, townships, and villages, two-hundred on the state level and fifty on the Federal level. A breakdown of the 39,750 local agencies shows 3,050 located in counties, 3,700 in cities, and 33,000 in townships and villages.[2]

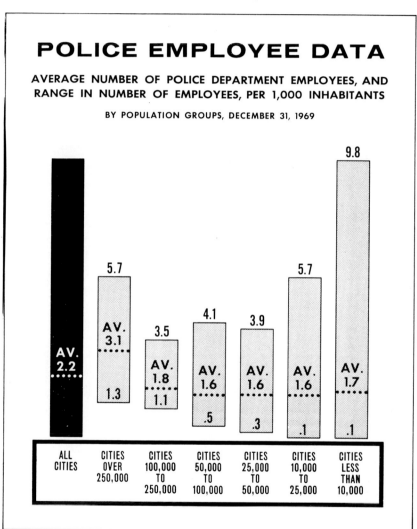

POLICE EMPLOYEE DATA

AVERAGE NUMBER OF POLICE DEPARTMENT EMPLOYEES, AND RANGE IN NUMBER OF EMPLOYEES, PER 1,000 INHABITANTS

BY POPULATION GROUPS, DECEMBER 31, 1969

ALL CITIES	CITIES OVER 250,000	CITIES 100,000 TO 250,000	CITIES 50,000 TO 100,000	CITIES 25,000 TO 50,000	CITIES 10,000 TO 25,000	CITIES LESS THAN 10,000
AV. 2.2	5.7 / AV. 3.1 / 1.3	3.5 / AV. 1.8 / 1.1	4.1 / AV. 1.6 / .5	3.9 / AV. 1.6 / .3	5.7 / AV. 1.6 / .1	9.8 / AV. 1.7 / .1

(Courtesy of the FBI's *Uniform Crime Reports*)

[2]The President's Commission on Law Enforcement and Administration of Justice, *Task Force Report: The Police* (Washington: U. S. Government Printing Office, 1967), pp. 7-9.

Police agencies may easily be classified by level of government; however, in order to study the vast system of policing in this country and to include private and special police forces in the survey, a more realistic breakdown is necessary. Thus, the following seven classifications of law enforcement will be discussed: (1) township, village, and contract police, (2) special protection districts, (3) municipal police, (4) county police, (5) state police, (6) Federal police, and (7) private police.

Township, Village, and Contract Police

Townships and villages that have minimal occurrences of crime and only occasional need for police service often do not have a police force, choosing to depend on the sheriff's department for patrol and criminal investigation, and the state highway patrol for traffic enforcement and accident investigation. Those communities which do maintain a police force usually rely on one man to do the job.[3] In the case of the one-man police force—of which there are thousands—the officer may well work out of his home because of the lack of a police station, and patrol in his private car, which has probably been equipped with police paraphernalia at community expense. A majority of police departments in the country employ less than ten men. These agencies probably present the greatest obstruction to police professionalization because of low pay, poor training, high rates of personnel turnover, outdated equipment, politics, and a lack of advanced education. Some townships and villages, and for that matter small cities, have arranged with sheriffs' departments to fulfill all police functions in the community by entering into a contract to buy police services from the county. Those municipalities fortunate enough to be located in a county which boasts a competent, professional sheriff's department—like the Los Angeles County Sheriff's Department—are able to contract for urban police services they could never provide for themselves.

Special Protection Districts

Over 15,000 special districts have been established in the

---

[3]Samuel G. Chapman and T. Eric St. John, *The Police Heritage in England and America* (East Lansing: Institute for Community Development, Michigan State University, 1962), pp. 32-33.

country for the purpose of providing services that would ordinarily go unfulfilled: housing, sanitation, fire protection. While special districts have been created to offer police services, they are few in number and have thus far had little impact on the overall police system.

Municipal Police

The heart of the American law enforcement system is the municipal police. Although there are more than 17,000 municipal police departments in the United States, it is law enforcement in the fifty-five cities of over 250,000 population with which most people are concerned. And for good reason! A major city's police department may dominate a region and set the tenor for an entire metropolitan area. A professional police department can have a positive effect on police operations in a hundred communities; while a poorly run department may have a devastating impact on a region. The City of Chicago, for example, has but one police force,

Police rookies, representing every segment of their community, graduate from the police academy, where they are prepared for a career in "the domestic peace corps." *(Courtesy of the Montgomery, Alabama, Police Department)*

but the Metropolitan Chicago area consists of 119 municipalities, employing over 2,000 full-time policemen.[4] The Chicago Police Department has, over the years, served as a model for most of the agencies in its metropolitan area. Municipal police departments are usually headed by a chief of police—he may be referred to as a superintendent, commissioner, or director in some communities—who in almost all cases is appointed by the city's chief executive, pending approval of the legislature. Depending on the law, the chief will be appointed either for a specific term of office or "during good behavior." He is rarely protected by civil service. Some cities choose their chiefs exclusively from within the command ranks of their departments, others pick only "outsiders," while others appoint the most qualified man available, either within or outside the agency. Rank on municipal agencies is generally patterned after the military, with sergeants, lieutenants, captains, and even majors and colonels. The military influence does not end here, however, as police departments consider themselves to be semimilitary organizations, with all the accompanying discipline, policies, and courtesies. Part III offers a detailed study of municipal police operations.

County Police

There are four general types of county law enforcement agencies; the full-service sheriff's department, the limited-service sheriff's department, the county police department, and the office of constable.

The Full-Service Sheriff's Department

In most communities the sheriff is an elected public official who serves a four-year term of office. Full-service sheriffs' departments usually police the unincorporated areas of the county and the county courts, run the county jail, and serve criminal and civil process. Although sheriffs' departments have legal authority to police municipalities, they rarely do unless requested by public officials because of political ramifications to which they are most sensitive because of the elected status of the sheriff. Some jurisdictions—notably Dade County, Florida—have changed the status of the sheriff from elected to appointed, to the benefit of

[4]*Supra* note 1, p. 9.

the department and the community. Still others have consolidated fragmented local police departments into one countywide force, ending duplication of effort, waste, and jurisdictional difficulties.

The Limited-Service Sheriff's Department

A number of counties have relegated their elected sheriff to the role of keeper of the jail, process server, and bailiff, as has Mecklenberg County, North Carolina. This is a limited-service sheriff's department. Where this type of department exists, there is either no unincorporated area to police or a county police force has been assigned to police the unincorporated area. Limited-service sheriffs are almost always elected officials.

The County Police Department

In those counties that have a limited-service sheriff's department and an unincorporated area, the job of policing the jurisdiction has been placed in the hands of a county police department, which is administered by an appointed chief executive. In these instances, the duties and responsibilities of the county police and the sheriff's department are separate and distinct.

The Office of Constable

The constable is a minor county law enforcement officer—generally elected—whose duties vary from jurisdiction to jurisdiction. Many counties have no constable and appear to suffer little from it. Constables may execute civil process issued by a justice of the peace, collect taxes, issue election notices, enforce traffic ordinances, or even patrol a designated area. Some constables, because of limited duties, are only part-time policemen. Many rely on the "fee system" for income, i.e. they receive in pay a percentage of the money generated through their activities. The office of constable is a foreign creation, and perhaps the most incisive commentary on it was made recently by an English police scholar:[5]

> The typical rural constable is the true descendant of Shakespeare's Dogberry, with about the same degree of efficiency: he is almost always untrained and often incompetent; and his law enforcement activities are almost nil.

[5]Delmar Karlen, *Anglo-American Criminal Justice* (New York: Oxford University Press, 1967), p. 9.

State Police

There are five types of state law enforcement agencies: the highway patrol, the state police, the general investigative bureau, miscellaneous state law enforcement agencies, and law enforcement support units.

The Highway Patrol

State highway patrols have as their primary responsibility the protection of motorists traveling on state roads and interstate highways. Preventive patrol, traffic enforcement, accident inves-

The state highway patrolman *(Courtesy of the Florida Highway Patrol)*

tigation, and driver aid make up a highway patrolman's responsibilities. Officers patrol in uniform, in either marked or unmarked cars, or on motorcycles. A very small percentage of officers may be assigned as plainclothes detectives to conduct follow-up investigations of hit-and-run accidents, serious injury accidents, fatalities, or traffic related crimes. With the advance of technology, many highway patrols have made good use of such hardware as computerized information systems, helicopters and aircraft, electronic detection gear, such as radar and other sophisticated devices to make it less profitable for the traffic violator to operate. The California Highway Patrol is considered a leader in the field of traffic enforcement, and some states have used it as a model for their agencies.

The State Police

While state police forces may also have a primary responsibility to enforce traffic laws, they differ from the highway patrol in that they are provided, through legislative enactment, with general police powers to enforce all state criminal statutes and, in some cases, selected health and safety codes (e.g. narcotics violations). The state police may have significantly larger detective staffs than do highway patrols because of their increased authority. The function of the state police varies from state to state, with some forces serving as the dominant law enforcement agency in the state, while others are assigned specific but limited duties such as the maintenance of security on state property and in government buildings. Some states may have only a highway patrol (as in Florida), others only a state police (as in Michigan), while others have both a highway patrol and a state police force (as in California). In the latter case the duties and responsibilities of both components are clearly delineated by state statute, and the state police, while having general police powers, perform a sharply limited function.

The General Investigative Bureau

Most states have established elite state investigative agencies to detect and investigate crimes which fragmented local agencies are ill-equipped to handle and to provide aid to communities in need of experienced investigative assistance or technical help. Many state investigative bureaus maintain comprehensive criminal records, a crime laboratory, and mobile lab units for their own use and as a service to communities who request aid. Applicants for a job as a state investigator must usually possess a baccalaureate degree and some police experience. With the worsening of the country's narcotics problem and the almost unchecked growth of organized crime, the role of state investigative bureaus will probably be expanded significantly. The Florida Department of Law Enforcement is fast becoming one of the most respected general investigative bureaus in the nation and one which is earning a reputation for imaginative programs, investigative excellence, and innovative leadership.

Miscellaneous State Law Enforcement Agencies

All states have law enforcement divisions with limited police powers, whose job it is to enforce specific state codes. Some agencies maintain uniformed forces, others only plainclothes investigative units, while others have both uniformed officers and plainclothesmen. Examples of miscellaneous agencies include state beverage departments, game commissions, conservation units, racing commissions, and public health departments. Recent tumultuous events dictate that in this category state national guard units be included, for their use in quelling civil disorders and riots qualifies them as a state public safety component.

Law Enforcement Support Units

The tremendous complexity of contemporary policing, coupled with the growing sophistication of criminals, has made it necessary for states to establish certain centralized law enforcement support agencies. Although not generally staffed by individuals with police powers, these agencies perform specialized functions critical to state law enforcement. Some of the functions of support units are fingerprint collection and classification, criminal record keeping, and the collection, interpretation, and dissemination of crime statistics. Often, though, these activities will be part of a state investigative bureau's service role.

Federal Police

Most Federal law enforcement agencies are *ad hoc* bodies with relatively limited powers and with a rather narrow scope of inquiry, the notable exception being the FBI, which employs more than 7,000 agents and thousands of support personnel, and has investigative jurisdiction over 160 Federal matters.[6] It should be stated that information regarding careers with Federal law enforcement agencies may be obtained from college placement officers, local branches of the agency in question, or by corresponding with the appropriate headquarters in Washington, D. C. The most prominent Federal agencies are located in the Department of Justice, the Executive Office of the President, the Department of the Treasury, the Department of Defense, the Department of State, the Department of the Interior, the Department of Agriculture, the Department of Commerce, the Department of Labor, the Department of Transportation, the Department of Health, Education, and Welfare, and the Post Office Department.

The Department of Justice

The Attorney General of the United States is the government's chief legal officer and, as such, his department houses many Federal police agencies. The Department of Justice, besides conducting its own investigations, also coordinates investigative activities of other departments concerned with overlapping problems, notably in the area of racketeering and organized crime.[7] The Department of Justice has enjoyed a good deal of success over the years, thanks in no small measure to the quality and competence of its investigative components.

THE FEDERAL BUREAU OF INVESTIGATION. The FBI, led to prominence by the late John Edgar Hoover, is considered by many to be the finest investigative body in the world. American policemen hold it in such esteem that it is often referred to as "The Bureau." The FBI is responsible for the investigation of all Federal laws not assigned to other agencies and for violations committed on Government property and Indian reservations. Thefts of government property are also investigated by the FBI. In addition the FBI's jurisdiction includes matters of internal security (espionage, sabotage, treason); bank robbery; kidnapping; extortion; interstate transportation of stolen autos, aircraft, cattle, or property; interstate transportation or transmission of wagering information,

[6]John L. Sullivan, *Introduction to Police Science* (New York: McGraw-Hill, Inc., 1966), p. 152.

[7]A. C. Germann, Frank D. Day, and Robert R. J. Gallatti, *Introduction to Law Enforcement and Criminal Justice,* (Springfield: Charles C Thomas, Publisher, 1970), p. 171.

The late John Edgar Hoover, former Director of the FBI. *(Courtesy of the FBI)*

gambling devices, and paraphernalia; interstate travel in aid of racketeering; fraud against the government; violations of election law; civil rights violation; and assaulting or killing a Federal officer or the President of the United States. The FBI also operates a national crime laboratory for its use and for use by police departments at all levels of government, and publishes the monthly *Law Enforcement Bulletin.* The FBI collects crime statistics and publishes them in the *Uniform Crime Report,* and maintains a central fingerprint repository. The Bureau engages in the training of local police officers through the National Academy and through schools conducted by traveling teams of agents.[8] FBI

[8]*Ibid.*

Pictorial representation of the new FBI Academy to be located in Quantico, Virginia. *(Courtesy of the FBI)*

agents often possess law degrees or degrees in accounting; however, applicants with baccalaureate degrees and various amounts of police and military experience are occasionally considered for appointment.

THE DRUG ENFORCEMENT ADMINISTRATION. The D.E.A. was established as a result of several reorganization plans, one of which transferred the Bureau of Narcotics from the Department of Treasury, and the Bureau of Drug Abuse Control from the Department of Health, Education, and Welfare, consolidating them into one agency in the Department of Justice. The new agency's functions include the enforcement of laws controlling narcotics, marijuana, stimulants, depressants, and hallucinogenic drugs. The D.E.A. also conducts a vigorous drug education program.

THE BORDER PATROL. The United States Border Patrol is the law enforcement component of the Immigration and Naturalization Service. The Border Patrol is a mobile uniformed police organization whose principal purpose is to prevent the smuggling and illegal entry of aliens into the United States and to Detect, apprehend, and initiate the departure of aliens illegally in this country. Border Patrol agents are generally assigned along international boundaries and coastal areas, but they are also stationed in other areas of the country, such as rural communities where aliens often seek employment. Agents may patrol in cars, on foot, on horseback, or in aircraft.

UNITED STATES MARSHALS. United States Marshals are officers of the Federal courts. They are assigned to maintain order in the court, handle prisoners, serve court orders, and implement court decisions, a task which has taken on added significance in the last two decades as a result of Federal court mandates.

The Executive Office of the President

Within the Executive Office of the President, the Central Intelligence Agency (CIA), under the direction of the National Security Council, acts to insure national security by performing critical intelligence functions. Its scope of operation includes the integration of foreign, domestic, and military policies relating to the national security.

The Department of the Treasury

The Department of the Treasury employs approximately 90,000 people, more than 5,000 of whom are Treasury enforcement agents in the following units.

THE BUREAU OF CUSTOMS. Special agents in the Bureau of Customs make certain that the Government receives its revenue on incoming goods, and that narcotics, drugs, and defense materials neither enter nor leave the country's borders illegally.

THE INTERNAL REVENUE SERVICE. IRS investigators are assigned to the Alcohol, Tobacco, and Firearms Division, the Internal Security Unit, or the Intelligence Division. Special investigators with the ATFD, or "Revenooers" as they have come to be known, are responsible for the investigation, detection, and prevention of violations of the liquor, tobacco, and firearms laws. The unit's major job in the past involved the tracking down of "moonshiners"; however, times have changed and special investigators now spend a good deal of time enforcing the Federal laws relating to the sale, transfer, manufacture, and possession of firearms. These activities range from background investigations of applicants for a firearms license to investigations of subversive or paramilitary organizations acquiring automatic weapons. Internal Security

Inspectors staff the IRS' own investigative unit. They insure that the integrity of the service is upheld by investigating prospective employes and by inquiring into allegations of misconduct involving Service employes. Special agents in the Internal Revenue Service's Intelligence Division investigate cases involving tax fraud and related criminal violations.

THE SECRET SERVICE. The primary responsibilities of the Secret Service's special agents are twofold: The protection of the President of the United States, the Vice President, the President-elect, the Vice President-elect, former Presidents at their request for a limited period of time, and the immediate families of these public officials; and the suppression of counterfeiting of U. S. currency and other securities. In addition, the Secret Service investigates forgeries of Government checks.

EXECUTIVE PROTECTIVE SERVICE. The Executive Protective Service, a uniformed force, is supervised by the Secret Service. Its duties are to protect the White House, buildings in which Presidential

The Secret Service in action. *(Courtesy of the St. Petersburg Police Department)*

offices are located, the President and his immediate family, foreign diplomatic missions located in the District of Columbia and in such areas in the United States, its territories and possessions as the President may direct.

The Department of Defense

Within the Department of Defense, the four service branches— Army, Navy, Marines, and Air Force—all maintain law enforcement components. Although the functions differ a good deal from municipal police agencies, the general structure is the same, each having uniformed policemen and plainclothes follow-up investigators. The four branches have necessarily large intelligence units because of the nature of their operations.

The Department of State

The State Department operates a small but vitally important program within the Office of Security. At present some threescore security officers are stationed at overseas posts, as well as twenty electronic engineers and technicians serving at U.S. embassies abroad. A primary job of the engineers and technicians is to insure that embassies remain free from electronic surveillance and foreign eavesdropping devices.

The Department of the Interior

The Department of the Interior, the guardian of this country's natural resources, has sixteen bureaus. Several divisions within the bureaus fulfill a law enforcement function: the Division of Security scrutinizes internal affairs; the Fish and Wildlife Service oversees commercial and game fish, and wildlife; the National Park Service patrols national parks and monuments, and the Division of Inspection conducts internal investigations and departmental inspections.

The Department of Commerce

The Department of Commerce maintains two law enforcement components under the Assistant Secretary of Commerce for Administration: the Office of Security Control, which is responsible for physical and personal security; and the Agency Inspection Staff, which investigates misconduct by employes.

The Department of Labor

The Office of the Solicitor coordinates investigative activities for the Department of Labor. Both civil and criminal cases are investigated in the areas of child labor, workman's compensation, unfair labor practices, and minimum wages, to name a few of its activities.

The Department of Transportation

The Department of Transportation contains four law enforcement branches: the United States Coast Guard, the Federal Aviation Administration, the Federal Highway Adminstration, and the Air Security Program.

THE UNITED STATES COAST GUARD. The Coast Guard operates within the Department of Transportation during peace time. The Coast Guard engages in a port security program and enforces Federal laws on the high seas.

THE FEDERAL AVIATION ADMINISTRATION. The FAA enforces regulations relating to the manufacture, registration, safety, and operation of aircraft. In addition, it investigates air crashes and inspects air navigation facilities.

THE FEDERAL HIGHWAY ADMINISTRATION. The Administration's National Highway Safety Bureau oversees a program designed to reduce deaths, injuries, and accidents on the nation's highways.

THE AIR SECURITY PROGRAM. The Air Security Program is one of the newest and one of the most critical programs in the Federal Government. Prompted by aircraft hijackings, the Department of Transportation is conducting a massive and intensive training program aimed at monitoring airports in order to forestall hijacking. The program is a unique experiment involving the private sector (airline companies), professional organizations (airline pilots associations), other components of Government (FBI), and other nations, both friendly and otherwise.

The Department of Health, Education, and Welfare

HEW has the critically important function of promoting the public welfare in the fields of health, education, and social security. Its primary law enforcement body, the Food and Drug Administration, investigates truth in labeling, product purity, standard potency, and related matters.[9]

[9]*Ibid.*, p. 174.

The Post Office Department

The Bureau of the Chief Postal Inspector investigates postal laws and regulations, including schemes to defraud, lotteries, obscene matter, and certain kinds of extortions.[10]

Private Police

Although the idea of private police forces is not uniquely an American phenomenon, no country matches this nation's reliance on parapolicemen. Private police officers, numbering in the tens of thousands, have as their primary responsibility the safeguarding of billions of dollars in cargo and merchandise. Although some large companies maintain their own security forces, many enter into contracts with private detective or protective agencies to perform services ranging from simple guard duty to complex investigatory work. With the advent of technology, private security firms have led the way in adopting sophisticated devices aimed at detecting and apprehending criminals. It is not the purpose of private police forces to replace formally constituted law enforcement, but to supplement the local police. In most communities there exists a spirit of friendly cooperation between local authorities and security administrators, both of whom have totally compatible goals.

POLICE JOURNALS

It stands to reason that because of the fragmentation and isolation of the American police some effective means of communication is necessary to keep officers informed of contemporary ideas and emerging issues in the field. In this regard law enforcement is fortunate to have a number of fine professional periodicals which cover every facet of the police profession. It is essential that students of law enforcement be made aware of the existence of the major police journals. Although few individuals have the finances to subscribe to all available publications, most police departments and college libraries stock at least several professional magazines. Some of the major law enforcement and law enforcement related journals are described below.

[10]*Supra* note 5, p. 153.

Criminology

Criminology, an interdisciplinary journal devoted to crime and deviant behavior, is the official publication of the American Society of Criminology. Subscriptions are also available to non-members. The periodical, published quarterly, places major emphasis on empirical research and scientific methodology. Articles reporting on original research in sociology, psychology, psychiatry, law, social work, urban design, and systems analysis are given priority by the editors, although occasionally theoretical treatises are published.

The Enforcement Journal

Formerly known as *Valor, The Enforcement Journal* is the voice of the National Police Officers Association of America. The periodical, published six times a year, is a journal of conservative police and academic opinion, although feature departments cover such subjects as enforcement tactics, prison reform, recent court decisions, industry news, and new police products.

FBI Law Enforcement Bulletin

The *Bulletin* is published by the FBI as a service to local law enforcement. Policemen and personnel in related fields are urged to contribute articles, which range from descriptions of community-relations programs to news on advanced crime-detection techniques. One of the most noteworthy features of the publication, which is issued monthly, is the "Message from the Director" column, written by the Director of the FBI, John Edgar Hoover.

Federal Probation

Federal Probation is a journal of correctional philosophy and practice published monthly by the Administrative Office of the United States Courts in cooperation with the Bureau of Prisons, Department of Justice. Useful information in the area of crime, law, corrections, rehabilitation, juvenile delinquency, and deviancy is available therein.

The Journal of Criminal Law, Criminology, and Police Science.

This journal, published by the Northwestern University School of Law, is probably the most scholarly periodical in the police field. Articles are written by international experts in the field of law, science, criminology, law enforcement, penology, and the social sciences. During the past few years the periodical has emphasized the sociological aspects of the criminal justice system, although not to the exclusion of innovative technology.

Law and Order

Law and Order magazine is an independent journal which is published monthly. Although most professional topics are covered, special emphasis is placed on the technical aspects of police work. Monthly columns are devoted to such subjects as police technology, weapons, in-service training, and new hardware. Unlike some of .the other major periodicals, lower-echelon officers often contribute articles to *Law and Order.*

The Law Officer

The Law Officer is the official quarterly publication of the International Conference of Police Associations, an organization made up of hundreds of local police associations. The magazine is concerned with the bread and butter, "gut" issues of the day. Its pages abound with stories of police officers killed and injured in the line of duty; the status of pro-police legislation; and instances of police labor militancy. Although some of the readership labors at executive and command levels, most are rank-and-file policemen.

The Police

The Police, published monthly by Charles C Thomas, Publisher, is a scholarly police journal covering the professional interests of law enforcement personnel. Most articles deal with the administrative or social aspects of law enforcement. Contributing writers come from all phases of police work; however, many articles are contributed by criminal justice professors, giving the publication an academic orientation.

The Police Chief

Published monthly by the International Association of Chiefs of Police, The *Police Chief* is one of the oldest and most respected police periodicals in circulation. Its content is of a relatively high level and contributors represent the entire spectrum of the police craft. Many articles are also written by those on the periphery of law enforcement: academicians, attorneys, architects, planners, and public officials.

The Police Journal

The Police Journal is a British publication described as "a monthly review for the police of the world." The *Journal* offers students of the art an excellent opportunity to keep abreast of issues in European law enforcement without subscribing to a foreign language magazine. It also presents European perspectives on the police in America. The *Journal* maintains an office in Canada to serve its American and Canadian subscribers.

Security World

Although not a police journal per se, *Security World* presents police-related information available in no other periodical. It is the magazine of professional security administration and practice, and as such, it surveys some of the most innovative techniques and devices available in the crime fighters' arsenal.

Traffic Safety

Sold monthly by the National Safety Council, *Traffic Safety* is dedicated to the prevention of traffic accidents through the presentation of responsible opinion and objective information. Departments are concerned with, among other things, legislative news, traffic records, and safety equipment.

THE INTERNATIONAL ASSOCIATION OF
CHIEFS OF POLICE (IACP)

The contribution of the International Association of Chiefs of Police to American law enforcement has been of such major significance that its internal workings should be known by all criminal justice students. From its meager beginnings in 1893 the IACP, under the able leadership of its Executive Director, Quinn Tamm, has become a dynamic force for police professionalism. The Association is made up of five classes of members: (1) active members, who must be of command rank on a public enforcement agency, or be a chief executive of a railroad police or railway express company police system, (2) associate members, who are those endorsed by active members, (3) sustaining members, who are individuals interested in advancing and improving the police profession, (4) elected life members, and (5) distinguished service life members. Approximately eighty-six percent of the total membership is comprised of active members. The IACP is

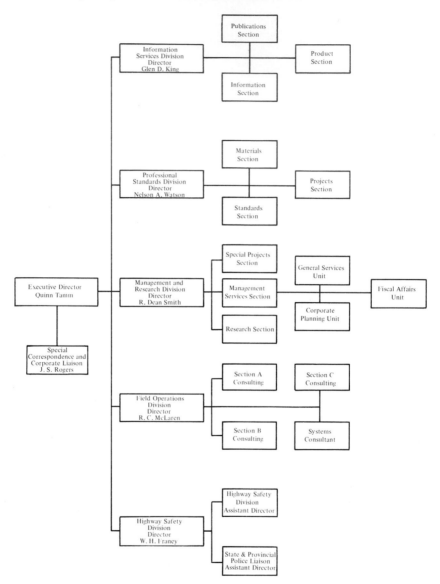

Organization chart of the International Association of Chiefs of Police *(Courtesy of the IACP)*

financially supported in a number of ways: by membership dues, by income from publications, through grants from public and private sectors, and through self-supporting field projects. The International Association of Chiefs of Police is divided into five separate divisions, each with a distinct function. The bulk of the

IACP's work is performed by these components and it is appropriate that each be studied.

The Management and Research Division

The Management and Research Division oversees the planning, research, and administration of the Association, including financial management. The division reviews grants, proposals, contracts, and requests for funds. Furthermore, the Division conducts research on a variety of subjects ranging from curriculum development for police recruits to behavioral analysis. The Division's general purpose is to "contribute to the effort to answer some of the problems of law enforcement, develop new techniques and methods, and provide assistance to law enforcement agencies as they reach for innovations."

The Field Operations Division

The Field Operations Division is the heart of the International Association of Chiefs of Police. The Division, staffed by a distinguished lineup of former professors, police commanders, and public administrators, conducts management and reorganizational studies of police departments. When an agency expresses an interest in commissioning the IACP for a survey, a preliminary investigation is conducted by a member of the division to determine whether IACP assistance is necessary. If it is, a team of consultants is sent to scrutinize the department's operations and to prepare a report of its findings together with a list of recommendations for improvement. The Field Operations Division also assists in the development of information and record systems, evaluates personnel and training programs, provides guidance in the design and construction of physical structures, and engages in state planning assistance.

The Highway Safety Division

The Highway Safety Division is staffed by nationally renowned experts in the field of traffic safety. Like the Field Operations Division, the Highway Safety Division engages in extensive consulting activities with local and state police agencies. The Division also maintains a liaison with organizations—both public and private—which work on Federal, state, and local governmental safety problems, conducts midyear conferences on highway safety and auto theft, and produces a manual entitled "Highway Safety Policies for Police Executives." An administrative entity has recently been established to work with state and provincial police departments.

The Professional Standards Division

The Professional Standards Division develops and disseminates a bimonthly training bulletin called the "Training Key" to subscribers, along with filmstrips and synchronized sound tapes on selected training subjects. The Division also stimulates the development of college police science, law enforcement, and criminal justice programs and conducts schools and conferences aimed at improving the skill of middle managers and police executives. A placement service is maintained to recruit and examine candidates for police chief positions at the municipal, county, and state levels.

The Information Services Division

The mission of the Information Services Division is twofold: to assist law enforcement in its relations with the citizenry and to improve the standing of the police in the community. The foundation of the Division is the Center for Law Enforcement Research and Information (CLERI), a major library and police research center which contains books, articles, theses, and monographs. The Division also publishes the *Police Chief* and *The Police Yearbook* and conducts programs and conferences relative to its mission.

Other activities of the IACP are too numerous to mention. It will suffice to say that the IACP is the greatest single force in the move to professionalize the nation's police, and one whose duties and responsibilities will continue to expand.

THE POLITICAL CLIMATE OF MUNICIPAL POLICE ADMINISTRATION[11]

Police administration does not operate in a vacuum. And it follows that the nature of the organizational environment in which

---

[11]Reprinted with permission from V. A. Leonard's *The Police Enterprise* (Springfield: Charles C Thomas, Publisher, 1969), pp. 29-35.

a police department finds itself may condition, either one way or the other, the caliber of police service that is delivered to the community.

Obviously, the form of municipal government is an important part of the climate of police administration. It is important, therefore, to consider the prevailing patterns of local government in this country because, without a sound administrative structure at the top, no police organization can be administered and controlled

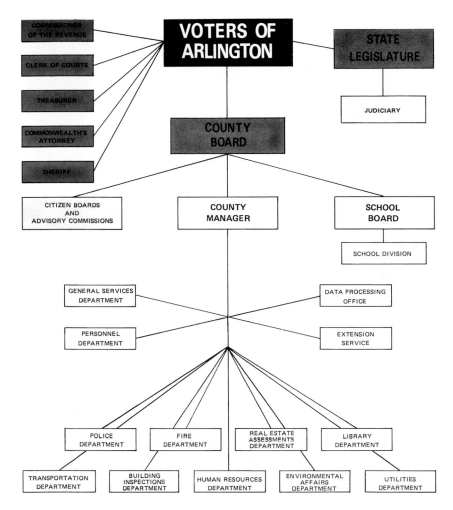

An organization chart showing the place of the police in the governmental structure. *(Courtesy of the Arlington, Virginia, Police Department)*

with efficiency and integrity. The type of administrative climate in which a police department finds itself compelled to function may prove to be a serious handicap, or it may foster a high degree of competence and efficiency. Within this frame of reference, it is pertinent to examine the three major forms of local government to be found in this country—the mayor-council type, the commission plan, and the city manager form of municipal government.

The Mayor-Council Type

The traditional pattern of municipal organization is the mayor-council form. Under this plan the members of the council are elected. They represent the political aspect of local government and in a democracy, provide the opportunity for the flow of control and responsibility between government and the electorate. Through its ordinance-making power, it exercises the legislative function. In addition to legislative and policymaking functions, the council—in common with most legislative bodies—holds the purse strings and exercises control over appropriations.

Executive power is vested in the mayor, who may be chosen by the council or elected directly by the people. Upon the mayor is conferred the power of appointment and removal of the heads of administrative departments, including the police, subject in most instances to the approval of the council. Ideally, the department head whom the mayor appoints should be an expert in those functions over which he has jurisdiction. There are instances where the office of mayor is held by a man with a strong personality, endowed with those qualities of leadership, integrity, and vision which are necessary for the successful administration of an important business enterprise. Under these conditions, capable leadership may be reflected in the competence of the police executive and the heads of other municipal departments. Unfortunately, however, such a happy condition is a rare occurrence. The history of police administration in the United States points up the frequency of failure in the mayor-council form of municipal government. As often as not, the mayor is largely a figurehead while the line departments of government are dominated and even corrupted by legislative interference. It was under such conditions of incompetence in local government that new forms of municipal administration were born.

The Commission Plan

In 1900 Galveston, Texas, was one of the most miserably governed cities in the United States. Enjoying a low tax rate, operations were financed largely through increasing the bonded indebtedness. Department heads were elected and municipal government was run largely for personal profit. Then, in that year came the great tidal wave which resulted in a staggering loss of life and destruction of property. It was a tremendous crisis demanding brains and energy; municipal officials could furnish neither.

A group of businessmen drew the blueprints for a new form of municipal government—the commission plan—and moved it through the legislature for approval. The distinguishing feature of the commission plan was that it combined both the legislative and administrative functions of government in an all-powerful body of five members—the commission—chosen by popular election. As a group the commission constituted the legislative and policymaking body of local government: singly each commissioner was the administrative head of one or more municipal departments. Thus the commissioner of public safety exercised administrative control over the police and fire departments.

Featured in the public press, the commission form of municipal government was hailed by students of municipal affairs as the reform that would bring light out of darkness and end the dominion of the professional politician. This was good news for police administration. By 1909 twenty-eight other American cities adopted the commission plan, and by 1917 the total number of commission-governed cities had risen to five hundred.

However, the commission plan possessed fatal defects in its original structure, and in recent years it has been rapidly losing ground. Although the commission plan held forth considerable promise for a new era in police administration, subsequent events exposed it as a new device for corrupt exploitation. The dual role of the individual commissioner as both legislator and administrator opened wide the door for the play of political influence and pressure. Of even greater significance it set up plural command over the police force, in violation of the law of unity of command. Police organization under conditions of dual control tends to become a divided house. A part of departmental personnel becomes devoted to the interests of the commissioner, with the other members of the department directing their allegiance toward the chief of police.

Another liability of the commission plan was the fusion of police and fire administration under single executive control. Among other things, this served to handcuff the police salary structure to salaries prevailing in the fire department.

Both the mayor-council and the commission plans of municipal government were shortly to be challenged by a new pattern of control in the administration of municipal affairs—the council-manager or city manager plan. A tidal wave swept the commission plan into Galveston. Thirteen years later a flood on the Miami River confronted the citizens of Dayton, Ohio, with a tragedy of major dimensions. The flood crisis brought out into bold relief the incompetence of existing local government and revealed its inability to deal with either the crisis or the routine responsibilities of municipal administration.

As a result of this emergency situation a committee of five, under the leadership of John H. Patterson of the National Cash Register Company, was appointed by the local chamber of commerce to study the possible application of a city manager plan to the management problems of Dayton. The committee reported favorably on the plan and it was subsequently approved by the voters by a vote of two to one.

The City Manager Plan

The new pattern provided an outstanding demonstration of efficiency in the administration of municipal affairs. By 1969 there were more than 2,000 cities and thirty counties in the United States operating under the city manager form of local government.

Under this arrangement, the city council functions in much the same manner as the board of directors in a corporate enterprise. The council determines public policies and then chooses the city manager to carry them out. Once chosen, he is given wide administrative control and authority to select his subordinates, including the executive heads of the various departments of municipal government.

The city manager plan has served to produce trained administrators for a very technical job in public management and has given American municipal government its first professional touch.

Among its recommendations is the fact that the plan has from the beginning been consistently opposed by the professional politicians whose interests are not too often in harmony with the development of high standards in the public service.

While it is possible to develop an efficient police service within the framework of the mayor-council or the commission plan, it is patent that the city manager form fosters professionalization in the various municipal departments. A professional administrator with full administrative power and responsibility would, by the very nature of his training and position, endeavor to place at the head of each department the most capable individual available. Hence, the city manager would obviously be interested in the appointment of a chief of police qualified for the delivery of a professional grade of management.

With the complete separation of the legislative and administrative functions of government provided by this form of municipal organization, political interference with police administration is reduced to a minimum. Under this form of administrative control, police administration finds itself in a professional atmosphere where it is less likely to be burdened by the inhibitions which in the past have retarded the professionalization of this branch of the public service. It is significant that city managers have uniformly sought for the position of police chief executive men who were professionally qualified for the task, and that they have, in most instances, based their selection on the professional qualifications of the candidate rather than upon political and other considerations that have governed appointments to this position in the past.

The city manager form of local government is being adopted on an increasing scale by the smaller communities of the nation. The police are indeed fortunate where they are able to operate in this type of administrative climate. The officials of local government and civic leaders in those communities still working under the mayor-council or commission plan would do well to look into the advantages of the city manager form of municipal government with its demonstrated offer of both economy and efficiency in the administration of local affairs.

Pressure Groups

Special-interest and pressure groups are a part of the climate of police administration. It is a basic principle of democratic government that administration must be responsive to public control. This is especially true of the police because of the unique powers with which they are entrusted. Basic also is the fact that such control must find expression through the formal channels of governmental structure, descending vertically from the people by way of the ballot box, through the legislative body, to the appointing officer, and through him to the police chief executive. It is likewise essential that responsibility flow vertically upward from the police to the appointing authority, and then from him to the legislature, and finally to the people. These controls should be out in the open where they are exposed to observation and appraisal.

Violations of this principle take the form of pressures and controls generated by special-interest groups in the community. They are usually brought to bear upon the weakest point or points in the organizational structure. The influence of special-interest or pressure groups may be constructive or it may be illegitimate and corrupt. It is a necessary characteristic of corrupt controls that they operate under cover because of fear of exposure. This alone is sufficient to place the public service and the people it serves on guard. This is best understood by examining the nature of a few representative special-interest groups.

Although the strength of political party organization varies from city to city and from community to community, political influence in any form is a direct threat to sound public management, including police administration. It is suspect all the way, and its presence should be observed with considerable concern. Vice interests, including gambling and prostitution, may constitute a potent pressure group even in the smaller cities and communities. The situation is not limited to communities in any particular population group nor to any particular section of the country. In every community, regardless of size, are to be found those whose standards are in the marginal zone of morality, and who are constantly on the alert for the relaxation in enforcement pressures which will permit them to open the doors for business.

Interference with local police administration expresses itself in many different forms. Occasionally it is well-intentioned, but frequently it is ill-conceived and misguided. Chambers of commerce and the constellation of service clubs that characterize the American scene may affect the quality of police administration one way or the other. These organizations, as rule, exert a constructive influence in municipal affairs. Most service clubs attempt to remain politically neutral. They should also remember that political neutrality is an absolute prerequisite of successful police administration. Service clubs and organizations can do much to promote the cause of good government in the community by prevailing upon the city council to see to it that the conditions and the climate for professionalized police service are made available.

The churches in a community represent a potential pressure group of considerable proportions. If their members are aroused, their influence can be a controlling factor in some areas of administrative policy determination. The voting power of active church members in an average American community may on occasion turn the tide. However, church membership includes a fair cross section of most interest groups in a community, which complicates the pooling of their resources. Nevertheless, the influence of churches in municipal affairs should not be underestimated. A man's thinking can be shaped by the impact of principles enunciated by the Man of Galilee, and a transformation in viewpoint on the part of an individual may have important implications at the ballot box.

(Courtesy of the Law Enforcement Assistance Administration, United States Department of Justice)

Chapter 15

THE COURTS

The courts are the core for justice administration in America, the hub of the wheel of criminal justice. Criminal courts were established for three basic reasons: (1) to administer justice in a fair and impartial way, (2) to provide an authority for controlling crime, and (3) to protect the liberties of citizens.[1]

THE LEGAL FOUNDATION

The authority for creating courts is derived from three sources: the United States Constitution, the state constitutions, and legislative enactments.

The United States Constitution

Article III, Sections 1 and 2 of the United States Constitution, specifically provides for a Federal court system.

Article III

Section 1. The Judicial Power of the United States shall be vested in one supreme court, and in such inferior Courts as the Congress may from time to time ordain and establish. The Judges, both of the supreme and inferior Courts, shall hold their Offices during good Behaviour, and shall, at Times, receive for their Services, a Compensation, which shall not be diminished during their Continuance in Office.

Section 2. The judicial Power shall extend to all Cases, in Law and Equity, arising under this Constitution, the Laws of the United States, and Treaties made, or which shall be made, under their Authority;—to all cases affecting Ambassadors, other public Ministers and Consuls;—to all Cases of admiralty and maritime Jurisdiction;—to Controversies to which the United States shall be a Party;—to Controversies between two or more States;—between a State and Citizens of another State;—between Citizens of different

[1]R. Gene Wright and John A. Marlo, *The Police Officer and Criminal Justice* (New York: McGraw-Hill Book Co., 1970), pp. 16-18.

States;—between Citizens of the same State claiming Lands under Grants of different States, and between a State, or the Citizens thereof, and foreign States, Citizens or Subjects.

In all Cases affecting Ambassadors, other public Ministers and Consuls, and those in which a State shall be Party, the supreme Court shall have original Jurisdiction. In all the other Cases before mentioned, the supreme Court shall have appellate Jurisdiction, both as to Law and Fact, with such Exceptions, and under such Regulations as the Congress shall make.

The Trial of all Crimes, except in Cases of Impeachment, shall be by Jury; and such Trial shall be held in the State where the said Crimes shall have been committed; but when not committed within any State, the Trial shall be at such Place or Places as the Congress may by Law have directed.

The State Constitutions

The authority for establishing state court systems is found in the state constitutions. State courts, although created by different authority, are integrated to a degree with the Federal system because of the appellate function performed by Federal courts.

Legislative Enactments

The United States Constitution and the state constitutions authorize the creation, through legislative enactment, of certain classes of inferior courts, an authority most of the states have exercised. If the experts are right and the nation's courts need to be coordinated and/or consolidated, legislative enactment is the one vehicle that can accomplish this kind of reform.

ORGANIZATION OF THE COURTS

When compared to the organization of the American police, the Federal and state court systems are strikingly simple, although, like the police, there is some duplication of service, and a good deal of isolation. The major problem facing the courts is probably a sharply increasing workload, a problem complicated by cumbersome court procedures which cause trials to drag on, occasionally for months; endless delays in bringing cases to trial, and the policy of relying on judges to supervise the actual administration of the courts. A trend toward creating professional court administrators to deal with the administrative aspects of justice is freeing judges to pursue the task for which they were chosen.

FEDERAL JUDICIAL SYSTEM

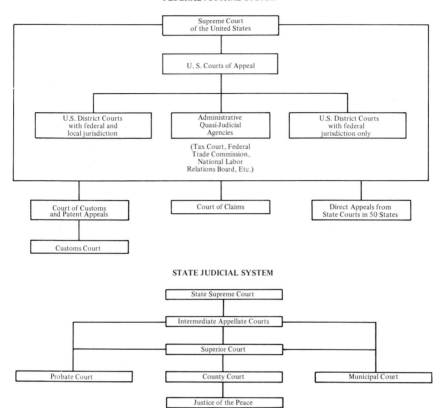

STATE JUDICIAL SYSTEM

The Federal Judicial System

The Supreme Court of the United States

The United States Supreme Court is the nation's highest court. The Supreme Court takes its authority not only from the Constitution but also from the precedent set in the case of *Marbury* v. *Madison* (1803), in which Chief Justice Marshall ruled that the court had the power of *judicial review*. The Supreme Court has appellate jurisdiction over the United States District Courts and the United States Courts of Appeal. There are nine Supreme Court Justices, who are appointed for life by the President with the advice and consent of the Senate. One Justice is selected as Chief Justice. When the court is in session in the ornate Supreme Court Building, the judges conform to a rather rigid protocol. The Chief Justice sits in the center and the others are distributed on his left and right according to seniority. The Supreme Court may exercise discretionary jurisdiction over judicial matters, which means that it may hear or refuse to hear any case appealed to it. It is the court of final appeal.

The United States Courts of Appeal

There are eleven United States Courts of Appeal, each serving a judicial district. The Courts of Appeal handle routine appeals from lower Federal courts and review and enforce the orders and action of many Federal administrative agencies and commissions. The court employs seventy-five judges. Decisions are generally made by a panel of three judges.

The United States District Courts

The United States District Courts, with ninety-one districts and 311 judges, were established by congressional statute. They are the principal trial courts in cases of Federal jurisdiction, trying violators of the United States Code and administrative orders. The District Courts are considered the workhorse of the Federal judicial system, hearing better than 100,000 cases annually. The United States District Courts in the fifty states and Puerto Rico have Federal jurisdiction only, while those in the District of Columbia, the Virgin Islands, the Canal Zone, and Guam have both Federal and local jurisdiction.

Special Federal Courts

A number of lower Federal courts have been established to hear special types of cases. These include (1) the Court of Claims, which hears claims for damages against the United States, (2) Customs Court, which hears cases involving customs duties, and (3) the Court of Customs and Patent Appeals.

The State Judicial System

State Supreme Court

The State Supreme Court is the highest tribunal in the state judicial system. The court, often called the "court of last resort," may also be called Supreme Court of Errors, Court of Appeals, Supreme Judicial Court, or Supreme Court of Appeals, depending on the state it serves. Its primary function is to hear appeals from lower state courts.

Intermediate Appellate Courts

These courts also hear appeals from lower state courts. Only about one third of the states have Intermediate Appellate Courts, which are tribunals between trial courts and the State Supreme Court. In those states in which this court functions, a majority of cases are finally decided therein, taking much of the appellate burden from the "court of last resort."

Superior Courts

Superior Courts—also called Circuit Courts, District Courts, Courts of Common Plea, and in New York, Supreme Courts—are the highest state trial courts with general jurisdiction. Besides acting as a trial court for serious crimes, the court will also hear major civil cases and act as reviewing authority over inferior courts.

Local Courts of Limited Jurisdiction

Courts of Limited Jurisdiction are so named because they generally handle minor misdemeanor cases and preliminary

A municipal courtroom scene.

hearings involving felonies. There are three types of local courts of this type.

MUNICIPAL COURT. Municipal Courts are city and town tribunals which hear less important cases, such as traffic offenses, minor civil actions, and violations of municipal ordinances.

COUNTY COURT. Like the Municipal Court, the County Court has a very limited jurisdiction over both civil and criminal cases.

PROBATE COURT. This is a special court which handles wills, the administration of estates, and guardianships of minors and incompetents. In some jurisdictions it is called Surrogate Court or Orphans' Court.

Justice of the Peace Court

Justice of the Peace Courts are the lowest in the judicial hierarchy. They have sharply limited jurisdiction over minor civil and criminal matters. Some may be empowered to hold arraignment hearings and hear traffic cases. They have come under a good deal of criticism lately for acting as bill collectors for companies victimized by bad-check artists.

THE ADMINISTRATION OF CRIMINAL JUSTICE[2]

Court actions fall into two general classifications: civil and criminal. According to the American Bar Association: "Civil cases are those in which an individual or business or agency of government seeks damages or relief from another individual or business or agency of government."

Although the great bulk of court cases in America are civil in nature, police officers deal almost exclusively with violations of the criminal law, making it appropriate that the administration of criminal justice be discussed at some length.

The administration of criminal justice generally follows the following form: (1) the arrest, (2) preliminary hearing, (3) bringing the charge, (4) the trial, (5) sentencing, and (6) appeal.

---

[2]The American Bar Association, *Law and Courts in the News* (Chicago: The American Bar Association, 1960), pp. 4-13; Martin R. Haskell and Lewis Yablonski, *Crime and Delinquency* (Chicago: Rand McNally & Co., 1970), pp. 14-17; The President's Commission on Law Enforcement and Administration of Justice, *Task Force Report: The Courts* (Washington: U. S. Government Printing Office, 1967); Paul B. Weston and Kenneth M. Wells, *The Administration of Justice* (Englewood Cliffs, New Jersey: Prentice-Hall, Inc., 1967).

The Arrest

An arrest is the seizing of a person and detaining him in custody for the purpose of charging him with a crime. Police officers may make an arrest with or without a warrant and, in some states, private citizens may make an arrest.

Arrest by Police Officer Without Warrant

A police officer may make an arrest without a warrant when he has reasonable cause to believe that the person to be arrested has committed a felony (a serious crime—one for which a person may be confined in the penitentiary) whether or not a felony has in fact been committed. An officer may also arrest without a warrant when a misdemeanor (a less serious crime-one for which a person may be confined in the city or county jail) has been committed in his physical presence.

Arrest by Police Officer with Warrant

A warrant of arrest is an order signed by a magistrate and issued by a court clerk directing a police officer to arrest an individual and bring him before said magistrate. A warrant is initiated by the filing of a written complaint with the prosecuting attorney in the county of the alleged offense.

Arrest by Private Citizen

A number of states allow a private citizen to arrest another (1) when a felony has been committed and he has reasonable cause to believe that the person arrested committed it, (2) when the person has committed a felony, although not in his physical presence, and (3) for a public offense committed or attempted in his presence. In those states in which citizens' arrests are allowed, they need not be accompanied by a warrant.

Preliminary Hearing

A person who has been arrested may either request or waive his right to a preliminary hearing before a magistrate. In any event he must be charged with a crime or released from custody without unreasonable delay—usually within twenty-four hours. If he requests a preliminary hearing, the state must present evidence to convince the magistrate that there is reason to believe that the defendant has committed a crime. Although the defendant must be present at the hearing, he does not have to present evidence on his own behalf. It is here that the defendant is arraigned, i.e. the charges are read to him and he is asked to plead guilty or not guilty. In some jurisdictions the arraignment and the plea are separate proceedings. If the magistrate believes the evidence justifies it, he may order the defendant bound over for trial in the appropriate court. In this case the person is either admitted to bail or held without bail if the crime is of sufficient gravity. Conversely, insufficient evidence may cause the magistrate to order the release of the defendant from custody.

Bringing the Charges

Criminal charges are instituted against a person in one of two ways: through an indictment or through the filing of an information.

Indictment

When a prosecuting attorney seeks an indictment against a person, he presents his case to a grand jury, a panel made up of from five to twenty-three citizens (but usually sixteen) who have been summoned by the court to inquire into crimes committed in the jurisdiction. Grand jury proceedings are held in private and in secret to protect the accused. If the grand jury decides to indict the person for the alleged crime, it returns a *true bill*. If it concludes that the evidence does not warrant an indictment, it returns a *no bill*.

Information

In many jurisdictions the prosecuting attorney may bring the accused to trial by filing an information with the appropriate court, based on the results of the police investigation. An information is nothing more than an accusation that is supported by evidence, such as that which is presented before a grand jury. Although most states allow the prosecuting attorney to choose the way in which he will institute the criminal charge against an individual, in serious cases, such as murder, the accused may be charged only by indictment.

The Trial

After the accused is arraigned, he may plead guilty. If he does, the trial ends and he is sentenced. If he pleads not guilty, the trial proceeds. In the American system of criminal justice the burden of proof is on the state to prove the guilt of the defendant beyond a reasonable doubt.

Officers of the Court

THE JUDGE. The judge, who may be either elected or appointed to his position, presides over the trial. If the case in question is to be tried before a jury, the judge rules on points of law dealing with trial procedure, presentation of evidence, and the law. If the case is to be tried without a jury, the judge determines the facts in the case in addition to his other duties.

THE COURT CLERK. The court clerk administers the oath to prospective veniremen (jurors). In taking the oath, the jurors promise to answer truthfully questions about their fitness to serve which are posed by the prosecution and defense. After the appropriate number of jurors are chosen, the court clerk administers an oath to the persons so chosen "to well and truly try the cause."

THE BAILIFF. The bailiff's duties are (1) to keep order in the courtroom, (2) to call witnesses, and (3) to take charge of the jury when the jury is not in the courtroom. The bailiff acts to insure that no outside influences are brought to bear on the jury.

THE COURT REPORTER. The reporter's mission is to record all of the trial, including the testimony of witnesses and the attorneys' objections to the presentation of evidence and court rulings. Court reporters also may list for identification exhibits introduced into evidence.

THE ATTORNEYS. In a criminal trial the state is represented by the prosecuting attorney (he may also be called district attorney, state's attorney, or county solicitor, depending on the jurisdiction), while the defendant is represented by either a private attorney or the public defender—the defense attorney. Only in extraordinary situations will the court allow a defendant to defend himself. Indigent defendants are appointed an attorney free of charge. Preparation of a case ordinarily requires a considerable amount of time and work, so it is essential that both defense and prosecution have adequate time before trial to make use of the investigative techniques at their disposal.

The Jury List

The trial jury, called a petit jury, is chosen by lot from a list (a venire) of prospective jurors. Although the method of compiling the list varies from one state to another, many states rely on tax assessment rolls or voter registration lists. Most jurisdictions, as a rule, exclude some persons from jury duty because of their occupations. A few of the most common exemptions are lawyers, physicians, teachers, clergymen, firemen, and policemen.

Occasionally, an entire jury panel may be challenged if, in the opinion of the defense attorney, the panel was selected in an illegal manner. This is called a *challenge to the arrays.*

Selecting the Jury

In most cases a jury in a criminal proceeding is made up of twelve persons; however, Florida, in what could become a trend, has allowed six-member juries to hear criminal cases, a decision which has been upheld by higher court rulings. Jury selection begins with the random selection of names—six, twelve, or what-ever the law states in that particular jurisdiction—from a box or drum by the clerk. The attorneys are then allowed to question each prospective juror to determine his or her fitness to serve. This questioning is called the *voir dire.* When a venireman exhibits a prejudice or an opinion that could affect his or her judgment in the case in question, the court will then excuse the juror for cause. There is no limit on the number of jurors who can be dismissed this way. The peremptory challenge permits each attorney to excuse a particular juror without having to show cause. The number of peremptory challenges is limited. As each juror is dismissed, another name is read to replace him or her. When the regular jury is selected, the court clerk administers the oath. In some cases, such as crimes of major importance that are expected to last for an extended period of time, a number of alternate jurors are chosen to replace regular jurors who may become disabled in midtrial. Alternate jurors sit with regular veniremen, but do not participate in the deliberations.

Separating the Witnesses

In certain criminal cases, an attorney—either the prosecutor or the defense counsel—may inform the court that he is *calling for the rule,* which is legal parlance meaning that he wishes to have all witnesses who are scheduled to give testimony excluded from the courtroom until they are called to testify. The rule is invoked so that witnesses are not swayed by the testimony of others.

Excluded witnesses are not permitted to discuss the case with anyone except the attorneys.

Opening Statements

After the jury has been selected and the oath administered, the attorney for the state and the defense attorney can, if they choose, make opening statements to the jury. The prosecuting attorney may advise the jury of what he intends to prove in the case, although his remarks are restricted to what later will be elicited in evidence. The defense attorney may offer the jury a preview of his case. In some states the defense attorney can reserve his opening statement until after the end of the state's case, a distinct advantage for the accused. Both sides can waive the opening statements if they so desire.

Presentation of Evidence

In a criminal case the state will begin presenting evidence by calling witnesses. Witnesses, whether they be testifying for prosecution or defense, may testify to matters of fact, i.e. what

Some police agencies take great pains to reconstruct a crime scene for jurors. Above, FBI technicians prepare a scale model for use in court. *(Courtesy of the FBI)*

they actually saw, heard, smelled, or touched. Witnesses are generally not allowed to state opinions or offer conclusions unless the court recognizes them as expert witnesses in a particular field. Only in extraordinary instances can witnesses testify to hearsay, which is what someone else might have said or witnessed— "second-hand evidence." Witnesses will not be permitted to testify on matters that are irrelevant or immaterial to the case being tried. An attorney may not ask leading questions of his witnesses. Leading questions are queries that suggest an answer. Counsel for the defense may voice objections to the testimony of witnesses, but the objections must be specific (i.e. hearsay, irrelevant, or immaterial evidence). If the judge sustains the objection, a new line of questioning is undertaken by the prosecutor, the jury is instructed to disregard the portion of the testimony in question, and it is stricken from the official record of the proceeding. If the objection is overruled, the state may continue the questioning. The defense attorney may take an exception to the judge's ruling, meaning that he thinks the judge erred and he wants to preserve a record of the ruling for purposes of a later appeal. In addition to testifying, witnesses are often asked to identify pictures, documents, or other physical evidence.

Cross-Examination

When the prosecuting attorney has concluded his direct examination of a witness, the defense attorney may then cross-examine the witness about any matter about which the witness testified in direct examination. The cross-examining attorney may ask leading questions in order to discredit the witness' testimony. Opposing counsel can object to some of the questions being posed to witness on the grounds that they are improper questions because they deal with facts not touched on in direct examination, or on the grounds previously discussed. Witnesses are not generally required to answer the same questions more than once.

Redirect Examination

When the opposing attorney has finished with the witness, the attorney who called the witness may, if he chooses, conduct redirect examination, which covers new matters brought up under cross-examination. It is a device used by an attorney to rehabilitate a witness whose testimony was weakened by cross-examination. When the prosecuting attorney has concluded his case, he will announce that the state rests.

Motion for Directed Verdict

When the state rests, the defense can, out of the jury's presence, demur to the state's case on the grounds that the charges against the defendant have not been proved. This is known as a motion for a directed verdict. The judge will either overrule the motion, in which case the trial goes on, or he will sustain the motion, releasing the defendant and ending the trial. Although the motion for a directed verdict is optional, the defense attorney almost always makes it, for he has nothing to lose and everything to gain by it.

Presentation of Defense Evidence

The defense attorney begins presenting evidence by calling witnesses, or he may elect to present no evidence if he believes that the state has not proved its case to the jury beyond a reasonable doubt. He may also present certain evidence, but not call the defendant as a witness. The defendant does not have to take the stand unless he wishes to, for he need not prove his innocence; the burden of proof is on the state. If the defense decides to present evidence, he does so in the same manner and under the same basic restrictions as the opposition. The state may cross-examine defense witnesses.

Rebuttal Evidence

When the defense rests his case, the state may present rebuttal witnesses or evidence to refute the defendant's case. If the defense has produced a so-called surprise witness—one that the state had not known would testify—rebuttal evidence is generally aimed at attacking the credibility of the witness. At the conclusion of the rebuttal evidence, the defense can present additional evidence to contradict it. At the conclusion of all the evidence, the defense, out of the jury's presence, may renew his motion for a directed verdict. If overruled, the trial proceeds.

Closing Arguments

Both sides are allowed to make closing arguments to the jury for the purpose of summarizing and placing their case in the best possible light. The prosecuting attorney, who proceeds first, will try to comment on the strength of his evidence. He may neither discuss evidence that was not presented nor make comment on the defendant's failure to testify, if that was the case. If he does, the defense can move for a mistrial and the trial will be terminated and set for retrial at a later date. When the prosecuting attorney has finished his closing argument, the defense will present argument in the defendant's behalf, summarizing the facts favorable to his client and pointing up what he considers to be defects in the state's case. Thereupon, the state makes the concluding argument, in which answers are directed at the defense attorney's closing argument. If the defense chooses not to make a closing argument, the state loses the right to the second argument.

Instructions to the Jury

Before the jury begins its deliberation, the judge gives it certain instructions concerning the law as it applies to the case. This is generally referred to as the judge's charge to the jury. Some states allow the attorneys to submit a list of suggested instructions to the judge who reviews it to determine which, if any, he will give to the jury. The attorneys may object to the judge's instructions in much the same way that they object to the presentation of evidence in the earlier stages of the trial. In giving the jury its instructions the judge (1) states the issues in the case, (2) defines legal terminology, (3) explains what verdicts the jury may reach, and (4) tells jurors that they are the sole judge of the facts and the credibility of witnesses. The judge's instructions to the jury are read in order to preclude reversible errors.

The Jury's Deliberations

After the jury is charged, it is taken to the jury room to begin deliberation. Generally its first act is to elect a foreman. The bailiff's assignment is to sit outside the jury room to see that no one enters or leaves. Most jurisdictions furnish jurors written verdict forms which contain all possible decisions that they can reach. Ordinarily, the verdict must be unanimous, and the verdict form must be signed by the foreman. If the jurors cannot agree on a verdict, the jury is termed a hung jury and the trial is over. The case will be retried before a new jury at a later date.

Juries in first-degree murder cases may choose from a variety of verdicts, each of which is contained on the following form, which was furnished by the state attorney of the Ninth Judicial Circuit of Florida. Each juror receives a copy.

FORMS OF VERDICT

If you find the defendant guilty of murder in the first degree, the form of your verdict will be:

"We, the jury, find the defendant, JOHN DOE, guilty of murder in the first degree, as charged in the indictment. So say we all."

In capital cases, where a jury convicts a defendant of murder in the first degree, a majority of their number may recommend him to the mercy of the Court, and such recommendation reduces the punishment from death to life imprisonment. In the event you find the defendant guilty of murder in the first degree and a majority of you recommend him to the mercy of the Court, the form of your verdict shall be:

"We, the jury, find the defendant, JOHN DOE, guilty of murder in the first degree, as charged in the indictment, and a majority of our number recommend mercy. So say we all."

If you find the defendant guilty of murder in the second degree, the form of your verdict shall be:

"We, the jury, find the defendant, JOHN DOE, guilty of murder in the second degree. So say we all."

If you find the defendant guilty of murder in the third degree, the form of your verdict shall be:

"We the jury, find the defendant, JOHN DOE, guilty of murder in the third degree. So say we all."

If you find the defendant guilty of manslaughter, the form of your verdict shall be:

"We, the jury, find the defendant, JOHN DOE, guilty of manslaughter. So say we all."

If you find the defendant not guilty, the form of your verdict will be:

"We, the jury, find the defendant, JOHN DOE, not guilty. So say we all."

The Verdict

If the jurors are able to reach a verdict they are returned to the courtroom where it is read or announced aloud in open court by either the foreman or the court clerk. After the verdict is read, the jurors may be polled individually to determine the validity of the verdict. When the verdict is accepted, the jury is dismissed and the trial is concluded.

The following is a sample of a jury verdict in a capital case:

IN THE CIRCUIT COURT OF THE NINTH
JUDICIAL CIRCUIT, IN AND FOR ORANGE
COUNTY, ORLANDO, FLORIDA

CASE NUMBER _____

STATE OF FLORIDA	:
Plaintiff	:
vs.	:
JOHN DOE	:
Defendant	:

VERDICT

We, the jury, find the defendant, JOHN DOE, Guilty of Murder in the First Degree, as charged in the indictment.

"So say we all."

Dated this _____ of May, 1971 _____

FOREMAN

Sentencing

If the defendant is convicted, the judge will set a date for sentencing. In most states the judge imposes the sentence; however, in some states the jury is delegated that responsibility. For serious crimes, such as murder, a few jurisdictions extend the trial process to include a penalty phase, in which the jury hears evidence presented on the issue of penalty. Four states employ administrative agencies, independent of the court, to fix prison terms. Regardless of who imposes the sentence, the time between the verdict and the sentence is generally devoted to a presentence investigation of the convicted man's background to determine what course of action should be taken regarding sentencing. The offender may, during this interim period, be committed temporarily to a medical diagnostic facility where psychiatric testing is conducted.

Appeal

The defense can appeal a conviction by filing a transcript of the record of the trial court with the appropriate appellate court. The prosecution may not appeal an acquittal. The most common grounds for appeal are errors in trial procedure and errors in substantive law. The appellant must also file his brief setting forth the reasons for his appeal and the law upon which he is seeking a reversal of the trial court. The appeals case may be set for an oral argument before the appellate court, but often appeals are submitted on the briefs, without argument. Not every error committed at the trial is a reversible error. Some are considered harmless errors (i.e. the right of a defendant to a fair trial was not jeopardized). Appellants may be released on bail pending their appeal if either the trial judge or an appellate judge allows it. An appeal may be taken all the way to the United States Supreme Court if a Constitutional question is involved.

THE JUVENILE COURT

Juvenile courts are tribunals that handle cases involving young people. Although the term "juvenile" is variously defined in the states, the courts generally designate the age of juveniles as under sixteen, seventeen or eighteen, although a few jurisdictions have set the age limit at twenty-one. Juvenile courts concern themselves with three types of cases: (1) delinquency, which is unlawful

(Courtesy of the National Council on Crime and Delinquency)

conduct, truancy from school, or unmanageability, (2) parental neglect, and (3) dependency, a term used to describe juveniles who, for a variety of reasons, have no natural parental support, or at least not enough to sustain them.

Juvenile courts are characterized by special procedures not found in criminal courts, and special terminologies are aimed at lessening the negative impact that is present in impersonal, rather cold, trial courts at other levels. According to the President's Commission on Law Enforcement and Administration of Justice:

> In short, children were not to be treated as criminals nor dealt with by the processes used for criminals. . .A new vocabulary symbolized the new order: petition instead of complaint, summons instead of warrant, initial hearing instead of trial, finding of involvement instead of conviction disposition instead of sentence.

Because of the informal nature of juvenile court hearings and the emphasis on protecting children, judges have been granted a good deal of authority over the child, authority which has not always been wielded wisely. Some civil libertarians, while agreeing

St. Louis Juvenile Court Building, completed in 1965, includes detention units, classrooms, kitchen, dining room, recreational facilities, and offices for the Court's 130 employes. *(Courtesy of the City of St. Louis, Office of the Mayor)*

STATE OF ILLINOIS
YOUTH COMMISSION

Order (Warrant) For Return Of Ward

To: ALL LAW ENFORCEMENT OFFICERS OR PEACE OFFICERS

_____ being a
(Name of ward)

ward and presently under the custody and guardianship of the YOUTH COMMISSION of the State of Illinois, and

it appearing to said YOUTH COMMISSION that said

_____ IYC Number_____
(Name of ward)

has_____
        (Violated his parole)   (escaped from institution)

_____ ;
        (Institution and location and approximate date)

NOW THEREFORE, the YOUTH COMMISSION of the State of Illinois does command you to forthwith take in cus-

tody and hold the said_____
                        (Name of ward)

to be returned to the said YOUTH COMMISSION of the State of Illinois by any duly authorized agent thereof.

YOUTH COMMISSION
of the
STATE OF ILLINOIS

_____
Chairman

By_____

Please notify:

_____

_____

_____

Telephone_____

A warrant commanding the police to take a juvenile into custody. *(Courtesy of the State of Illinois Youth Commission)*

with the original philosophy of juvenile courts, have become convinced that the very system that was founded to protect children actually violates their rights by failing to provide for basic Constitutional guarantees. Two recent Supreme Court decisions, made by the Warren Court, seem to agree with this contention. In *Kent* v. *United States,* the court, divided five to four, held that a juvenile court must conduct a hearing prior to the entry of a waiver order transferring jurisdiction to a criminal court. In re Gault the high court held that the juvenile code of the State of

Arizona deprived delinquents of the procedural safeguards guaranteed by the due process clause of the Fourteenth Amendment.

Reaction to these two landmark decisions has been mixed. Civil libertarians claim it is a victory for children and goes a long way toward extending to them the protection of due process of law. Others, however, sound portentious warnings that the juvenile system of justice, based on compassion, concern, and treatment, may be destroyed, to the everlasting detriment of America's children.

THE NEED FOR COURT REFORM

The absolute necessity for meaningful court reform is indisputable. In 1967 the President's Commission on Law Enforcement and Administration of Justice, in *Task Force Report: The Courts,* pointed up areas of judicial weakness and recommended reasonable—though comprehensive and expensive—solutions to the problems. Probably the most concise statement concerning the need for court reform was made by Chief Justice of the U. S. Supreme Court, Warren E. Burger, when he said that the American judicial machinery was facing an impending crisis due to "deferred maintenance." The consequences of this deferred maintenance are (1) those who are charged with crimes must suffer through unconscionable delays before they are finally brought to trial: (2) convicted persons are not punished promptly after conviction, and (3) those sentenced to confinement are not generally rehabilitated. The problem is caused primarily because the machinery is being asked to carry too heavy a workload, a problem not unique to this criminal justice component.

A key to criminal court reform is, surprisingly, civil court reform, for the entire judicial system is bogged down by clogged civil court calendars. If one is to take a systems approach to court reform, as experts have unanimously advised, then it is self-defeating to fragment reform efforts by attacking problems piecemeal as if they can be separated and isolated from the total machinery.

One of the most encouraging signs of impending court overhaul came March 11-14, 1971, in Williamsburg, Virginia, at the National Conference on the Judiciary—the first such conference ever held. In attendance were more than five hundred court administrators, attorneys, and judges, including a majority of chief justices from the state supreme courts; United States Attorney General John Mitchell; retired Supreme Court Justice Tom C. Clark, and Chief Justice Warren Burger. President Richard Nixon gave the opening address in which he stated, "Justice delayed is not only justice denied, it is also justice circumvented, justice mocked, and the system of justice undermined." The President also pledged the Federal Government to a vigorous court reform effort.

Some of the points discussed and acted upon at the conference included:

1. The formation of a national center to act as a clearinghouse for information and a service agency for state courts.
2. State adoption of the American Bar Association's Standards for Criminal Justice as a first move toward reform.
3. The appointment of state judges to long terms in office as an alternative to elections.
4. The selection of judicial discipline panels to remove unfit judges from office.
5. Mandatory retirement of judges at a certain age (70 was generally accepted).
6. Greater use of "paraprofessionals: in the law, especially "parajudges" to handle administrative matters.
7. The exploration of ways to quickly clear the courts of less serious "victimless" crimes (i.e. loitering, drunkenness, minor traffic cases).
8. An extension of the court executive officer concept, in which trained management personnel are hired to see that the resources of the court are administered efficiently.
9. An extension of the "rulemaking power" of state judges.
10. Increased use of technical advances, such as electronic information-retrieval systems.

Not one of the points made at the conference was new; however, with the weight of the President, The Attorney General, and the Supreme Court behind them, and with the resources of the Federal Government's Law Enforcement Assistance Administration being brought to bear, there is now hope that the dream of "equal justice under the law" can be made a reality.

Probation officer conducting a presentence investigation. *(Courtesy of the Florida Parole and Probation Commission)*

Chapter 16

PROBATION

HISTORICAL SUMMARY

Probation is the process whereby a man convicted of a crime is returned to society during a period of supervision rather than being committed to prison. The term "probation" comes from the Latin word *probare,* meaning to test or to prove. Although the concept of probation was both an English and an American creation, it is generally conceded that its father was John Augustus, a nineteenth-century Boston cobbler. In August, 1841, Augustus, while attending Boston's police court, decided to stand bail for a man who had been arrested for drunkenness. The court allowed it, and the accused was instructed to come back for sentencing in three weeks. Touched by Augustus' gesture, the defendant "took the pledge" and when he reported back to the court, the judge was so impressed by the obvious improvement in the man that he imposed a fine of one cent and court costs in lieu of the imprisonment that was traditional for that offense.[1]

Buoyed by this experience, Augustus began to stand bail for other defendants, at first only adult males charged with drunkenness, but later he extended his philanthropy to persons— men, women, and children—charged with a variety of offenses. The Boston cobbler, in these early days, developed several principles which are in effect to this day. He knew that he assumed a risk in each case, but he sought to minimize the risk factor by establishing certain guidelines:[2]

1. Efforts are confined mainly to first offenders.
2. Background investigations are conducted of each prospective probationer to determine the character of individuals under consideration.

[1]United Nations, Department of Social Affairs, *Probation and Related Measures* (New York: United Nations, 1951), pp. 29-31.

[2]*Ibid.,* pp. 29-42.

3. Individuals accepted as probationers are counseled to enter school or seek gainful employment.
4. Probationers are supervised and kept away from those influences which might adversely affect their rehabilitation.

John Augustus died but, owing mainly to his charitable work, the State of Massachusetts in 1878 passed the country's first probation law. The law provided for the appointment, by the Mayor of Boston, of a probation officer to perform the following duties.[3]

1. Attend court on a continuing basis.
2. Investigate cases of persons charged with or convicted of crimes.
3. Make recommendations to the court regarding the advisability of using probation.
4. Submit periodical reports to the Boston Chief of Police.
5. Visit probationers.
6. Render assistance and encouragement to probationers.

The first formal probation officer in the United States was the distinguished former police chief of Boston, *Edward H. Savage,* who was appointed following the passage of Massachusetts' law. Two years later, in 1880, the law was extended to apply to other communities in the state. In 1891 Massachusetts passed another law which required the extension of probation into the criminal courts.[4]

The concept of probation took on added scope and dimension when in 1899 Cook County, Illinois, created the juvenile court, thereby treating juveniles as a separate and distinct class of offenders for the first time. Although the idea of probation was slow to catch on—only five states had provided by statute for the new technique by 1900—the advent of the juvenile court system in America gave impetus to probation and within three decades all states except one had juvenile probation laws and all but thirteen had adult probation laws, a figure that was cut to five in 1950. By 1956 juvenile probation and adult probation were available in every state.

Over the years scholars on the subject have had widely differing perspectives on what probation was and what it ought to be. Some have viewed it as a basically humanitarian gesture, while others

[3]*Ibid.*

[4]Lewis Diana, "What is Probation?", *Journal of Criminal Law, Criminology, and Police Science* (Northwestern University School of Law, July-August 1960), pp. 189-190.

looked on it in a more pragmatic way. Following is a summary of six prominent historical definitions of probation:[5]

1. **As Legal Disposition Exclusively.** One viewpoint sees probation exclusively as a suspended sentence in which the offender, instead of going to jail, is allowed to remain in the community under supervision until his sentence has ended. In this context, probation was a policing procedure whereby the probationer was given another chance, but never allowed to forget that should he fail he would be summarily incarcerated. This theory, put forth primarily by attorneys and judges, was popular around the turn of the century.

2. **As a Measure of Leniency.** This view looks on probationers as people who have simply made a mistake and need another chance, rather than treatment. This definition represented a widely held lay belief that was in vogue during the 1920s and beyond.

3. **As Punishment.** Although this definition never had widespread support, some writers of the past half-century viewed probation as a punitive measure which allowed the probationer to escape confinement but made certain rigid demands on him which had to be faithfully and promptly fulfilled lest he be severely punished.

4. **As a Bureaucratic Process.** This idea defined probation as an administrative process in which certain systematic procedures were carried out—arranging medical treatment, administering tests, seeking employment—in the hope that the probationer would in some way be deterred from returning to crime. This process, popular during the first three decades of the century, was a negative one which believed—although not strongly—that if enough was done for a probationer, in some way he would be rehabilitated.

5. **As Social Casework Treatment.** This theory became popular after 1940. It had strong clinical overtones in which the resources of community service agencies were fully utilized and deep therapy—the process of changing attitudes—was relied on heavily. The probationer was induced to develop his latent abilities and to behave responsibly.

6. **As a Combination of Administration and Casework.** This view integrates the bureaucratic process and the casework method, emphasizing whichever approach is appropriate in specific cases. Probation, by this definition, is viewed as a simultaneous application of methods.

[5]*Ibid.*, pp. 191-204.

PROBATION TODAY

Today, although the system of probation varies from jurisdiction to jurisdiction, adult probation services are generally state functions, while juvenile probation tends to be a local function. There also exists a Federal probation component to service the Federal courts. Two agencies are thought to be the proper bodies to control probation work: the courts and independent county or state administrative entities. In many states and communities probation officers can be appointed only by the court.[6] Probation officers, regardless of the placement and structure of their agency, are considered an extension of court services. The question of whether an individual is eligible for probation usually lies with the court; however, in some instances the court may face statutory limitations in selecting cases for probation. Some serious offenses, such as violent crimes, crimes against morals, or crimes involving the use of deadly weapons, may specify by law that guilty persons are not eligible for probation.

There is and always will be a risk factor in probation work. Contemporary probation officers have undertaken to lessen that risk by establishing systematic procedures for the selection of probationers. Furthermore, certain "conditions" to probation are stipulated so that the probationer has rather firm guidelines regarding what he can and cannot do and what will cause his probation to be revoked. Jail terms are often routinely imposed as a "condition" to probation, as is financial reimbursement to victims of crimes.

PRESENTENCE INVESTIGATIONS AND SUPERVISION

The primary duties of probation officers are presentence investigations and supervision. Presentence investigation is ordinarily initiated, upon a judge's command, after the defendant in a case has been convicted. Probation will not succeed unless the presentence investigation report reflects an accurate view of the offender. The presentence investigation report is an essential aid in the selection process of probationers, although that is not its only purpose. The report, in fact, performs five functions: (1) aids the

[6]Edwin H. Sutherland and Donald R. Cressey, *Principles of Criminology,* 6th ed. (New York: J. B. Lippincott Co., 1960), p. 425.

court in determining an appropriate sentence, (2) assists penal institutions in classifying prisoners, (3) furnishes parole boards with information pertinent to its consideration of parole, (4) aids the probation officer in his rehabilitation efforts during probation supervision, and (5) serves as a source of research data.[7] The primary purpose of the report is to focus light on the offender's personality and character. The probation officer's task is to gather pertinent information on the subject, evaluate, assimilate, and interpret the data, and reduce it to a logically organized, readable, objective report.[8]

The weakest point in the probation process is probably supervision because of oversized caseloads and governmental austerity programs which preclude the hiring of more manpower, a problem not unknown to other components in the criminal justice system. After an offender has been granted probationary status, he is assigned to a probation officer for supervision. Some years ago the concept of an "average caseload" was stated. Fifty was the recommended number of probationers to be assigned to one officer. However, during the past decade there has been a movement away from doctrinaire principles regarding caseload assignment. Studies are now underway to determine what caseloads are appropriate in selected circumstances. Three general systems of probation assignment are used: by district; by sex, race, and religion, and by problems.[9] A probationer is required to report to his probation officer at regular intervals. Often these reports are made weekly or twice monthly, but they may be monthly or even daily, in selected cases. Contacts are generally made in the office of the probation officer or in the home of the probationer. The latter place is considered the more desirable location because it allows the officer to view first-hand the most crucial facet of the individual's environment. Occasionally the probation officer may choose another location for the visit.

It is the probation officer's job to see that his charge lives up to

[7]Division of Probation, Administrative Office of the United States Courts, *The Presentence Investigation Report* (Washington: U. S. Government Printing Office), pp. 1-5.

[8]*Ibid.*

[9]*Supra* note 6, p. 430.

the conditions of his probation. The officer tries to provide personal assistance and guidance where appropriate. Accordingly, the probation officer may employ four central techniques:[10]

1. **Manipulative Techniques.** The environment may be physically manipulated in the interest of the probationer. For example, financial assistance may be provided, or an employer may be persuaded to hire or rehire him. In any event, something tangible will be received by the individual.
2. **Executive Techniques.** The officer may refer the individual to another social service agency—either public or private—to make use of services unavailable in the probation department (i.e. Legal Aid Society, drug rehabilitation clinic, welfare department).
3. **Guidance Techniques.** The probation officer may give personal advice on problems not requiring complicated psychological counseling. The advice will probably center around an economic problem, such as a financial issue, or a relatively simple marital dispute.
4. **Counseling Techniques.** Counseling, in this context, is an extremely complex endeavor which demands a good deal of skill on the part of the officer. It has a psychological orientation and is aimed at working toward the solution of deep-seated emotional problems.

ADVANTAGES OF PROBATION

There appears to be widespread public distrust of the probation system, caused in large measure by a general lack of knowledge of its limitations. Citizen fear of violent crimes, much of it being committed by repeaters, has led to a wholesale loss of confidence in the courts, especially that component which appears to be turning criminals loose to ravage society. But with all its faults—some human, some administrative—probation can work to lower the crime rate and return an offender to a useful and productive life. Briefly, some of the advantages of probation are as follows:[11]

1. It affords an individual not considered a danger to society another chance.

[10]David Dressler, *Practice and Theory in Probation and Parole* (New York: Columbia University Press, 1959), pp. 151-152.

[11]Harry Elmer Barnes and Negley K. Teeters, *New Horizons in Criminology,* 3rd ed. (Englewood Cliffs, New Jersey: Prentice-Hall, Inc., 1959), pp. 556-557.

2. It allows an individual to continue life habits that meet the approval of society (work, school, family obligations, etc.).
3. It averts the erasable stigma of a prison term.
4. It is financially less expensive than institutional confinement.
5. It allows the probation officer to use community rehabilitation facilities not available to institutionalized offenders.

SOME BASIC PROBLEMS

To paint a completely rosy picture of probation is to do a disservice to students, for although the concept is sound, the application of it does not always meet the standards necessary for consistent success. Even the most enthusiastic advocates of the system admit that some probation departments have been badly administered. Some years ago the American Bar Association conducted a comprehensive survey of the probation systems in selected Western and Midwestern states. Although the survey is somewhat dated, its findings point out dilemmas encountered by communities to this day. A number of basic problems were uncovered by the survey, including the following eleven:[12]

1. Probation was granted without sufficient knowledge of the defendant and his background.
2. Presentence reports lacked objectivity.
3. Presentence reports were not treated as confidential information.
4. Determination of sentences was sometimes made a public spectacle.
5. Probation was used as a device to induce defendants to plead guilty, or to alleviate crowded conditions in prisons.
6. Probation was used as a device to collect money to reimburse complaining witnesses.
7. The cost of probation was charged to defendants.
8. Probation officers played a dwindling role, sometimes relegated to a position similar to that of prison guard.
9. Supervision was neglected.
10. There was a tendency to overlook the law enforcement role of the probation officer.
11. There was an appalling lack of reliable statistics to evaluate probation's overall effectiveness.

[12]Sanford Bates, "When Is Probation Not Probation?" *Federal Probation,* Dec., 1960, pp. 15-20.

CAREER ORIENTATION

The strongest part of the American probation system is personnel. Probation is one of the most professional criminal justice components; this is due mainly to the competent, energetic, and dedicated people who have been attracted to it as a career. The job is fraught with frustrations and heartbreaks, but the rewards are great for a young man or woman desirous of pursuing a career in the service of others. Although the qualifications of probation officers may vary in each community, it would behoove prospective applicants to adhere to the standards set by the American Correctional Association for probation officers, supervisory personnel, and chief probation officers.

Probation Officer

The preferred qualifications are a baccalaureate degree with two full years of graduate study in an accredited school of social work or comparable studies in criminology, psychology, sociology, or a related field in the social sciences. The minimum requirements are graduation from an accredited college or university with a major in the social or behavioral sciences or one of the following: one year of graduate study in social work or a related field, or one year of professional full-time paid social work experience in a recognized agency. Some agencies employ trainees. Trainees need only possess a degree from an accredited four-year institution with a major in the social or behavioral sciences. All applicants, trainees included, must display emotional maturity, integrity, the ability to establish constructive interpersonal relationships, a genuine interest in helping people, intellectual ability, mature judgment, and a continuing interest in professional development.

Supervisory Personnel

It is recommended that supervisory personnel possess the same preferred educational standards as probation officers—two years of acceptable graduate study, plus three years of continuous full-time supervised experience in a recognized agency. Personal qualities should be the same as for probation officers, but candidates for supervisory positions should demonstrate an ability to teach, to develop social work skills in an authoritative setting, and to interpret agency policies and procedures to staff; administrative and organizational abilities; the ability to speak and write effectively, and the ability to establish and maintain effective working relationships.

Chief Probation Officer

Chief probation officers are expected to have earned an advanced degree in the behavioral sciences, or a master's degree in social work, and a minimum of three years' successful supervisory experience. Personal qualities should include a demonstrated ability to plan, organize, and direct; the ability to interpret programs of the agency to the public, and the ability to work with related agencies. In addition he or she must possess those qualities of leadership demanded of command personnel in other agencies, both public and private.

Historic Walnut Street Jail, Philadelphia.

Chapter 17

CORRECTIONAL INSTITUTIONS AND JAILS

In the United States today there are more than 15,000 detention facilities.[1] Responsibility for administering these institutions is divided not only among levels of government but within single jurisdictions. A county which contains ten municipalities may very well contain ten separate and distinct detention facilities—or more. And each institution will probably operate independently of the others. Correctional institutions and jails in this country are, to say the least, fragmented. To understand this massive contemporary correctional system it will do well to review certain historical highlights.

HISTORICAL SUMMARY

While the concept of detention facilities can be traced back to Mesopotamia and ancient Egypt, widespread use of extended imprisonment as a form of punishment did not develop until the late eighteenth century. Early social philosophy generally held that punishment for a crime should be administered promptly— and with enthusiasm. Long-term confinement was considered neither swift nor severe enough to retaliate for a person's transgressions, so prisons had little place in ancient societies. Torture, public embarrassment, corporal punishment, mutilation, and execution were the devices that most communities used to punish wrongdoers. A system of *gaols* (jails) was developed in medieval England, but these facilities were simply cellars and gatehouses that had been pressed into service to store individuals awaiting punishment or execution. The gaols, maintained by private keepers rather than by official law enforcement personnel or magistrates, were "operated at a profit by charging inmates fees

[1]The President's Commission on Law Enforcement and Administration of Justice, *Task Force Report: Corrections* (Washington: U. S. Government Printing Office, 1967), pp. 4, 79.

for admission and discharge.[2] If a prisoner possessed coin of the realm in sufficient quantity, he could pay to have his chains removed, purchase the services of a prostitute, buy liquor and a soft bed, and make his life in gaol, if not pleasant, then at least tolerable. From the sixteenth century until the latter half of the eighteenth century in England, prisoners were stored anywhere that space was available. Many simply awaited transportation to the New World where they were sold into slavery or indentured servitude. Favorite "temporary expedients" for the detention of prisoners were the hulks of derelict ships on the Thames in London. The age of exploration also led to the idea of penal colonies, and Gibralter and Sidney, Australia, were pressed into service for that grim purpose.

In colonial and post-Revolutionary America some significant modifications in the idea and philosophy of confinement occurred. These changes, like so many other American social innovations, were motivated by deep religious beliefs and by an abiding faith that all men were children of God and deserving of help—whether they wanted it or not. In 1762 William Penn restricted the death penalty to murder alone. A system of fines and incarceration was stipulated for lesser offenses, thus creating a need for long-term detention facilities. In 1787 the Quakers achieved a milestone in correctional history by founding the Philadelphia Society for Alleviating the Miseries of Public Prisons, a humanitarian organization dedicated to the very purpose that its name implied. That same year the Society converted Philadelphia's squalid Walnut Street Jail into America's first penitentiary.[3] A panel of supervisors was placed in charge of the jail, and prisoners—except those who were considered dangerous—were allowed to do manual labor—carpentry, weaving, shoemaking. In fact, the sentences of many prisoners stipulated toil of some description. Prisoners were paid a wage comparable to that earned by honest citizens, out of which they had to pay room, board, court costs, and fines. Religious services were held periodically, and in the Quaker tradition, the guards carried no weapons.

By the turn of the century control of the Walnut Street Jail had

---

[2]Elmer Hubert Johnson, *Crime, Correction, and Society* (Homewood, Illinois: The Dorsey Press, 1968), pp. 477-479.

[3]*Ibid.,* p. 482.

been wrested from the Quakers by city officials, who soon encountered penological problems not uncommon to contemporary correctional institutions: extreme overcrowding, riot, and a cessation of industrial activity due to cramped quarters and lack of funds and materials. During the first decade of the nineteenth century the Quakers began campaigning vigorously for an end to prison labor and a system of solitary confinement, again an idea based on their religious philosophy.[4] The Quakers asserted that a man should be truly penitent for his sins, so it was only appropriate that offenders be isolated where they could reflect on their misdeeds and achieve a moral regeneration. In 1818 Pennsylvania passed a law modeled after the Quaker idea of solitary confinement. The Western Penitentiary of Pittsburgh was constructed in 1827 and the idea was operationalized. In 1829 the Eastern Penitentiary was built in Cherry Hill. Although the Western Penitentiary was demolished in 1833, the Eastern Penitentiary survived and perpetuated the concept of solitary confinement.[5]

In the meantime, another notion, totally incompatible with Quaker beliefs, was beginning to surface, this time in New York's

Western State Penitentiary at Pittsburgh, constructed in 1827. *(Courtesy of the Charles M. Unkovic Collection)*

[4]*Ibid.*, p. 483.

[5]*Ibid.*

Auburn Prison. Auburn Prison had been opened in 1819 under the Quaker plan of solitary confinement. Within a decade, however, penal reformers in New York began to take a more secular view of confinement and a congregate system was developed in which prisoners were allowed to work together, silently, but were separated and locked in individual cells at night. Strict discipline was maintained through floggings. A raging controversy erupted over the merits of the Pennsylvania and Auburn systems, and studies were undertaken by penal experts to determine which was preferable.[6] An interesting survey of both prisons indicated that although the inmates at Auburn Prison were treated brutally, their morale was infinitely higher than that of their counterparts at Eastern Penitentiary, thereby pointing up the importance of physical labor in the prisoners' daily routine. Auburn Prison was run by the infamous warden Elam Lynds. Lynds firmly believed that in order to reform a prisoner you first had to break his spirit, a task which the warden undertook with relish. Lynds felt that, as warden, he had *carte blanche* to do with his charges what he felt was appropriate.

The architectural design of Auburn Prison was unique. The designers of the institution used "inside-cell architecture." Narrow rows of multitiered cells ran the length of a cell block. Cells were completely indoors, sheltered from light and all but impervious to the elements, including fresh air. Cells were small—seven feet long and three and one-half feet wide—and the dampness of the place often led to widespread sickness. When the prisoners moved from place to place in a body, they employed the "lock step" which is a single- or double-file formation of inmates walking in a slow motion shuffle with each man's hand placed on the shoulder of the person in front of him. Under no circumstances was conversation tolerated.[7]

The "Auburn system" became the model for other prisons for decades. Ten states in rapid succession followed New York's lead. By the middle of the nineteenth century America, for good or ill, had a true penal system. When in 1866 overcrowded conditions

[6]Harry Elmer Barnes and Negley K. Teeters, *New Horizons in Criminology,* 3rd edition (Englewood Cliffs, New Jersey: Prentice Hall, Inc., 1959), pp. 339-340.

[7]*Ibid.,* pp. 340-341.

forced Eastern Pennsylvania Penitentiary to move two men into each cell, the solitary confinement system in the United States came to an end.

During the decade following the Civil War, brutal conditions in prisons brought on a virtual flood of humanitarian concern. State boards of charities were organized in a dozen states to inquire into crime, poverty, insanity, and the conditions in penal institutions.

In 1877 Zebulon Brockway, a new breed penal reformer who had organized the Detroit House of Corrections' strong industrial program during the preceding decade, was assigned as superintendent of New York's Elmira Reformatory. The reformatory was the culmination of years of effort on the part of the progressive New York Prison Association. Located on farm land in upstate New York, the institution limited commitments to first-felony offenders from sixteen to thirty-one years of age. Brockway set up a three-step grading system for inmates. Upon commitment each prisoner was assigned automatically to the intermediate grade. Within six months, through good conduct and satisfactory performance at work, he could attain grade two. Six months of good conduct in this grade made prisoners eligible for the most sought prize—parole. Just as good conduct meant rewards, bad conduct could cause a prisoner to lose honor points and drop to a lower grade. Brockway provided industrial training, but the emphasis of his training program was on academic subjects and religion. Professionals from the community—professors, attorneys, bookkeepers, clergymen, doctors—came to the prison to teach inmates. A trade school was created and instruction was offered in plumbing, carpentry, telegraphy, and printing. Mornings in the prison were devoted to exercise, military drill, and schooling, while the afternoons were reserved for work. By the turn of the century the reformatory idea had caught on and a score of like institutions were developed in other communities. The reformatory concept never lived up to its expectations though, as the personnel who staffed the prisons were generally incompetent and either unwilling or unable to make the system work.

By the 1920s prisons had again (with some exceptions) become storing houses for unwanted humanity. In 1923 the Federal Government had in its employ one Inspector of Prisons. In what may be a bit of an overstatement the Inspector, Joseph F. Fishman, wrote a book in which he defined "jail" as:[8]

> An unbelievably filthy institution in which are confined men and women serving sentence for misdemeanors and crimes, and men and women not under sentence who are simply awaiting trial. With few exceptions, having no segregation of the unconvicted from the convicted, the well from the diseased, the youngest and most impressionable from the most degraded and hardened. Usually swarming with bedbugs, roaches, lice, and other vermin; has an odor of disinfectant and filth which is appalling; supports in complete idleness countless thousands of able-bodied men and women, and generally affords ample time and opportunity to assure inmates a complete course in every kind of viciousness and crime. A melting pot in which the worst elements of the raw material in the criminal world are brought forth, blended and turned out in absolute perfection.

On May 14, 1930, Congress created the Federal Bureau of Prisons. The Bureau has been a positive force in prison reform, aiding institutions and administrators at all levels of government.

During the New Deal the Works Progress Administration (WPA) constructed new prisons from one end of the country to the other. But only a slight improvement resulted; for what was needed, even more than structures, were innovative programs and highly trained, competent, well-paid personnel to staff the institutions. Austin MacCormick, a giant figure in corrections, constantly bemoaned the Government's practice of spending millions on physical facilities, and only a pittance on programs and personnel.

TYPES OF CONFINEMENT INSTITUTIONS

The term "correctional institution" is often used automatically by laymen to describe facilities where prisoners are confined. In most cases, however, detention facilities are not correctional facilities, for the overwhelming number of penal institutions in this country are short-term holding facilities where virtually no rehabilitative work is undertaken. Institutions are generally classified by the clientele they serve (i.e. juvenile institutions, misdemeanant facilities, women's prisons, male adult felony institutions); or by their security (i.e. minimum, medium, and maximum). Yet these, or any other "pat" classifications, give one a muddled view of the vast field. Likewise, to survey institutions by level of government fails to give students a clear-cut view of the

---

[8]Joseph F. Fishman, *Crucibles of Crime* (Montclair, New Jersey: Patterson Smith Publishing Corp. Originally published in 1923, reprinted in 1969), pp. 13-14.

system or, more correctly, the nonsystem. Accordingly, for the purpose of a more comprehensive overview, this discussion will center around five general types of confinement institutions: (1) lockups and city jails, (2) county jails, (3) juvenile institutions, (4) state prisons, and (5) Federal prisons.

Lockups and City Jails

Lockups are the most numerous type of confinement institution. They are almost always located in police stations or in precinct houses where they are used for holding persons for short periods of time. Arrested persons, regardless of their status (misdemeanant, felon, traffic violator, etc.), may be confined in lockups because they cannot post bail, to await transportation to a more appropriate facility, to sleep off a drunk, or to wait for morning court. Lockups rarely are staffed by trained personnel. Policemen or administrative employes keep a watchful eye on prisoners and provide meals, but little else. No rehabilitative programs are available; exercise is all but impossible, and only the barest sanitary facilities exist. Most lockups have fewer than seven cells, each containing sparse furniture—two wall beds, a chair, recessed lighting, and maybe a table. Under extraordinary

One small city's lockup. *(Courtesy of the Altamonte Springs, Florida, Police Department)*

Cell block in a city jail. *(Courtesy of the Fort Lauderdale Police Department)*

The booking desk in a municipal jail. *(Courtesy of the Wallace N. LaPeters Collection)*

conditions, or when mass arrests have been made, prisoners may be forced to sleep on mattresses on the floor. Many towns look on lockups as an evil made necessary by the unavailability of a centrally located confinement facility. Small town officers and patrolmen in big city precincts cannot tie themselves up for inordinate periods of time transporting prisoners, so the lockup provides a convenient alternative. Lockups have very low priority at budget time, and their physical appearance and staffing reflect that fact. Some officials have proposed to eliminate lockups by creating state operated regional jails staffed by professional personnel; however, there has been widespread resistence to the idea for a number of reasons, not the least of which is politics.

County Jails

The county jail is America's oldest type of confinement institution. It is generally under the control of the county sheriff, who will staff it with deputies or civilian custodial personnel. County jails serve three entirely different functions: (1) lockups for persons arrested by the sheriff's department, (2) confinement facilities for people convicted of misdemeanors and some classes of felonies (those who have been sentenced to less than one year in jail), and (3) detention facilities for defendants awaiting trial but who are unable to or are restrained from posting bail.[9] Many counties have created satellite facilities, such as inmate-operated farms, to supplement their main jail. Although some county jails and prison farms have instituted meaningful rehabilitation programs, they are few and far between. Most treatment programs are aimed at revolving-door alcoholics.

Juvenile Institutions

Juvenile institutions have a long history of protecting and treating children; consequently, many contemporary institutions emphasize rehabilitation through vocational training and academic education. But in some jurisdictions juveniles are still confined in city or county jails, although there appears to be some movement away from this practice. The mere fact that a community estab-

[9]Edwin H. Sutherland and Donald R. Cressey, *Principles of Criminology,* 6th ed. (New York; J. B. Lippincott Co., 1960), p. 363.

lishes a juvenile detention facility does not necessarily mean that youngsters will be treated much differently from the way they were in adult facilities. Some juvenile facilities, while physically

Inmates installing air-conditioning equipment during a sheet metal class at a vocational institution. *(Courtesy of the State of California Department of Corrections)*

more attractive than jails, do little more than hold children for specified periods of time. Yet, there is a significant amount of rehabilitative work going on in juvenile institutions, be they juvenile halls, detention homes, or training schools. Unlike laws pertaining to adult offenders, statutes that apply to juveniles permit children to be taken into custody for their protection. Therefore, two distinct types of confinement may be employed by the courts: (1) *detention,* for delinquent children and (2) *shelter,* for dependent children.

State Prisons

Each state maintains a prison system where felony offenders—adult men and women—are confined for a period of not less than one year (except under extraordinary circumstances). Some institutions also hold misdemeanants, but very few. By and large, state prisons confine individuals who the court believes are a danger to society. There is a great divergence in programs from state to state, and although the emphasis is on treatment; budgetary restraints, shortages of trained personnel, and public and legislative apathy have made the job of rehabilitating offenders a tough one indeed for the many dedicated correctional administrators. State institutions have consistently been plagued by collective inmate violence—prison riots—pointing up the frustration and helplessness that exists behind the familiar grey walls.

Federal Prisons

Federal prisons house some 25,000 convicted violators of Federal laws. Federal prisons have a reputation for being the toughest institutions in the country, a reputation not entirely unearned because of their functions during the gangster era in which hardened gangsters were incarcerated when no other prisons could hold them. Today, the "Alcatraz image" (Alcatraz has now been closed) of maximum security, hardline custodial practices, grim-faced guards, and solitary confinement is passing. In fact, the Federal system is now generally considered the most effective and the most diversified correctional system in America. It is, of course, a highly centralized operation. The Federal prison system employs a number of different institutions, including (1) maximum security penitentiaries, (2) medium security penitentiaries, (3) reformatories for inexperienced offenders, (4) correctional institutions for short-term offenders, and (5) honor camps. In addition, prerelease guidance centers and a medical facility are maintained.[10]

BASIC FUNCTIONS OF CONTEMPORARY CORRECTIONAL INSTITUTIONS

The philosophy of corrections has evolved into one that recognizes the need for punitive restrictions but sees as an absolute necessity the need for individual rehabilitation. In this context extreme punishment is neither a means nor an end. Penological thinking now stresses constructive treatment programs within an environment characterized by humane restraint. Of course, philosophies are not always easily translated into workable programs, but there is more hope now than ever before that correctional institutions can be transformed into bridges to the community—one-way bridges. American correction institutions now perform three basic functions: protection, punishment, and rehabilitation.[11]

The Protective Function

Insuring the safety and security of society is a major function of correctional institutions. If a man who is convicted of a crime presents a clear and present danger to his fellow citizens, then regardless of humanitarian concern over his plight, society's welfare comes first and the offender should be incarcerated. While the ultimate aim of the corrections process may be to return a useful individual to a productive life in society, the system's immediate aim is to protect the community from dangerous individuals, and it must fulfill this function if it hopes to have any long-range success.

The Punitive Function

The punitive function will always be a part of correctional institutions, for it is built into the system. To be in prison against

[10]Delmar Karlen, *Anglo-American Criminal Justice* (New York: Oxford University Press, 1967), p. 79.

[11]Martin R. Haskell and Lewis Yablonsky, *Crime and Delinquency* (Chicago: Rand McNally and Co., 1970), pp. 392-393.

one's will, regardless of how pleasant the enviornment, is punishment. And while the idea of punishment as a deterrent to crime is open to discussion, the general public appears to be demanding punishment for certain classes of criminals, so the punitive function will continue to play a major role in the system, at least until society rejects retaliation as a necessary element of corrections.

The Rehabilitative Function

The trend in the corrections field is toward individual or group therapy aimed at rehabilitation. There are indications, though, that the public views with suspicion programs which stress treatment. This view may be based partly on religious orientations which emphasize "an eye for an eye" philosophy, and partly on a lack of information on what the programs are and what they can and cannot do. Whether or not a majority of citizens are hostile to treatment programs, there is a growing body of evidence that suggests that the rehabilitative function of corrections offers one of the best methods of lowering the country's spiraling crime rate.

CLASSIFICATION OF OFFENDERS

There is, and has always been, a need to develop a reliable and accurate system of classifying offenders. Dozens of classification systems and nonsystems now exist, some of which fail to take into consideration anything but the basic characteristics of inmates. Years ago classification was undertaken in order to determine which prisoners should be segregated, disciplined, or closely watched. Today, classification of offenders is necessary for an entirely different reason: to "individualize" the inmate so that proper rehabilitative methods may be employed. It is essential that inmates be classified upon commitment in correctional institutions; however, it may even be desirable, under certain circumstances, to classify offenders before they are incarcerated (i.e. while on or being considered for probation). The National Institute of Mental Health has proposed a preliminary typology that was endorsed by the President's Commission on Law Enforcement and Administration of Justice. Following is a preliminary grouping of major types of offenders.[12]

[12]Reprinted from *Task Force Report: Corrections*, pp. 21-22.

A classification hearing in which a prisoner *(back to camera)* is interviewed by a sociologist, a psychiatrist, the director of prisoner education, a vocational counselor, a diagnostician, and the head of social services. *(Courtesy of the Charles M. Unkovic Collection)*

The Prosocial Offender

Most offenders of this type are viewed as "normal" individuals, identifying with legitimate values and rejecting the norms of delinquent subcultures. Their offenses usually grow out of extraordinary pressures. They are most frequently convicted of crimes of violence, such as homicide or assault, or naively executed property crimes, such as forgery. Some prosocial offenders, while attached to the legitimate system, may exhibit various neurotic manifestations. They are referred to in the descriptive typologies as "intimidated," "disturbed," "overinhibited," "anxious," "depressed," or "withdrawn." Many of these offenders, it seems agreed, really need no rehabilitative treatment at all. The problem with some of them is to get them out of the correctional cycle before they are harmed by contact with other offenders. For example, one study of prosocial offenders in a reformatory setting found that the lowest recidivism rates occurred among the members of this type who served the briefest possible sentences and who were isolated and not involved in therapy programs. By contrast, those who stayed longer and took part in treatment programs—i.e. participated actively with other inmates—did less well.

The Antisocial Offender

This type of offender identifies with a delinquent subculture, if he resides in an area which has a subculture, or exhibits a generally delinquent orientation by rejecting conventional norms and values. He is usually described as primitive, underinhibited, impulsive, hostile, negativistic, or alienated. It is generally agreed that he does not see himself as delinquent or criminal but rather as a victim of an unreasonable and hostile world. His history often includes patterns of family helplessness, indifference, or inability to meet needs of children, absence of adequate adult-role models, truancy in school, and inadequate performance in most social speheres. The antisocial offender, it is agreed in many of the typologies, should be provided an environment with clear, consistent social demands but one in which concern for his welfare and interests is regularly communicated to him. Methods of group treatment are recommended in order to increase the offender's social insight and skill. In the last analysis, however, the offender's value system must be changed. The attempt to get him to identify with a strong and adequate adult-role model is an important part of most treatment programs designed for this group.

The Pseudosocial Manipulator

This type of offender is described as not having adopted conventional standards, as being guilt-free, self-satisfied, power-oriented, nontrusting, emotionally insulated, and cynical. Personal histories reveal distrustful and angry families in which members are involved in competitive and mutually exploitative patterns of interaction, parents who feel deprived and who expect the children to meet their dependency needs, parental overindulgence alternating with frustration and inconsistent patterns of affection and rejection. Many and diverse recommendations are made for handling this type. Some investigators recommend long-term psychotherapy. Others encourage the offender to redirect his manipulative skills in a socially acceptable manner. Still others call for the establishment of a group setting in which the offender's capacity for playing contradictory roles is immediately discovered; he is confronted with evidence of his inconsistent conduct and is forced to choose among the alternatives. In general, the investigators give a rather discouraging picture of prospects for successful treatment.

The Asocial Offender

Another type of offender is one who acts out his primitive impulses, is extremely hostile, insecure, and negativistic, and demands immediate gratification. An important characteristic is his incapacity to identify with others. This distinguishes the asocial from the antisocial type who, although committed to delinquent values, is often described as being loyal to peers, proud, and capable of identifying with others. The asocial offender requires elementary training in human relations. The most striking characteristic of this group is an inability to relate to a therapist or to the social world around them. Most investigators recommend a simple social setting offering support, patience, and acceptance of the offender, with only minimum demands on his extremely limited skills and adaptability. Before pressures toward conformity can be exerted, the asocial offender needs to learn that human interaction is always a two-way process. Methods need to be used which reduce the offender's fear of rejection and abandonment. When these fundamentals have been learned, he is probably ready for more conventional therapy in both group and individual settings.

TREATMENT OF OFFENDERS

A variety of treatment methods are employed by corrections personnel trying to restore inmates back to society. The amount and kinds of treatment used will depend on the individual subject, but sociological, psychological, economic, and medical techniques may all be employed in an individual or group setting. It must be said that prison is not a desirable place to obtain positive results— most experts prefer community-based treatment programs—but the people most in need of therapy are often in prison, so many programs must surmount a negative physical environment in order to be successful. Treatment services in a correctional institution may be of three general types: (1) clinical services, (2) religious programs, and (3) educational and vocational programs.

Clinical Services

The success or failure of an inmate's rehabilitative program often depends on his physical and emotional well-being. A

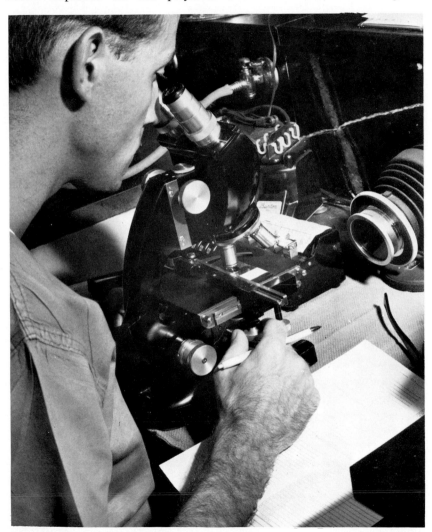

Innovative correctional institutions have comprehensive hospitals and laboratories to meet the health needs of inmates and to offer vocational training to prisoners interested in a medical career. *(Courtesy of the State of California Department of Corrections)*

comprehensive physical and psychological examination must be given to each prisoner as soon as possible after his admittance to prison. It is not rare to find that an individual's whole outlook on life can be changed by eliminating a congenital anomaly or an acquired physical infirmity (e.g. a limp, scars, a speech impediment, bad teeth). Trained medical personnel can detect physical problems, treat them, and improve a man's chances for successful rehabilitation. Clinicians also identify psychological problems and prescribe appropriate psychotherapy. In psychotherapy, whether it is individual or group therapy or counseling, the offender plays the major role. Communications must be established with him and he should share in the planning of his program. He must want to be helped before real progress can be made. Unfortunately, trained clinicians are in short supply in prisons, and the inmate population, and society, are worse off because of it.

Religious Programs

The influence of religion on an offender cannot be overlooked as a rehabilitative measure. An adequate chaplaincy staff can have a positive impact on the inmate population by administering to the spiritual needs of prisoners, by assisting clinicians, by involving themselves in needed counseling services, and by making contacts in the community for prospective parolees. Most correctional institutions are legally required to have two chaplains: one a Protestant and one a Catholic. Visiting chaplains from other faiths insure that the religious needs of all inmates will be served. Terms in prison leave inmates with a good deal of time to reflect on their past and future, and the role of the clergy in giving guidance and direction can be a critically important one.

Educational and Vocational Programs

Many inmates lack formal education and even the most basic skills necessary for gainful employment. Although vocational training programs have been employed in correctional institutions for years, a good deal of criticism has been leveled at prisons that teach inmates trades they cannot use in the community. During the past decade, research has been undertaken to determine what vocational training programs should be established in institutions desirous of providing inmates with usable trades. Most would

Prisoners in class. *(Courtesy of the Charles M. Unkovic Collection)*

agree that although shoemaking may hold an inmate's interest, the market for professional shoemakers outside of prison is limited. Some of the most exciting contemporary institutional programs are in the field of education. Now, in many prisons inmates can earn not only a high school diploma but also credits toward a college degree, an immensely important innovation.

THE COLLABORATIVE INSTITUTION

Traditional correctional institutions were characterized by an authoritative regime that ruled by fiat, brutal inmate subcultures, kangaroo courts, and mutual hostility and suspicion between staff members and prisoners. During the past few decades, however, the traditional prison has undergone significant modifications and a more democratic institution is emerging, a collaborative institution which "is structured around the partnership of all inmates and staff members in the process of rehabilitation.."[13]

[13]*Supra* note 2, p. 47.

Simply stated, the collaborative institution seeks to create a community atmosphere by employing methods aimed at bringing people together. The collaborative institution attempts to reduce mass treatment and depersonalization. For example, changes are made in dining procedures. Prisoners are allowed to talk during meals. They are not marched in long lines to the dining hall. Four-man restaurant tables are utilized. Some institutions have replaced the traditional cells with individual housing units that provide prisoners with privacy.

Another feature of the collaborative institutions is increased communication with inmates. Group counseling sessions are held at regular intervals to encourage inmates to frankly express their feelings on the issues that affect them. All suggestions made by inmates are considered by the staff before a decision is made to accept or reject them. In any case, the inmate is notified of the final disposition of his suggestion.

Probably the most important aspect of the collaborative institution is its policy of shared decision-making. Inmate advisory committees are established for the purpose of organizing inmate recreational activities, scheduling cultural programs, and advising on inmate-related problems connected with prison management. The committees may perform an ombudsman function, although on a sharply limited basis. Some committees are staffed jointly by inmates and staff members.

CONCLUSION

The most difficult criminal justice component to reform is probably that which confines the nation's criminals: lockups, jails, and correctional institutions. It is the component which citizens know the least about and the one which evokes the least empathy. During the past decade there has been a great deal of emphasis on the rights of accused persons, caused in no small measure by Supreme Court decisions and work by civil libertarians. There also has been an increase in serious crimes. The result is a citizenry that is fed up with the "coddling" of criminals and one that feels the pinch of inflation and has little sympathy toward legislators who would spend tax dollars on convicted felons. The most pressing reason for prison reform—a high rate of recidivism—is the very thing that seemingly retards reform, for to the public it appears that the new programs are not working, when in reality money and trained personnel are in such short supply that ambitious programs rarely got beyond the pilot project stage. A good deal of effort is being expended to professionalize the police and update outmoded court procedures. While this is a most worthwhile idea, it can serve only to put more pressures on confinement institutions, many of which are badly overcrowded, understaffed, and in need of renovation.

ADDENDUM

A NATIONAL JAIL CENSUS CONDUCTED BY THE LAW ENFORCEMENT ASSISTANCE ADMINISTRATION, UNITED STATES DEPARTMENT OF JUSTICE IN COOPERATION WITH THE BUREAU OF THE CENSUS.

Introduction and Summary

The national jail census of 1970 revealed that there are 4,037 locally administered jails in the United States which have the authority to retain adult persons for forty-eight hours or longer. Not included in this number are Federal and state prisons or other correctional institutions; institutions used exclusively for juveniles; the state-operated jails of Connecticut, Delaware, and Rhode Island; nor drunk tanks, lock-ups, and other facilities which retain persons for less than two full days.

As of March 15, 1970, these local jails held a total of 160,863 persons, including 153,063 adults and 7,800 juveniles. One in every twenty of the adults held on that date was a female. Those incarcerated included 83,079 (52%) who were pretrial detainees or otherwise not convicted; two thirds of the juveniles were in this category. Another 5 percent of the adults (8,688) had been convicted but were awaiting further legal action such as sentencing or appeal; the remaining 43 percent (69,096) were serving sentences of varying lengths.

Of the 4,037 adult jails, about 70 percent also receive juveniles. There are 765 institutions which have the authority to retain juveniles serving sentences of a year or less; a total of sixty-seven jails hold juveniles serving sentences of longer than one year.

In March, 1970, 205 (5%) of the jails in the United States contained more inmates than they were designed to hold. Of these, seventeen jails designed to hold one hundred or more persons exceeded their capacity by 100 to 299 persons, and an additional fourteen institutions intended for three hundred or more inmates were overcrowded in excess of three hundred inmates. For those jails which are designed to hold three hundred or more persons, nearly thirty percent are overcrowded.

There are 3,319 jails in the United States which are either county level or located in municipalities of 25,000 or greater population. Eighty-six percent of these institutions provide no facilities for exercise or other recreation for their inmates. Nearly ninety percent have no educational facilities. Only half provide medical facilities; one in four has no visiting facility; and there are forty-seven institutions (about 1.4%) which are without an operating flush toilet. These 3,319 county and urban institutions contain nearly 100,000 cells. One in every four of these cells has been in use for longer than fifty years, including more than 5,000 cells that are over one hundred years old.

The nation's jails employed 28,911 full-time equivalent persons on March 15, 1970, for an average of about 5.5 inmates per jail employee. The fiscal year 1969 operating costs amounted to $324 million, with planned construction expenditures for fiscal year 1970 anticipated at $171 million. The March, 1970, payroll was $18 million for an average of $617 per full-time employee.

Detailed Findings

General

Jails in the United States confined 160,863 inmates on March 15, 1970—an average of about forty inmates each in the 4,037 local jails with forty-eight-hour retention authority. The overwhelming majority of the inmates were adult males—nine out of ten. Others included juveniles as well as adult females—each accounting for about one in twenty of the inmate population. The State of California contained the largest inmate population with 27,672, or seventeen percent of the total. The only other states with more than 10,000 inmates were New York and Texas with 17,399 and 10,720, respectively.

Altogether, however, six states—the three already named plus Florida, Pennsylvania, and Georgia—accounted for 78,829 inmates, or about half the total number confined in the United

States. These same six states, on the other hand, contain about one-fourth of the United States population, according to preliminary figures from the 1970 Decennial Census. Vermont, by contrast, had only twenty-two inmates in its jails on the survey date.

By region, the South had by far the largest number of inmates on March 15—a total of 61,655 (see Text Table A). By comparison, the Northeast and North Central each had only about half as many inmates, 31,458 and 29,209, respectively. There were 38,541 in the West.

Juveniles in Adult Institutions

Every state, except Connecticut, Delaware, and Rhode Island which do not have locally administered jails, contained some adult jails which have the authority to incarcerate juveniles for varying types of retention. On the census date, March 15, there were 7,800 juveniles confined in the 4,037 jails. Over 4,500 juveniles were reported in the State of New York. A large number (3,943) of these, however, were confined in the New York City Reformatory and the New York City Adolescent Remand Shelter. While these inmates are sixteen to twenty-one years old and, therefore, legally adults, according to New York State Law, they are regarded by New York officials as "youthful offenders." For survey purposes they were classified as juveniles.

Including New York, only twelve states had as many as one hundred juveniles confined in their adult jails on March 15. Pennsylvania, Indiana, and Ohio were the only other states with more than two hundred juvenile inmates.

Inmates by Type of Retention—Adults and Juveniles

There are four basic categories of retention—sentenced prisoners, convicted persons under appeal or awaiting sentencing, pretrial detainees, and persons either not yet arraigned or being held for other authorities. The last two groups make up a "not convicted inmate" category, which accounted for just over half (52%) the total inmates in jail. For adult females this percentage was slightly higher at fifty-five percent. For juveniles the proportion was much higher. Two out of three young people in adult jails were pretrial detainees or were otherwise not convicted.

TABLE A
NUMBER AND PERCENT OF JAIL INMATE
POPULATION NOT CONVICTED, BY AGE
(ADULT OR JUVENILE) AND BY REGION–MARCH 1970

Region	Total	Adult Inmates			Juvenile Inmates		
		Total	Not Convicted[1]	Percent not Convicted	Total	Not Convicted[1]	Percent not Convicted
Total, U.S. ..	160,863	153,063	77,921	50.9	7,800	5,158	66.1
Northeast ...	31,458	26,526	13,648	51.5	4,932	2,684	54.4
North Central	29,209	28,226	14,654	51.9	983	816	83.0
South	61,655	60,330	31,797	52.7	1,325	1,152	86.9
West	38,541	37,981	17,822	46.9	560	506	90.4

Table A shows regional differences in the proportion of adult and juvenile inmates who had not been convicted of a crime.

There is very little variation by region in the proportion of adult inmates who were not convicted. Only the West region was under half, however, with 46.9 percent. As for juvenile inmates, however, differences vary widely by region and except for the Northeast region the proportion of juvenile inmates not convicted is dramatically higher than the corresponding adult figure. Overall, sixty-six percent of the juveniles are in the "not convicted" category. For the Northeast this proportion drops to fifty-four percent, which is comparable to the fifty-two percent adult figure for that region. A sharp departure from the National pattern is evident in the other three regions. In the North Central five out of six juvenile inmates are detained in jail without a conviction; in the South the proportion is about seven out of eight; and in the West it is nine of every ten.

Among the many states, the District of Columbia has the lowest percentage (29%) of its inmates in the "not convicted" category. This is partly due to the Federal Bail Reform Act of 1966 which is binding on the District of Columbia. This act curtails considerably the use of pretrial detention and especially money bail.

Of the 27,460 persons being held for other authorities or not yet arraigned, eight states—California, Texas, Florida, Illinois, Ohio, New York, Georgia, and Pennsylvania—account for 15,132

---

[1]Not convicted inmates include persons held for other authorities, those not yet arraigned, and those arraigned and awaiting trial.

(55%). These same states contain forty-six percent of the United States population.

Pretrial detainees were concentrated largely in just six states. California, New York, Texas, Pennsylvania, Florida, and Michigan accounted for over half the total U.S. inmates in this category—29,829 out of 55,619. Likewise, the five states of New York, Texas, Florida, California, and Virginia contained about half—4,461 out of 8,688—the convicted inmates who were awaiting further legal action. New York has more than two and a half times as many persons in this category as the second highest state—Texas.

Of those inmates who are serving sentences, fifteen percent are jailed for longer than a year. Altogether, 69,096 persons are serving sentences of varying lengths in the nation's local jails. California has the largest number of sentenced prisoners in its local jails serving one year or less—14,076. Next is New York with 5,309, followed By Florida with 3,821. Those three states, together with Michigan, Georgia, and Ohio contribute 30,007 (51% of the 58,600 prisoners serving sentences of a year or less. Although the District of Columbia, Georgia, Pennsylvania, New York, and South Carolina contain only two out of ten of the nation's citizens, they contain seven out of ten of the local-jail prisoners serving sentences of more than one year.

Facilities Available and Age of Cells

For those jails located either in cities of 25,000 or greater population or in counties, information was obtained in the census relating to the presence of various facilities, as well as the ages of the cells in the institutions. There are 3,319 jails which are either county-operated or are located in municipalities of 25,000 or more people. For the U.S., eighty-six percent of these jails were found to be without facilities for exercise or other recreation. Many states have ninety-five to one hundred percent of their local jails lacking in recreational facilities. There are some exceptions to this widespread absence. The District of Columbia has only one of its five jails without some recreational facilities. Fourteen of eighteen jails in Massachusetts do provide recreation facilities; forty-four of New York's seventy-four jails have facilities of this type, as do thirty-five of Pennsylvania's seventy-three jails, six of

New Hampshire's eleven, and seventy-one of California's 134. Hawaii has only four local jails, two of which have recreation facilities.

Educational facilities are even rarer than recreation facilities; nearly nine in every ten jails are without any kind of educational facility. The most notable exception in this instance is Massachusetts, which has thirteen of its eighteen local jails providing educational facilities of some kind. About half the jails in New Jersey and New York provide educational facilities.

Medical facilities exist in slightly more than half the nation's jails. The states with the highest proportion of jails providing medical facilities are New York and Maine (86% each), New Hampshire (82%), New Jersey (81%), California (79%), Massachusetts (78%), and Virginia (74%). All five District of Columbia jails and the two urban jails of Alaska reported the presence of medical facilities.

The states with the smallest proportion of jails containing medical facilities are Vermont (20%), Hawaii (25%), Tennessee (27%), Kentucky and Arkansas (27% each), Alabama (28%), and Mississippi (29%). It should be noted that Vermont and Hawaii also had the smallest inmate populations of all the states—twenty-two and ninety-seven respectively. Tennessee, Kentucky, Arkansas, Alabama, and Mississippi, however, all had sizable numbers of jail inmates—ranging from about 1,200 in Arkansas to about 3,600 in Tennessee.

Visiting facilities in a jail are more likely to be present than the other types of facilities discussed thus far. Three fourths of the United States jails contain visiting facilities. Only five states have fewer than sixty percent of their jails providing facilities for visiting. They are Idaho (43%), Nevada (47%), Missouri (50%), Kentucky (52%), and Mississippi (53%). There are forty-seven jails throughout the nation which do not have toilet facilities. These institutions are scattered over twenty-one states.

Table B displays differences in the lack of selected facilities by region.

On a regional basis the Northeast has the fewest local jails (226) but the highest proportion of such institutions providing recreational, educational, or medical facilities. Whereas the United States as a whole has eighty-six percent of its jails lacking in recreational facilities, about fifty percent of the Northeast jails are

TABLE B
PERCENT OF JAILS WITHOUT SELECTED FACILITIES IN
CITIES OVER 25,000 POPULATION AND IN COUNTIES,
BY REGION–MARCH 1970

Region	Number of Insti- tutions	Percent Without Recreational Facilities	Percent Without Educational Facilities	Percent Without Medical Facilities
Total U.S.	3,319	86.4	89.2	49.0
Northeast	226	49.6	57.1	22.6
North Central ..	1,028	91.3	91.9	46.3
South	1,574	90.5	92.7	57.3
West	491	80.0	87.2	40.3

without these facilities. Educational facilities are to be found in only eleven percent of the United States jails, but they are present in forty-three percent of the jails of the Northeast region. Medical facilities vary somewhat more by region, again with the Northeast having the lowest proportion of jails totally lacking such facilities. Twenty-three percent of the Northeast jails have no medical facilities, compared with forty percent in the West, forty-six percent in the North Central, and fifty-seven percent in the South.

Across the United States, in county and large urban jails there are nearly 25,000 cells being utilized which were built more than fifty years ago. This accounts for more than twenty-five percent of the 97,891 cells located in these same jails. Nearly 12,000 of these cells are over seventy-five years old, and 5,416 have been in use longer than a century.

On a state-by-state comparison, there are six states where more than seventy percent of the jail cells are not over twenty-five years old. All fifty-seven cells in Alaska's two jails are in this category. About eighty-two percent of Florida's 2,744 cells are twenty-five years old or younger; seventy-seven percent of California's 7,858 cells are, seventy-six percent of the 1,219 cells in Maryland, seventy-five percent of the 3,054 cells in Virginia, and seventy-one percent of Wisconsin's 1,973 cells were constructed since 1945.

By contrast, there are seven states with more than half their jail cells being over fifty years old. In New Hampshire, eighty-eight percent of the cells are older than fifty years. In Massachusetts, Vermont, and Maine, the percentages are seventy-eight, seventy-two, and sixty-eight, respectively. Sixty-one percent of

Pennsylvania's cells exceed fifty years of age, as do fifty-five percent of the cells in Montana and fifty-two percent in Kentucky.

Overcrowding

Across the United States, one in twenty of the local jails holds more inmates than it was designed to hold. Altogether, 205 institutions reported overcrowding, of which fifteen percent are exceeding their capacity by one hundred persons or more. Fourteen institutions, all located in very large metropolitan areas, reported overcrowding in excess of three hundred inmates.

The figures presented on the extent of overcrowding refer only to each institution as a complete entity. Although absolute overcrowding may not occur for a given jail, it is possible for the same jail to be overcrowded in selected quarters. For example, the section of a jail used for adult males may exceed its capacity but the female or juvenile sections may be underutilized so that, overall, the facility may or may not be overcrowded.

The states with the largest proportion of their jails reporting overcrowding conditions are the District of Columbia (2 of its 5 jails or 40%), New Jersey (25%), New York (20%), and Maryland (17%). By contrast, seventeen states reported either no jails or only one jail that exceeds its design capacity.

Table C shows regional comparisons of overcrowding in local jails.

TABLE C
PERCENT OF JAILS THAT ARE OVERCROWDED FOR THEIR DESIGN CAPACITY, BY REGION–MARCH 1970

Region	Number of Institutions	Percent Over-Crowded	Design Capacity					
			1-99 Inmates		100-299 Inmates		300+ Inmates	
			Number of Institutions	Percent Over-Crowded	Number of Institutions	Percent Over-Crowded	Number of Institutions	Percent Over-Crowded
Total U.S. ...	4,037	(205) 5.1	3,532	(128) 3.6	374	(39) 10.4	131	(38) 29.0
Northeast	235	(32) 13.6	151	(7) 4.6	54	(12) 22.2	30	(13) 43.3
North Central .	1,178	(40) 3.4	1,092	(25) 2.3	71	(10) 14.1	15	(5) 33.3
South	1,914	(92) 4.8	1,686	(69) 4.1	178	(13) 7.3	50	(10) 20.0
West	710	(41) 5.8	603	(27) 4.5	71	(4) 5.6	36	(10) 27.8

Numbers in parentheses are the number of institutions upon which the percents are based.

Table C shows that large jails are more likely to be overcrowded than smaller ones. Considering all jails in the United States, one in twenty is overcrowded. Those jails, however, which are designed to hold between 100 to 299 inmates are twice as likely to exceed capacity. One in ten of such jails reported overcrowding. For those jails designed to hold three hundred or more inmates, nearly three in ten are overcrowded.

By region, the Northeast reported the highest percentage of jails with overcrowding—about fourteen percent. The North Central was lowest at less than four percent. In the largest jails—three hundred or more capacity—about four in nine of the Northeast jails are holding more inmates than design capacity permits. In the North Central this ratio is one in three. In the West it is slightly more than one in four, and in the South one in five.

TABLE D
NUMBER OF JAILS BY DESIGN CAPACITY BY
OVERCROWDING FOR THE U.S.—MARCH 1970

Design Capacity (Number of Inmates)	Number of Institutions	Number at or Below Capacity	less than 10	10-24	25-99	100-299	300 or more
Total	4,037	3,832	92	35	47	17	14
Less than 10 ...	594	572	21	1	- -	- -	- -
10-24	1,327	1,273	39	14	1	- -	- -
25-99	1,611	1,559	26	11	15	- -	- -
100-299	374	335	3	8	21	7	- -
300 or more ...	131	93	3	1	10	10	14

(Institutions over Capacity by: less than 10, 10-24, 25-99, 100-299, 300 or more)

Table D shows the extent of overcrowding by the actual design capacity. Thirty-one jails which, by design, can accommodate one hundred or more persons were overcrowded in excess of one hundred persons on the survey date. This includes fourteen institutions which were built for three hundred or more inmates but which exceeded their capacity by a like amount.

Jails by Type of Retention Authority

Of the 4,037 jails in the United States, 3,807 (94%) have the authority to hold persons who have not been arraigned or who are being held for other authorities. Of these, five are exclusively for females and 2,785 have the authority to hold juveniles under the same conditions. A total of 3,614 (90%) of the jails have the authority to hold arraigned persons who are awaiting trial, including eight institutions that are used exclusively for females and 2,289 that hold juveniles.

Convicted persons awaiting further legal action are held in 2,745 jails (68% of the total). Nine such institutions hold females only, and 856 also hold juveniles. Eighty-seven percent (3,531) of all jails have the authority to hold sentenced prisoners for terms of one year or less. Sentenced prisoners serving more than a year are found in only 572 (14% of all jails), sixty-seven of these jails also hold juveniles.

Employment, Expenditures, and Planned Construction

The number of employees in the country's jails in March, 1970, was 33,729, including 5,676 part-time employees. Full-time equivalent personnel amounted to 28,911. Over thirty percent of the full-time equivalent work force is located in only two states—New York and California with 4,477 and 4,474 employees, respectively.

The ratio of inmates to full-time equivalent employees averaged 5.56 for the United States. Variation in this number among states was considerable, however, ranging from high ratios of 11.44 in Mississippi, 10.63 in Idaho, and 10.22 in Texas to low values of 1.31 in Hawaii, 2.70 in Massachusetts, 3.27 in Maine, 3.40 in the District of Columbia, and 3.43 in New Hampshire.

The average earnings of full-time employees was $617 for the month of March, with the overall March payroll exceeding $18 million. Three eighths of the March payroll was expended in California and New York, each with over $3.3 million. The average monthly earnings of full-time employees is almost fifty percent higher in cities over 25,000 population and in counties than in cities under 25,000—the figures being $620 and $419, respectively. The highest average salaries are paid in the District of Columbia ($849), California ($760), New York ($745), and Wisconsin ($705). The lowest are found in Arkansas ($338), South Dakota ($350), West Virginia ($369), Idaho and South Carolina ($380 each), North Dakota ($392), and Mississippi ($397).

Fiscal year 1969 operating costs amounted to $324 million, of which forty-two percent was expended in California, New York, and Pennsylvania. Anticipated construction expenditures for fiscal year 1970 were $171 million, with forty-eight of that total expected to be spent in New York, Washington, California, Illinois, Maryland, and New Jersey.

Mrs. Amy Stannard, a member of the first United States Board of Parole—1930. *(Courtesy of the U.S. Board of Parole)*

Chapter 18

PAROLE

There are four methods by which a prisoner can be released from a correctional institution: (1) conditional pardon, (2) mandatory (conditional) release, (3) discharge, and (4) parole. Parole is generally conceded to be the best form of release. Parole may be defined as "a procedure by which prisoners are selected for release and a service by which they are provided with necessary controls, assistance, and guidance as they serve the remainder of their sentences within the free community."[1]

HISTORICAL SUMMARY

Although philanthropic societies attempted to assist former prisoners to adjust to social life as early as the sixteenth century, it was not until 1820 that a true parole system was developed. In that year the English created a plan called ticket-of-leave, whereby men were granted early release from penal colonies with little aftercare or supervision. Some years later the Irish adopted the system, and in 1865 the Massachusetts Prison Board recommended, without success, that the English plan be adopted in that state.[2] In 1867 *Zebulon R. Brockway,* superintendent at the Detroit House of Correction for over a decade, presented a bill to the Michigan legislature to provide that prostitutes be sentenced to a three-year term, but empowering his institution to release them, under certain conditions, before the end of their terms. The legislature passed the bill, giving Michigan the distinction of being the first state to provide for the indeterminate sentence through legislative enactment. In 1870 during the first meeting of the National Prison Association, several penologists, including

[1]American Correctional Association, *Manual of Correctional Standards* (Washington: American Correctional Association, 1968), pp. 113-114.

[2]Edwin H. Sutherland and Donald R. Cressey, *Principles of Criminology,* 6th ed. (New York: J.B. Lippincott Co., 1960), pp. 567-568.

Brockway, presented scholarly papers expounding the idea of a parole system. It was not until 1876 that the concept was operationalized. In that year New York's Elmira Reformatory adopted a parole procedure, the first developed form of parole in American history. Although Brockway took credit for its invention, it had been in operation in Europe for a half-century. The Elmira plan provided for released prisoners to remain under the jurisdiction of the institution for six months.[3] Juvenile parole was established during the latter part of the nineteenth century as a part of the country's general child welfare movement.[4] In 1884 Ohio became the first state to pass a law extending parole to all state-run penal institutions. The idea spread fast and by 1898 twenty-five states had passed parole laws. By 1922 forty-five states enacted parole legislation. Twenty-two years later parole laws had been passed in all the states.[5]

THE LEGAL FRAMEWORK OF PAROLE[6]

The contemporary legal framework within which parole decisions are made varies widely from one jurisdiction to another.

Parole for Adults

Basically, the parole decision for adult offenders may depend on (1) statutes enacted by the legislature, (2) on the sentence imposed by the court, or (3) on the determination of correctional authorities or an independent parole board. For certain offenses some statutes require that various amounts of time must be served before parole can be considered, or they prohibit parole entirely. The basic trouble with such restrictions is that they allow no consideration of individual circumstances. . .In a few states indeterminate sentencing is authorized, permitting consideration for parole at any time, without service of a minimum term. "Good

[3]Harry Elmer Barnes and Negley K. Teeters, *New Horizons in Criminology,* 3rd ed. (Englewood Cliffs, N.J.: Prentice-Hall, Inc., 1959), pp. 569-570.

[4]The President's Commission on Law Enforcement and Administration of Justice, *Task Force Report: Corrections* (Washington: U.S. Government Printing Office, 1967), p. 60.

[5]*Supra* note 2, p. 568.

[6]Reprinted from *Task Force Report: Corrections,* pp. 62-63. (Editorial Adaption)

(Courtesy of the Florida Parole and Probation Commission)

time" or other credits earned by conduct during imprisonment may reduce the time that must be served in some jurisdictions prior to eligibility for parole. Under any such variant, eligibility for parole does not, of course, mean that parole will in all cases be granted. In some states offenders may be released outright at the end of their term. The requirement of mandatory supervision in force in the Federal system and several states is one attempt to deal with this problem. In general, mandatory supervision laws require that any prisoner released prior to the expiration of his term by reason of having earned good time or other credits during imprisonment must be released to a parole officer subject to parole supervision and conditions.

Parole for Juveniles

With respect to juveniles a number of legal issues are involved in commitment and subsequent release. Those which most directly

(Courtesy of the National Council on Crime and Delinquency)

affect parole practices are restrictions as to when a juvenile can be released. Of these the most important are (1) stipulated periods of time a youth is required to stay in a training school, and (2) the requirement of approval from a committing judge before release can be authorized. . . . Three states stipulate by law a minimum period of confinement before parole can be considered for a youngster. . . In many other states minimum terms are established by administrative action. More widespread. . .is the procedure. . . under which committing judges must become officially involved before juveniles can be released on probation. . .With this approach. . .a judge must be aware of a child's behavior in an institution after commitment by the court as well as current factors in the community situation. Since it is difficult at best to provide both kinds of information to a judge, he is apt to have the act on the basis of incomplete information.

ESSENTIAL ELEMENTS OF AN ADEQUATE PAROLE SYSTEM

Parole, like other criminal justice components, is a system within a system. Not only should each element in the overall criminal justice system respond to and interact with the others, but the elements within each component must maintain working and workable relationships. To overemphasize one element or subordinate another will eventually mean that the entire component will suffer, for like a pipeline, one leak, however small, can mean weakness, waste, and eventual collapse. Parole, in order to be an effective force for positive social change, must possess certain internal and external elements, each working toward the elimination of goal impediments. According to the American Correctional Association, there are nine essential elements of an adequate parole system:

1. Flexibility in the sentencing and parole laws.

2. A qualified parole board.

3. A qualified parole staff.

4. Freedom from political or improper influences.

5. Parole assigned to a workable position in the governmental administrative structure.

6. Proper parole procedure.

7. Prerelease preparation within the correctional institution's program.

8. Parole research.

9. A proper public attitude toward the parolee.

THE PAROLE BOARD

All states have a board whose primary duty is to determine when a prisoner should be released on parole. In most states the

The eight member United States Board of Parole. *(Courtesy of The U.S. Board of Parole)*

[7]*Supra* note 4, p. 65.

board operates as an independent state agency; however, in some it functions as a unit in a larger state department. In a few states the board is the same body that regulates penal institutions.[7] Boards are staffed with from five to ten members generally appointed by the governor. Often, too often, appointments to a parole board are politically motivated. Terms of office vary, but most members serve terms of six years or less. Several states—notably Michigan and Wisconsin—have adopted a "merit system" for appointment of parole board members whereby appointees are required to illustrate, through education and experience, their fitness to serve. Florida demands that board members pass a criminal justice examination before appointment. About half the states maintain a part-time parole board, a situation the President's Commission on Law Enforcement called "a pervasive problem in the adult field." Part-time board members devote only a limited share of their time to parole activities, and as a result the whole system suffers. One device that may help these jurisdictions is the idea of using parole examiners—professional corrections personnel who conduct hearings and interviews for the board, which delegates the authority to make certain decisions regarding the selection of parolees. The functions of parole boards in the states vary considerably and there are only slight signs of a movement toward uniformity. Ideally, however, the parole board's functions should include (1) reviewing cases to fix the time of parole when supervision is no longer needed, (2) assuming a major policymaking role, (3) determining conditions of parole, (4) relating the concept of parole to the public, and (5) promoting sound parole administration.

THE MECHANICS OF PAROLE

Superior parole practice consists of three basic procedures: (1) preparation, (2) selection, and (3) supervision. Although the formal parole machinery does not begin until the parole board fixes the conditions of parole and sets the date that the inmate

Parole Form H-8
(Rev. Dec. 1970)
(Formerly Parole Form 17)

The United States Board of Parole

Washington, D.C. 20537

Certificate of Parole

$SAMPLE$

Know all Men by these Presents:

It having been made to appear to the United States Board of Parole that

...., Register No. ...., a prisoner in

the ....,
is eligible to be PAROLED, and that there is a reasonable probability that he WILL REMAIN AT
LIBERTY WITHOUT VIOLATING THE LAWS and it being the opinion of the said United States Board of
Parole that the release of this person is not incompatible with the welfare of society, it is ORDERED by the

said United States Board of Parole that he be PAROLED on ...., 19......,

and that he remain within the limits of...until

...., 19........; or in the event of a committed fine or a committed fine and costs, until
the same have been paid or he has been discharged under the provisions of Section 3569, Title 18, U.S. Code, or
until other action may be taken by the said United States Board of Parole.

Given under the hands and the seal of the United States Board of Parole

this .... day of ...., nineteen hundred and ....

UNITED STATES BOARD OF PAROLE,

By ....
Parole/Youth Division Executive.

[SEAL]

ADVISER   ....

PROBATION OFFICER   ....

    This CERTIFICATE OF PAROLE will become effective on the date of release shown on the reverse
side. If the parolee's continuance on parole becomes incompatible with the welfare of society, or if he fails
to comply with any of the conditions listed on the reverse side, he may be retaken on a warrant issued by a
Member of the Board of Parole, and reimprisoned pending a hearing to determine if the parole should be
revoked.

CONDITIONS OF PAROLE

1. You shall go directly to the district shown on this CERTIFICATE OF PAROLE (unless released to the custody of other authorities). Within three days after your arrival, you shall report to your parole adviser if you have one, and to the United States Probation Officer whose name appears on this Certificate. If in any emergency you are unable to get in touch with your parole adviser, or your probation officer or his office, you shall communicate with the United States Board of Parole, Department of Justice, Washington, D.C. 20537.

2. If you are released to the custody of other authorities, and after your release from physical custody of such authorities, you are unable to report to the United States Probation Officer to whom you are assigned within three days, you shall report instead to the nearest United States Probation Officer.

3. You shall not leave the limits fixed by this CERTIFICATE OF PAROLE without written permission from the probation officer.

4. You shall notify your probation officer immediately of any change in your place of residence.

5. You shall make a complete and truthful written report (on a form provided for that purpose) to your probation officer between the first and third day of each month, and on the final day of parole. You shall also report to your probation officer at other times as he directs.

6. You shall not violate any law. Nor shall you associate with persons engaged in criminal activity. You shall get in touch immediately with your probation officer or his office if you are arrested or questioned by a law-enforcement officer.

7. You shall not enter into any agreement to act as an "informer" or special agent for any law-enforcement agency.

8. You shall work regularly unless excused by your probation officer, and support your legal dependents, if any, to the best of your ability. You shall report immediately to your probation officer any changes in employment.

9. You shall not drink alcoholic beverages to excess. You shall not purchase, possess, use, or administer marihuana or narcotic or other habit-forming or dangerous drugs, unless prescribed or advised by a physician. You shall not frequent places where such drugs are illegally sold, dispensed, used or given away.

10. You shall not associate with persons who have a criminal record unless you have permission of your probation officer.

11. You shall not have firearms (or other dangerous weapons) in your possession without the written permission of your probation officer, following prior approval of the United States Board of Parole.

I have read, or had read to me, the foregoing conditions of parole. I fully understand them and know that if I violate any of them, I may be recommitted. I also understand that special conditions may be added or modifications of any condition may be made by the Board of Parole at any time.

_____
(Name)

_____
(Register No.)

WITNESSED _____

_____
(Title)

_____
(Date)

UNITED STATES BOARD OF PAROLE:

The above-named person was released on the _____ day of _____, 19____ , with a total of _____ days remaining to be served.

_____
(Warden or Superintendent)

will be released from custody, the actual process ideally commences when the offender is admitted to the institution, for it is then that he is psychologically tested, medically evaluated, interviewed, and classified, a procedure that will have a significant impact on the eventual decision regarding parole. When an inmate has prepared himself for parole, i.e. he appears ready to again return to society, he will be eligible for parole, assuming that his release would be consistent with sentencing requirements, state policy, and legislative enactment. Over ninety percent of all prisoners are eventually released from institutions, so the selection procedure is concerned more with *when* than with *who.*

Several weeks prior to an inmate's release a preparole plan is drafted and sent to the parole agency in the community that the inmate specifies as his place of future residence. The inmate will play an active role in the preparation of his plan, as it is based largely on his work and residence plans. When the agency receives the plan, a parole officer is assigned to evaluate it. The officer can accept, reject, or recommend modifications in the plan. Under no circumstances should a prisoner be admitted to parole without this initial approval by the parole officer.

Many correctional institutions have sought to help the inmate make a smooth transition from prison to the community by allowing prospective parolees to spend a preliminary period of near-normality while still being confined. Some prisons have honor blocks, where inmates awaiting release enjoy special privileges. Other states maintain separation centers to which prospective parolees are transported just prior to release. Similar devices include minimum custodial facilities, honor camps, community dormitories, work release programs, and furloughs.

Once released, a parolee is assigned to a parole officer for supervision. The conditions of parole are carefully explained by the officer to preclude any misinterpretation. Although the parole officer will guide and assist the parolee, the ultimate success or failure of the venture will depend on the parolee. It is generally conceded that the chance of a successful parole experience decreases as the number of unreasonable conditions of parole are increased. Accordingly, it is self-defeating to demand of parolees standards of conduct that are significantly higher than those demanded of the general citizenry. Although the law will probably stipulate that any violation of parole conditions will result in the revocation of parole and the return of the offender to prison, in reality parole officers distinguish between technical violations and major violations. But, though the officer has a duty to his charge, he must also have the community's welfare at heart and when a number of violations are observed a formal declaration of violation of parole should be made, the end result of which will be the issuance of an arrest warrant for the parolee and his eventual return to prison.

OBJECTIVES OF PAROLE

There are two extreme views of the objectives of parole: one sees parole as a way in which society can become more humane by granting, through administrative action, the unfortunate and downtrodden another chance; the other holds that parole offers a way in which an offender can be kept under close surveillance without having to expend vast sums of money on his upkeep. Although these two views may be desirable side effects of parole, they are not the direct objectives of the system. The objectives of a model parole system may be listed as follows:[8]

1. Release of each person from confinement at the most favorable time, with appropriate consideration to requirements of justice, expectations of subsequent behavior, and costs.

2. The largest possible number of successful parole completions.

3. The smallest number of new crimes committed by released offenders.

4. The smallest number of violent acts committed by released offenders.

[8]*Supra* note 4, p. 185.

Probation and Parole
Form 17

FLORIDA PROBATION AND PAROLE COMMISSION

To: _____   Date_____,19_____
(Probation and Parole Supervisor)

_____   ___ Month
(Address)   ___ Quarter   Check one
                                     ___ Semi-Annual of these

Sir: I respectfully submit my written report for the month ending_____,19_____

Name and Address of Employer _____
(If unemployed or job change – explain)_____
Type Work_____. I (have) (have not) worked full time. If not,

explain why_____

INCOME		EXPENSES	
Wages or Salary (Gross) $_____		General Living Expenses $_____	
Borrowed $_____		Court Costs of Fines $_____	
Other _____ $_____		Restitution $_____	
(Identify) TOTAL $_____		Support $_____	
Savings (Total) $_____		TOTAL $_____	

I (did) (did not) go into debt. If so, explain:_____

_____

I (have) (have not) bought and drunk intoxicants. If so, how much and reason:_____

_____

I (have) (have not) bought, sold or used narcotics. If so, explain:_____

_____

My health (is) (is not) good. My trouble is_____
I (have) (have not) been arrested or had trouble with anyone. If so, explain:_____

_____

Name and Address of Church (If in attendance)_____
I (do) (do not) have special problems or trouble to talk over with supervisor. If so, explain:__

_____
_____
_____

Signature of Advisor, if you have one.   I certify the above to be true and complete

Name:_____   Signature or Mark_____
                                            (Probationer or Parolee)
                                 Mailing Address:_____
Address:_____   Residence Address:_____

                                 City_____State_____

                                 Initial of Supervisor_____

A report submitted to parole supervisors on a monthly basis by parolees. *(Courtesy of the Florida Parole and Probation Commission)*

PROBATION & PAROLE
FORM NO. 3B

FLORIDA PROBATION AND PAROLE COMMISSION
PROGRESS REPORT . . . PERIOD COVERED_____

NAME_____DISTRICT NO._____ CO NO._____

HOME ADDRESS_____

EMPLOYER_____ADDRESS_____

PROBATIONER_____ PAROLEE_____ PROGRESS: EXC._____ GOOD_____ FAIR_____ POOR_____ VIOL._____

CONTACTS_____

_____

DATE OF REVIEW_____ **Area Supervisor's Review**
_____TYPE OF SUPERVISION MIN._____ MED._____ MAX.____

A quarterly report prepared by parole supervisors to keep track of the progress of parolees. *(Courtesy of the Florida Parole and Probation Commission)*

5. An increase of general community confidence in parole administration.

These objectives are humane but pragmatic, for they allow that saving a human being is not only a desirable end but a way in which society can take positive steps toward ending the holocaust of crime.

CAREER ORIENTATION[9]

1. **Parole Officer Qualifications**

   (a) **Preferred**: Possession of a master's degree from an accredited school of social work or comparable study in correction, criminology, psychology, sociology, or a related field of social science.

   (b) **Minimum**: Possession of a bachelor's degree from an accredited college, with a major in the social or behavioral sciences and one of the following: (1) one year of graduate study in an accredited school of social work or comparable study in correction, criminology, psychology, sociology, or a related field of social science or (2) one year of paid full-time casework experience under professional supervision in a recognized social agency.

2. **Supervisor Qualifications**: Possession of at least the parole officer's minimum educational requirements, and two years of paid full-time casework experience in a recognized social agency.

3. **Administrator Qualifications**: Possession of the educational and experience qualifications required for supervisor and, in addition, three years of paid full-time experience in a supervisory capacity in a recognized social agency.

4. A parole officer's workload should not exceed fifty units a month.

---

[9]Reprinted from *Corrections in the United States* by the National Council on Crime and Delinquency (1966) as contained in *Task Force Report: Corrections*, pp. 208-209.

A parole officer–overburdened by a caseload three times what it should be. *(Courtesy of the Florida Parole and Probation Commission)*

5. One full-time supervisor should be assigned for every six full-time parole officers.

6. A minimum of one supporting position (stenographer, clerk, or receptionist) should be provided for every three parole officers.

7. An employment specialist should be on the staff of the adult parole agency to serve as liaison between the agency and outside employment agencies, union officials, and employer organizations.

(Courtesy of Florida Technological University)

Chapter 19

CRIMINAL JUSTICE EDUCATION

Advanced educational programs for students interested in pursuing careers in criminal justice agencies—police, courts, and corrections—have arisen in a rather haphazard fashion. A basic problem surrounding the development of these types of academic programs is a lack of research on just what type of education is necessary for a career in criminal justice, especially as regards the police. Very little scholarly inquiry has been undertaken to determine what college curriculums should contain, although since the report of the President's Commission on Law Enforcement in 1967, there has been a movement toward serious research in this area. However, there still exists a multiplicity of ideas and schools of thought regarding criminal justice education.

SCHOOLS OF ACADEMIC THOUGHT

During school year 1970-1971, 890 colleges and universities had applied for and received awards from the Law Enforcement Assistance Administration for use as student financial aid. Some 50,000 students benefited from this windfall. A breakdown of that figure reveals that approximately 41,000 were in-service personnel, with the remaining 9,000 being pre-service persons. Of the 41,000 in-service people 35,000 were police personnel, 5,000 were employed in corrections, and 1,000 were court employees.

Furthermore, the overwhelming number of participating colleges were two-year institutions—junior colleges, community colleges, or technical institutes. Approximately one-third of the participating schools offer programs which lead to a degree in a subject only indirectly related to their students' career orientations. To better understand these rapidly expanding educational programs, it is necessary that one survey certain schools of academic thought. The following educational approaches represent the dominant schools of thought:

1. The liberal arts approach.

2. The area of concentration.
3. The interdisciplinary approach.
4. The police science approach.
5. The law enforcement or police administration approach.
6. The criminology approach.
7. The criminal justice approach.

The Liberal Arts Approach

The philosophy behind the liberal arts approach is that students desiring a career in criminal justice should seek an education that will cover a breadth of disciplines. In this way a student's perspectives are broadened and his or her intellectual development is along general lines. Although proponents of this approach realize that specific occupational knowledge is also needed, they argue that this is a task that may be more appropriately fulfilled in recruit academies and in in-service training schools. Students graduating from institutions employing this approach will usually receive a baccalaureate degree in liberal arts, general studies, or social science. The liberal arts approach received some support from the President's Commission on Law Enforcement when it stated that until the educational needs of field officers are more fully evaluated "educational programs should emphasize the. . .liberal arts."

The Area of Concentration

In this approach, which is generally aimed at police and parole and probation students, instead of forming a special academic department to serve criminal justice students, a subfield is created within an existing department, such as sociology or political science. For example, although a student's major will be sociology, his area of concentration within the sociology department will be law enforcement. Certain courses—e.g. juvenile delinquency, criminology, social problems, alcoholism—will be required. No special courses are usually drafted for inclusion in the curriculum. Instead, courses which are considered relevant to a student's career pursuits and which existed within the college structure before the creation of the area of concentration are required. Though some institutions view an area of concentration as a permanent academic entity, many have chosen to use it as a stopgap measure

(Courtesy of Florida Technological University)

to fill the void until a full department can be established. The area of concentration approach is most often found at the state university level.

The Interdisciplinary Approach

This approach is a variation of the area of concentration, with the major exception being that two or more academic departments are involved in administering the major. Again, new courses are not generally drafted, as courses from other disciplines thought to have special application to the major make up the curriculum. For example, a law enforcement student may be required to take an equal number of stipulated courses in sociology, political science, psychology, and history. Specialized law enforcement coursework will probably not be offered. The interdisciplinary approach is also found primarily at state universities.

The Police Science Approach

The police science approach is the one most utilized by junior colleges. It is a rather specialized program of study designed to provide the technical skills necessary in performing line police functions. The overwhelming number of in-service law enforcement students begin their academic careers in a junior college police science program, where they take coursework in criminal law, police administration, patrol tactics, criminal investigation, police procedures, criminalistics, and like subjects. Police science programs, which usually lead to a two-year degree or to a certificate of completion, are often aimed primarily at the working policeman, and therefore offer both morning and evening classes to facilitate students who are assigned to shiftwork. Most junior college police science programs were originally established as terminal programs; but with the growth of four-year institutions, many two-year police science departments are restructuring their curricula so that full transferability of credits is achieved.

The Law Enforcement or Police Administration Approach

Generally this approach, found occasionally at the two-year level but primarily undertaken by four-year institutions, is a pro-

(Courtesy of the St. Petersburg Police Department)

The Southern Police Institute in Louisville, Kentucky, a leader in the field of high-level law enforcement training. The Institute is housed in the University of Louisville, which also offers a distinguished academic program in the School of Police Administration. Its father was Dean David A. McCandless, whose recent passing saddened the entire law enforcement community. *(Courtesy of the Southern Police Institute, University of Louisville)*

gram of study aimed at producing graduates who someday aspire to leadership roles on police agencies. Advanced coursework is offered in the management and administrative sciences, with allied courses required to impress upon the student his social responsibilities. The curriculum is internally oriented, i.e. students are provided with an up-to-date learning experience on how to fulfill the role of major policymaker. One of the most distinguished programs to employ this approach is the School of Police Administration at the University of Louisville.

The Criminology Approach

The main thrust of most criminology programs is toward corrections, although professional law enforcement practitioners are also accommodated, but to a lesser degree. Criminology majors are often those persons who seek careers in counseling, research, university teaching, parole and probation work, and in treatment-oriented correctional tasks. It is not unusual to find a graduate program in the curriculum, and many criminology components offer doctorate study. Criminology differs most from many of the other approaches in its emphasis on theory and research. A number of very distinguished criminology programs exist across the country, including the one at the University of California at Berkeley.

The Criminal Justice Approach

The criminal justice concept, a popular idea that gained widespread support during the post-1967 period, is a systems approach to education. Its proponents argue that the police, the courts, and correctional agencies operate quite independently thereby isolating themselves from one another and from the general community. Although criminal justice majors pursue some specialized study in their respective fields, they also take coursework that will bring them into contact with students aspiring to careers in all components of criminal justice and with students of other disciplines. In this regard, the criminal justice curriculum is believed to work toward abating the isolation problem. Many criminal justice programs employ a modified interdisciplinary approach. Some were coverted from police science, or police administration programs. Criticism has been leveled at the name "criminal justice" because it does not aptly describe the career pursuits of students and it has a negative connotation. The venerable program at San Jose State College employs the approach but not the title, choosing instead to name the department the Administration of Justice. Some of the country's most distinguished police programs have adopted the criminal justice approach, including Michigan State University, the John Jay College of Criminal Justice, Georgia State University, Northeastern University, the University of Missouri, and the State University of New York (Albany).

OBJECTIVES OF HIGHER EDUCATION

As can be seen from the great divergence of thought on the subject, there exists no consensus on how educational programs for criminal justice students should be structured. There is no right or wrong way of drafting programs, for even those institutions which appear to have what some would condemn as a "defective" curriculum may very well be responding to a definite need in their region. For example, it is very easy to criticize a junior college for offering "nuts and bolts," "how to handcuff" courses, but if little recruit or in-service training is available to policemen in the area, then the junior college is filling a felt need, albeit a fundamental one.

The basic argument heard in the academic community, one that may never totally be resolved, involves the theorist and the pragmatist. The former feels that advanced education should stress theory courses and research-oriented curricula. Among other things, students should delve into correctional theories, the historical roots of policing, avenues of jurisprudential thought, the paradigmatic underpinnings of public safety, the philosophy of parole and probation, and philosophical methods of social control, so says the theorist. In this context the "why" questions of the discipline are answered. The pragmatist, on the other hand, feels that students should be provided with more "usable" knowledge. Accordingly, a useful curriculum is seen as one that contains subjects of practical worth, with only a minor emphasis on theory. Students aspiring to careers as police administrators are offered coursework directly applicable to their field. In this context the "how" questions of the discipline are offered.

Regardless of what main thrust an academic program takes— either theoretical or pragmatic—it is a sad program indeed that does not include to some degree the divergent philosophy in its curriculum. The academic program that can blend the two schools of thought is well on its way to success. A degree program will have, regardless of its orientation, a number of clearly defined goals, although the various institutions may stress one above the other. Accordingly, criminal justice education has the following general objectives:

1. To produce well-qualified professional practitioners who will seek careers either in a criminal justice agency or in teaching.

2. To make students aware of their social responsibilities to the community.

3. To impress upon students the importance of viewing the American criminal justice apparatus as a system made up of functional components.

4. To produce students who are cognizant of the role of all components in the criminal justice system and who are qualified to conduct research in their own field.

5. To equip students with the intellectual tools to become useful and productive citizens.

CRIMINAL JUSTICE APPRENTICESHIPS

In the past there has been little opportunity for pre-service students to engage in apprenticeship training in a criminal justice agency prior to graduation. This has been especially true of police students. Now, however, things are changing and the prospects are bright for this type of training. There exist two ways in which agencies allow apprentices to train in the criminal justice service: as cadets and as interns.

Cadet Training

The first cadet was appointed in Lincolnshire, England, in 1935. The English idea was to select a young man of approximately sixteen years of age to train for the police service. The concept has come to America virtually intact, with the one major difference being age. American police cadets are generally eighteen years old and above. A cadet program may be academically oriented, community oriented, or both. If it is academically oriented, candidates will often be expected to be enrolled in a college or university program that is compatible with police employment. The cadet's work week will be between ten and twenty hours, with his or here shift modified to accommodate school attendance. Pay is nominal. If the program is community oriented, college attendance may not be compulsory, although after being admitted into the program, cadets will probably be encouraged to enroll in advanced study. Some community-oriented cadet programs will offer full-time employment, but at a significantly lower pay scale than patrolmen. These types of programs are often used as devices to stimulate minority recruitment into police ranks.

The police department library. *(Courtesy of the Metropolitan Police Department, City of St. Louis)*

Occasionally, cadets are utilized exclusively to perform clerical tasks; but if the program is to be of maximum effectiveness, a broader range of duties should be assigned. A model cadet program exists in the Orlando, Florida, Police Department where cadets undergo basically the same entry-level tests and training as do patrolmen. Recruitment is conducted within the community and at the area's colleges and universities. Sex and race are not factors in consideration for employment. Once hired, the cadet will rotate duty assignments each month until he or she has built up experience in each division of the agency. When the cadet turns twenty-one and has shown satisfactory progress, the department will welcome him or her into its ranks.

Internships

Internships are joint police department-college ventures. The mechanics of the program vary across the country, but traditionally a school will contract to furnish for a period of time— often one or two school terms—a group of candidates from which the department selects its choice. The intern may work for pay,

Police cadets. *(Courtesy of the Orlando Police Department)*

(Courtesy of the Dallas Police Department)

for college credit, or for a combination of both. An intern generally works at higher-level administrative tasks than does a cadet. Other criminal justice agencies also employ interns, especially parole and probation agencies, wherein they perform a valuable investigative service. The internship program is closely supervised by colleges, so scholarship is an important factor in determining which students will be selected for appointment.

THE LAW ENFORCEMENT EDUCATION PROGRAM

The Law Enforcement Education Program (LEEP) is administered by the Law Enforcement Assistance Administration's Office of Academic Assistance, U.S. Department of Justice. LEEP provides two types of financial aid to students enrolled in colleges and universities: (1) loans of up to $1,800 per academic year to

DEPARTMENT OF JUSTICE
LAW ENFORCEMENT ASSISTANCE ADMINISTRATION

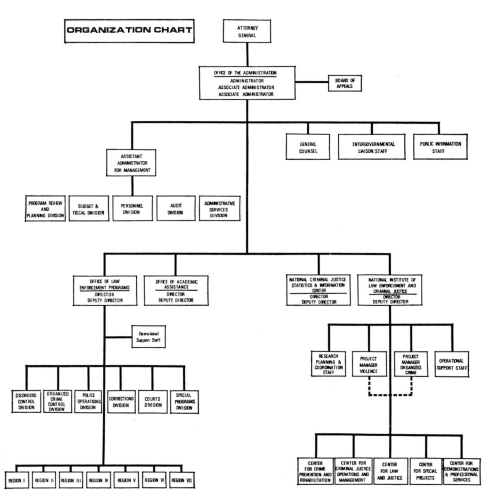

(Courtesy of the Law Enforcement Assistance Administration, U.S. Department of Justice)

students preparing for criminal justice careers and (2) grants of $300 per semester for students presently employed in criminal justice agencies. LEEP offers attractive forgiveness features. The loan obligation is canceled at the rate of twenty-five percent for each year of service in a criminal justice agency. The grant has no repayment provisions, providing the student remains with his agency for two years after completing courses paid for by LEEP.

The responsibilities of the Office of Academic Assistance are grouped into five categories:

1. Processing, supervising, and administering of loans and grants.
2. Assisting in the development of criminal justice education on a nationwide basis, recommending areas for research and action programs relating to education and training.
3. Providing for follow-up on student obligations and for recovery of Federal funds when obligations are not met.
4. Encouraging careers in law enforcement as a supplement to state and local efforts and stimulating the attainment of higher education by in-service and pre-service personnel.
5. Administering for the Office of Law Enforcement Programs a graduate fellowship program for command and middle-management police and correctional personnel.

The Law Enforcement Education Program has had a positive and measurable impact on the public and on criminal justice, especially the police. More officers are in school than ever before, and more schools are now opening their doors to criminal justice students. The benefits to all—the police, the courts, corrections, and the community—are abundantly clear.

CONCLUSION

Criminal justice education is on the move, but it is experiencing growing pains. If one is to consider (as these authors have) education as a functional component in the system of criminal justice, then many institutions of higher learning must take their own advice and insure that they do not isolate themselves from the other components. Programs too preoccupied with theory and pure research may find themselves contributing to the very problem they seek to eliminate. In addition, more coordination is needed between two-year and four-year programs. It is safe to predict that within the next decade criminal justice educational programs will remain dynamic and fluid as the divergent academic theories blend into an acceptable mix.

(Courtesy of the Arlington County [Virginia] Police Department)

Chapter 20

THE COMMUNITY AND CRIMINAL JUSTICE

Criminal justice in this nation, or any other democratic society, must enlist the support of its citizens if it ever hopes to be successful. Crime is not exclusively the business of the police, the courts, and correctional institutions, for the citizenry has a stake, occasionally a life-and-death stake, in the administration of criminal justice. Criminal justice agencies, especially the police, need help from citizens, from private organizations, and from municipal agencies in order to attack the causes of crime and criminality. It is the intention of this chapter to survey the historical role of citizen involvement in criminal justice, and to discuss some of the noteworthy community-based programs that have been created nationally.

HISTORICAL SUMMARY

History shows that American citizens have involved themselves deeply in criminal justice systems although that involvement was often a negative one as men sought to preempt legally constituted institutions for their own ends, or they acted collectively to take extreme action in the absence of effective criminal justice machinery. In times of lawlessness citizens were occasionally forced to engage in direct action. During the violent era of the Old West this action took the form of vigilantes, who in many cases did not preempt criminal justice, they were criminal justice—the police, the courts, parole and probation agencies.

Early police forces in this country were civilian operations, as able-bodied men banded together in watches to protect their communities. When formal criminal justice systems were created, citizen involvement did not end; it simply took other, less dominant, forms, at least for a time. The post-Civil War period saw private public-spirited groups formed in great profusion. Many of these groups had strong religious orientations and had as their goal the elimination of various forms of immorality.

In 1873 citizen antivice crusades became popular. During that year *Anthony Comstock,* special agent for the Postmaster General, began a movement to fight for legislation aimed at prohibiting the mailing of obscene matter and lottery tickets. As a direct result of Comstock's campaign, the Society for the Suppression of Vice was formed in conjunction with the New York City YMCA. Other communities soon followed New York's lead.

In 1878 the New England Watch and Ward Society was organized in Boston to "promote public morality," a task it undertook with great gusto. That same year a wealthy Baltimore philanthropist, Goldsborough S. Griffith, founded the Maryland Society to Protect Children from Cruelty and Immorality. Its mission was to "apply the arm of the law to protect helpless children." It placed minors in foster homes, protected children from cruel punishment, and fought against the abduction of young women for immoral purposes. Eight years later, in 1886, private citizens created the Society for the Suppression of Vice in Baltimore City to secure the enactment of antivice laws and to see to it that they were rigidly enforced.

Aside from vice suppression, citizens banded together in groups to tackle other *ad hoc* problems. In New York the Anti-Horse Thief Society was formed. In Baltimore, the Society for Promoting the Observance of the Lord's Day was created. A later goal of this organization was to protect the public from the evils of Sunday baseball games. In 1908 the Charity Organization Society of New York City created a Committee on Criminal Courts to investigate the corrupt and inefficient justice-of-the-peace courts in that city. Significant court reform was undertaken as a result of their actions.

When the Prohibition Law was enacted, much of the work of vice-suppression groups tapered off. However, committees on criminal justice were formed, by entirely different kinds of citizens, to combat the effect of prohibition on the administration of justice and to investigate the rising tide of gangsterism. During the twenties and thirties citizen crime commissions were created in Philadelphia and Washington. The commissions acted as watch dogs over criminal justice agencies, pointing up corrupt practices and recommending meaningful reform measures. Citizens who staffed these panels were usually responsible business, professional, and academic types who had stakes in their communities and who possessed the expertise to do a good job of overseeing criminal justice. The commissions had a secular bent and seemed to be interested more in institutional honesty and efficiency than in the enforcement of morality on the community.

The early 1950s saw major exposés on the existence of organized crime and its corrupting influence on municipal criminal justice. Citizen crime commissions popped up in Miami, New Orleans, Wichita, St. Louis, Dallas, Burbank, and Gary, to mention but a few cities. Beginning in 1951 a National Association of Citizens Crime Commissions was organized for the purpose of holding annual conferences wherein representatives from crime commissions not affiliated with government could meet and exchange ideas. The Association's existence had four purposes:

1. To facilitate exchange of information between commissions in order to better carry out their individual objectives.
2. To educate the public on the nature and control of organized crime and racketeering.
3. To arouse public interest in clean government.
4. To encourage and assist in the formation of citizen crime commissions throughout the nation.

CONTEMPORARY CITIZEN INVOLVEMENT

The dominant social issues of bygone eras motivated specific public concern over matters, a concern that eventually translated itself into citizen involvement with criminal justice. Today, the crime commission idea is still growing because the problems that spurred their creation are still around, but new issues in society have stimulated the establishment of other forms of citizen involvement. Contrary to popular opinion, citizens have never before been so closely and so significantly involved with agencies of criminal justice. Americans are a public-spirited people and crises—war, depression, social problems—always seem to bring out the best in them. With the rise of crime, violence, narcotics addiction, and drunkenness, citizens have rushed to the aid of besieged institutions at an unprecedented rate.

Yet, government, especially municipal government, is a sensitive animal. Civil servants jealously guard their independence and tend to look on citizen committees as a threat to their hard-won autonomy. The resistance of the police to the formation of citizen-complaint review panels illustrates this new sensitivity. So citizens now have to surmount internal resistance to their activities. But with all the difficulties encountered by public-spirited community members, unexampled numbers of people still flock to join civic groups and criminal justice associations, on which they serve without pay. Criminal justice agencies need all the help they can get, and in many communities citizens are rolling up their sleeves to pitch in. Although the following grouping of police, courts, and corrections programs does not represent the complete spectrum of citizen involvement, the projects and programs are representative of a pervasive public concern and a national citizen commitment.

Police-Related Programs

A score of cities have instituted a program called crime check. The motto of crime check is "If you see it, report it." The program is aimed at preventing crime by educating the public about the critical importance of immediately reporting criminal acts to the police. Citizens' groups get this message across through television spot announcements, newspaper advertisements, speeches, window posters, auto decals, and billboard advertisements. The Committee on Law, Order, and Justice of Alton, Illinois, even produced a fifteen-minute color movie to publicize citizens' responsibilities in preventing crimes. Other communities who have initiated a crime check program are Hartford, Indianapolis, Minneapolis, Omaha, and Peoria.

Citizens in a number of communities, including Buffalo, Norfolk, Cincinnati, and Honolulu have initiated a community radio watch whereby business firms whose vehicles are equipped with two-way radios are urged to report to their dispatchers fires, crimes in progress, and suspicious incidents. The dispatchers then call the police.

People in dozens of communities, often instigated by local Chamber of Commerce units, have embarked on lighting programs that have brought improved street lighting to cities. In Indianapolis, a women's Anti-Crime Crusade was instrumental in having installed 9,000 new street lights over a six-year period, an action which was said to have brought a sixty to ninety percent reduction in some classes of street crimes.

Shoplifting, one of the nation's most expensive and tragic non-violent crimes, has been the target of a good deal of citizen action aimed at preventing offenses and quickly apprehending violators. A chain-call warning system has been developed in many communities, notably Decatur, Illinois, that notifies businessmen of professional shoplifters at work. The police will call a designated business which will in turn notify two other businesses and so on. Within a brief period of time, hundreds of merchants may be alerted, with a minimum of effort on the part of the police.

Probably no single phenomenon in recent years has aroused public concern like the problem of drug abuse. Concern over this vexing question has led citizens to undertake extraordinary narcotics programs. In Flint, Michigan, a mobile drug education center was commissioned to travel to neighborhoods and schools for the purpose of disseminating information on drug abuse. In Kent, Ohio, the American School Health Association, in conjunction with the Pharmaceutical Manufacturers Association, drafted a curriculum guide for a public school drug education program. The U.S. Chamber of Commerce sponsored an Action Forum on narcotics in which representatives from a number of communities described what their cities were doing to combat the problem. In New York State, Narcotic Guidance Councils were established to receive confidential information about drug use in order to coordinate governmental treatment and enforcement efforts.

Citizens have also become deeply involved in the struggle to professionalize the nation's law enforcement agencies by assisting the police in very tangible ways. In Indianapolis financial contributions from the Chamber of Commerce supported specialized training courses for sixty policemen, some of whom were given college scholarships. In Shelby, Ohio, a group of public spirited citizens raised $2,600 for a fund to educate officers. When the city of Detroit could not reach a decision on whether to purchase thirty-three badly needed motor scooters, the Board of Commerce stepped in and furnished the needed money. In Peoria the Association of Commerce sponsored weekend "retreats" wherein minority group representatives and the police met in private group discussions.

Court-Related Programs

A number of communities have established court-watching programs in which members of civic groups are assigned to observe the criminal courts in action. Court data sheets are furnished so that even inexperienced "watchers" can spotlight judicial weaknesses.

The Chamber of Commerce in Omaha contributed $6,700 for a study of the county's juvenile court. The finished study report resulted in a wholesale reform of the court.

In Onondaga, New York, a citizens' committee was created to view the day-to-day operations of the County Childrens' Court in order to assist court personnel and public officials in bringing about needed changes made necessary by the burgeoning caseload.

In New York City the Vera Institute of Justice, a private foundation, sponsored the Manhattan Bail Project, a three-year program which saw 3,500 defendants freed on bail in order to determine the desirability of releasing certain classes of offenders on their own recognizance. The Institute also embarked on the Manhattan Court Employment Project in which counselors contacted persons awaiting trial with offers of jobs and assistance. If prior to trial a defendant showed promise of permanent change, the district attorney and the judge were contacted and requested to display leniency.

NOTICE TO APPEAR - MISDEMEANOR - VIOLATION	MUNICIPAL COURT FOR OAKLAND-PIEDMONT JUDICIAL DISTRICT COUNTY OF ALAMEDA, STATE OF CALIFORNIA	OAKLAND CITATION NO. No 3152
NAME		DATE AND TIME OF VIOLATION
RESIDENCE ADDRESS	TELEPHONE	LOCATION OF VIOLATION
BUSINESS ADDRESS	TELEPHONE	VIOLATION CODE NUMBER AND NAME
SEX RACE HEIGHT WEIGHT DATE OF BIRTH AGE		DESCRIBE VIOLATION:
IDENTIFICATION: DRIVER'S LIC.: OTHER:		
YOU ARE HEREBY NOTIFIED TO APPEAR IN THE MUNICIPAL COURT FOR THE OAKLAND-PIEDMONT JUDICIAL DISTRICT, DEPARTMENT NO. ____ 600 WASHINGTON ST., OAKLAND ON THE DAY OF 19 AT A.M.		
WITHOUT ADMITTING GUILT, I PROMISE TO APPEAR AT THE TIME AND PLACE INDICATED. SIGNATURE:		ISSUED BY SER. NO. DATE ISSUED
WITNESS: GIVE NAME, ADDRESS AND TELEPHONE		

Many communities issue misdemeanor citations for violations of municipal ordinances, in lieu of a physical arrest. *(Courtesy of the Oakland Police Department)*

Correction-Related Programs

Correction is a difficult criminal justice component in which to involve citizens, for it is the one which deals with offenders after they have been convicted of a crime. Furthermore, interested citizens do not always have access to those who need help most— prison inmates. Yet there is citizen involvement in this area, too.

Prison Citizens' Committees have been set up in dozens of communities and, although the function of these committees differs in each jurisdiction, the accomplishments of the Bucks County (Pennsylvania) Prison Citizens' Committee is 'in many ways typical of other programs. The Bucks County Committee, comprised of businessmen, educators, professional men, and governmental representatives, has accomplished the following:

1. Worked with individual inmates on personal problems.
2. Volunteered to help prison personnel with clerical and administrative tasks, such as typing, filing, the administration of tests, library expansion, and education.
3. Helped fund in-service training courses for prison employes.

In Malden, Massachusetts, a group of concerned citizens raised funds to support a local drug abuse facility. In Manchester, Connecticut, a Drug Advisory Council was created to coordinate an effort to form a drug education center for addicts in need of treatment. Cleveland's Criminal Justice Coordinating Council opened a free medical clinic to provide drug users with day-to-day care. Citizens in Boulder, Colorado, support neighborhood residences wherein selected juvenile offenders are allowed to reside in lieu of detention.

A rapidly expanding corrections program called Volunteers in Courts* has enlisted 25,000 citizen volunteers nationwide. Citizens may work in various detention facilities, or they may choose to employ their talents in parole or probation agencies. Approximately twenty-five percent of the country's juvenile courts have volunteers. Florida's Volunteers in Probation and Parole, some 2,000 strong, assist the state's Probation and Parole

---

*The name may be misleading because of the word "court" in the title. It is indeed a corrections program. The title merely signifies that those who work in it are responsible to a judge.

A criminal court judge and a housewife who serves as a volunteer court aid. *(Courtesy of the Florida Parole and Probation Commission)*

Parole volunteer teaches reading to illiterate parolees. *(Courtesy of the Florida Parole and Probation Commission)*

Commission by aiding professional personnel in supervising parolees. The Volunteers, who save the state $250,000 annually, have the following duties:

1. To act as court aids by observing and recording court proceedings for probation officers.

2. To assist in making community contacts.

3. To act as professional assistants—e.g. counseling, teaching, testing.

4. To evaluate methods of offender treatment and make recommendations for improvement.

One of the thorniest problems facing parolees is finding gainful employment. It is also a critical problem for society, for so much depends on the parolee's reintegration into a community. Citizens have moved to meet this challenge. In St. Paul, Minnesota, an Employers' Council for Equal Employment Opportunity was established to serve as a liaison between prison inmates and prospective employers. The Illinois State Chamber of Commerce is exploring ways of providing more jobs for ex-offenders. California has formed trade advisory committees staffed by representatives from business, labor, and government. Their job is to advise correctional officials about the quality and appropriateness of vocational training programs in prisons. The National Alliance of Businessmen provides on-the-job training for the disadvantaged, as well as procuring employment for recently released offenders.

CONCLUSION

There is no doubt about the desirability of encouraging constructive citizen involvement in the affairs of criminal justice agencies. But the questions of just what constitutes "constructive involvement" and who should provide the impetus for that involvement are not easily answered. In the case of the police, for example, there is a thin line between enthusiastic public cooperation and vigilanteism. Furthermore, citizen advisory commissions which perform their tasks too strenuously may have a negative impact on the morale of the agency they have undertaken to help. The movement toward police professionalization makes it

A municipal judge in Montgomery, Alabama, opens his courtroom to young citizens. *(Courtesy of the Montgomery Police Department)*

essential that law enforcement be granted a high degree of operating independence, and although the police must be held accountable for their actions, it is vital that citizen involvement be oriented more toward advisement than supervision.

There is danger in citizen involvement in other criminal justice agencies, too. Overenthusiastic citizens can actually trample the rights of those they wish to help by unwittingly preempting due process of law. So citizen action in this area should not be headstrong, unrestrained, and directionless. Certain guidelines must be articulated by agencies desirous of receiving public support but anxious to channel unbridled enthusiasm into meaningful assistance. Citizens should be given creative freedom, but not license. Their job descriptions must be as clearly delineated as those of the full-time staff. Goals should be set so that tasks are not completed just for the sake of making the participants feel better. Chains of command should be established. The creation of firm operating policies is essential. Principles of sound management will insure that manpower is allotted properly and that maximum efficiency and productivity are achieved. Because citizen committees generally work without pay is no reason for criminal justice administrators to waste their considerable talents on meaningless jobs. Citizens who volunteer for public service work can see through this tack and will deplore and resent it. Men and women with advanced education and professional experience are highly sought after in the private sector, and to squander their abilities is to do a disservice to them and to the agency.

Formidable criminal justice problems face this nation, problems that cannot be solved by government alone. Citizen power must be marshaled to join the fight on crime. The price tag for crime in dollars, in broken dreams, and in lives lost is too high not to allow citizen involvement. The words of Warren E. Burger, Chief Justice of the United States Supreme Court, puts the matter in perspective: "If we do not solve. . .the problems of criminal justice, will anything else matter very much?"

PART III

ELEMENTS OF

LAW ENFORCEMENT

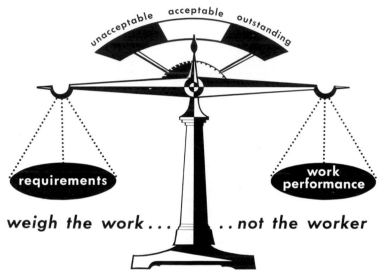

(Courtesy of the United States Air Force)

Chapter 21

POLICE ORGANIZATION
AND ADMINISTRATION

Historically, police departments were run by the rule-of-thumb method in which problems and issues were encountered and solved through a device which may accurately be referred to as "muddling through." Over the years, however, the law enforcement task has become too dynamic, too complex, too basic to the very survival of an entire society to be administered by incompetent executives using hit-or-miss methods. Therefore, certain rules have been promulgated to insure that police departments will be organized and administered along lines consistent with principles of sound management. It must initially be stated that the most important factor in police administration is the selection of a chief administrator with the education, training, experience, competence, and courage to fulfill his role as top executive. Without a chief executive of talent and vision, little else will matter. It is the purpose of this chapter to give students of the discipline an insight into the administrative elements that go into the making of superior police departments.

LEADERSHIP IN LAW ENFORCEMENT

There are several categories of leadership on any sizable police agency, each of which requires certain very specific talents. However, before examining these levels of leadership, it will do well to look at the general functions of police leadership. In any summary of the traits of leadership, the following should be possessed or acquired through a combination of education and experience before a person is allowed to ascend to a role of leadership on his agency:

1. Decisiveness—the knack of being able to make forthright decisions based on the pros and cons of a situation.
2. Judgement—the ability to weigh alternate courses of action.

3. Drive—vigor, enthusiasm, and the ability to inspire action in others.
4. Vision-the faculty for long-range and broad perception.

On police departments, leadership is situational, i.e. its requirements vary in time and place due to the nature of the police task. Different leadership behavior patterns are called for in differing situations, making it essential that men chosen for promotion are men who can adapt to a constantly fluid environment. Furthermore, the day of the old line leader who ruled by fiat is passing from the scene. In his place is appearing a "new breed" leader who places an emphasis on administrative skill and who believes in concepts such as shared decision-making, interpersonal relations, compromise, and persuasion. In this context the prime leadership strategy is manipulation rather than command.

Police leadership is divided into three broad categories: top management, middle management, and first-line supervision. Each category requires different personal qualities.

Top Management

Top management on a police department is the chief and his immediate subordinates—generally deputy or assistant chiefs, inspectors, or majors. Top managers determine policy, direct program execution, harmonize varying viewpoints, coordinate the processes of administration, and are responsible for the attainment of the department's goals. Probably no department head in government is delegated the authority and responsibility of top police managers, so it is absolutely essential that they possess qualities befitting their position. According to Professor Roscoe Martin, top managers must have the following qualities:

1. The faculty of generalizing or abstracting general rules from analysis of large quantities of data.
2. High intelligence combined with imagination and willingness to accept new ideas.
3. Determination to operate at their own levels and to delegate performance of operational level to others.
4. Capacity of dealing with other men and judging them correctly.
5. Willingness to accept responsibility for important decisions.

6. Skill in communication and negotiation.
7. Orientation toward public service.

Top managers must delegate certain tasks to others; however, there are some functions that they cannot delegate. These are the fiscal function (deciding on what funds the agency needs to operate and how they should be distributed), the personnel function (measuring the personnel needed by the department and assigning manpower on some logical basis), and the planning function (approving, modifying, or rejecting future programs).

The environmental conditions of a large police agency require that top managers be generalists who can view their department and its programs as a whole, rather than specialists who see the institutional enterprise in the narrow perspective of particular functional duties. A police officer who is promoted to a top management position after long service in one assignment may not bring to his new job the generalist view that it needs. To preclude this problem many police departments regularly reassign their personnel to prepare them for future executive duties.

The essence of high level leadership is influencing the actions of people. To influence people top managers must know and understand the general theories of human motivation, for men and women are not stamped from a single mold. An understanding of the needs of human personality can go a long way toward helping top managers bring their agencies closer to the citizenry, as well as lessening the chances of internal rank-and-file militancy.

Middle Management

Middle managers—usually captains and lieutenants—primarily function to activate the department's policies by adapting the organization to particular tasks, by meshing personnel with methods and procedures, by maintaining operational control, and by setting standards and reviewing accomplishments. Simply stated, middle management directs the agency's operations. Although policy is made by top management, middle managers translate it into action.

Middle managers must possess great skill in devising specific work programs that will blend with the total departmental program. It is this level of management, more than any other, that will determine whether the police department operates as a functional system or as a group of semirelated divisions working at cross-purposes. It is essential that middle managers have a flair for organizing and the capacity to inspire group loyalty.

First-Line Supervision

First-line supervisors are those leaders who operate at the performance level. Usually uniformed sergeants, first-line supervisors are the ones who actually oversee the work of line officers. Their counterparts in industry are foremen. Part of their duties include devising work plans, laying out beat assignments, training and evaluating those they supervise, maintaining records, developing team spirit, presenting departmental policy to patrolmen, and cooperating with managers above them and with other supervisors. First-line supervisors must possess a good deal of technical competence and be thoroughly familiar with line tasks.

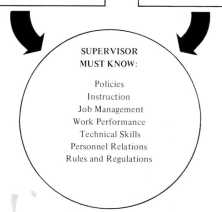

MANAGEMENT EXPECTS THE SUPERVISOR TO:	WORKER EXPECTS THE SUPERVISOR TO:
Get Out Production (Quantity and Quality)	Give On-the-Job Training
Settle Problems	Give Fair Treatment
Explain and Carry Out Policies	Represent Him to Management
Enforce Regulations and Rules	Interpret Rules and Regulations
Promote Safety	Provide Safe Working Conditions
Plan and Improve Work Methods	Use Improved Work Methods
Get Workers' Cooperation	Give Advice
Induct New Workers	Listen to His Suggestions and Problems
Represent Management to Worker	Provide Good Working Relations
	Be a Good Leader
	Plan His Work
	Consider Mental and Physical Ability

SUPERVISOR
MUST KNOW:

Policies
Instruction
Job Management
Work Performance
Technical Skills
Personnel Relations
Rules and Regulations

The duties of a first-line supervisor. *(Courtesy of the United States Air Force)*

In fact, a major portion of a promotional examination for sergeant is designed to measure technical ability. Only master patrolmen should be considered for promotion, and even then the final weeding out process, if undertaken properly, will eliminate most of them.

A recurring problem in police management, one that will never completely be resolved, is the failure of sergeants to view themselves as part of management's team, rather than just promoted patrolmen. Sergeants are so close to the action and emotions of everyday police work that they often find it difficult to identify with the administrative hierarchy, especially when they have worked for years with the patrolmen they are assigned to supervise. The protective instinct that occurs from supervising men who risk their lives daily often outweighs the tenets of sound management, however well trained the sergeant may be. In this regard, one of the most valuable supervisory traits may be the capacity to switch roles, to "wear two hats" as some scholars have put it. As the most direct management link with uniformed patrolmen, sergeants have an incredibly important function, one which, if not properly fulfilled, can mean failure for the department in eliminating goal impediments. Current research indicates that there is a direct correlation between small-group efficiency and the quality of supervision. Police squads have higher morale, greater effectiveness, and better production records when the first-line supervisor is liked and respected by his subordinates. As planner, coordinator, team leader, and management representative, the supervisor must possess more than the ordinary dynamic traits and should excel the average squad patrolman in intelligence, dependability, and intellectual integrity.

SOME ORGANIZATIONAL PRINCIPLES

Contemporary police theorists have attempted to formulate organizational principles flexible enough to apply to all law enforcement agencies. The final test of whether or not organizational rules are correct is if they contribute in some way to the accomplishment of the police task. Apparently no single "right" form of organization has yet been devised, but in order to insure a healthy agency, certain administrative postulates should be adopted by chief executives desirous of professionalizing their departments. The following organizational principles reflect current scholarly thought on the subject of sound management:

1. Personnel performing like duties should be grouped together to insure more effective productivity.

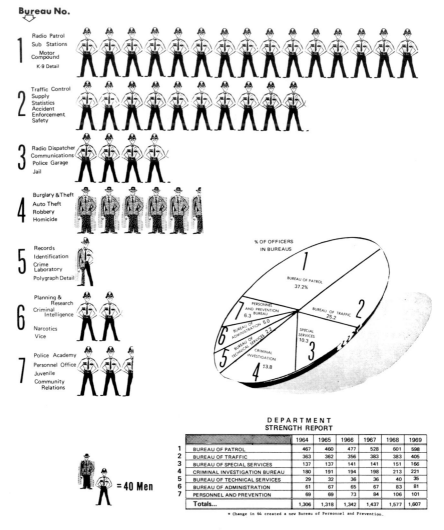

STRENGTH REPORT

Bureau No.

1 Radio Patrol / Sub Stations / Motor Compound / K-9 Detail

2 Traffic Control / Supply / Statistics / Accident Enforcement / Safety

3 Radio Dispatcher / Communications / Police Garage / Jail

4 Burglary & Theft / Auto Theft / Robbery / Homicide

5 Records / Identification / Crime Laboratory / Polygraph Detail

6 Planning & Research / Criminal Intelligence / Narcotics / Vice

7 Police Academy / Personnel Office / Juvenile / Community Relations

% OF OFFICERS IN BUREAUS

BUREAU OF PATROL 37.2%
PERSONNEL AND PREVENTION BUREAU 6.3
BUREAU OF ADMINISTRATION 5.0
BUREAU OF TECHNICAL SERVICES 2.2
BUREAU OF TRAFFIC 25.2
SPECIAL SERVICES 10.3
CRIMINAL INVESTIGATION 13.8

= 40 Men

DEPARTMENT STRENGTH REPORT

		1964	1965	1966	1967	1968	1969
1	BUREAU OF PATROL	467	460	477	528	601	598
2	BUREAU OF TRAFFIC	363	362	356	383	383	405
3	BUREAU OF SPECIAL SERVICES	137	137	141	141	151	166
4	CRIMINAL INVESTIGATION BUREAU	180	191	194	198	213	221
5	BUREAU OF TECHNICAL SERVICES	29	32	36	36	40	35
6	BUREAU OF ADMINISTRATION	61	67	65	67	83	81
7	PERSONNEL AND PREVENTION	69	69	73	84	106	101
	Totals...	1,306	1,318	1,342	1,437	1,577	1,607

* Change in 64 created a new Bureau of Personnel and Prevention.

A departmental strength report which graphically depicts manpower allotment by bureau. *(Courtesy of the Houston Police Department)*

2. The department's major divisions should be established according to the functions for which they will be responsible, i.e. bureau of investigation, bureau of administration, bureau of operations, etc.

3. The responsibilities to be performed by each manager or unit should be defined in as clear and definite a manner as possible. Furthermore, two managers or two units should not be assigned the same duties, because such duplication produces confusion and makes it difficult to hold either fully responsible for performance.

4. No person should ordinarily have to take orders from more than one supervisor.

5. When responsibility for a task is assigned, corresponding authority should also be delegated. It is best not to accept responsibility for a mission unless it is coupled with the authority to act with some discretion.

6. Administrators should always have a means at their control whereby they can check on the quality of their agency's work.

7. A manager should have under him and reporting to him only that number of subordinates that he is capable of adequately supervising. His span of control should not be overextended.

8. The department's positions should be set up in accordance with the various classes of work to be accomplished rather than being related to particular men and women. The demands of the work, rather than personal considerations, should determine the number and types of positions in the department.

9. The organization of the department and its operating policies should be delineated in writing and disseminated to all members of the agency.

10. There should be a recognized chain of command and the lines of authority should be as clear and direct as possible.

11. The department's enterprise should be fully coordinated.

ORGANIZATIONAL CLARIFICATION

Internal conflicts often develop in police departments because personnel do not fully understand their duties and the assignments of others. Regardless of how well conceived the structure of an organization is, if employes do not fully comprehend their roles in it, it will not work. Two administrative devices are used to see to it that personnel are informed of their functions in the agency: organization charts and position descriptions.

Organization Charts

There are a number of types of organization charts, each serving a specific need; however, no purpose would be served by introducing them into this section, so only brief, general explanation of the broad concept of charting will be discussed.

There can be no acceptable reason for a sizable department not to chart its organization. Charts map lines of authority and point up organizational inconsistencies. They avoid conflict by clarification and serve as aids in orienting new employes to their jobs. According to the International City Management Association (ICMA), an organization chart is a pictorial representation of personnel distributions. Manager-subordinate relations do not exist because of organizational charts but they are strengthened because of charting, for uncertain decisionmaking often results when officers do not know how they tie into the entire structure. Yet, as invaluable as charts are, they have limitations: (1) they point up formal authority relationships, but they do not show how much authority exists at each point in the organization, (2) they omit, by necessity, unofficial or informal relationships, and (3) charts often depict organizations as they are supposed to be rather than as they are.

Position Descriptions

Each position on a police department, especially managerial positions, should be specifically defined in a position description, although not in minute detail. Basic job functions and the relationship to others are generally included in the description. A good position description will inform a new jobholder what he is

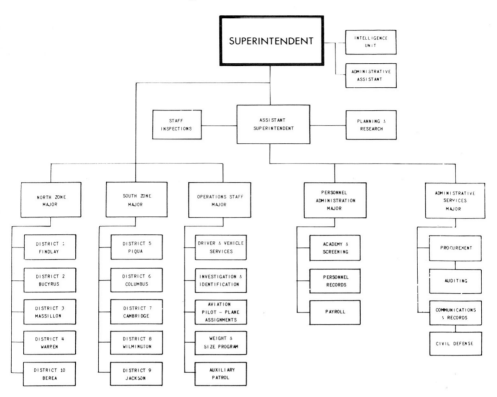

A highway patrol force is scattered throughout the state, making it a difficult public safety component to keep track of. A sound organizational structure and a true organization chart, as above, can foster staff control and eliminate confusion. *(Courtesy of the Ohio State Highway Patrol)*

supposed to do, to whom he reports, and who reports to him. There is no need for each uniformed patrolman in a police department to have a position description, but the general position of patrol officer should have one. On departments that have a civil service system, it is not generally necessary for an agency to have position descriptions as such, for jobs are classified into civil service classes to which descriptions are attached.

105.14 Duties of Identification Officers*

a. A member of the identification section shall become proficient in the science and techniques of fingerprinting and photography and the collection, preservation and presentation in court of all physical evidence, including trace evidence.

*A typical position description. *(Courtesy of The Orlando Police Department)*

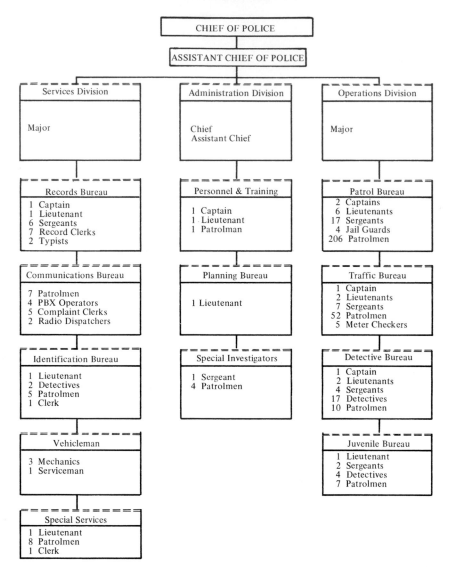

A structural organization chart and manning for a police department serving a city of 225,000. *(Courtesy of the Charlotte, North Carolina, Police Department)*

b. The identification technician shall have the duty of searching crime scenes for physical evidence in conformity with the established and approved procedures set forth by recognized authorities.

c. He shall process all evidence brought to the section; classify

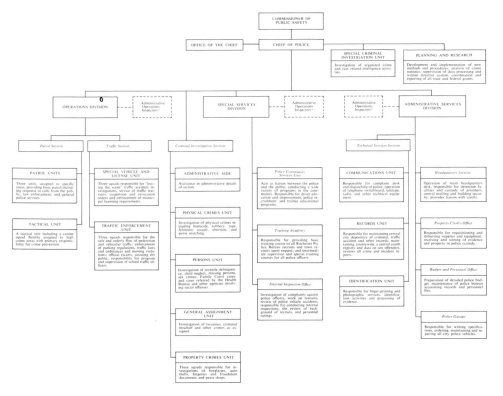

A functional organization chart for a police department serving a city of 300,000. *(Courtesy of the Rochester Police Bureau)*

fingerprints and search the files when necessary; shall file all fingerprint records and photographs. He shall photograph and process persons taken into custody by the members of the department and shall take such other photographs as required by the commanding officer.

d. He shall preserve the chain of custody of evidence by issuing or receiving a receipt whenever evidence is received or transferred to another.

e. He shall assist investigating officers in identifying, marking, preserving and packaging all physical evidence requiring further processing or analysis by another laboratory and shall assist in any other way possible.

f. He shall conduct only authorized searches of the various files maintained by the section and he is prohibited from divulging

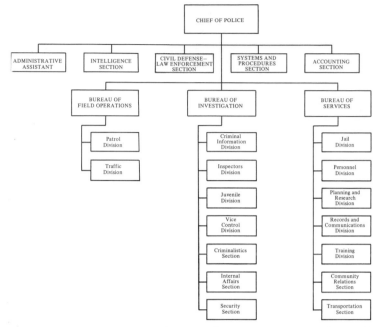

A structural organization chart for a police department serving a city of 375,000. *(Courtesy of the Oakland Police Department)*

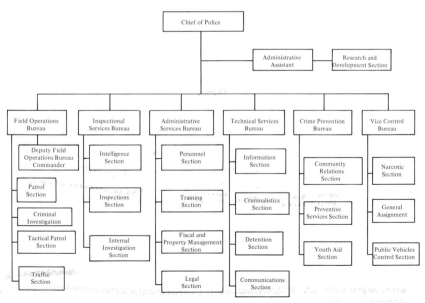

A structural organization chart for a police department serving a city of 500,000. *(Courtesy of the Cincinnati Division of Police)*

information to persons other than those authorized by the commanding officer.

g. A member of the section shall keep himself informed of all improved scientific methods and investigative techniques with regard to police identification and laboratory procedures.

h. He shall conduct such examinations and identification processes of all firearms involved in the commission of criminal acts as directed by the commanding officer.

THE ADMINISTRATIVE PROCESSES

Probably the most clear-cut definition of the term "administrative process" was given by the ICMA, who termed them "those interrelated means employed on a continuing basis by which an administrator achieves his organizational goals and objectives." The kinds of actions covered by this definition may number several score, or more. But it is generally thought that there are five major processes that universally apply to police departments: *planning, organizing, staffing and assembling resources, direction,* and *control.* Again, it should be emphasized that these processes are all interrelated.

Planning

Planning is the process of deciding on the objectives of a police department and of programming effort as the means of accomplishing the agency's mission. Planning is the first step which must be taken by an administrator in preparing for action because it is the process of formulating goals toward which the department's resources will be directed. Since the planning phase is such an important one, it is one element that the chief of police must personally spend a good deal of time thinking about. The chief, in his planning activities, performs the significant function of applying foresight to his department's activities. Planning may either be long- or short-ranged in nature and it should relate to both policy and programming. Broad policy planning must be followed up with program planning in which the more specific

SALARY SCALE AND DISTRIBUTION OF PERSONNEL

TITLE	NO.	MONTHLY SALARY	ADMINISTRATIVE DIVISION				DETECTIVE DIVISION			PATROL DIVISION				SERVICE DIVISION	
			OFFICE OF CHIEF OF POLICE	PERSONNEL AND TRAINING	COMMUNITY RELATIONS	POLICE RESERVES	INSPECTORS BUREAU	JUVENILE BUREAU	SPEC. INVESTIGATION	PATROL BUREAU	TRAFFIC BUREAU	WARRANT BUREAU	REPT. TRANSCRIBING	RECORD BUREAU	IDENTIFICATION BUREAU
Chief of Police	1	1625-2200	1												
Captains	5	1453-1603	1	1a			1a			1a				1a	
Lieutenants	7	1286-1418		1			1			4				1	
Inspectors	10	1138-1255					10								
Juvenile Bureau Director	1	1286-1418						1							
Special Investigations Director	1	1138-1255							1						
Sergeants	25	1084-1195	1	1	2	1	1			15	1	1		2	
Identification Expert	1	1084-1195													1
Jr. Traffic Police Director	1	1084-1195									1				
Patrolman-Sr. Ptm.	149	849-1084	1	2	1		5	6	3	101	6	4		15	5
Policewoman-Sr. Pwn.	2	849-1084						2							
Ass't Policewoman	9	634-809	1	1				2					2	2	1
Inter. Steno Clerk*	5	562-619	1	1	1		1			1					
Inter. Account Clerk*	1	562-619	1												
Inter. Typist Clerk*	19	535-590					2	1				3	8	4	1
Community Service Assistants	4	590-650			4										
Police Serv. Ass't.*	1	590-650												1	
Trainees & Aides**	13			13											
TOTALS	256		6	20	9	2	21	12	4	122	8	8	10	26	8

*   Civilian employees.
** Each Trainee and Aide works half time. Two persons fill one full time position.
a   Indicates Division Commander.

CITY ANIMAL SHELTER *		
Poundmaster	(1)	full time
Ass't Poundmaster	(4)	full time
Pound Attendant	(1)	full time

PART TIME PERSONNEL *		
Librarian	(1)	1/8 time
Clerk Bicycle Bureau	(1)	1/4 time
Key Punch Operator	(2)	1/2 time each
Typist-Rept. Transcribing	(1)	1/4 time

A chart depicting the distribution of personnel by division, and pay scale. *(Courtesy of the Berkeley Police Department)*

steps toward long-range goals are taken and actual work plans are laid out. Accordingly, there are three basic steps in planning: (1) formulation of objectives, (2) assessment of the means that can be assembled to achieve the objectives, and (3) the careful preparation of work programs devised to accomplish the objectives.

Public administrator H. S. Person views planning as a continuing process concerned with dynamic situations, a method for keeping to a minimum the frictions, confusions, and losses resulting from variability. Person has formulated eight postulates of planning:

1. The foundation of good planning is the laying out of the goals in as clear-cut and comprehensive a manner as possible by those possessing this authority.

2. The formulation of broad policies governing achievement of objectives must be undertaken.

3. It is essential that there be joint analysis by top management of alternative means and methods by which objectives can be accomplished.

4. A major step in planning is the setting up of an organization within which administrators can divide up the different functions—all of which together will amount to a synthesis of effort by all organizational segments.

5. After the initial synthesis comes further detailed examination of ways and means which will result in specifying the work flow.

6. Particular duties must be assigned to specific personnel and units in order to translate procedure into action.

7. A sense of responsibility for performing the various tasks must be infused into the organization so that work is undertaken pursuant to prescribed procedure—not according to individual whim.

8. Work measurement should be provided for so that the operations of various subdivisions and the results of their efforts can be examined with some precision.

Organizing

Organizing (as a process) is the method by which group activity is structured and authority relationships are formalized. The logic behind organizing is that departmental objectives will not be met unless the total resources of an agency are arranged and utilized in a way that is consistent with efficiency and economy. Police work is a fluid task with, for example, crime patterns constantly changing. Police administrators must look on organizing as an "action process" by which the dynamic internal and external

DEPARTMENT SPECIAL ORDER	DATE OF ISSUE 22 June 1964	EFFECTIVE DATE 23 June 1964	SPECIAL ORDER NO. 64-39
SUBJECT CHICAGO TRANSIT AUTHORITY INCIDENTS		AMENDS	
REFERENCE	RESCINDS Department Memorandums 61-197 & 62-110		

1. PURPOSE

    This order is intended to:

    a.   guide officers in the handling of incidents involving the Chicago Transit Authority.

    b.   familiarize officers of the Department with those operations of the Chicago Transit Authority of importance in the proper handling of police incidents.

2. HANDLING INCIDENTS

    a.   An officer who responds to an incident on a C. T. A. bus, train, or an elevated or subway platform will immediately request assistance if there is any doubt that he is able to handle the incident rapidly and safely.

    b.   The Communications Center will inform the C. T. A. Radio Room of all incidents which affect C. T. A. service or the safety of employees or passengers.

3. RADIO & TELEPHONE COMMUNICATIONS

    a.   The C. T. A. Radio Room, located in the Merchandise Mart, has a direct telephone line to a number of positions in our Communications Center. In the event of an emergency, radio equipped C. T. A. Police and supervisors' vehicles, and many elevated and subway trains can contact the C. T. A. Radio Room to relay a message to the Department's Communications Center for dispatch to our radio units. Eventually all elevated and subway trains will be equipped to communicate with the C. T. A. Radio Room.

    b.   When there are emergencies in the subway or on elevated tracks, officers may request motormen or conductors on C. T. A. trains, equipped with radio-telephone, to have calls for assistance relayed to our Communications Center by their Radio Room.

4. BUSES

    Many C. T. A. buses are equipped with two amber flashing lights mounted both on the front and rear of the vehicle. All new buses are so equipped before being placed in service. Bus drivers are instructed to use all these lights simultaneously to summon police in emergencies. Since all buses are not so equipped at this time, officers will be alert to both the amber flashing signals and any other indications by C. T. A. bus drivers that assistance is necessary.

5. C. T. A. POLICE

    a.   The C. T. A. police office is located in room 429 of the Merchandise Mart. Pax 358 and MO 4-7200, ext. 2300, are answered at any time. When incidents requiring police action are expected or have occurred on C. T. A. property, the C. T. A. Police will be notified so that they may assist our Department in properly handling the incident.

    b.   C. T. A. Police officers are assigned in citizen's dress, both in unmarked cars and on foot patrol. They are peace officers for the purpose of protecting C. T. A. property and the persons and property of C. T. A. passengers and employees.

    c.   The Department will accept prisoners from C. T. A. Police officers. The C. T. A. Police will be required to sign complaints, unless a citizen will do so, and provide all necessary information for the completion of an arrest report.

Authenticated by:

O. W. WILSON
Superintendent of Police

Distribution: "E"   All units and each police officer.

Special order. A device for transmitting departmental policy down the chain of command. *(Courtesy of the Chicago Police Department)*

JAIL DIVISION GENERAL ORDER   I - 2
OAKLAND POLICE DEPARTMENT

Index as:
      Arrest Reports, Incomplete
      Corrections to Arrest Reports
      Errors in Arrest Reports

INCOMPLETE OR INADEQUATE ARREST REPORTS

The purpose of this order is to establish a procedure for correcting errors on Arrest Reports received by the Jail Division.

I.   Jail Division personnel who discover a material error or
    omission on an arrest report will bring the matter to the
    attention of a Watch Supervisor.

I.   The Watch Supervisor will evaluate the discrepancy and if
    additional information is needed for clarification, he will
    contact a command or supervisory officer of the arresting
    officer and ask their cooperation in obtaining the necessary
    information.

    A. Minor errors or omissions in any of the boxes
       except the "Charge" box (No. 13) and the narrative
       portion of the report (No. 49) may be corrected
       by the Jail Division Watch Supervisor.

    B. Changes in the "Charge" box or narrative portion of
       the report will not be made by personnel assigned to
       the Jail Division. Corrections in the "Charge" or
       body of the report must be made by the arresting
       officer or his supervisor or commanding officer. The
       identity of the officer making alterations or additions
       to these two items must be noted on the arrest report.

                              By order of

                              PALMER STINSON
                              Captain, Commanding
                              Jail Division

General order. Originating at either the top- or middle-management level, the general order apprises police personnel of policies and procedures to be followed in specific instances. *(Courtesy of the Oakland Police Department)*

environment with which they must grapple may be properly handled, even under constantly changing conditions.

Staffing and Assembling Resources

The assembling of men and materials to successfully complete the police task is a high-priority process. A certain amount of money is allotted to police departments each year to perform rather specific functions. It is critical that these tax dollars be used in such a way that waste is minimized. Only those programs that are necessary to the public safety should be created, and glamorous but frivolous equipment should not be purchased. In lean budget years essential programs may have to be cut back, but even then some system of priorities must be established to insure that the most-needed programs are kept alive. As far as manpower is concerned, the same principle applies. Personnel who have received specialized education or training (e.g. at Northwestern Traffic Institute or Southern Police Institute, or an advanced academic degree) should be assigned to those units where they can best put their knowledge to work.

Direction

The function of direction is to get employes to fulfill their duties. Direction involves working relationships at each departmental level, but it especially concerns commanding officers, whose job it is to guide the department on a true course. Orders are important in directing subordinates. A police department's orders may be either oral or written, although written orders are generally preferred. Written orders may be transmitted in a number of ways, including (1) in training bulletins explaining departmental procedure in specific field situations (e.g. use of the long baton), (2) in general orders describing permanent departmental policies (e.g. internal investigation procedures), (3) in special orders applying to *ad hoc* incidents (e.g. traffic assignments at a parade), (4) personnel orders notifying members in changes of status (e.g. transfers, promotions, disciplinary action), and (5) in memos directing operational changes.

Control

Control is a managerial function which measures and corrects the performance of subordinates. According to Henri Fayol, the father of modern management theory, control "consists of verifying whether everything occurs in conformity with the plan adopted, the instructions issued, and principles established." There are certain systematic ways in which chief executives exert staff control over their departments. The most popular method, at least on large departments, is the creation of a special unit to inspect departmental operations on a continuing basis. Even smaller departments often either assign one man to the job or place in the job description of a middle manager the authority and responsibility to perform that task.

POLICE POLICYMAKING

In 1967 the President's Commission on Law Enforcement took the nation's police chiefs to task for failing to assume the role of major policymakers. From an administrative standpoint, no more serious charge can be made against a chief executive than that of shirking his decision-making function, which is exactly what the Commission was referring to. There were reasons for this widespread failure, none of which is tenable; however, there is nothing to be gained here by a discussion of past neglect. Many, though not nearly all, departments have since corrected this weakness.

Sound policy has six essential characteristics:

1. It should be based on clearly defined objectives.
2. It should be as simple as possible.
3. It should establish standards.
4. It must be flexible.
5. It ought to be well-balanced.
6. It should use available resources before creating new authority and new resources.

Volumes have been written on the art of policymaking, so it is impossible to do little more than introduce some of the basic ideas relating to the subject. Accordingly, the following are some propositions respecting the making and expressing of policy:

1. Vagueness about general policy objectives renders administration almost ineffectual.
2. Basic policy statements should permit middle managers and field supervisors to act freely within broad limitations.
3. Policymaking is a continuous, cumulative, and collective process, widely diffused throughout a police department.
4. A police chief in his policymaking role is as dependent on middle managers and first-line supervisors as they are on him.

5. Sound policy can be made only on the basis of adequate information, detailed analysis, and careful research.
6. Nothing is more destructive of confidence in an agency and internal morale than policies which cannot be relied upon.
7. It is not enough for administrators to simply approve policy; they must also express it clearly and impart it throughout the police department.
8. Policies should generally be in writing.
9. Highly competent administrators will anticipate needed policy changes and keep policies up to date.

COMMUNICATION IN POLICE ADMINISTRATION

The element of communication, which may be defined as the functional process by which personnel from top to bottom of the administrative pyramid are kept informed, is inextricably bound up with every task in a police department. Communication brings understanding and dispels ignorance. When officers understand what they are doing and why, they are more productive. Conveying information from top management down is only part of the communication process; its essence is the will to listen and take in the interests and concern of personnel throughout the agency. This kind of reverse, or upward, communication is called feedback. Communication may be formal—a planned system of procedures and channels flowing along lines of formal authority with the object of transmitting information to all levels of the department; or it may be informal—a web of interpersonal contacts and personal relations which serves as a transmitting device for information. Police managers will never be able to eliminate the latter type, so they often learn to use it to the department's advantage.

One of the principal obstacles to communication is gobbledygook or "bureaucratic officialese," which is language which becomes jargon because of its overexactness, overabstractness, and overimpersonalization. The classic example of this problem, often quoted by public administrators, is the case of the San Francisco plumber who wrote the Bureau of Standards to ask if it was permissible to use hydrochloric acid to clean drains.

Replied the Bureau: "The efficacy of hydrochloric acid is indisputable, but the chlorine residue is incompatible with metallic permanence."

The plumber replied that he was happy the Bureau agreed the acid was a good drain cleaner.

The Bureau wrote again: "We cannot assume responsibility for the production of toxic and noxious residues with hydrochloric acid, and we suggest you use an alternative."

The plumber wrote back that he was happy the Bureau still agreed with him.

Whereupon, the Bureau frantically replied: "Don't use hydrochloric acid; it eats hell out of the pipes!"

(Courtesy of the Los Angeles County Sheriff's Department)

Chapter 22

POLICE INTEGRITY[1]

Exacting ethical standards and a high degree of honesty are perhaps more essential for the police than for any other group in society. Because the police are entrusted with the enforcement of the fundamental rules that guide society's conduct, a policeman's violation of the law or his corrupt failure to enforce it dishonors the law and authority he represents. Dishonesty within the police agency can, almost overnight, destroy respect and trust that has been built up over a period of years by honest local government and police officials. Nothing undermines public confidence in the police and the process of criminal justice more than the illegal acts of officers. Support for the police in their work, and the bringing about of crucial changes such as those recommended by the Commission to strengthen the police, can easily be impaired by a belief that the police themselves are not taking every possible measure to eradicate corruption and unethical conduct.

Although the policeman is no more resistant to temptation than anyone else, his position exposes him to extraordinary pressures. In many cases practices that are accepted in other fields and occupations—such as tipping and doing favors—are particularly difficult to avoid in police work. Conflicting pressures are often placed upon the police. For example, police are required to enforce parking and gambling laws, though most of the community might prefer them not to. Public resistance to the enforcement of such laws greatly increases the temptation to accept favors, gratuities or bribes, or simply to ignore violations. Police dishonesty is, of course, a series of private tragedies for the officers who become involved. It also affects the morale of thousands of honest policemen who suffer from popular identification with those involved in corruption or misconduct. When the

---

[1] Reprinted with editorial adaption from *Task Force Report: The Police*, pp. 208-215.

"dishonest cop" headline appears, honest police officers through-out the country are adversely affected.

PATTERNS OF DISHONESTY

The violations in which police are involved vary widely in character. The most common are improper political influence; acceptance of gratuities or bribes in exchange for nonenforcement of laws, particulary those relating to gambling, prostitution, and liquor offenses, which are often extensively interconnected with organized crime; the "fixing" of traffic tickets; minor thefts; and occasional burglaries.

Political Corruption

Government corruption in the United States has troubled historians, political reformers, and the general public since the middle of the nineteenth century. Metropolitan police forces—most of which developed during the late 1800s when government corruption was most prevalent—have been deeply involved in corruption. The police are particularly susceptible to the forms of corruption that have attracted widest attention—those that involve tolerance or support of organized crime activities. But the police, as one of the largest and most strategic groups in metropolitan government, are also likely targets for political patronage, favoritism, and other kinds of influence that have pervaded local governments dominated by political machines. Against both forms of corruption responsible police leaders have fought a continuing battle—one that appears to be steadily gaining.

The remnants of corrupt political control allied with organized crime and vice operations have, however, continued to plague some cities—as evidenced by widely publicized incidents during the past ten years, particularly concerning organized crime activities.

Police Appointments

Another form of political corruption—where police appointments are considered a reward for political favors and police officials are consequently responsive primarily to the local political machine—is still fairly open and tacitly accepted practice in many small cities and counties. It recurs too, from time to time, in larger cities, though generally in less conspicuous form.

Even in some cities where reforms have ended open political control of the police, policemen who make trouble for businessmen with strong political influence may still be transferred to punishment beats, and traffic tickets may still be fixed in some places through political connections. Honest and conscientious police chiefs often have an extremely difficult time eliminating these practices.

Such assignment practices may be present in the lower ranks of individual precincts or bureaus and, if detected, are often difficult to prove with the certainty needed to take action under cumbersome civil service regulations. Appeal to a mayor, city council, or prosecutor may of course be fruitless, since they themselves may be involved in such practices or condone them. The general public often accepts this style of city government as simply "the way things are," and the policeman who tries to buck such a system is likely to be ostracized by his companions and lose any chance he may have had to advance in his career. Political corruption in police personnel practices, although rarely dramatic enough to make headlines, can in itself destroy the morale of the honest and conscientious officer, and deter able men from careers in law enforcement.

Nonenforcement of the Law

Problems often confront the police when they are faced with enforcement of laws in such areas as gambling, prostitution, liquor, and traffic. In many cases there are strong community pressures against enforcement of such laws. In others neither the police nor the rest of the criminal justice system have the resources or ability to attempt full enforcement, and in these cases a pattern of selective nonenforcement prevails. Some prosecutors and judges react to selective enforcement problems by dropping cases or imposing fines low enough to be accepted as part of the overhead of illegal business. This can create an environment in which dishonesty thrives.

Enforcement Policies

Sometimes enforcement policies are decided openly and rationally; in such instances selective enforcement is properly regulated. But in others, nonenforcement may become the occasion for bribery or other corruption. Thus, in the prohibition era millions of people sought and found ways to disregard the ban on liquor, and police attempts at enforcement were met with citizen condemnation and offers of payment for tolerance of community norms.

Illegitimate Nonenforcement

While the wholesale corruption of prohibition days has passed, illegitimate nonenforcement remains a problem. One West Coast police official described in his fashion how a bookie once attempted to influence him:

> These people really work on you. They make it seem so logical—like you are the one that is out of step. This bookie gave me this kind of a line: "It's legal at the tracks, isn't it? So why isn't it legal here? It's because of those crooks at the Capitol. They're gettin' plenty—all driving Cads. Look at my customers, some of the biggest guys in town—they don't want you to close me down. If you do they'll just transfer you. Like that last jerk. And even the judge, what did he do? Fined me a hundred and suspended fifty. Hell, he knows Joe citizen wants me here, so get smart, be one of the boys, be part of the system. It's a way of life in this town and one you're not gonna change. Tell you what I'll do. I won't give you a nickel; just call in a free bet in the first race every day and you can win or lose, how about it?"

Theft

The problems of theft by police officers sometimes takes a form less blatant than the occasional well-publicized burglary such as the Summerdale incident, which resulted in the reorganization of the entire Chicago police department in 1960, and the 1961 apprehension in Denver of a ring of police burglars, which resulted in dismissal of fifty-two men.

Pattern

A pattern that has been described by more than one police official was that of storekeepers who also take the attitude that insurance will cover losses and, as a mark of appreciation when policemen discover an unlocked door or investigate a burglary, invite them to help themselves to merchandise that can be reported as having been stolen.

Some officers have also been known to take building material and actually transport it in police vehicles. In one city, officers picked up nails, tools, bundles of shingles, roofing paper, and other items from the "midnight" supply company. They were all remodeling their houses and rationalized their act on the basis of numerous reports of stolen property from building contractors, presumably much of it taken by workman on the job. One of the officers was a former building-trade worker and looked upon this form of toting as an accepted practice.

Kickbacks

Particularly in the case of traffic offenses is there an opportunity, which has sometimes resulted in publicized incidents, for policemen to receive payments for referring business to others such as towing companies, garages, and lawyers who specialize in traffic accident damage suits. In one large city, for example, lawyers' "runners" with radio equipped cars sometimes showed up at accidents. The result was an automatic twenty-five dollars for the police officer handling it if the victim could be influenced to accept the attorney. Licensing, inspection, and truck-weighing duties also have afforded opportunities for this sort of unethical conduct.

THE BACKGROUND OF THE PROBLEM

Since such conduct continues to be a problem of concern for police officials, inquiry is required into the underlying factors that contribute to dishonesty and violation of ethics.

Political Domination

The problem of old-style domination of the police by political machines has attracted the most intensive reform efforts from the police themselves. As a result, the effort to establish independent professional law enforcement has made considerable headway over the past thirty years. This movement has not been without its own problems, however; the tradition of improper political interference is deep rooted.

Civil Service Regulations

Further, civil service regulations in many jurisdictions have sometimes restricted the reform attempts of honest police executives. In many cities, for example, it is extremely difficult to remove officers who have engaged in serious acts of misconduct.

Political Interference

It is obvious that improper political interference contributes to corruption. Patronage appointments lower the quality of personnel and encourage all officers to cooperate with politicians, even in improper circumstances. Although a man might withstand this temptation for himself, it may be impossible or even pointless for him to separate himself from the practice of his superiors or partners.

Dishonest Superiors and Fellow Officers

Not long ago the police commissioner of a large city expressed publicly his pessimism about the ability of training to protect recruits from the pressures of improper conduct. He preferred to assign his best young officers to a tactical force that operated as a unit entirely separate and apart from the traditional organization. In that way, he said, it kept them out of "the system," where a new man was sometimes subjected to heavy pressures to conform to unethical practices, such as splitting tow-truck rebates and accepting gifts from merchants.

In many cases, of course, an honest recruit if properly trained and motivated will decide to report a matter to his superiors and assist in prosecuting disciplinary action.

Superiors

In some cases superiors too may be involved in dishonesty. When this is known to the officer, he should report the incident to a superior he trusts, even if he must go as high as the chief himself or to an outside agency. To protect the officers supervisors can, in most instances, develop a case without revealing the identity of the reporting officer.

Support of Regulations

All police officers have taken an oath to uphold the law and to support the regulations of their department. While in some cases proper action may be difficult and require considerable fortitude, the general problem cannot be overcome until there is a strong determination within all law enforcement agencies to get rid of the "rotten apples." Failure to do so by witholding information should be cause for severe disciplinary action. This rule is firmly enforced within the FBI and may be one of the strongest factors responsible for its outstanding record of integrity.

Ethical Standards

The personal ethical standard of police supervisors and executives exerts great influence in establishing an agency's attitude toward dishonest behavior. If an officer suspects that others support or simply condone dishonesty, his own definition of what comprises proper conduct may shift to accord with his concept of departmental norms.

Atmosphere

Supervisors may create an atmosphere that supports corruption if they place popularity among patrolmen above their supervisory responsibilities. Such an official may be willing to excuse infractions of departmental rules. He may keep from the police chief information that an officer accepted a number of small items from a local merchant. He may realize that a patrolman is engaging in misconduct, but to avoid controversy and to maintain what he considers a good working relationship, he may remain silent.

Chief of Police

Chiefs of police who are suspected of improper action can exert even more serious influence. Such men may symbolize to young officers the standard for reaching the top. When the chief is known to be responsive to improper political pressure or even to take orders from criminal elements, corruption can be considered a necessary route to promotion. At the least, the existence of dishonesty at the top levels of command may influence an officer to accept favors.

Public Participation

One major reason why police dishonesty continues is that large sections of the public contribute to it or condone it.

Gifts and Gratuities

It is not merely the professional gambler offering a patrolman a free bet who promotes corruption, but the motorist who thinks little of offering a traffic officer five-dollars to avoid a ticket, or the businessman who presses gifts and gratuities on police in return for indulgences or other favors.

Lack of Enforcement Policy

A considerable number of the most serious and persistent kinds of unethical conduct are connected with failure to enforce laws that are not in accord with community norms. Among these are laws concerning gambling, prostitution, liquor, and traffic. The failure of police administrators and other law enforcement officials and ultimately of legislators and the general public to acknowledge frankly the paradoxes confronting enforcement officials has meant that only rarely have explicit policies and guides to enforcement in these areas been developed and enforced.

Recruitment, Training, and Compensation

The inability to attract and retain men of higher character and the failure to screen applicants carefully enough contribute to the problem of dishonesty. A failure to confront in training the various ethical dilemmas that may be faced by a policeman can compound this situation. Recruits may get the idea that a departments command really does not care about ethics in borderline situations, or they may simply never realize that some practices constitute ethical violations, especially if they have not been so informed, and if they see other officers engaging in such practices.

Salaries

Low salaries may also contribute to police dishonesty, both by making it more difficult to recruit able men and by providing a convenient rationale for illegal enrichment.

Isolation

The climate of isolation between police and community that exists in some places, particularly in slum neighborhoods, has a pervasive influence in supporting misconduct. In such neighborhoods a policeman tends to see only the bad and to have contact with residents only when they have committed an offense. He may come to feel that the problems he has to deal with are insoluble and that he has no support or cooperation from the community. It is easy for the man who feels himself to be an outcast to react by disregarding standards of ethics and law.

MAINTAINING POLICE INTEGRITY

It is the police themselves, in the vast majority of cases, who are ridding their profession of the unethical and the corrupt. An ever increasing number of law enforcement leaders are realizing that vigilance against such practices is a continuing part of their responsibilities.

Law Enforcement Code of Ethics

As a Law Enforcement Officer, my fundamental duty is to serve mankind; to safeguard lives and property; to protect the innocent against deception, the weak against oppression or intimidation, and the peaceful against violence or disorder; and to respect the Constitutional rights of all men to liberty, equality and justice.

I will keep my private life unsullied as an example to all; maintain courageous calm in the face of danger, scorn, or ridicule; develop self-restraint; and be constantly mindful of the welfare of others. Honest in thought and deed in both my personal and official life, I will be exemplary in obeying the laws of the land and the regulations of my department. Whatever I see or hear of a confidential nature or that is confided to me in my official capacity will be kept ever secret unless revelation is necessary in the performance of my duty.

I will never act officiously or permit personal feelings, prejudices, animosities or friendships to influence my decisions. With no compromise for crime and with relentless prosecution of criminals, I will enforce the law courteously and appropriately without fear or favor, malice or ill will, never employing unnecessary force or violence and never accepting gratuities.

I recognize the badge of my office as a symbol of public faith, and I accept it as a public trust to be held so long as I am true to the ethics of the police service. I will constantly strive to achieve these objectives and ideals, dedicating myself before God to my chosen profession . . . law enforcement.

Law enforcement pins its recruitment hopes on young people. *(Courtesy of the Los Angeles County Sheriff's Department)*

Chapter 23

RECRUITMENT AND SELECTION OF PERSONNEL

MUNICIPAL POLICE RECRUITMENT AND SELECTION

The recruitment of qualified police personnel has always been a difficult task; however, in the years to come the shortage of qualified manpower may become critical. Each year in America from 30,000 to 50,000 new police officers are required to keep pace with population increases and the problems of an increasingly mobile nation. Approximately five percent of the nation's police officers leave the service annually, and compensation must also be made for this loss. Policing is a demanding task, making it mandatory that only the finest applicants be hired. Even though the best candidates are selected and trained, some will eventually leave police work for a variety of reasons. Occasionally a dedicated officer will terminate his services because of family pressures. Prior to accepting a position in a law enforcement agency the applicant and his family should consider the many facets governing the duties of a police officer. Rotating shifts, health and injury hazards, and extra hours devoted to training and education are but a few of the factors that may strain personal relationships. When a man accepts a position in a police agency, in many ways his family also serves. The secret of success as a police officer may well be an understanding wife who is proud to see her husband dedicate his life to the service of others.

Complicating the demand for police manpower is the fact that many urban police agencies will in the near future experience a mass exodus of veteran officers because of retirement. Those officers who entered the police service shortly after the end of World War II are fast becoming eligible for their well-deserved retirements. Not only will this cause vacancies at the line level, but opportunities for promotion will also occur, as many of these prospective retirees are ranking officers.

Job Announcements

To meet the critical need for more personnel, police agencies utilize a variety of methods to recruit qualified applicants. Probably the most widespread method is an announcement in the local newspaper. Furthermore, recruitment posters may be cir-

LAW ENFORCEMENT - CAREER WITH A FUTURE

BUREAU OF POLICE
RICHMOND, VIRGINIA

BENEFITS

GOOD PAY - starts at $6,864.00 - goes to $8,970.00

40 HOUR WEEK - job security and advancements

PAID VACATION - up to 18 working days per year

PAID HOLIDAYS - 9½ days per year

SICK LEAVE - 1 day accumulated per month

GROUP INSURANCE - financial savings to employee

TRAINING - intensive 16 weeks training program for all recruits which includes college credited, in-service training courses designed to keep the police officer abreast of the continual changes in law enforcement

MILITARY LEAVE WITH PAY - up to 15 days per year

VETERANS ON THE JOB TRAINING - tax-free subsistence allowance up to $100.00 a month for the first 18 months - over and above salary

QUALIFICATIONS

MALE - must be at least 21 years of age and not more than 35 (special consideration given experienced applicants up to 40 years of age)

PHYSICALLY FIT - strong, active, good appearance, and free from body defects

EDUCATION - at least a high school graduate or must be able to show documentary evidence of equivalency

CHARACTER - a thorough background investigation will be made on each candidate

FOR FURTHER INFORMATION, CALL OR WRITE:

RICHMOND BUREAU OF POLICE

POLICE ACADEMY - MOSQUE

LAUREL AND MAIN STS.

RICHMOND, VIRGINIA 23220

PHONE 703.649-5691

A simple, yet concise and effective one-page job announcement inviting young men to seek a career in the police service. *(Courtesy of the Richmond Bureau of Police)*

A mobile police recruitment van. *(Courtesy of the Police Department, City of Baltimore)*

culated on military bases and on college campuses. Spot announcements on television have also proved effective. The ultimate goal is to attract qualified individuals to a career in law enforcement.

Minority Recruitment

Police departments are now embarking on extraordinary programs aimed at recruiting minority-group citizens into law enforcement. Although some would set strict quotas of black-white ratios on police agencies, quotas have proved, in varying ways, unworkable. Those police departments that have experienced success in minority recruitment have done so not by setting quotas, dropping standards, or instituting heavy-handed recruitment devices.

If an applicant is able to meet strict, but fair standards, race, creed, and nationality considerations should be ignored. When reasonable employment qualifications are lowered to induce minority applicants, the good that results is more often offset by the devastating effect that double standards have on an agency and on the community.

Two prospective policewomen applicants question a recruiter. *(Courtesy of the Metropolitan Police Department, Washington, D. C.)*

Basic Requirements

The requirements for police applicants vary from agency to agency; however, some basic standards are uniformly found in most good departments. Again because of personnel shortages certain requirements have been lowered to allow more applicants to apply for available positions.

Citizenship

A uniform requirement is for the applicant to be a citizen of the United States of America.

Age

The minimum age is usually twenty-one years, although some departments accept eighteen- or nineteen-year-old applicants. Maximum age requirements vary, with the average range being from twenty-nine to thirty-five years of age. Many police agencies will increase their maximum age if an applicant has prior police experience and/or some college education.

Education

The basic requirement for most police agencies is high school graduation or equivalent, although an increasing number of municipal agencies are moving toward varying amounts of college education as an entry level requirement. Because of the many law enforcement college programs throughout the country and the desire of the police community to raise its standards, certain police agencies have two- and four-year-degree requirements for entry level. Police departments in California, Oregon, Florida, and elsewhere have established the baccalaureate degree as a minimum entry-level requirement.

Height

The generally acceptable minimum height requirement is 5'7" to 5'9". Some may argue that the height of an individual does not measure his ability and intelligence; however, a reasonable minimum height requirement is essential. Studies have shown that physical appearance can often have a dampening effect on a potentially violent situation.

Weight

The generally acceptable minimum weight is 135 to 150 lbs. The important factor in most agencies is weight in proportion to height.

Vision

Vision requirements have almost universally been relaxed across the country. Many departments no longer demand perfect eyesight of applicants, although certain correctable standards have been set. Safety glasses and contact lenses have positively affected

A nationwide recruitment program is conducted by Washington's Metropolitan Police in its search for qualified personnel. *(Courtesy of the Metropolitan Police Department ,Washington, D.C.)*

the standards in vision requirements. Applicants may not be color blind, and their depth perception must be "normal."

Hearing

Normal or uncorrected hearing is the requirement for entry levels in almost all agencies.

Pay and Benefits

Most police departments offer benefits which assist in attracting many fine applicants into the police service. Although altruism and dedication are expected of all applicants, personal situations dictate that law enforcement agencies express their gratitude for faithful service in tangible ways. Following is a discussion of some of the material considerations offered police officers.

Salary Considerations

One of the most encouraging signs for law enforcement has been the recent increase in wages for line personnel. In the labor market law enforcement must consider itself a competitor with other occupational groupings. With the entry salary level of some police agencies surpassing one thousand dollars a month (without overtime), one can see that a number of communities have placed a high value on police manpower. As more communities realize the worth of a police officer then decent competitive wages will increase throughout the nation. Many police agencies are now paying college graduates higher entry level salaries than their non-degreed counterparts.

Job Security

One obvious advantage to a career in the police service is that of job security. To many thousands of workers each year in our country a layoff is an impending threat. In such areas as the defense industry, layoffs are a reality that must be faced at the termination of each government contract. Law enforcement has no threat of layoffs or seasonal work assignments. As long as a man or woman remains productive and does not violate a major rule or policy of the agency, continued employment is of little concern. Even if a cutback in personnel occurred in some agencies, the need for qualified police personnel throughout the country insures continued employment for those who wish to serve.

Promotional Opportunities

As a police agency grows, so too, does its need for more supervisory, administrative, and command personnel. In law enforcement today a man's ability to compete through advanced testing and proven accomplishments generally determines the level that he will attain, although some departments still employ archaic promotional practices.

Specialization of various law enforcement tasks also offers possibilities for those interested and qualified. Investigation, criminalistics, polygraph testing, and data processing are but a few of the opportunities offered to line officers who wish to specialize. Many specialized tasks offer a man a higher wage or rank along with a more desirable work shift.

Sick Leave

Sick leave is generally accrued at the rate of one day per working month. In the majority of the police departments sick leave may be accumulated in case of serious sickness at a later date. Should injury occur in the performance of an officer's duties, there is generally no limit to the amount of recuperative leave he is allowed.

Vacation Time

A majority of major police agencies offer vacation leaves competitive with those offered in the private sector. Some agencies offer the recruit a day of vacation for each working month, as does the Albuquerque Police Department (twelve-and-a-half working days a year). Other agencies may follow a more liberal vacation schedule like the Oakland, California, Police Department (fifteen working days for recruits; twenty-one for veterans). As service time increases, additional vacation time is often allotted.

Retirement

Every person contemplating a police career should consider the advantages or disadvantages offered in the various retirement plans. A great majority of law enforcement agencies have established realistic and rewarding retirement plans. An excellent program demonstrating the above statement can be found by examining the current program offered by the city of Oakland, California:

1. One-half pay after twenty-five years service or one-half at age fifty-five with twenty years service.
2. Retirement pay of fifty percent of whatever the current pay is, i.e. an officer who retired in 1950 receives fifty percent of today's top pay, or $512.50.
3. Seventy-five percent to an officer who is retired for service-incurred disability. Upon reaching his normal retirement date he assumes the normal fifty percent salary.

4. Seventy-five percent to dependents of a retired officer who dies as a result of service-connected injuries. Upon normal retirement date this amount reduces to the normal fifty percent.
5. One-third salary to an officer with nonservice-connected disability who has over ten years service.

Overtime Considerations

In most occupations a worker is expected to occasionally devote extra hours to his job. In law enforcement agencies overtime is often required. Police work is no nine-to-five job! Historically, overtime in police work has been considered a part of the job. In an effort to compete for qualified personnel many of the country's police agencies have initiated extra pay for hours worked in excess of forty hours per week. Usually the wages paid for extra hours of duty are computed on the regular hourly wage of the individual. Progressive police agencies such as the Tucson Police Department offer time-and-one-half pay for extra duty hours. Some departments compensate their officers for overtime work by giving them credit time on vacations.

Uniforms

The accepted practice regarding uniforms is for the police department to either issue a man his full uniform or to compensate him for the expenditure of monies to buy uniforms and equipment.

The Selection Procedure

Once an individual has weighed the advantages and disadvantages of a police career and has decided that he wishes to become an officer of the law his next step is to apply for a position on the agency of his choice. An excellent example of the type of information usually requested of applicants may be found in the application form used for the County of Arlington, Virginia (see Appendix E). Following are the steps which most applicants must successfully complete prior to appointment.

The Written Test

A written test is usually administered to candidates shortly after they apply for a position. Out of a possible score of 100, the basic passing percentile is usually 70. Although many different types of

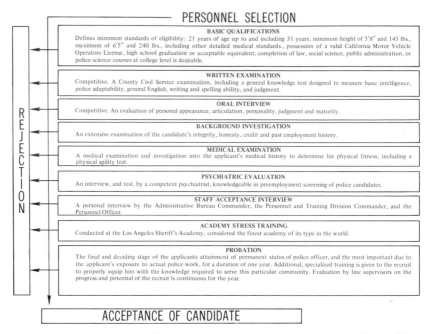

PERSONNEL SELECTION

BASIC QUALIFICATIONS
Defines minimum standards of eligibility: 21 years of age up to and including 31 years, minimum height of 5'8" and 145 lbs., maximum of 6'5" and 240 lbs., including other detailed medical standards., possession of a valid California Motor Vehicle Operators License, high school graduation or acceptable equivalent; completion of law, social science, public administration, or police science courses at college level is desirable.

WRITTEN EXAMINATION
Competitive. A County Civil Service examination, including a general knowledge test designed to measure basic intelligence, police adaptability, general English, writing and spelling ability, and judgment.

ORAL INTERVIEW
Competitive. An evaluation of personal appearance, articulation, personality, judgment and maturity.

BACKGROUND INVESTIGATION
An extensive examination of the candidate's integrity, honesty, credit and past employment history.

MEDICAL EXAMINATION
A medical examination and investigation into the applicant's medical history to determine his physical fitness, including a physical agility test.

PSYCHIATRIC EVALUATION
An interview, and test, by a competent psychiatrist, knowledgeable in preemployment screening of police candidates.

STAFF ACCEPTANCE INTERVIEW
A personal interview by the Administrative Bureau Commander, the Personnel and Training Division Commander, and the Personnel Officer.

ACADEMY STRESS TRAINING
Conducted at the Los Angeles Sheriff's Academy, considered the finest academy of its type in the world.

PROBATION
The final and deciding stage of the applicants attainment of permanent status of police officer, and the most important due to the applicant's exposure to actual police work, for a duration of one year. Additional, specialized training is given to the recruit to properly equip him with the knowledge required to serve this particular community. Evaluation by line supervisors on the progress and potential of the recruit is continuous for the year.

REJECTION

ACCEPTANCE OF CANDIDATE

Requirements and steps for permanent employment as a police officer. *(Courtesy of the Torrance, California, Police Department)*

written tests are utilized, the goal of any written test should be to measure general intelligence and aptitude, not knowledge in a specialized area. Although there are some books on the market that claim to prepare police applicants for civil service examinations, their reliability must be questioned, though they may assist in psychologically preparing those who have been out of an academic setting for an extended period.

The Initial Personal Interview

The initial personal interview is usually conducted by members of the local civil service board and/or representatives of the city, county, or state personnel board. The primary purpose of this first oral interview is to eliminate those candidates who appear to have difficulty in communicating or who have obvious personal traits objectionable to the civil service and/or personnel representatives.

Physical Examination

After successfully completing a written test and passing the initial oral interview, the next logical step for most agencies is the physical examination. In some cases a local doctor may be designated by the agency. In larger cities full-time doctors and assistants are available to determine the physical condition of candidates. Naturally, obvious health problems are enough to eliminate a candidate. This phase of testing is structured to eliminate personnel who are physically unable to meet the requirements of the agency.

Physical Aptitude Test

Besides demonstrating excellent physical health, a candidate may be asked to prove his physical fitness. Physical fitness is tested by a series of exercises. An example of what may be expected of a potential police officer is shown in a representation of the form used by the Las Cruces Police Department, New Mexico.

LAS CRUCES POLICE DEPARTMENT
ACADEMY
PHYSICAL APTITUDE TEST FOR APPLICANTS

NAME   ADDRESS

AGE   HEIGHT   WEIGHT   GRADE

TEST #1—VERTICAL JUMP—MEASURES HEIGHT THAT CANDIDATE CAN JUMP FROM STANDING POSITION. SEVENTEEN (17) INCH SPAN IS MINIMUM NEEDED TO QUALIFY.

GRADE

TEST #2—PRONE PUSH-UPS—MUST COMPLETE SIX MOVEMENTS IN 15 SECONDS.

GRADE

TEST #3—DYNAMIC FLEXIBILITY—EMPHASIS ON FLEXIBILITY AND SPEED OF MOVEMENTS. STANDS WITH BACK TO WALL, FEET SLIGHTLY SPREAD, HANDS TOGETHER, BENDS FORWARD, TOUCHES FLOOR, STANDS, AND THEN TOUCHES WALL TO RIGHT, THEN LEFT, ALTERNATING. MUST COMPLETE 14 REPETITIONS IN 20 SECONDS.

GRADE

TEST #4—ROPE CLIMBING—HAND OVER HAND—MUST NOT USE FEET OR LEGS. MUST CLIMB MINIMUM. ONE POINT FOR EACH OVER MIN.

GRADE

TEST #5—CHIN UPS—MIN. OF TEN—ONE POINT FOR EACH CHIN-UP OVER MIN.

GRADE

TEST #6—JUMPING ROPE—TEST TO DETERMINE COORDINATION. MIN OF 30 TO PASS. ONE POINT OFF PER MISS. MUST COMPLETE MIN. IN ONE-HALF MINUTE.

GRADE

TOTAL GRADE FOR ALL TESTS   DATE

REMARKS   EXAMINING OFFICER

117 POINTS MINIMUM REQUIRED TO PASS: SATISFACTORY
                                             UNSATISFACTORY

The City of Los Angeles does not have a physical agility test as such; however, the day before a recruit class convenes, recruits are required to perform the following exercises:

1. Run one-and-a-half miles in less than twelve minutes.
2. Two pull-ups, palms forward.
3. Ten push-ups, body straight with no swaying or arching.
4. Twenty-five sit-ups, hands behind the head, feet held by another.

Polygraph Examination

Some police agencies utilize a polygraph examination as part of their testing process. A polygraph test may be able to determine the honesty of the candidate, and even latent homosexual tendencies. Because it is an expensive process, the polygraph test is usually given only to candidates who have successfully passed other lower-cost tests and requirements. Some agencies have eliminated polygraph testing because of the inconsistency of the device.

Background Investigation

The extent of the background investigation varies with the ability of the agency to spend manhours and finances to check into the background of the police candidate. Almost all agencies send a fingerprint card to the FBI for a criminal record check. The agency may also wish to have departmental personnel talk to the candidate's family, friends, neighbors, previous employers, and other acquaintances. Many times vital information needed for proper consideration of the candidate's character is determined by patient questioning of people who have a personal knowledge of the candidate.

Psychological Interview

Some agencies have additional requirements in that the candidate must be examined by a trained psychologist or psychiatrist. Potential personnel problems are many times eliminated at this phase of testing. The main objective is to detect those candidates with negative personality traits which may later lead to brutality charges.

Departmental Interview

The last phase of the testing process is usually the second oral interview, conducted by departmental staff members. It is at this time that the administrative staff is able to interview those men and women who have passed all the prior required tests. Experienced police personnel are often able to spot weaknesses that did not show up in earlier tests and interviews. Departmental interviews are rigorous and demanding, for they are designed to observe the applicant in a stress situation.

Appointment

After all the testing phases are completed and the candidates are graded and listed in order, appointments are made. If fifty applicants have completed all the testing phases successfully and twenty-five openings are available, the top men on the list are usually selected for employment. An eligibility list may be kept to fill vacancies as they occur throughout the year. This type of procedure assists in keeping costs down by not requiring the complete testing process each time a vacancy occurs.

A patrolman candidate undergoes a preliminary employment interview, one of a number of steps he must successfully complete. *(Courtesy of the Orlando Police Department)*

Recruit Academy

After the police candidate is selected to become part of the agency, he is enrolled in a course of basic police study. The primary purpose of the police academy is to establish a basic understanding in those areas which will become an important part of the officer's professional life. Subjects such as police patrol procedures, ethics, criminal law, arrest techniques, investigation, community relations, and self-defense techniques are but a part of the many courses designed to assist the beginning officer understand his professional role. Even though the academy is set to establish guidelines, the final testing ground is the street, where policemen must put to work what they have learned. Most police academies have the police officer for a period of only five to sixteen weeks, depending on the policies and budgets of the various police departments.

The Probationary Period

Almost all police departments have a probationary period for recruit officers. During this period the agency can release the employee on general grounds and the officer has no legal recourse to appeal his termination. This is the final phase in the selection of the permanent police officer and it must be a meaningful experience. If the probationary period becomes just a routine part of the selection process and is not utilized as a final check on the fitness of an officer, it may just as well be eliminated from the hiring process.

The period of probation usually runs from six to twelve months, during which the officer is not protected by civil service. It is during this time that any negative traits possessed by the police officer which had been overlooked should come to the front. Many men can pass all the tests to become a police officer, but cannot adequately handle field assignments.

Once the officer survives the probationary period, he is given a permanent appointment as a police officer. At this point his job should be secure unless he violates a policy or law to the extent that he must be discharged.

Even though all police agencies do not go through each of the above phases in their hiring process, more and more departments are becoming aware of the need to select their personnel with care.

FEDERAL POLICE RECRUITMENT AND SELECTION

Each year an increasing number of men are needed to investigate and enforce laws at the Federal level. Many of the problems encountered in municipal police recruitment are of little concern to the various Federal law enforcement agencies. The beginning wage is often much higher than that of a municipal police recruit. The overall image of Federal law enforcement also assists in obtaining qualified personnel. Agencies such as the FBI, the CIA, and the Treasury Department enjoy positions of prestige in the police community. Naturally, many potentially excellent municipal police officers are attracted into the area of Federal law enforcement. Concentrated recruitment efforts are made to entice college seniors into Federal enforcement careers.

Benefits

The benefits of a Federal law enforcement career are numerous. Among the most outstanding are the higher salary levels, advancement opportunities, and travel. Security of position is also a major consideration, as the threat of a layoff is never present. Liberal fringe benefits and a generous retirement plan are attractive inducements to those seeking careers in the Federal Service.

Federal law enforcement salary structure is generally superior to that of most local police departments. In those agencies where the starting wage is low, the advancement possibilities must be considered. In local law enforcement a man usually moves up in rank and salary by competing with his fellow rank holders for the next promotional level. Thus if three openings are available for the position of sergeant, although fifty patrol officers may apply and compete for the position only three will be appointed. In Federal law enforcement, advancement is based on competing against a raw score on a test. Ranking by salary is based on a rating system and one can continue to raise his rating by passing the required scores in advanced-level tests. This salary advancement is based on individual ability and not solely on competition with fellow employees.

Because of the broad scope and jurisdiction of Federal law enforcement agencies, investigative personnel have the opportunity to travel and transfer to various locations throughout the United States and foreign countries.

Career Opportunities

The Federal Bureau of Investigation

Probably the most widely known and respected Federal law enforcement agency is the FBI. Its exalted position can be largely attributed to its first and only director J. Edgar Hoover. Since taking over the administration of the FBI, Hoover has made a legend of both himself and his agency. Agents enjoy high wages, a challenging career, excellent retirement benefits, and are sought by many business concerns for executive-level positions.

Basic applicant requirements are excellent health, impeccable character, and a four-year degree from an accredited college. A major in law or accounting is desirable; however, other areas such as law enforcement, criminal justice, and police science are acceptable, along with police experience. Additional information can be obtained by writing to:

> The Federal Bureau of Investigation
> Ninth and Pennsylvania Avenue, NW
> Washington, D.C. 20535

Drug Enforcement Administration

D.E.A. agents are stationed in most major cities throughout the United States and in some major cities overseas. Workload determines where positions are available, but it is quite possible that an applicant will eventually be able to find a position in the location where he wishes to work. Employees must be available for transfer between offices as the needs of the service require. Frequent travel and substantial amounts of irregular, unscheduled overtime work are also required. Shortly after appointment, agents undergo a formalized training program in Washington, D.C. The training includes instruction in self-defense tactics, use of firearms, laws, court procedures, criminology, investigative techniques, drug and narcotics identification, and other courses of value to investigative personnel.

The appointments are made at grades GS-7 and GS-9. In addition to base pay, all agents receive premium pay for irregular, unscheduled overtime. Liberal amounts of annual leave and sick lcave are earned, depending upon the employe's years of creditable service. There is also the opportunity to participate in low-cost group health benefits and insurance plans and a special plan which allows retirement at age fifty with twenty years of service. Promotions to higher-grade positions are normally made at one-year intervals, provided the employe is performing his duties satisfactorily. Promotion beyond the GS-12 level (currently $12,174 per annum) is made through the competitive procedures of the Federal Merit Promotion System, and are usually based on supervisory or specialized responsibilities of the position.

QUALIFICATIONS. To become a GS-7 special agent, an applicant must have established eligibility for this grade level through the Federal Civil Service Entrance Examination. Appointment at the GS-9 level requires eligibility on the Mid-Level Examination. Both examinations are administered by the United States Civil Service Commission, and information about these examinations can be obtained from local Civil Service representatives. Employment is without regard to race, religion, or national origin. Because of the nature of the duties involved, however, special agent positions are restricted to males. Since performance of these duties frequently require personal risks, exposure to all kinds of weather, considerable travel, and arduous exertion, candidates must also pass a rigid physical examination.

Further information can be obtained by writing to the Drug Enforcement Administration domestic regional offices, the addresses of which are listed below.

BALTIMORE
    Room 945 Federal Building
    31 Hopkins Place
    Baltimore, Maryland 21201

BOSTON
    John F. Kennedy Federal
    Building
    Room G-64
    Boston, Massachusetts 02203

CHICAGO
    Suite 1700
    Engineering Building
    205 West Walker Drive
    Chicago, Illinois 60606

DENVER
New Custom House
1950 Stout Street
Denver, Colorado 80202

DETROIT
602 Federal Building and
United States Courthouse
231 West Lafayette
Detroit, Michigan 48226

KANSAS CITY
United States Courthouse
811 Grand Avenue, Suite 115
Kansas City, Missouri 64106

NEW YORK
90 Church Street, Suite 605
New York, New York 10014

PHILADELPHIA
605 United States Custom
House
Second and Chestnut Streets
Philadelphia, Pennsylvania
19106

SEATTLE
311 United States Courthouse
Seattle, Washington 98104

NEW ORLEANS
939 Federal Office Building
600 South Street
New Orleans, Louisiana 70310

MIAMI
1515 Northwest Seventh Street
Room 205
Miami, Florida 33125

Treasury Department

Since there are many law enforcement opportunities in the various Treasury Department divisions, the qualifications vary from high school diplomas or equivalent for the Executive Protective Service to a college degree for Treasury Enforcement

Agent. For further information contact the Treasury College Recruitment Coordinators for Law Enforcement at one of the locations given below.

ADDRESSES

AREAS COVERED

Atlanta
    P.O. Box 926
    Atlanta, Georgia 30301

Alabama, Florida, Georgia, Mississippi, North Carolina, South Carolina, Tennessee

Boston
    John F. Kennedy Federal Building
    Government Center
    Boston, Massachusetts 02203

Connecticut, Maine, Massachusetts, New Hampshire, Rhode Island, Vermont

Chicago
    35 East Wacker Drive
    Chicago, Illinois 60601

Illinois, Iowa, Minnesota, Missouri, Nebraska, North Dakota, South Dakota, Wisconsin

Cincinnati
    P.O. Box 2119
    Cincinnati, Ohio 45201

Indiana, Kentucky, Michigan, Ohio, West Virginia

Dallas
    1114 Commerce Street
    Dallas, Texas 75202

Arkansas, Colorado, Kansas, Louisiana, New Mexico, Oklahoma, Texas, Wyoming

New York
    90 Church Street
    New York, New York 10007

New York State, Puerto Rico, Virgin Islands

Philadelphia
    2 Pennsylvania Center Plaza
    Philadelphia, Pennsylvania 19102

Delaware, Maryland, New Jersey, Pennsylvania, Virginia, District of Columbia

San Francisco
    870 Market Street
    San Francisco, California 94102

Alaska, Arizona, California, Hawaii, Idaho, Montana, Nevada, Oregon, Utah, Washington

Border Patrol

Persons selected for appointment as border patrol agent, GS-7, report to the Border Patrol Academy for approximately three months of intensive training. While in attendance at the training school, appointees are required to devote full-time to their studies. They are taught history and responsibilities of the Service and instructed in immigration and nationality laws, Spanish, physical training, marksmanship, and other courses pertinent to the work of the patrol. During the balance of the probationary year, their intensive training program is continued under the direction of a sector training officer and in the company of a senior officer. The new employees are given further written and oral examinations at the conclusion of five-and-a-half and ten months service. Those candidates who do not succeed during the course of the probationary period are dismissed.

Salaries are based on the standard Federal work week of forty hours. Additional compensation is provided for authorized overtime worked in excess of the forty-hour week.

The basic entrance salary is $8,098 a year (grade GS-7). Officers who have completed their first or probationary year successfully have built firm foundation for advancement. In recognition of this they are promoted to the journeyman position of border patrol agent (GS-8, $8,956 a year). Those who display ability for independent action, mature judgment, and willingness to accept greater responsibility may be promoted to the higher-level journeyman position (grade GS-9, $9,881 a year) after two years at the grade GS-8 level. As they gain additional experience officers become qualified for promotion to supervisory positions in other activities, even up to executive levels.

WRITTEN TEST. All competitors for the position of border patrol agent are required to take a written examination designed to measure verbal abilities and judgment. The written examination requires about two hours.

Competitors are rated on the basis of the written examination on a scale of 100. To pass the written examination, competitors must attain a rating of at least 70 on the examination as a whole.

ORAL INTERVIEW. Competitors who qualify in the written test are required to appear for an oral interview in the order of their standing on the register and only as the needs of the Service may require. The oral interview is designed to determine if applicants possess the personal qualities necessary for successful performance of the duties of the position.

AUTOMOBILE DRIVING EXPERIENCE. Applicants must possess a valid automobile driver's license and must have had at least one year of licensed automobile driving experience. After entry on duty, appointees will be required to pass a road test before being issued a U.S. Government Motor Vehicle Operator's Identification Card.

CITIZENSHIP. Applicants must be citizens of, or hold permanent allegiance to, the United States.

AGE LIMITS. Applicants must have reached or passed their twenty-first birthday on the date of appointment. However, persons between twenty and twenty-one years of age may apply for this examination. Such persons will be examined and, if qualified in all other respects, may be tentatively selected but may not enter on duty prior to attaining the age of twenty-one years. There is no maximum age limit.

PHYSICAL REQUIREMENTS. Since the duties of these positions involve physical exertion under rigorous environmental conditions; irregular as well as protracted hours of work; patrol duties on foot, motor vehicle, and/or aircraft, applicants must be in excellent physical condition and be of good muscular development.

For further information write to
Interagency Board of United States Civil Service Examiners
1930 E Street N.W.
Washington, D.C. 20415

Department of Justice, Bureau of Prisons

DUTIES. Some of the duties of employees of the Bureau of Prisons are the following:

1. Enforcing the rules and regulations governing the operation of a correctional institution and the confinement, safety, health, and protection of inmates.

2. Supervising the work assignments of inmates.

3. Counseling inmates on personal and family goals and problems.

4. Being a member of the treatment team of social workers, psychiatrists, psychologists, teachers, and others working to change the behavior of the individual offender.

POSITIONS FOR WOMEN. Women are employed as correctional officers by the Bureau of Prisons at Anderson, West Virginia, and

Terminal Island, California, and by the District of Columbia Department of Corrections, Washington, D.C.

Qualifications

1. No written test is required.

2. Supervisory or leadership experience in the armed forces and/or civilian employment.

3. Education successfully completed in an accredited college or university may be substituted on the basis of one year of college for nine months of experience, up to a maximum of three years.

For further information contact
Interagency Board of United States Civil Service Examiners
1930 E Street, N.W.
Washington, D.C. 20415

or

Bureau of Prisons
101 Indiana Avenue
Washington, D.C. 20537

Department of State

SECURITY OFFICER. The Department of State offers a unique opportunity for those who can qualify, for travel and a career with the diplomatic service of the United States. It is one of the smallest law enforcement agencies, employing approximately sixty security officers and twenty electronic engineers serving overseas, with an unknown number in the States.

Qualifications

Education—A minimum of a bachelor of arts degree from an accredited university.

Physical—Complete medical examination for overseas travel.

Background—Thorough background investigation.

Age—Prefer under thirty-five years of age.

Sex—Because of nature of the job, male only.

For further information write to
        Office of Security
        Department of State
        Washington, D.C. 20520

Police recruits parade in review at the world-renowned Los Angeles County Police Academy. *(Courtesy of the Los Angeles County Sheriff's Department)*

Chapter 24

TRAINING

Regardless of how inherently talented a person is, he is not equipped to perform police tasks on intrinsic ability alone. Pre-service preparations notwithstanding, a period of training is necessary before one is minimally equipped to engage in police work. Training is one of the most important means of upgrading the police service and, as such, should be a continuing process whereby men of all ranks and assignments are afforded an uninterrupted training experience from selection to retirement. The State of Florida, like many other progressive states, is embarking on such a career development program.

TYPES OF TRAINING

There are four general types of police training: recruit training, in-service training, specialized training, and command training.

Recruit Training

Most communities either maintain or have access to a recruit academy where rookie patrolman are sent for formal entry-level training. A number of states, following the lead of New York and California, have passed laws establishing police training programs. Although the standards differ in the various states, the minimum training period is often between two-hundred and three-hundred hours. Some police agencies require their recruits to complete from twelve to twenty weeks of training (480 to 800 hours). Recruit training, regardless of the length of the academy, is an intensified period of instruction which covers a breadth of subjects. Officers are not expected to achieve a level of expertise in any one subject, for the entire curriculum simply provides a foundation to build on in later years. Some of the courses offered in a recruit academy include:

History of police

Human relations

Recruit training. Police recruits are subjected to a rigorous, demanding, and highly intensified period of training. *(Courtesy of the St. Petersburg Police Department)*

Firearms
Preliminary investigation
Patrol techniques
Accident investigation and reporting
Criminal law
Road blocks and raid techniques
Narcotics investigation
Forensic sciences
Duties at the crime scene
Courtroom demeanor and testimony
Court organization
Crowds and their behavior
Aspects of riot-control operation
Criminal investigation
Report writing
Mechanics of arrest
Laws of arrest
Handling disturbance and prowler calls
Sex crimes
The Nation's training academies are in no way identical. The

Newly commissioned special agents receive training in defensive tactics from an instructor at FBI Headquarters, Washington, D.C. *(Courtesy of the FBI)*

thrust of each individual academy will reflect the needs of the community and the function of the department. Obviously, a state highway patrol academy will stress courses in traffic, while an urban police academy may emphasize community relations and criminal law. Training classes will probably be fifty minutes in length, with ten-minute breaks each hour. Due to the great mass of material that must be covered, tests and quizzes are administered with great frequency. Besides the academic role of the police academy, it performs another valuable function by allowing police supervisors to scrutinize recruits in a controlled environment. Many academies also utilize stress training techniques to evaluate the emotional stability of the recruits, before they are released on patrol. Recruit officers who fail to meet the rigid standards set in the academy will find themselves screened-out before graduation.

In-Service Training

The weakest part of the police training process is in-service, or refresher, training. Police departments operate around the clock and find it difficult and expensive to systematically conduct in-service training, especially for extended periods of time. Yet it

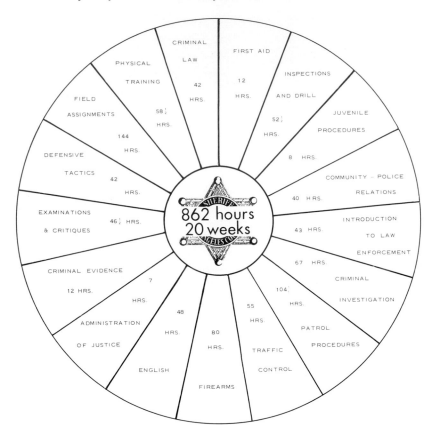

Law enforcement recruit training categorization. Note the emphasis on both technical and academic subjects. *(Courtesy of the Los Angeles County Sheriff's Department)*

is a critical undertaking. To ask a policeman to competently fulfill his assigned tasks equipped with only the formal training which he received in the recruit academy is to place an unreasonable burden on him. Some police departments have initiated roll call training periods to take advantage of the fact that this is one of the few instances in which a large group of policemen are assembled. These training periods usually run from fifteen to thirty minutes prior to patrol duty, and they are usually conducted by the watch commander or his representative. When formal in-service classes are held, they are usually of short duration—rarely over forty hours—and small in size. Departments have found that they can

Roll call training. (Courtesy of the Police Department, City of Baltimore)

spare a few men on each patrol shift for school attendence without seriously affecting the agency's operations. Another device used by police departments is the issuance of written training bulletins, which are prepared and disseminated by the training division. The Oakland Police Department is considered a leader in this area. Experts feel that a minimum of forty hours of in-service training should be required of all officers yearly.

Specialized Training

The need for special training commences once an officer is permanently assigned to a departmental division, although many agencies make an exception for patrol officers. Each division in a police department has its own unique operating procedures and techniques, making it necessary that specialized training be conducted on a continuing basis. Often departments must seek outside experts to conduct some of the complex training courses. The FBI sends teams of agents around the country to conduct,

DEPARTMENTAL TRAINING BULLETIN
OAKLAND POLICE DEPARTMENT

BARRICADED SUSPECTS

Bulletin Index Number: III - B. 1

                                              Manual III, Patrol Procedures

                                              Section B, Apprehending, Searching and Transporting Suspects

                                              Sub-section 1, Barricaded Suspects

Master Alphabetical Index:
                                              Apprehending Suspects, Barricaded

                                              Barricaded Suspects

Distribution Information:

This bulletin will be distributed to all organizational units on 14 Apr 67 and is to be presented as line-up training material during the period of 17-30 Apr 67. Organization units shall distribute copies of the bulletin to all members and communications dispatchers for inclusion in Manual III, Patrol Procedures, at the conclusion of the line-up presentation period.

Publication Date: 14 Apr 67

The cover sheet on this departmental training bulletin illustrates the lengths to which superior police agencies go to keep their men well trained. *(Courtesy of the Oakland Police Department)*

free of charge, short-term training schools. Many police agencies have also found it necessary to send personnel away to school where they are taught skills that are passed on to other members

In-service training. A California patrolman seeks cover and concealment as he brings his weapon to bear during a training exercise. *(Courtesy of the Torrance, California, Police Department)*

Specialized training. A weary group of policemen receive specialized training in the techniques of riot and crowd control. *(Courtesy of the St. Petersburg Police Department)*

of the agency when they return. Some of the most distinguished specialized training programs are at Northwestern University's Traffic Institute (personnel management), the Southern Police Institute in Louisville (personnel management and supervision), Indiana University (supervision), and The University of Southern California (Delinquency Control Institute). Some critics of the practice of sending officers away to school argue that this expensive tactic is simply a reward for good service rather than a meaningful attempt to upgrade the department. In any event, specialized training is critically needed by police departments which, because of escalating public demands for increased services, must react by creating new kinds of specialists trained to give citizens the best service possible for their tax dollar.

Command Training

Formal training is at least as important to command personnel as it is to lower-ranking officers. The President's Commission on Law Enforcement found a disappointing absence of executive development programs, as the following statement indicates:

> Many departments lack qualified leadership. Police chiefs and personnel in middle management ranks should be required to have sufficient education and training to enable them to administer the complex affairs of a police force. . . .

Command training may best be undertaken by large universities, either in the regular curriculum or in short-term noncredit seminars. Command training is also conducted by the FBI, The International Association of Chiefs of Police, and The Southern Police Institute.

METHODS OF INSTRUCTION

Training programs, regardless of the group at which they are aimed, must make use of up-to-date devices and instruction methods in order to be successful. Years ago, police training programs were taught almost exclusively by lecture method, but lately other educative techniques have been used, not to replace lectures but to supplement them. There are eight general methods of instruction, each of which should be utilized, in varying degrees, in police instruction:

1. Lectures.

2. Demonstrations.

3. Films and recordings.

4. Field trips.

5. Simulations and role-playing.

6. Discussions.

7. Conferences.

8. Actual Practice.

The police task, with its diversity and complexity, lends itself admirably to all eight methods of instruction, although not in equal amounts. The successful training program will synthesize these methods to insure maximum efficiency and a superior learning experience. The training of police personnel is too important a task to be conducted in a haphazard fashion.

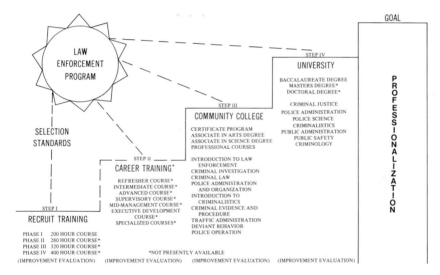

A law enforcement career development program. *(Courtesy of the Florida Police Standards Board)*

The patrol division—Where the action is! *(Courtesy of the Los Angeles County Sheriff's Department)*

(Courtesy of the St. Petersburg Police Department)

Chapter 25

PATROL

T he work horse or backbone of any police department is the patrol division. It is this division that represents law and order to the average citizen and is the determining factor in whether or not a police agency will successfully fulfill its obligations to the community. Few policemen assigned to other divisions encounter the action and the variety of assignments of the police patrol officer. Police patrol is where the action is, and that is where most good policemen want to be.

In small communities the entire police force may be assigned as uniformed patrol officers. In such instances one will find police officers not only responding to calls and writing reports but also conducting detailed follow-up investigations. As the community grows in size more police personnel will be needed. In urban areas where police duties are more complex and time consuming, specialization is undertaken and some patrol officers will be assigned to perform secondary duties, i.e. investigation, traffic, juvenile, vice, training, intelligence, and community relations. The purpose of establishing secondary units is to assist the patrol division in a specialty area. There are dangers to overspecialization though, and the police administrator who neglects the patrol function by assigning his best men to specialized tasks may very well be engaging in a self-defeating activity.

The great majority of recruit police officers will begin their law enforcement careers as a patrol officer. This is not only the logical division in which to start a new police officer's professional life, but it is also the best test of a new officer's ability, courage, and intelligence.

In no other division is a man expected to handle every type of call or assignment and to make split second decisions that patrol officers routinely make. If the new officer has a natural aptitude for law enforcement and he displays courage and good common sense, he will soon become one of the most valued men in the police agency—a street police officer.

BASIC OBJECTIVES

Patrol officers are expected to accomplish a number of clearly defined objectives while on patrol, some of which follow:

1. **The protection of life and property.** Democratic government must guarantee to all citizens the right to be secure in their persons and property. The task of securing these rights rests squarely on the shoulders of our police agencies; however, it is accomplished basically through the efforts of the patrol division. Good overt patrol techniques and alert observations by patrol officers help keep a community's citizens safe from personal danger and property loss.

2. **The prevention of crime.** Patrol officers will, because of their uniforms, marked police units, and aggressive patrol techniques, eliminate a certain number of opportunities for criminal actions. Because an experienced patrol officer may give the impression that he can be anywhere on his beat at any time, the observant criminal will avoid this officer's area.

3. **The enforcement of laws.** A patrol officer is expected to know municipal, county, and state laws as well as some Federal statutes. He must also know the difference between written law and the spirit of the law.

4. **The detection and apprehension of criminals.** When crime prevention fails and a criminal violation occurs, the patrol officer is expected to possess the skills and knowledge to detect the crime and apprehend the offender. Naturally, many hours are spent by dedicated police personnel learning the various techniques of crime detection and the prompt apprehension of the guilty suspects.

5. **Miscellaneous tasks.** A great amount of time is dedicated to providing various service to the public. These services may range from providing directions to a lost citizen to helping a fallen invalid back to his bed. Assisting citizens is not only a duty but a rewarding experience.

METHODS OF PATROL

Foot Patrol

Naturally, the oldest method of patrolling is foot patrol. Even though automobiles, airplanes, helicopters, boats, and other methods are used today, foot patrol is still important in fulfilling police tasks. Because of physical limitations foot patrol officers can cover only a small area compared to a patrolman in a police car, making it a very costly proposition. But there is and always will be a need for foot patrolman, especially in light of the fact that many citizens are in downtown areas in large metropolitan cities. Many police administrators are anxious to "humanize" the police by bringing them closer to the community. There are certain advantages in using a foot patrol officer in an area:

1. **The ability to obtain information.** It is difficult for an officer assigned to an automobile to build up rapport with people on his beat. The areas patrolled by officers in cars are large, making it difficult for patrol officers to cultivate personal relationships. A foot patrol officer is not tempted to stay in the safety and comfort of a police vehicle. He is on the street literally brushing shoulders with every citizen who lives or works in the area. Because of a closer contact with the people on his beat, he can build up rapport which will assist him in obtaining information. By doing this the foot patrol officer is a personal entity and not just a figure emerging from a police vehicle.

2. **Knowledge of the area.** Because the foot patrol officer has a limited area, he soon learns his assigned neighborhood. Items which may be overlooked by an officer in a police car are carefully noted by the foot patrolman who intimately knows his beat.

3. **Less Conspicuousness.** By varying his route of patrol the foot patrolman increases his chances of being on the scene during an attempted holdup or burglary. He is more difficult to observe than an officer in a police unit and can take advantage of this fact.

4. **Traffic control.** By knowing his beat he can predict traffic hazards or congestion problems. His unique perspective of the area often helps him alleviate a potentially dangerous traffic situation with ease.

5. **Community relations**. Officers on walking beats are in a unique position to interact meaningfully with the citizenry, whose support police agencies desperately need.

Horse, Motor Scooter, and Bicycle Patrols

In many cities there are locations which cannot be easily patrolled by police cars or motorcycles. Large parks, rocky terrain, and waterfront areas are but a few of the types of locations which

A motorscooter officer assigned to crowd control at a recent demonstration in the Nation's Capital. *(Courtesy of the Metropolitan Police Department, Washington, D. C.)*

may require a special patrol technique. The New York Police Department is well known for its mounted horse patrols. Besides being able to patrol difficult terrains, the horse patrol has been quite successful in crowd-control duties.

Motor scooters and bicycles may not carry the same prestige as do the heavier traffic motorcycles; however, their value in some areas is above question. Among other advantages they are inexpensive, and the officer is able to patrol difficult areas effectively. An example of how motor scooters can be used effectively is found by studying the Metropolitan Police Department, Washington, D.C. There, police administrators have found motor scooters to be of particular help during recent mass demonstrations.

Bicycle patrol—convenient, silent, inexpensive, and effective. *(Courtesy of the Los Angeles Police Department)*

Helicopter Patrol

Some law enforcement agencies have experienced a degree of success in utilizing helicopters for concentrated patrol in high-crime areas. City parks, often the scene of muggings, may be made safer by police helicopters patrolling with high intensity lights. Studies show that high-burglary areas, both residential and commercial, show definite signs of a crime-rate drop after short periods of helicopters patrol. In 1948 the New York Police Department became the first agency in the United States to employ a helicopter for police patrol purposes.

The police helicopter—a valuable tool for modern police agencies. *(Courtesy of the Los Angeles County Sheriff's Department)*

Traffic Utilization

One of the major uses and benefits of a police helicopter is in the area of traffic accident prevention. A primary duty in this regard is the observation of potential traffic hazards. In 1956 The Los Angeles Police Department began employing helicopters to observe rush hour freeway traffic, motivating other agencies to follow its lead. With the ability to remain suspended in a location directly over a traffic hazard, the helicopter pilot has an opportunity to observe and report on the accurate traffic picture at a given roadway or at a specific intersection. To substantiate his observations, photographs are often taken for further evaluation.

In many areas a police vehicle is unable to arrive at a traffic accident scene or a local disaster because of roadway conditions and traffic congestion. A police helicopter is not restricted to the use of city streets and can easily arrive at any reasonable location in short order. The ability to land in a limited space also adds to the value of this recent police tool. The rapid arrival of a police helicopter assures almost immediate first aid to isolated accident victims.

Plasma Runs

From time to time patrol officers are requested to make emergency runs to pick up and deliver a rare blood type to a hospital. This assignment is usually a prolonged one in which the officer must travel many miles at high speed to hasten the delivery process, but it can be done in relative safety. Police records abound with descriptions of lives being saved by competent, efficient helicopter crews.

Searches

In isolated areas such as deserts or mountainous terrain occasionally a lost person becomes the subject of an intensive search. Inclement weather and special conditions, such as lack of food, wild animals, special medical problems, or age, may make it essential that the lost person be located in the shortest possible time. Naturally police cars will be of little value in desolate areas. Horse patrol can assist, but it takes precious time to transport the horses to the search scene. With a map and some basic information a well-trained helicopter unit can soon be in the area trying to locate the subject. Once located, the subject of the search can be transported quickly and safely to a medical facility by the helicopter.

Marine Patrol

Many cities throughout the country have lakes, rivers, or oceanfronts within their jurisdictions. Although waterfront is desirable to a city, it also presents special problems to local law enforcement agencies, for the waterways within a jurisdiction must also be patrolled. Patrol activities are geared to regulate legal shipments of goods and attempt to halt illegal shipments of contraband and narcotics. The prevention of accidents is also of concern.

Large bodies of water are natural locations to utilize in disposing of incriminating evidence. Police underwater recovery teams such as those in Lansing, Michigan; Los Angeles; Dade County, Florida, and Flint, Michigan, are invaluable components of any law enforcement agency. When not in official use recovering evidence, marine patrolmen are of considerable value in water-safety programs, which not only add to good police community relations but can also save many lives through proper

One city's marine patrol. *(Courtesy of the Fort Lauderdale Police Department)*

The Police Water Rescue Team on a mission. *(Courtesy of The Los Angeles County Sheriff's Department)*

education. Members of the Norwalk, Connecticut, Police Department water team lecture before community groups, students, and other organizations on swimming safety, and proper boating procedures. Other police agencies have found that, like traffic safety programs, programs in boating safety can reduce accidents on waterways.

K-9 Patrol

Police dogs (K-9) are a most valuable asset to a law enforcement agency, but one that is often misunderstood. Police agencies throughout the nation have found K-9's to be a useful and functional crime-fighting tool. It is unfortunate that some groups have chosen to oppose the use of police dogs out of fear or ignorance of their use. Police administrators have often bowed to the wishes of the antidog lobby by eliminating K-9 teams already in use in their agency or by refusing to implement dog patrols for fear of political pressure. It must be stated that police dogs have been misused by a few police departments who have loosed their animals on citizens in crowd-control situations; however, properly utilized and deployed, police K-9 patrol, like any police device, may be a valuable tool in the war on crime, and one that can gain a measure of acceptance in the community.

The police dog—a valuable asset to a police department when trained and used properly. *(Courtesy of the Miami Police Department)*

Preventive Patrol

Whether on foot patrol or riding in a police unit the police dog can be a deterrent to crime. A criminal may be able to elude an officer but not the keen senses of a police dog. The K-9 gives an added advantage to the already alert and competent officer.

Building Searches

There are times when a criminal has a definite advantage over a patrol officer, such as the burglar hidden in a building. The suspect has a choice of hiding places, he knows that he is being sought, and his eyes are adjusted to the dimly lit conditions. Although a building search is never easy, it is less hazardous when a police dog is available. The dog is fast, he adapts quickly to the surroundings, and he can flush out a suspect without the necessity of using deadly force. In this context the use of K-9's may very well be the most humane way of handling this difficult and dangerous situation, not to mention an effective crime-prevention device.

Protection of Officers

Properly trained police dogs offer considerable personal protection to police officers. A K-9 is quick to react to an overt action, and people are aware of that fact. A criminal may take his chances with one or two officers, but he will probably hesitate matching his speed with that of a police dog. The elimination of this desire to try to outshoot or outrun the police has probably saved many officers from death and serious injury.

Automobile Patrol

The most common method of police patrol today is the automobile patrol. An officer in a vehicle is able to cover a large area, thus making auto patrol the most inexpensive method of accomplishing the goals of the patrol division. An automobile also offers a shelter from weather conditions which lessens patrol officers' absences from duty due to illness. The automobile often lends protective shelter during a shooting incident and provides the officer with radio communications and other needed equipment and weapons. The balance of the chapter refers to those functions and techniques utilized by patrol officers assigned to automobile patrol.

Patrol diminishes the potential offender's belief in the existence of an opportunity to successfully violate the law. The policeman should be constantly alert for conditions and circumstances which may facilitate or promote the commission of crimes and other incidents that require police service. Observation is the function that most completely describes the policeman's job—most of his other duties depend on what he observes. The extent and accuracy of his observation influences his ability to discover unsecured premises, unwholesome conditions, questionable individuals, and other hazards. His power to observe also enables him to detect offenders, to learn the habits of persons living on his beat, to be familiar with the residential and commercial districts that are the most frequent scenes of crime, and to evaluate the social environment and influences which must be controlled if crime is to be prevented. His power of observation assists him in the effective performance of his first and most important task—the protection of life and property. It also makes him more useful to follow-up units, who depend on him in complex investigative work. The policeman thus serves as the eyes and ears of the department, providing that he reports what he observes. His functional observations make him the focal point of police operations.

THE FIELD INTERROGATION

One of the many self-initiated activities that an officer may perform is the field interrogation. Field interrogations, like traffic citations, should never be placed on a quota basis. Only when an officer feels strongly that an individual's presence in an area is suspicious, should a field interrogation be accomplished. Many police departments have established general orders informing officers of their rights and responsibilities in conducting field interrogations.

Although a number of factors may constitute a suspicious person, it is generally conceded that he is one who does not fit into a particular situation or area, based on information possessed by an officer and his professional experience. In all cases the interrogation must be consistent with departmental policy, statute, case law, and common sense.

The basic purpose of field interrogation is to find out who a person is and what his intentions are. After a short conversation if it is discovered that the person does belong in the area, the interrogation may be completed quickly and courteously with the officer returning to his police unit to continue on routine patrol. When handled correctly, the citizen will feel no imposition, and may actually be grateful that an efficient officer is protecting his community.

If after a brief conversation with a suspicious person the officer is not convinced that the subject belongs in the area, he will expand the simple field interrogation to satisfy his need for further information. He may wish to have the subject's name and date of birth checked out by his agency. This action accomplishes two purposes: (1) if the subject has an outstanding warrent on file, he will be arrested and (2) if the subject has a record, the information will assist the officer in determining the final disposition of the interrogation.

To accurately record a field interrogation, the patrol officer will want to have a written record of the event and information concerning the subject. Most police agencies have a convenient form commonly called the Field Interrogation (F.I.) card. The purpose of the F.I. card is to keep a written record regarding a suspicious person and the circumstances under which he was contacted. Information on an F.I. card includes the name and address of the subject or subjects, and the F.I. cards are turned in along with the officer's reports at the end of his shift. The cards are forwarded either to a central repository or to the appropriate investigative unit.

NAME (LAST)			(FIRST)		(MIDDLE)		NICKNAME			

RESIDENCE	PHONE

DAY / DATE / TIME	DRIVER'S LIC. #	DRIVER	PASS.	PED.

PLACE OF OCCURRENCE

RACE	SEX	AGE	D.O.B.	HGHT	WGHT	HAIR	EYES	COMP	SCARS, MARKS

CLOTHING WORN

YEAR & MAKE OF CAR	BODY TYPE	COLOR	TAG #	STATE	YR.

SUBJECT'S BUSINESS ADDRESS	OCCUPATION	NAME OF SCHOOL — JUV.

OFFICER REPORTING	I.D. NO. O.R. NO.

DISPOSITION

NAMES & ADDRESSES OF PERSONS WITH SUSPECT AT TIME

DETAILS OF INTERROGATION OR REPORT

Sample field interrogation (F.I.) card used by a majority of law enforcement agencies to convey information obtained by the patrol officer to the various auxiliary units. *(Courtesy of the Broward County [Florida] Sheriff's Department)*

BUILDING CHECKS

During nighttime and early morning shifts patrol officers must maintain the security of businesses and commercial buildings. Besides routinely patrolling their beats, officers are expected to leave the comfort and safety of their police vehicles and personally check as many buildings as possible. Many burglars have been apprehended in the act of perpetrating crimes because an efficient patrol officer checked a building and found signs of an illegal entry.

The extent to which an officer can make building checks depends on the amount of time the patrol officer has free from responding to assigned calls. Usually a search for open windows and doors is all that is required for a normal building check. Naturally this type of activity tends to become routine and many police officers do not enjoy checking out buildings. It is, however, one of the best methods of insuring building security, and often results in the business community's appreciation for their local police department.

TRAFFIC DUTIES

Among other activities, the patrol officer will engage in traffic enforcement functions. Even though traffic units may be working his beat, the patrol officer is expected to perform some traffic duties. The two obvious duties are traffic control in congested areas and warning and issuing citations to traffic violators. Directing traffic and working traffic violations are not widely enjoyed tasks, but the patrol officer is expected to add traffic duties to his overall workload.

EMERGENCY OR "CODE THREE" CALLS

A major portion of a patrol officer's calls will be assigned by the dispatcher (rather than self-initiated). Of these assigned calls some will be classified as emergency calls, which are usually termed "code three calls." Emergency or code-three calls are to be expedited and the rule of thumb is to arrive at the scene as quickly as possible without risking the safety of citizens or the officer. The emergency lights are activated to visually warn motorists that the police vehicle has an emergency call. The siren is also utilized to warn of an approaching emergency run by a police unit. Siren and emergency lights, however, do not give the officer an obsolute right of way.

The code-three call is a constant test of a patrol officer's driving ability and common sense. He is expected to arrive as quickly as he can, taking into consideration the safety factor and also mentally planning what he will do when he arrives at the scene. Some instances justifying an emergency run are transporting a rare blood type to a hospital, an injury accident, a possible suicide, medical aid to the sick or injured, and aiding another officer who is in need of assistance.

HOT PURSUIT

Sometime during a patrol officer's career he will be faced with the situation of a chase. A chase (or hot pursuit), unlike the call received by the dispatcher, is self-initiated. The same general rules apply in a pursuit as in all other emergency or code-three calls. The patrol officer must not jeopardize the safety and welfare of others while in pursuit. Many officers have the misconception that to break off pursuit is an act of cowardice; nothing could be further from the truth.

Some basic suggestions to use for hot pursuit are the following:
1. Check for departmental guidelines regarding hot pursuit.
2. When a pursuit begins, use the radio; give the dispatcher your location; direction of travel; make, model, and license number of vehicle; the number of occupants, and (if known) whether they are armed.
3. Keep the dispatcher posted as to your progress. If you stop the vehicle notify the dispatcher of your location so that a back-up unit can be assigned.

NONEMERGENCY OR "CODE TWO" CALLS

Code-two calls require a speedy arrival at the scene but do not justify the use of emergency lights and siren. The officer in a code-two call must pay particular attention to road conditions and other vehicles, as he is not requesting a right of way, even though he is attempting to arrive at the call as quickly as possible. Some police agencies use a rear amber flashing light on the police cruiser to communicate to the drivers being passed that the officer needs to arrive at the call as soon as possible. Some examples of a code-two call are family, neighborhood, and landlord-tenant disputes where there is a possibility of injury; and following-up another officer assigned to a code-three or trouble call, such as a bar fight involving a number of combatants.

ROUTINE OR "CODE ONE" CALLS

A code-one call is to be regarded as a routine assignment where the officer should arrive as soon as possible, but in strict compliance with all traffic signals, signs, and speed limits. Most assigned calls are routine or code one in nature. Minor disturbances, common drunks, noninjury accidents, and theft reports are examples of routine assignments to which patrol officers may be dispatched.

CONTROL OF PUBLIC GATHERINGS

The policeman is frequently assigned to public meetings and assemblies. He may be sent to a regularly scheduled meeting, to maintain order at the entrances and exits of the building and to quell disturbances which may occur, or he may be called upon to handle a spontaneous gathering of persons which have assembled on the street or on other public property for some particular purpose. Usually the policeman is concerned only with preventing violence; and if the situation is tense, he may require assistance, which should be requested before the situation becomes critical. Sometimes the assembly must be dispersed either because it is obstructing traffic or because it is trespassing on private property. In such cases great tact is required to avoid an incident between police and citizens. In all cases the policeman must keep in mind

Crowd control for a Presidential motorcade. *(Courtesy of the St. Petersburg Police Department)*

that free speech and peaceful assembly are important Constitutional rights which should not be denied.

BEAT DESIGNATIONS

Beat or zone designations are geographical areas for which the patrol officer will be responsible. When he is assigned to a specific area, he is expected to handle all calls and problems within those boundaries. The patrol officer is the local vice officer, traffic officer, juvenile specialist, intelligence officer, and community-relations officer to all persons living or working in his assigned area or beat. No matter what type of police problem is reported, the patrol officer is usually required to be the first law enforcement officer on the scene. He represents not only the police department but local government as well. Even though the case may later be assigned to another division, his initial contact and observations may be the most important factor in the successful conclusion of the investigation.

Beat or Zone Determination

There are many items to be considered in determining the size and locations of the patrol areas. Naturally, smaller communities have less of a problem in establishing zones, as a simple assignment

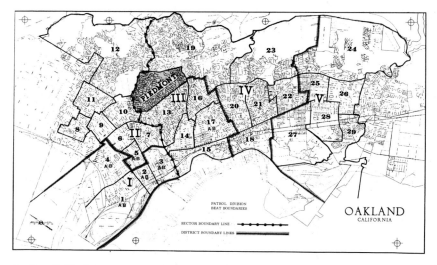

A city divided into geographic entities—beats, sectors, and districts—to facilitate systematic police patrol. *(Courtesy of the Oakland Police Department)*

of north car, south car, east car, or west car, may be all that is required. In larger communities, however, factors such as natural boundaries, density of population, hazard or trouble areas, and criminal activity will have to be evaluated prior to the creation of zones.

Natural Boundaries

Frequently, natural boundaries, such as a river, railroad tracks, or major streets, will determine the limits of a patrol area. Major streets are often used as beat boundaries to insure double patrols where they are needed most. In assigning beats, it is also advantageous to have well-known streets as boundaries, for they form manageable work areas which are easily understood by the patrol officer and the dispatcher.

Density of Population

Patrolling a beat in a crowded downtown area of a large city is a difficult task. Among other problems heavy traffic conditions slow down response time. Beat assignments must be structured in a manner that assures the citizens that a police officer will be able to

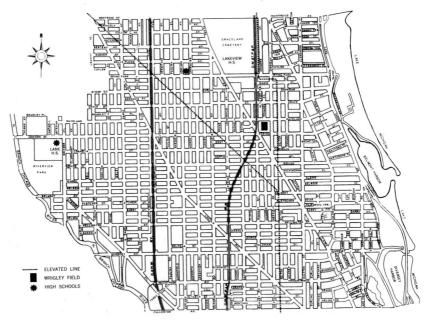

Nineteenth Police District, Town Hall, Chicago. (From *Task Force Report: Crime and Its Impact—An Assessment*)

respond to a call in a reasonable amount of time. Downtown beat areas must therefore be smaller in size than those located in less-traveled zones.

Besides traffic conditions the mere fact that large numbers of people work and live in an area makes it necessary to decrease the size of beats. High-density population usually leads to slum conditions which are expected to produce more street crimes than other more affluent sections. Living in close proximity seems to increase the likelihood of the need for police services. Domestic disturbances are a frequent problem under these conditions.

Hazard or Trouble Areas

High-crime areas exist in many cities and sections of communities, creating a hazardous situation for police officers. Many of these areas are natural traps for the patrol officer during his tour of duty. Beats in these locations should purposely be small in size and well staffed to insure that adequate assistance is close by. The patrol car assigned to such sections should also contain two or more patrol officers, depending on dangers involved.

A trouble area might include a strip of bars catering to a troublesome element, a residential area containing many narcotic addicts, neighborhoods containing political hate groups, or business and commercial zones which are constantly being burglarized. In police beats where hazards are present, constant protective measures must be taken by the patrol officer. He is a marked man driving a marked police vehicle.

Criminal Distribution

In many cities certain sections are heavily populated with boarding houses or low-rent hotels. These are usually areas where skid-row alcoholics, drug addicts, subjects fleeing from criminal prosecution, and like individuals reside. The rents are inexpensive and no one asks questions. For the criminal element these areas are havens. To police they represent difficult enforcement zones.

PIN MAPS

Pin maps play an important part in the patrol planning process. By geographically depicting city precincts, a supervisor and his patrolman can usually see their problem zones and natural patrol areas. Factors such as incidents of holdups, burglaries, traffic

Pin maps are used for many purposes, including the determination of beat or patrol areas. *(Courtesy of the St. Petersburg Police Department)*

accidents, disturbance-prone establishments, and other important considerations can be represented by various-colored pins placed in the proper position on the map. The end result is a visual picture of what has happened during a specified period of time.

POLICE RESERVES

To assist in overcoming manpower shortages many law enforcement agencies have initiated a police reserve force. The patrol division is often exclusively assigned police reservists. Police reserves are men twenty-one years of age and over who are not police officers by occupation. They are, however, dedicated citizens who serve their communities by becoming part-time police personnel.

Police reserves are usually assigned to ride with a regular officer. In many ways they are expected to be as qualified as a regular officer, and for all practical purposes they are considered one half of a two-man unit. Many agencies require from eight to forty hours patrol time from each reserve officer a month. In some smaller cities reserves are sometimes assigned police units and

Police reservist *(left)* rides with a veteran officer. *(Courtesy of the Metro-politan Police Department, City of St. Louis)*

work patrol beats by themselves, having the same responsibilities and police powers as a regular officer. Naturally a careful screening process is required to insure that only qualified reserve officers are employed. Only rarely are police reservists compensated for their work, although uniforms and equipment are generally provided.

(Courtesy of the Kansas City Police Department)

The old and the new of traffic enforcement. *(Courtesy of the Orange County [California] Police Department)*

Chapter 26

TRAFFIC CONTROL

T he traffic problem in the United States is increasing each year. Despite numerous automobile safety features, traffic deaths continue to rise. Of additional concern is the volume of motor vehicles utilizing streets and highways which were constructed for the needs of a less mobile society. Even though driver education and advance planning and engineering may assist in lessening the problem, the police have a major role in traffic regulation and one that will continue to expand.

TRAFFIC OFFICERS' DUTIES

A police department's traffic division is established to perform certain specific functions which are aimed at promoting safe motoring. Some of the major duties of a traffic officer are the following:

1. To obtain the best possible movement of vehicles and pedestrians consistent with safety. With traffic congestion increasing, this function becomes a definite challenge to the traffic officer.
2. To obtain compliance to the various regulations and traffic laws from as many motorists and pedestrians as possible. Enforcement is the main tool in this area of roadway supervision.
3. To assist at traffic accidents by rendering immediate care or first aid to motorists and/or pedestrians.
4. To investigate the causes of traffic accidents and report the findings for use in traffic enforcement, planning, and safety engineering.
5. To assist local traffic engineers in their research by providing information regarding the traffic flow, the number of accidents, and other pertinent data.
6. To plan for traffic direction in cases of safety hazards

431

caused by an unusual volume of vehicular traffic, malfunctioning traffic signals, and other emergency or temporary situations.
7. To assist lost or stranded motorists and pedestrians.

TRAFFIC ENFORCEMENT

To enforce traffic ordinances traffic officers utilize certain proven effective methods, some of which follow:

1. **Constant patrol aimed at creating the impression of omnipresence.** It is the goal of every police agency to secure voluntary compliance with traffic laws; however, human nature being what it is, certain sanctions are provided for violations and the police serve as a reminder that disobedience may be costly and time consuming.

2. **Operationalizing the concept of selective enforcement.** This method is a concentrated effort to enforce certain traffic laws at a location where violations frequently occur. When a number of vehicular accidents in a given area can be attributed to the violation of a certain law, the traffic commander may assign a detail to work the location for a specified period, usually a few days. This action generally results in numerous citations being issued for the specified offense, and a measurable reduction of accidents as motorists learn to expect a concentrated effort to apprehend violators at the given location.

3. **The issuance of traffic citations or warnings without employing selective enforcement techniques.** In this circumstance traffic officers are given a geographic assignment wherein they enforce all violations and handle traffic situations as they arise.

Citations or Warnings

The basic theory behind the issuing of citations for traffic offenses is that people usually respond to laws if they realize that punitive action will be forthcoming for failing to obey or comply with the rules of the road. Judicial action against traffic violators may include suspended sentence, fine, imprisonment, or the loss of driving privileges, depending on the severity of the offense. Driving is a privilege which may, if the situation warrants, be

To alleviate human suffering and loss from motor vehicle accidents by promoting and encouraging voluntary compliance with law through education and enforcement, and assistance to engineering.

To promote economical, beneficial and enjoyable use of the highways by reducing congestion and removing impediments which retard the smooth and rapid flow of traffic.

To assure inspired and dedicated service to the public by providing opportunity and encouragement, guidance and direction which make the development of each employee meaningful, purposeful, and valuable both to the public and himself.

To protect the public's investment by maintaining continuous vigilance to prevent damage, misuse and littering of the highways.

To further the efficient operation of the automotive transportation system by research and testing, and establishing new concepts in traffic control—gathering, analyzing, and disseminating technical information.

To protect the public against economic loss from theft and arson of vehicles and from failure of owners to properly license vehicles.

To assure the public maximum personal safety and convenience on the highways by providing protection and assistance night and day.

To encourage uniform application of the traffic laws by offering to all enforcement agencies the training capabilities of the California Highway Patrol Academy.

The objectives of the California Highway Patrol. *(Courtesy of The California Highway Patrol)*

suspended for a period of time determined by the court or an administrative agency of the state.

Some years ago city governments viewed traffic fines as an excellent source of badly needed revenue. Accordingly, ticket

POLICE DEPARTMENT
CITY OF WINTER PARK

CASE No._____DOCKET No._____ PAGE No._____

STATE OF FLORIDA, } SS.   **No. 12108**
CITY OF WINTER PARK

COMPLAINT-AFFIDAVIT

IN THE _____**MUNICIPAL**_____ COURT OF _**WINTER PARK, FLORIDA**_

The undersigned, being duly sworn, upon his oath deposes and says:

ON_____THE_____DAY OF_____19_____, AT_____A.M.
                                                          P.M.

NAME_____
     (Please Print)   First   Middle   Last

STREET_____

CITY-STATE_____

BIRTH
DATE_____ RACE_____ SEX_____ HT._____WT._____

DRIV.
LIC. No._____
                           State   Kind

VEH. LIC. No._____ STATE_____YR._____

MAKE_____ STYLE_____ COLOR_____

Upon a Public Street or Highway, namely (LOCATION)_____

DID UNLAWFULLY COMMIT THE FOLLOWING OFFENSE.

ACCIDENT CASE / Leading Causes of Accidents	UNLAWFUL SPEED_____ MPH SPEED APPLICABLE_____MPH
	Improper LEFT TURN ☐ No signal ☐ Cut corner ☐ From wrong lane
	Improper RIGHT TURN ☐ No signal ☐ Into wrong lane ☐ From wrong lane
	Disobeyed TRAFFIC SIGNAL (When light turned red) ☐ Past middle intersection ☐ Middle of intersection ☐ Not reached intersection
	Disobeyed STOP SIGN ☐ Wrong place ☐ Walk speed ☐ Faster
	Improper PASSING OR LANE USAGE ☐ At intersection ☐ Cut-in ☐ No passing zone / ☐ Between traffic ☐ On right ☐ On hill / ☐ Lane straddling ☐ Wrong lane ☐ On curve
	☐ Following too closely ☐ Failure to yield
	Other Violations:_____
	In violation of Section_____
	☐ State Statute ☐ Local Ordinance in such case made and provided.

(right margin, vertical: ☐ Arrest-Delivered to / ☐ Accepted Bond-Amt. or Type / Receipt No.)

THE UNDERSIGNED FURTHER STATES THAT HE HAS JUST AND REASON-
ABLE GROUNDS TO BELIEVE, AND DOES BELIEVE, THAT THE PERSON
NAMED ABOVE COMMITTED THE OFFENSE HEREIN SET FORTH, CON-
TRARY TO LAW.

SWORN TO AND ACKNOWLEDGED BEFORE ME

THIS_____DAY OF_____, 19_____

W. P. MUN. CT.
(Name and title)
                                    (Sig. & identity of officer)

I,_____ AGREE AND PROMISE TO APPEAR
          Signature of DEFENDANT

AT_____, BEFORE
       Location   Time   Date

_____ TO ANSWER CHARGES SPECIFIED IN THIS

HAROLD A. WARD, III
NOTICE. UNDERSTANDING THAT FAILURE TO APPEAR CONSTITUTES A SEPARATE OFFENSE

MUN. JUDGE

Conditions that Increased Seriousness of Violation		CAUSED PERSON TO DODGE		PD PI FATAL
PAVEMENT	☐ Rain ☐ Snow ☐ Ice	☐ Pedestrian		☐ ☐ ☐
DARKNESS	☐ Night ☐ Fog ☐ Snow	☐ Driver ☐ JUST MISSED ACCIDENT		☐ Ped. ☐ Vehicle ☐ Hit Fixed Object ☐ Right Angle ☐ Head on ☐ Sideswipe ☐ Rear end ☐ Ran off Roadway ☐ Intersection
OTHER TRAFFIC PRESENT	☐ Cross ☐ Oncoming ☐ Pedestrian ☐ Same Direction		TYPE ACCIDENT	
AREA ☐ Business ☐ Industrial ☐ School ☐ Residential ☐ Rural				
HIGHWAY TYPE ☐ 2 lane ☐ 3 lane ☐ 4 lane ☐ 4 lane divided				

A municipal traffic ticket. *(Courtesy of the Winter Park, Florida, Police Department)*

quotas were established for traffic officers. This, like many other undesirable police practices, has passed from the scene, with good reason, for there is nothing that will destroy public confidence in a police agency faster than a quota system. The value of both written and oral warnings for traffic offenses has been studied and

JUVENILE TRAFFIC CITATION

(DATE) _____

IN RE:

(TIME) _____

_____ _____ _____ _____
(OFFENDER'S NAME)　　　　　　　(SEX)　(AGE)

(DEPT.) _____

_____ _____ _____
(PARENTS)　　　　　　　　　　(STREET)　　　　　(CITY)

You and your parents are hereby ORDERED to, within 48 hours of receiving this Citation, present same in person at the Juvenile Court, 605 S. W. 26th St., (South off Road #84), Fort Lauderdale, Florida, between the hours of 8:30 A.M. and 4:30 P.M., Monday through Friday, or telephone 525-4731 (Lauderdale) for a specific time to appear.

TYPE AND PLACE OF VIOLATION _____

_____

_____

☐ ARREST
☐ WARNING (CHECK ONE)

_____ _____
(DRIVER'S LICENSE NO.)　　　　　　(PHONE)

_____ _____
(OFFENDER'S SIGNATURE)　　　　　(OFFICER'S SIGNATURE)

Failure to comply with instructions above will result in the issuance of legal processes for you and your parents or guardian. NOTE: If Citation is marked "warning" only, disregard instructions above.

OFFENDER'S COPY

Youthful traffic violators are usually handled differently from the way adults are handled, as this citation indicates. *(Courtesy of the Fort Lauderdale Police Department)*

evaluated by many law enforcement agencies and police scholars. The need for traffic enforcement is unquestioned; but as with most police activities, common sense must be applied in deciding whether a warning or a citation is the appropriate action for the given offense and traffic violator. Many good police agencies have articulated policies limiting the exercise of discretion in certain cases. An example of this would be a tolerance limit, in which the department conveys to its officers the point above the speed limit at which patrolmen are to warn a motorist or issue a citation to him. This is being increasingly used by metropolitan agencies and state highway patrols interested in giving consistency to enforcement activities through systematic action.

Electronic Speed Control

Electronic speed control is gaining increased popularity with law enforcement agencies. It is reliable, easy to use, and much more accurate than the mechanical check (pacing the vehicle). If it is used properly, it can be a valuable asset in reducing the number of

The mobile radar unit. *(Courtesy of the Los Angeles County Sheriff's Department)*

traffic accidents. There are two types of electronic speed control in general use:

Radar. This device is the most common and the oldest type used. It uses the "Doppler effect," which measures the difference in frequency between the transmitter and the receiver, one of which is in motion. When the radio waves return from the vehicle being monitored, they are computed and flashed on a radar panel in miles per hour.

Vascar® (**V**isual **A**verage **S**peed **C**omputer **A**nd **R**ecorder). The purpose of this unit is to replace the speedometer in the police car. It can clock a vehicle (whether the patrol car is moving or stationary) accurately. It is a time-distance computer which utilizes the mathematical formula: distance ÷ time = speed. Vascar is a mechanical computer which measures quantities of distance and time and computes the resultant speed.

Vascar. A state highway patrolman flicks time switch on electric Vascar to record the time it takes a speeding motorist to cover a certain distance on the highway. With distance already computed, the officer will receive an instant automatic digital readout of the motorist's speed on the module mounted on the dashboard. *(Courtesy of the Florida Highway Patrol)*

ACCIDENT-CAUSING VIOLATIONS

Even though state and local statutes contain numerous minor traffic offenses, such as parking violations, mechanical violations, and various moving violations, *the professional traffic officer will concentrate on enforcing traffic violations most likely to cause an accident.* In addition to driving while intoxicated, eight other offenses have been listed by the National Safety Council as the principle accident causing violations. Of major concern are the following offenses:

    1. Excessive speed.

    2. Driving over center lines.

    3. Failure to yield right-of-way.

    4. Not heeding stop signs.

5. Improper passing.

6. Disregarding signals.

7. Improper turning movements.

8. Following too closely.

ACCIDENT INVESTIGATION

A major task of a patrolman or traffic officer will be to investigate traffic accidents. Some of the most complex investigations handled by policemen, rivaling even murder cases, are traffic accidents. To reconstruct a multicar collision that has resulted in death or serious injury takes a special type of talent. In this context accident investigation is, in every sense of the term, an art! Upon receiving a fatal or injury traffic accident call the first consideration of the assigned officer is to reach the scene as

The end result of a traffic violation. *(Courtesy of the Los Angeles County Sheriff's Department)*

quickly and as safely as possible. Occasionally traffic accidents occur as the result of police officers responding to an injury accident without being aware of the special hazards a speeding police car can present to other motorists. A recklessly driven patrol car can do more harm than good.

Upon arriving at the scene the investigating officer's first concern should be for the injured. He must provide first aid for victims and make arrangements to transport the injured to a medical facility. The officer must also try to prevent another accident by obtaining a free flow of traffic. Although each accident is in its own way unique, certain investigative techniques remain constant. Depending on the severity of the collision, any or all of the following techniques may be employed:

1. Photographs covering the many angles of the accident must be taken.

2. All pertinent physical evidence must be marked and collected.

3. Statements from anyone observing the accident must be recorded.

4. Accurate measurements of the scene which clearly show, among other things, the point of impact must be taken.

5. In addition to completing the accident report, the officer should take complete and accurate notes for use at a later court trial.

A noninjury accident investigation has many of the same considerations and problems as the injury accident investigation except that it is not to be considered an emergency assignment. After safely arriving at the scene of a noninjury accident, the major problems will usually be connected with traffic congestion and with the efficient and prompt investigation of the collision.

DRIVING UNDER THE INFLUENCE

Driving under the influence (DUI) has become a massive social issue. The drinking driver has long been a problem to society; however, the rapid increase of drug use is also causing great concern. The officer must always take the possibility of the usage of drugs into consideration when questioning the suspect driver,

FLORIDA TRAFFIC ACCIDENT REPORT

MAIL TO: ACCIDENT RECORDS BUREAU, DEPARTMENT OF HIGHWAY SAFETY, TALLAHASSEE, FLORIDA

TIME and LOCATION

DATE OF ACCIDENT	DAY OF WEEK
	TIME OF DAY M
COUNTY	
	CITY, TOWN OR COMMUNITY

If accident was outside city limits, indicate distance from nearest town _____ ☐ Feet ☐ Miles North S E W Of _____ City, Village or Township

ROAD ON WHICH ACCIDENT OCCURRED _____ Use State or County road number or name ☐ Exit Ramp ☐ Entrance R AT ITS INTERSECTION WITH _____ Highway number or name of intersecting street

IF NOT AT INTERSECTION _____ ☐ Feet ☐ Miles North S E W Of _____ Show nearest milepost, intersecting street or highway, bridge, R.R. crossing, underpass or curve

IS ENGINEERING STUDY NEEDED (If so explain)

Do not write in space above

VEHICLE 1

TOTAL NO. VEH INVOLVED ____

YEAR	MAKE		TYPE (sedan, truck, bus, etc.)	VEHICLE LICENSE PLATE NO.		STATE		YEAR

PARTS OF VEHICLE DAMAGED Front | R Front | L Front | R Side | L Side | Rear | R Rear | L Rear | Top | Veh. rolled or burned. Total body damage | AMOUNT (approximate) | VEHICLE REMOVED BY

LIABILITY INSURANCE – Name of company   ☐ Yes ☐ No   ☐ Owner's request ☐ Other (explain)   ☐ Rotation list

OWNER – Print or type FULL name   ADDRESS – Number and street   City and State

DRIVER – Exactly as on driver's license   ADDRESS – Number and street   City and State

DRIVER'S LICENSE TYPE	DRIVER'S LICENSE NO.	STATE	DATE OF – Month – Day – Year BIRTH	RACE	SEX	INJURY	OCCUPATION

OCCUPANTS	Name	ADDRESS – Number and street	City and State	AGE	RACE	SEX	INJURY
Front center							
Front right							
Rear left							
Rear center							
Rear right							

VEHICLE 2 OR PEDESTRIAN

YEAR	MAKE		TYPE (sedan, truck, bus, etc.)	VEHICLE LICENSE PLATE NO.		STATE		YEAR

PARTS OF VEHICLE DAMAGED Front | R Front | L Front | R Side | L Side | Rear | R Rear | L Rear | Top | Veh. rolled or burned. Total body damage | AMOUNT (approximate) | VEHICLE REMOVED BY

LIABILITY INSURANCE – Name of company   ☐ Yes ☐ No   ☐ Owner's request ☐ Other (explain)   ☐ Rotation list

OWNER – Print or type FULL name   ADDRESS – Number and street   City and State

DRIVER – Exactly as on driver's license (Pedestrian)   ADDRESS – Number and street   City and State

DRIVER'S LICENSE TYPE	DRIVER'S LICENSE NO.	STATE	DATE OF – Month – Day – Year BIRTH	RACE	SEX	INJURY	OCCUPATION

OCCUPANTS	Name	ADDRESS – Number and street	City and State	AGE	RACE	SEX	INJURY
Front center							
Front right							
Rear left							
Rear center							
Rear right							

PROPERTY DAMAGED – Other than vehicles | AMOUNT | OWNER – Name | ADDRESS – Number and street | City and State

WITNESSES (other than occupants)

NAME	ADDRESS – Number and street	City and State

CODE FOR INJURY
(Use only the most serious injury)

K – Dead on arrival or before report was made
A – Visible sign of injury, as bleeding wound or distorted member, or had to be carried from scene
B – Other visible injury, as bruises, abrasions, swelling, limping, etc.
C – No visible injury but complaint of pain or momentary unconsciousness
O – No indication of injury

FIRST AID GIVEN BY   INJURED TAKEN TO   BY

INVESTIGATOR – Name and rank (signature) | BADGE NO. | I.D. NO. | DEPARTMENT | DATE OF REPORT

FOR ADDITIONAL INFORMATION USE *SUPPLEMENTAL REPORT (FHP 3A)*

FHP3 REVISED 1-1-71

particularly when there is no odor of an alcoholic beverage on the suspects breath. Observations concerning certain driving habits may lead to the suspicion of DUI, some of these are the following:

1. Speeding.

2. Driving on the wrong side of the roadway.

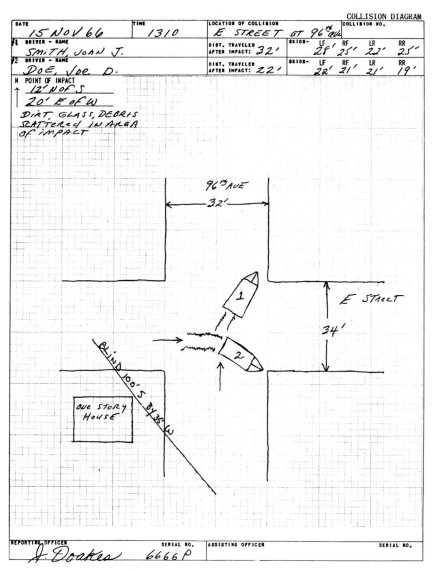

Accident investigator's collision diagram depicting a crash scene. *(Courtesy of the Oakland Police Department)*

3. Driving too slowly.

4. Inconsistent stopping and starting.

5. Driving at night without lights.

6. Swaying or weaving while on the roadway.

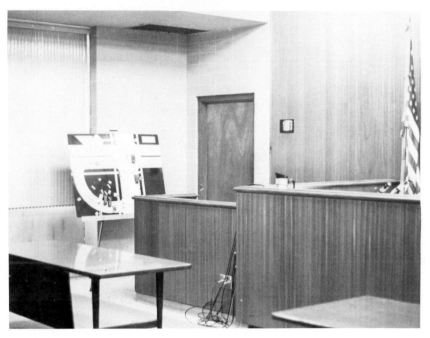

Most municipal courtrooms are equipped with a magnetic board suitable to reconstruct traffic accidents.

Chemical Tests

In order to measure to some degree the amount of alcohol in the suspect drivers system, three types of chemical tests may be used.

1. **Breath**. Balloon and Breathalyzer. They are as popular as they are easy to use, and give quick results.

2. **Blood**. This type of test is the most reliable method.

3. **Urine**. The urine test not only measures the alcohol content in suspect's body but can be used to determine the use of narcotics as well.

POLICE MOTORCYCLES

The police motorcycle has been utilized for a great many years by police traffic divisions. Yet, with all its value, the police motor-

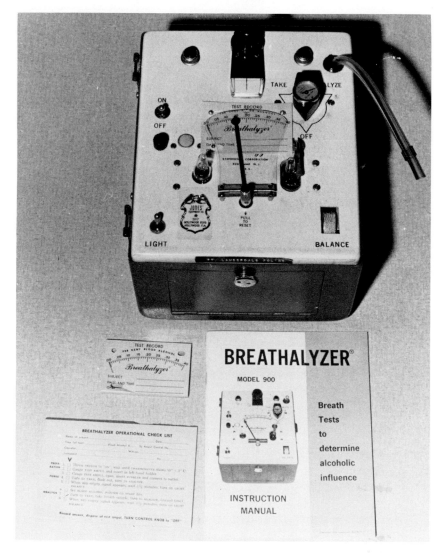

The Breathalyzer®. A breath sample is taken through the clear plastic hose at the top of the machine and in ninety seconds an accurate measurement of the alcoholic content in a suspect's blood system is available.

cycle is not without disadvantages, some of which have curtailed its use in large cities. Some of the advantages which make the police motorcycle a necessary and desirable device are

1. It allows easy access to accident scenes and congested areas

Roll call for the police traffic unit. *(Courtesy of the Montgomery, Alabama, Police Department)*

because of its size and mobility.

2. It affords a psychological advantage which serves as a deterrent to potential traffic violators.

3. It is readily available for escort duties and crowd control situations.

Some of the disadvantages of the police motorcycle are

1. It cannot be operated safely in inclement weather.

2. There is a high rate of injury for motor officers.

3. It does not afford ample protection or cover for the officer.

4. It cannot carry as much equipment as a police car (shotgun, first aid materials, emergency gear, etc).

THE MOVEMENT OF TRAFFIC

To control the flow of motor vehicles and pedestrians it

becomes necessary at times for traffic officers to personally supervise and direct traffic movement. Unfortunately there are no set standards of uniform methods of traffic direction which are utilized throughout the United States. The California Highway Patrol and many other California police agencies have adopted an agreed upon method of traffic direction to help establish some uniformity in their area. Many officers have found it necessary, or at least desirable, to adopt the tactics of the military police; however any method that works and is consistent with departmental policy is acceptable. Although state highway patrol academies devote a good deal of time to traffic direction, municipal agencies generally spend only a few hours on this subject.

CIVILIAN TRAFFIC OFFICERS

To assist in the growing vehicular parking problems in many of

The police meter maid. *(Courtesy of the Wichita Police Department)*

our larger metropolitan areas, police agencies have recently acquired the assistance of civilian traffic officers—both men and women. Those agencies, such as the Oakland, California, Police Department, that have hired civilians for this task have been able to release sworn officers for more critical functions.

PERSONNEL SELECTION

The position of traffic officer is a desired assignment in most police departments. Many patrol officers will apply for transfer into the traffic division. Accordingly, the traffic commander has the advantage of being able to select his manpower from the top men on the department. The great majority of law enforcement agencies have established certain requirements which must be met prior to any consideration of transfer. Usually the applicant must have served from one to five years with the agency and have proved himself to be a good street policeman. Rigid medical examinations are often part of the process, as physical condition is an important factor in considering a potential traffic officer. To be

A school for traffic violators sponsored by the police. *(Courtesy of the St. Petersburg Police Department)*

successful, a traffic officer must be mature, responsible, and dedicated to his job.

Fiber examination. *(Courtesy of the FBI)*

Chapter 27

CRIMINAL INVESTIGATION

When a police recruit is asked to what job he someday aspires, his immediate reply is usually, "I want to be a detective." This response is probably due to the fictionalized image of police detectives that television programs, paperbacks, and the movies have created. What the recruit perceives as a position of derring-do, of contacts, of informants, and of the capture of cunning criminal syndicate members is in reality a job of reviewing teletype messages; writing supplemental reports; tracing information through the various computer networks; interviewing witnesses, victims, and suspects; obtaining complaints from the district attorney, and testifying in court. This is not to say that the other picture is completely false, but rather that it occupies only a small portion of the detective's time and is the end result of the more routine aspects of his job.

Like other units, the primary function of an investigation division on a municipal police force is to assist the patrol division, to handle its "spinoff." The great majority of criminal investigations are initiated through the efforts of the patrol officer. When a victim of a crime calls the police, it is the patrol officer who will respond to the call. Occasionally the suspect is apprehended at the scene by the responding officer. More often, however, the suspect has to be identified and located. Because of time limitations, manpower restrictions, and the need for specialized knowledge, patrol officers are generally prohibited from conducting lengthy follow-up investigations, creating the necessity for the formation of a secondary line element which will perform that task. This element is the investigation, or detective, division.

THE INVESTIGATIVE MISSION

The police investigator's mission is threefold:
1. **To establish that a crime has in fact been committed.**

449

During this phase the investigator must establish sufficient facts to prove that the necessary legal elements were present to justify a criminal complaint and that the alleged offense was perpetrated by someone.

2. **To establish the identity of the suspect, locate the suspect, and bring about his apprehension.** This part of the investigation may take many man-hours to accomplish. Often there is more than one suspect to investigate. The professional investigator will attempt to prove innocence as well as guilt, to assure the prosecution of only the guilty.

3. **To collect, preserve, and transport to court evidence which will convict the defendant and to testify at the trial, when appropriate.** It is important to realize that the police only provide the evidence against the suspect and that it is the job

CRIMINAL INVESTIGATION DIVISION
INVESTIGATOR'S DAILY LOG

Mr. John L. Law   ID # 9716   Section C. A. Property   Unit 2   B&T / 7 am- 3 pm   Watch   Date 12-15-69

Car 691   Miles Out 27652   Miles In 27704   Total Miles 52

Offenses Assigned		Offenses Cleared		Offenses Unfounded		Offenses Filed		Total Offenses Supplemented
Part 1	Part 2	Part 1	Part 2	Part 1	Part 2	Part 1	Part 2	
3	1	2	1	1		2	1	4

PRISONERS ASSIGNED

Name	Charge	Disposition
Harry G. Hook	Burg. Bus. House Nighttime	Released
Joe C. Blow	Theft Over $50.00	Filed Theft Over $50.00

Activities Log: Record All Investigations, Calls, and Mark Outs

Time Out	Service #	Init. Inv.	Supp. Inv.	Nature and Location	Time In
9:00 am	699657A	X		Interviewed theft complainant, 5907	
				Gaston Ave.	9:25 am
9:35 am	756772A	X		Safe Burg. call, 4001 Main St.	10:05 am

Arrests

Time	Name	Charge
1:15 p.m.	John G. Crook	Inv. Burg.
1:15 p.m.	Mary R. Crook	Inv. Burg.

Special Assignments

Nature Surveillance of suspected fence of stolen property   Time Out 2:00 pm Time In 3:00 pm
Nature   Time Out   Time In
Unusual Arrests, Situations, or Information

USE REVERSE SIDE FOR ADDITIONAL INFORMATION 54

Signature   ID #

Reviewing Supervisor

(Courtesy of the Dallas Police Department)

of the district attorney to prosecute. The ultimate objective of any criminal investigation is to insure that the ends of justice are served.

The investigator's stock-in-trade is information. To locate the needed information in a criminal case the investigator must have the ability to know where to look and what to ask. In every case he will ask *who? where? when? why?* and *how?* His skill and ability will determine to a large extent whether these questions are answered correctly.

INTERVIEWS

Often the success of a criminal case will depend on what a witness to a crime observed, and the investigator's ability to locate the witness and gather the pertinent data. An interview may be defined as an informal conversation with a friendly witness or a victim. The subject has no reason to withhold information, thus the main problem is to see that the right questions are asked. An interview is usually not as difficult to conduct as an interrogation, but it is a good technique to establish rapport with the subject, even though a witness or a crime victim has no intention of withholding information. It is always more desirable to talk to a person who wants to help. To establish rapport an investigator finds a topic of mutual interest. Similar likes in furniture styles, automobiles, or hobbies are but a few items which may be initially discussed. Rapport is important because (1) the individual views the investigator as a person "who feels as I do" thus a bond of friendship is established and (2) the individual is at ease while talking to someone with whom he can "feel at home."

Even though a subject is willing to talk to an officer and good rapport has been established, the successful conclusion of an interview depends on the investigator's ability to properly question the witness or victim. To be considered, among other things, are the mental alertness and the educational level of the subject. The investigator must also remember some basic questioning techniques.

1. **Full answers.** The subject should be permitted to answer the questions fully and should be allowed to explain or expand on any items he considers important.

2. **Implied answers.** Even though an investigator feels that he already knows what response the subject will give to a question, he should not lead the subject. Questions should not be structured for an expected response.

3. **Simplicity of questions.** Complicated questions should be avoided. Having to explain questions only tends to make the interview more difficult. Questions must be geared to the ability of the subject so as not to confuse or embarrass him.

In addition to knowing the basic techniques of interviewing the investigator must also know how to question subjects, regardless of their age, race, sex, or background. To be able to expertly question all types and ages of subjects is an art which must be developed.

INTERROGATIONS

Interrogations are much more difficult to conduct than interviews, and thus demand more skill to bring about a successful result. An interrogation is the formal questioning of a criminal suspect or a hostile witness. Factors making an interrogation difficult include:

1. The subject is being questioned in a formal manner.
2. The subject is either a hostile witness or a suspect, and therefore is often unwilling to assist in the investigation.
3. The subject may be under orders from his attorney not to talk to the investigator.

The investigator in attempting to gain information during an interrogation must consider recent Supreme Court decisions that restrict his right to question persons suspected of crimes. When the process of an investigation shifts from the investigatory to the accusatory stage, the suspect must be apprised of certain legal safeguards. Accordingly, the investigator must furnish the suspect with the following information:

1. He has the right to remain silent—he is not obliged to say anything or to answer any questions.
2. If he waives his right to remain silent, any information obtained may be used against him at a later trial.
3. He has a right to have his lawyer present during any questioning.
4. If he cannot afford an attorney and would like to have one present, the state will provide one without expense.

chicago police department
INVESTIGATOR'S NOTEBOOK

No. 65-13
14 July 1965

O. W. WILSON
SUPERINTENDENT

STATEMENTS (Part III)

Only after the investigator is satisfied that he is armed with all the necessary information concerning the incident, should he begin the process of taking the formal statement. A thorough review of physical evidence, interview notes and the results of the interrogation will provide the investigator with all the necessary information for outlining the formal statement.

The presence of witnesses during the taking of the statement will increase the probability that the statement will be accepted by the court. In some cases the investigator may wish to have additional people present during the statement taking. The investigator must take the time to introduce everyone present so that each knows his particular role in the process of taking the statement. A NOTE OF CAUTION - Bear in mind that all witnesses to a confession may be called to testify. Limit the number of witnesses and select persons who will be available for the trial.

The statement may take one of three forms, that is, it may be strictly narrative or strictly question - answer or it may be a combination of narrative,question-answer. The narrative contains the "story" of the incident as it is told by the subject, either in his own handwriting or as it is dictated and later signed by him. The question-answer form is simply a series of questions put to the subject and his answers. From the standpoint of both completeness and admissibility the third form, a combination of narrative and question-answer, it is the most desirable.

The advantages of this third type are obvious when we consider that most people are not specific or clear in relating what they have experienced. Details are frequently omitted, for one reason or another in the telling of the experience. These details can be brought out by the investigator through the use of the question-answer method.

The use of this combination method in taking the statement can best be illustrated by considering the entire statement from beginning to end and indicating how this method is employed.

The statement can be divided into three parts, the heading, the body, and the ending.

THE HEADING - This is the first part which contains identifying data. The name of the person making the statement, what the statement is about, the date and time (always stated in civilian terms), and the location of the incident. The date and time as well as the location where the statement is taken must also be indicated in this portion of the statement. The names and identities of all persons present must be clearly stated. Occupations, home and business addresses should be included. The role that each person plays in the statement taking must be indicated; which person is typing

the statement, who are the witnesses to the statement and who was present when the crime was committed.

THE BODY - In this part of the statement all the elements of the offense and the facts associating the subject to the elements must be clearly indicated. The body of the statement contains the previously mentioned narrative, question-answer method of statement taking. The investigator should begin here with a series of directive questions. That is, questions which demand a specific answer. These questions should be directed toward establishing positive identity of the subject and to indicate that the answers he is furnishing is information which he alone would know. His answers should indicate that he is not being subjected to any form of duress, or that "words were not put into the subject's mouth".

Rather than using the indications; "Q" and "A" to show question and answer, the typist should indicate the name of the person speaking. This form clearly establishes who is asking the question and who is answering. It also makes it easier to indicate a change in persons questioning and makes it possible to question more than one person without becoming involved in lengthy explanations as to who is being questioned.

After this question-answer series, the investigator should allow the subject to tell what happened concerning the incident. This is accomplished by asking one or more non-directive statements, such as "Tell me what happened." or "Tell us about the incident." This type of question allows the subject to narrate his version of the incident without interruption.

When the subject has completed his narration, the investigator should return to the question-answer form to clarify any points which the subject did not mention or was not particularly clear in bringing out. This directive questioning should follow the same development of the incident given by the subject clearing up each point as it was given in the narration.

THE ENDING - When the investigator is satisfied that he has obtained an account of the incident which satisfies the legal requirements of the offense he should conclude with statements which will indicate that the subject was not denied any of his civil rights. Immediately following these concluding statements the subject should place his signature and the witnesses should sign the statement.

After the statement has been given, the investigator must verify every point made by the subject. The investigator must be able to prove each item mentioned and must not rely upon the word of the subject as to the truth of the statement.

This page from the Chicago Police Department's "Investigator's Notebook," a compilation of training materials, points up the importance that top agencies place on investigative excellence. *(Courtesy of the Chicago Police Department)*

The investigator must also make sure that the subject fully understands his rights.

ADMONITION AND WAIVER

Oakland Police Department

PART I

INSTRUCTIONS:

QUOTE TO ALL PERSONS ARRESTED AND ALL PERSONS TO BE QUESTIONED AS SUSPECTS IN CRIMINAL OFFENSES

1. You have the right to remain silent.

2. Anything you say can be used against you in a court of law.

3. You have the right to talk to a lawyer and have him present with you while you are being questioned.

4. If you cannot afford to hire a lawyer one will be appointed to represent you before any questioning. if you wish one.

PART II

INSTRUCTIONS:

1. ASK THE FOLLOWING QUESTIONS PRIOR TO QUESTIONING ANY SUSPECT. RECORD ALL ANSWERS VERBATIM.

Do you understand each of these rights I have explained to you?

_____

Having these rights in mind, do you wish to talk to us now?

_____

2. PRINT THE NAME OF PERSON ADMONISHED:_____

_____   _____
Signature of Officer   Date and Time

(Attach and Submit with Statement)

TF 361
(Rev. 8 66)

Police departments take great pains to see that the Constitutional rights of suspects are protected, as evidenced by the above admonition and waiver form. *(Courtesy of the Oakland Police Department)*

INFORMANTS

To be effective, an investigator must have good personal sources of information—informants. An informant is any person with information for the police; however, it is generally accepted that the term "informant" denotes someone who supplies information to the police over a period of time and is in some way paid or compensated for the service. Typical informants are prostitutes, drug addicts, pimps, bar owners and bartenders, pawn shop owners, local finance company personnel, and postal employes.

An important consideration for an investigator is the security of his informants. Naturally, any public knowledge of cooperation between the informant and the investigator will impair the detective's ability to gather future information from that informant. Even officers newly assigned as investigators will have informants, assuming that while in uniform they cultivated the informants on their beats.

A great deal of time and effort can often be saved if the investigator knows the many sources of information available to him. Every person from the time he is born until he dies leaves certain recorded facts—birth certificates, marriage licenses, health records, credit applications. Knowing where to go and what information is available is especially helpful in attempting to locate a suspect or a missing person.

CRIME SCENE DUTIES

Because of an emphasis on specialization many police agencies immediately assign important cases to investigators, who are dispatched directly to the crime scene. Murder, burglary, robbery, rape, and many other serious crimes are virtually assigned intact to the appropriate investigator. To obtain as much information as possible from the crime scene the detective must be expert in searching for and preserving evidence. He must also be accomplished in report writing and crime scene sketching. Larger metropolitan police departments may have photo technicians, however, in smaller agencies or during early morning hours, the investigator may also be expected to take crime scene photos which will be utilized later in court.

STAKEOUTS

Often the capture of a criminal will require an investigator to stakeout a location, to observe and wait at a location in anticipation of a suspect's arrival. As with many other aspects of an investigator's job, the stakeout is not an easy task. Complete

Homicide investigation. A murdered man lies face down on the sidewalk, shot in the back. The area has been roped off as patrolmen await the medical examiner, homicide detectives, and a mobile lab unit. *(Courtesy of the Wallace N. LaPeters Collection)*

planning is necessary to insure success. The investigator must station himself in a position that gives him the best possible vantage point, without being conspicuous.

Stakeouts are also used to obtain evidence in certain cases (e.g. bookmaking, prostitution, and narcotics purchases). Furthermore, they are often employed to capture a suspect in the act of committing a crime. When numerous robberies are occurring in a certain location or type of business, a stakeout can net the suspect or suspects and serve as a deterrent to future offenses.

THE MUNICIPAL POLICE DETECTIVE DIVISION

Large urban police agencies have detective divisions or bureaus which divide workloads among three subsections: (1) crimes

Burglars' tools and the men that use them, caught in the act of opening someone else's safe. *(Courtesy of the Montgomery, Alabama, Police Department)*

against persons, (2) crimes against property, and (3) general assignments.

Crimes-Against-Persons Section

The purpose of the division that investigates crimes against persons is to investigate all crimes committed, or any attempt to commit a crime, that will affect the health or safety of any person. Divisions under this category include:

1. Murder.
2. Rape.
3. Robbery.
4. Kidnapping.
5. Extortion.
6. Suicide.
7. Natural death.
8. Assaults.
9. Theft from person (including purse snatching).
10. Fondling.
11. Maiming.
12. Carrying a prohibited weapon.

An experienced officer gives recruit patrolman tips on investigating a safe burglary, a sensitive and highly complex art. *(Courtesy of the Detroit Police Department)*

Crimes-Against-Property Section

The purpose of the crimes-against-property section is to investigate all crimes committed, or any attempt to commit a crime, that will endanger or deprive a person of his property. Some divisions under this category include:

1. Burglary.
2. Theft (all, except theft from person).
3. Lost and found property.
4. Pawnbroker checks.
5. Bicycle license ordinance.
6. Explosions.
7. Bomb threats.
8. Receiving and concealing stolen property.
9. Breaking and entering a coin-operated machine.
10. Breaking and entering a motor vehicle.
11. Failure to pay for merchandise.
12. Shoplift offenses.

General-Assignment Section

The purpose of the general-assignment section is to investigate all crimes committed which are not assigned to either crimes-against-persons or crimes-against-property sections. The types of crimes vary in this assigned area. Some of the categories include:

1. Nonsufficient funds.
2. Forgeries.
3. No checking account.
4. Swindles.
5. Embezzlements (all types).
6. Accosting a female.
7. Malicious mischief.
8. Destruction of private property.
9. Animal bites.
10. Theft of credit cards.
11. Failure to pay (disorderly conduct).
12. Arson.
13. Indecent exposure.
14. Trespassing.
15. Obscene phone calls.
16. Accidental injury.

DAILY LOG

Among the many types of report forms that an investigator must fill out is the daily log. Like the patrol officer, police agencies often require the investigator to maintain a daily log to justify his time and workload. An example of this type of investigator's daily log is seen on page 450.

PERSONNEL SELECTION

After noting all the areas in which an investigator must be proficient, it is obvious that only the most qualified police personnel should be assigned to the investigative division. Traditionally, any candidate for a position as an investigator must have first proven his ability as a patrol officer. Now, however, some departments are allowing young men with unique qualifications to enter the agency as investigators. For example, The Lakewood, Colorado, Police Department allows this type of lateral entry. High intelligence, initiative, good report writing ability, and personal integrity are a few of the minimum prerequisites for the position. The candidate must also have the desire to be a detective, as it is not a position of sustained action. Personnel assigned to the investigation division should also have patience and maturity and be satisfied with many routine assignments.

CRIMINALISTICS

The age of mobility and technology has made the police crime laboratory and criminalistics of vital importance to the criminal investigator. The word "criminalistics" may then be defined as "the scientific examination of physical evidence."

The criminalist toils in the crime laboratory, where he is

Two criminalists at work in the police crime laboratory. *(Courtesy of the Wichita Police Department)*

concerned with analyzing evidence found at crime scenes. Some of the things which can be identified are blood groups, narcotics, paint, and most organic elements.

Equipment

Spectrograph

This unit has been an aid to the chemist for over fifty years and makes it possible to analyze minute samples, and provide photographic records of the sample being analyzed. Simply stated, the spectrograph is an optical device in which a narrow slit of light

Closeup of spectrograph during an examination. *(Courtesy of the FBI)*

is produced; the substance is then burned off in front of this slit, producing a luminous gas which is characteristic to that particular element. A photograph is taken which shows a series of black lines of varying degree, which is then compared to a standard for identification.

Spectrophotometer

Like the spectrograph, the spectrophotometer provides a record of the test being conducted. The spectrophotometer measures the intensity of the light transmitted or reflected by a substance at different wavelengths. Light from a standard source is divided into two beams. The beams are dispersed into spectra from which narrow wavelength regions can be isolated. One of the beams is transmitted or reflected by the sample. A photoelectric cell or photographic plate is used to record the transmitted or reflected beam and the direct beam. In this way a wavelength-by-wavelength comparison is accomplished.

X-ray Diffraction

The method of x-ray diffraction consists in sending a narrow beam of x-rays through the crystals of a substance and recording photographically the manner in which the crystal diffracts the rays. In this way the crystal structure of the substance is determined. The nature of the substance also is revealed because crystal structure has certain unique characteristics.

Electron Microscope

The electron microscope is capable of giving direct magnifications from 50X to 20,000X. Useful magnification of 100,000X is possible without employment of elaborate techniques.

Neutron Activation Analysis

Perhaps the most exciting device to come along in the field of analysis, the neutron activation analysis (or N.A.A.) makes it possible to provide positive identification of a substance. With N.A.A., for example, a suspect's hair is bombarded with neutrons which are absorbed like a sponge, at which time the rate that the neutrons begin to release themselves is measured and compared with the hair found at a crime scene.

There are only two of these machines in the United States. One

A demonstration of a Star-tron® amplificator, which allows viewing and photographing objects in almost total darkness. *(Courtesy of The Florida Department of Law Enforcement)*

is in the FBI Laboratory, and the other is owned by a private company.

The Crime Scene Unit

The crime scene technician has the responsibility of collecting and transporting evidence to the laboratory for analysis, and drafting maps and sketches. The crime scene technician is usually issued a kit for specific use at the crime scene. Listed below are some of the items found in the kit.

1. **Latent fingerprint equipment**—Various powders, chemicals, tape, fingerprint lifters, and brushes.

2. **Cameras**—Since most crime scene technicians have charge of photographing the crime scene, a variety of cameras are issued and used. The type of camera to be employed depends on the type of crime, conditions at the crime scene, and sometimes the technician's personal preference. There are many

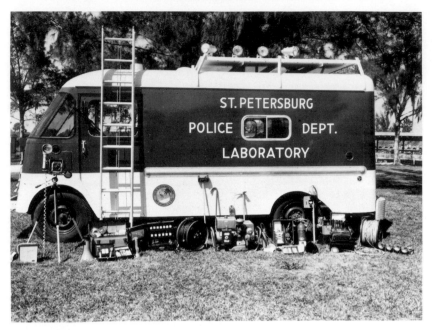

The mobile police crime laboratory. *(Courtesy of the St. Petersburg Police Department)*

types of cameras on the market, some of which are

    a. **The Speed Graphic** (sometimes called the 4 x 5 because of the film size)—Probably the most widely used and accepted, because the 4 x 5 negative can usually be enlarged and distortion is kept to a minimum.

    b. **35mm S.L.R.** (single lens reflex)—Popular because of its compactness.

    c. **Specialty cameras**—E.g. the fingerprint camera widely used by the technician at the crime scene.

    d. **Movie cameras**—Used in major cases, e.g. narcotics and gambling raids.

3. **Survey equipment**—A portable drafting table, tripod, measuring tape, compass, and a level for use in preparing an accurate diagram of the crime scene.

4. **Miscellaneous items**—Evidence bags, notebook, scribes, evidence tags, property receipts (to maintain chain of custody), fingerprint cards (for elimination prints), and rubber gloves.

Preparing evidence for serology examination. *(Courtesy of the FBI)*

Questioned Documents

The questioned-document expert examines the genuineness of documents or the identity of any of its parts. The common misconception is that the questioned document expert can instantly make an identification of bogus, forged, or altered papers. Nothing could be further from the truth! The true questioned-document expert uses many scientific tools and modern technology to make accurate identification of the item in question:

1. **Infrared photography**. This device is used in examining different inks, obliterations of the original document, erasures, secret writing, and so on. This is done by the use of filters, and special infrared film. One of the advantages of infrared photography is that it is inexpensive and requires no special camera.

2. **Electron radiography**. This technique uses secondary

radiation and is helpful in the identification of art forgeries.

3. **X-rays.** X-rays are used to identify fabrics and secret writing and are a great aid in determining art forgery.

4. **Ultraviolet light.** Ultraviolet light is used in the identification of inks to see if an attempt had been made to alter a document or reseal an envelope.

Firearms and Explosives Unit

Generally medium and large-sized police departments maintain a firearms and explosives unit, for it is a very specialized and expensive undertaking. The duties of this criminalistics component will range from ballistics testing to the dismantling of explosive devices. It is essential that the scientific equipment assigned to the staff be kept in perfect working order, as the life of technicians, especially those concerned with bomb disposal activities, may very well depend on how well their equipment functions.

The primary gear of firearms technicians is the comparison microscope, a device which can compare two bullets to see if they were fired from the same gun, and the bullet recovery tank, a large water-filled tank into which a bullet may be fired and recovered undamaged for analysis.

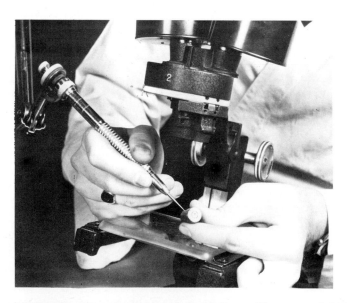

Engraving identification number on shell specimen. *(Courtesy of the FBI)*

Police technician examines spent bullets under a comparison microscope. *(Courtesy of the Metropolitan Police Department, City of St. Louis)*

Some departments take great pains to insure that recovered explosives are handled and deactivated as safely as possible. A device that is enjoying widespread use is the explosive carrier, a cylindrical container constructed of heavy steel and weighing approximately 1,500 pounds. The carrier is mounted on the bed of a truck so that inflammables and explosive devices can be transported quickly and with reasonable safety from where they were found. The Dade County (Florida) Public Safety Department

A member of the police bomb disposal squad plies his trade. *(Courtesy of the St. Petersburg Police Department)*

has employed this device, popularly referred to as a "bomb truck" for almost a decade.

Photography Unit

The photography unit takes the film from the crime scene technician, processes it, and makes enlargements for further investigation or for use in court. Personnel herein must insure that the film is developed free from distortion. The importance of crime scene films as evidence in court is indisputable.

Polygraph Unit

The polygraph operator is responsible for instrumental detection of deception. With modern scientific instruments designed to reveal physiological responses, the operator serves to aid the department's investigators in determining the truthfulness of victims, witnesses, and suspects involved in crimes. These instruments record physiological tracings of an individual's cardiac, respiration, and galvanic patterns. In test situations a norm is established for the subject. A series of questions relating to the incident are then asked. These questions are designed to

An FBI agent photographs a heel print left at the scene of a crime. *(Courtesy of the FBI)*

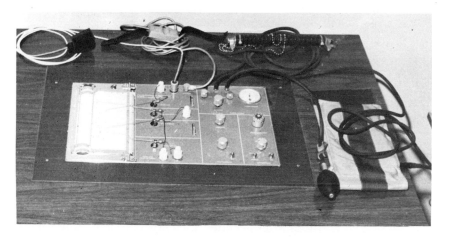

A closeup view of the polygraph.

A polygraph interrogation room. Note the sparseness of furnishings and the manner in which the furniture is arranged. Since it is essential that the subject be isolated from extraneous influences, he sits facing away from the polygraph and its operator.

elicit a physiological change in one who is concealing knowledge relative to the incident. Responses are recorded on a graph which is then evaluated by an examiner to serve as a basis for his opinion.

Fingerprint Unit

Personnel assigned to the fingerprint unit, or to duties as a fingerprint technician, work closely with the FBI, which maintains the most comprehensive fingerprint repository in the world. Fingerprint technicians must be thoroughly schooled in their job and be prepared to give expert testimony in court regarding the positive identification of fingerprints found at a crime scene. No more damning evidence (with the exception of the testimony of an eyewitness) exists than the discovery of an identifiable fingerprint on the scene of a criminal violation. A qualified technician can detect specific points of identification on a well-preserved fingerprint and thus furnish detectives with a clue of enormous importance. The Henry system of fingerprint classification, discussed in Part I, is still in existence.

A fingerprint expert is shown verifying an identification in the assembly section of the FBI Identification Division, Washington, D.C. *(Courtesy of the FBI)*

Vice problems and investigative devices are brought to the attention of the public by departments that realize that community support is the essence of successful law enforcement. *(Courtesy of the Orlando Police Department)*

Chapter 28

SPECIALIZED INVESTIGATIONS

INTELLIGENCE[1]

Most intelligence activities are popularly misconstrued as being a secret group conducting clandestine activities. This is not the case. Intelligence is hard work, involving the gathering and filtering of great volumes of data.

The patrol division is often referred to as the "workhorse" or the "backbone" of the police agency. One could just as appropriately say that the intelligence unit is the "nerve center" that supplies the police administrator with accurate information to combat organized crime, subversive organizations, and local disruptive elements.

History of Intelligence

The importance of intelligence to both the military and law enforcement is well documented in the pages of history. The success or failure of many battles was often determined by intelligence information rather than the force of numbers. Knowledge of the enemy's weakness is naturally vital data.

Some of the masters of intelligence will never be known and that is a tribute to their genius. Many within the ranks of agents or administrators are, however, well known. Some of these follow:

Moses. Moses undertook one of the first recorded formalized intelligence efforts when twelve intelligence agents were sent into Canaan to spy on that land.

Alexander the Great. Alexander, during his march into Asia, detected discontent in the ranks of his allies. He intercepted the mail of his officers and through this process was able to identify malcontents.

Genghis Khan. Prior to his invasion of Cathay, Genghis

---

[1]Information derived from D.O. Schultz and L.A. Norton's *Police Operational Intelligence* (Springfield: Charles C Thomas, Publisher, 1968).

Khan made use of paid informants for data on his adversaries.

Frederick the Great. Frederick the Great, the father of organized military intelligence, organized four classes of agents: (1) common spies recruited from the poor, (2) double spies, whose job it was to spread false information among the enemy, (3) spies of consequence—courtiers, noblemen, army officers, and (4) persons forced to engage in espionage against their will.

The Jesuits. Jesuit fathers were best known for their spiritual missions, but shortly after the invention of the printing press they set up a secret press and published clandestine messages which were widely distributed to the populace.

Joseph Fouché. Fouché, a Frenchman, was Minister of Police during the time of Roberspierre, whom he eventually overthrew. He then set up a system of *contre-espionnage* (counterespionage) that was to have a definite impact upon the history of France.

Karl Schulmeister. Schulmeister was Chief of Intelligence for Napoleon and creator of a military "secret service." He is credited with furnishing Napoleon with the necessary information to defeat the combined forces of Austria and Russia in the historic 1805 campaign.

Wilhelm Stieber. Stieber, often called the Prussian Master, was an intelligence agent for Bismarck. His two major contributions to the field were "military censorship" and "organized military propaganda."

Colonel William Donovan. During World War II Donovan was directed by President Roosevelt to draft a plan for an intelligence service. His creation was the legendary Office of Strategic Services (OSS).

Joseph Petrosino. Petrosino, a native of Italy, formed the New York Police Department's "Italian Squad" and gained a measure of immortality when he was ambushed and killed while on a visit to Sicily.

J. Edgar Hoover. The venerable Director of the FBI created the Special Intelligence Section (SIS) in 1940 for the purpose of gathering information in Central and South America during the war years.

Frank Ahern and James E. Hamilton. These two Los

Angeles Police Department Intelligence Officers were instrumental in founding the Law Enforcement Intelligence Unit (LEIU), a national organization dedicated to exchanging data and professionalizing the intelligence service.

Types of Intelligence

Strategic Intelligence

All intelligence data that is not of an immediate value, in most cases, can be categorized as strategic intelligence. The accumulation of physical descriptions of personalities who are engaged in major criminal enterprises, their vehicle descriptions, their telephone numbers, and known associates are classic examples of strategic intelligence.

Counterintelligence

Intelligence activity which is concerned principally with the defending of the department against a penetration by individuals and various groups who are inimical to the best interest and general harmony can be classified as counterintelligence. It is concerned with neutralizing and destroying attempts by individuals or groups that seek to discredit law enforcement. On many occasions it is difficult to separate counterintelligence activities from internal affairs areas of interest.

ELEMENTS OF POLICE INTELLIGENCE

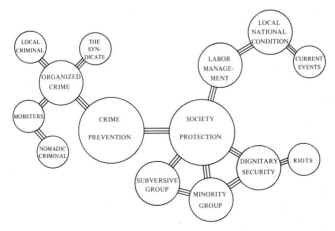

(Courtesy of The Dade County [Florida] Public Safety Department)

Line Intelligence

Line intelligence involves both a process and an immediate product. It can be said that all intelligence is an end product of gathering and processing information. That part of the product which is of an immediate nature and essential to more effective police planning and operations can be appropriately classified as line intelligence.

The Intelligence Officer

Selection of the intelligence division commander by the chief of police is probably one of the most important tasks to be performed. Coupled with other attributes, loyalty is paramount; however, loyalty should never be confused with blind obedience. The two are grossly different. He must be a person who consistently acts to provide truth, unshadowed and in its simplest form, regardless of personalities involved.

Once the chief has appointed the intelligence commander, he should at the same time give the commander wide latitude in selecting the personnel for this unit. Again, loyalty to the chief and to the agency plays a major role, perhaps only surpassed by personal and professional integrity.

One method of trait identification to be used in the selection of intelligence personnel can be expressed as the four "I's,"—*interest* in this type of work, *ingenuity, integrity,* and a high degree of *intelligence*—and the capacity for recall. A man who has little interest in this type of work, one who cannot quickly improvise or adapt to a rapidly changing situation, and one whose price of betrayal may be purchasable is a threat to the entire intelligence family. But how can one measure these items? A preassignment investigation of personnel, conducted by the staff or supervisors within the intelligence unit, is definitely an insurance policy in that regard. This could loosely be classified as a counter-intelligence activity. The intelligence commander cannot afford to have average policemen with average shortcomings. The candidate cannot be indiscreetly verbose, be dangerously in debt, or engage in adultery. Only the best may serve. Each must be a potential intelligence division commander.

VICE

Some of the most difficult types of crime for police personnel to deter are vice offenses. Part of the difficulty lies in the lack of victims or willing witnesses. Unlike robbery, burglary, assaults, and other types of crimes which have a criminal suspect and a victim, vice offenses have willing participants. There are sellers and users—e.g. the narcotic pusher and his customers, the addicts; the seller of obscene materials and his customers, the willing readers; the prostitute and her willing customers, commonly referred to as johns; the shylock and his willing customers, those who need the loan of money at any interest rate; and the purchaser of public officials and his willing partners, the crooked politicians.

There are other difficulties in trying to enforce vice ordinances.

VICE

Prostitution
and Sex Crimes

Drugs

Bribes to
Public Officials

Gambling

Obscene
Material

Shylocking

Illegal Liquor

Among them is the ability of those criminals engaged in vice activities to obtain money and political assistance to fight prosecution. The primary reason for this is that organized crime makes its basic living through vice operations and is more than willing to keep the "business" going. Another difficulty is the apathy of honest citizens and their reluctance to recognize the importance of enforcing vice laws. "If they want to do it, it's their business" is a dangerous attitude, for the final expense for vice activities will rest with the average taxpayer.

In smaller police agencies the chief may have vice officers report directly to him. In medium or larger agencies the responsibility may be assigned to a vice commander who will also report directly to the chief. The establishment of a vice unit places primary enforcement responsibility for vice conditions on those assigned to this division. The ultimate responsibility, however, will rest with the chief of police as the head administrator. Many chiefs of police have lost their positions because of their failure to effectively enforce vice laws or, in a corrupt city, for their success in enforcing them.

Vice Offenses

Prostitution and Sex Offenses

In the investigation of prostitution, homosexual acts, indecent exposure, some forms of child molestation, and lewd conduct, places wherein sex offenders visit and recreate—bars, parks, clubs—are kept under surveillance.

Narcotics

Larger agencies usually employ a separate unit of vice officers to combat this problem. The goal is the detection, apprehension, and successful prosecution of illegal drug users and suppliers. Naturally, the main emphasis should be in apprehending the "pushers" or the main sources of the illegal drug supply.

Shylocking

The lending of money at an illegal interest rate is generally found in larger metropolitan areas. Victims are often difficult to obtain because they fear bodily harm by the "enforcers" or collectors.

Evidence in a drug "bust." *(Courtesy of The Police Department, City of Baltimore)*

Illegal Liquor

The manufacture and sale of illegal liquor was a problem for law enforcement agencies prior to the prohibition era and is still of concern. The tax money lost to the government is of secondary importance to the possibility of injury or death which might occur should the illegal liquor be poisonous.

Gambling

This area encompasses many types or categories. Card games, lotteries, punch boards, illegal carnival gambling, and dice games are among some of the offenses of interest to the vice detail.

Obscene Material

Pornography might be considered the sale of literature, photos, or motion pictures which are lewd or obscene in nature. Because of Supreme Court decisions it is becoming difficult for anyone to determine what is obscene and what is not. The major emphasis for vice enforcement in this area is to attempt to deter sales to minors.

Bribery of Public Officials

Although this violation is of concern to the intelligence unit, vice officers are often involved in bribery investigations. Many times there is a direct connection between vice overlords and illicit money paid to politicians for protection.

Personnel Selection

The personnel selected to serve on vice details must be scrupulously honest and able to withstand tremendous temptation. The pressures to accept a bribe are ever present to officers assigned to the vice unit. Years of loyal dedication to the agency is an important consideration in the selection of personnel.

Vice investigators must work irregular hours and deal constantly with drug users, pimps, prostitutes, and other undesirable individuals. Constant observation must be maintained on vice personnel to determine if or when the assignment is affecting their mental well-being. Family pressures may also affect the performance level of the officer.

Vice officers will occasionally handle department funds for undercover activities and informant payoffs. Because of the very nature of the assignment, the vice officer must be the type of professional who requires little supervision.

Because vice crimes are usually surreptitious offenses involving willing buyers and sellers, vice investigators must, in order to be successful, either make on-the-scene arrests of crimes in progress or conduct lengthy continuing surveillances of undesirable places and suspected offenders. The former method is a procedure of only limited worth because of its inconsistency, making the latter device the most desirable investigative technique but also the most expensive and most time consuming. The police department cannot replace vice officers each time they are identified by their clientele, so a system of informants and undercover agents—some of whom are policemen, others may be citizens on the police payroll—are developed to give officers an insight into what is happening in their city. Some may decry this as "secret police" activity; however, vice purveyors—especially narcotic dealers—engage in clandestine activities, and traditional Sherlock Holmes techniques must be forsaken for more workable methods. Vice investigators often must qualify as expert court witnesses on the identification of certain narcotic or barbiturate substances, and officers should have an intimate knowledge of the penal code, especially search and seizure laws, for defense attorneys most often attack in court the constitutionality of the arrest rather than the facts in the case or the evidence at hand. A knowledge of human nature, an understanding of the law and the tools of the trade, lengthy experience, a healthy outlook toward ones job, a professional aloofness from offenders, and a sense of humor are handy tools for vice investigators to possess. Occasionally, in order to make use of a fresh face, officers from the police academy are assigned for a short period of time to the vice detail.

INTERNAL AFFAIRS

An internal-affairs unit is established to protect the interests of both the community and the police agency. It is the investigative arm of the chief of police and its assignment is to investigate allegations of misconduct lodged against police personnel by citizens and other officers. It is not instituted to condemn all officers charged with offenses or to single out department personnel to be terminated. The unit should operate free from political interference, and its personnel should be immediately responsible either to the chief or a deputy chief.

Some of the types of investigations which will be assigned to the internal affairs unit follow.

1. Any complaint by a citizen charging one or more of the department's personnel with misconduct.
2. Any suspected violations of morals by members of the agency.
3. Any situation where injury or death results from a citizen-police officer conflict. This conflict may be on or off duty.
4. Any situation where a police officer discharged his weapon.

The Investigative Process

Large, well-run police departments have adopted systematic procedures for investigating citizen complaints of police mis-conduct. Good police departments will accept a complaint from anyone, including anonymous complainants, and by any means—

OAKLAND POLICE DEPARTMENT

Police Administration Building, 155 7th St.
Oakland, California 94607

To the People of the City of Oakland:

I wish to assure you that your Police Department welcomes constructive criticism of Department procedures or valid complaints against police officers. Each criticism and complaint received will be investigated thoroughly and appropriate corrective action taken when warranted by the facts obtained. You will be informed of the results of the investigation when it is completed.

If you wish to make a complaint, you may come to my office on the 8th floor of the Police Administration Building, at 7th and Broadway, or phone 273-3365. You will be received by my Administrative Aide or by the Sergeant in charge of the Internal Affairs Section, whose job it is to investigate complaints. You will be treated courteously and thorough consideration will be given to the problem you present.

If you do not wish to come to the Police Department or telephone, you may register your complaint in writing to me. Just complete the form, seal the glued flap and mail this pamphlet. I am the only one who will open it. Please write as much information as you can; it will be helpful if you will give your name and address so that we may contact you for further information if needed. Any information you give will be kept confidential if you so request.

Please feel free to express yourself on any problem which you feel should be directed to my attention.

Sincerely,

C. R. Gain
Chief of Police

WRITE YOUR NAME, ADDRESS AND PHONE NUMBER

WRITE THE DATE THIS FORM IS FILLED IN   WRITE THE DAY & DATE OF INCIDENT OR ACTION   TIME OF INCIDENT

WHERE DID THE INCIDENT OR ACTION TAKE PLACE?

WRITE THE NAMES OF ANY WITNESSES, THEIR ADDRESSES AND TELEPHONE NUMBERS

IF A PERSON WAS ARRESTED, WRITE HIS NAME, ADDRESS AND PHONE NUMBER IF KNOWN

IF A POLICEMAN WAS INVOLVED, WRITE HIS NAME, BADGE NUMBER AND CAR NUMBER, IF YOU HAVE THIS INFORMATION

WRITE THE NATURE OF OPINION OR COMPLAINT

GLUE FLAP DOWN TO MAIL

The Oakland Police Department distributed within the community thousands of letters *(as shown here)* soliciting citizens' complaints. *(Courtesy of the Oakland Police Department)*

telephone, letter, personal contact. Many agencies even solicit complaints from the community. Some major police departments distribute letters informing citizens of their right to register a grievance and the procedure to follow in lodging it.

The investigative process in internal matters is basically the same as it is in criminal cases, with the exception that the accused (the policeman) enjoys none of the rights that a criminal suspect is afforded. The policeman does not have the right to remain silent. He may not be allowed to have his attorney present during questioning. What he says will be used against him at a later hearing. He can be forced to take a polygraph examination. He may be questioned and requestioned for extended periods of time. He need not be advised of the charge against him or of the complainant. In short, the internal investigation offers policemen none of the procedural safeguards or Constitutional guarantees

that are automatically granted to felons, although some departments afford their men a form of due process and rights to appeal
convictions.

The first step in the handling of a grievance is to assign a control
number and an investigator to the case. A statement, written and
signed if possible, is taken from the complainant. Witnesses are
located and statements are taken from them. Physical evidence is
marked and impounded, if practical. When the case against the
accused officer nears completion, he is asked to come to the
internal affairs office, wherein he is required to give a written
statement. Witnesses and evidence in his behalf are handled in the
same manner as is the complainant. When the investigation has
been completed, the results are transmitted through the chain of
command to the chief of police for review. The chief may find for
or against the officer, or he may order a further investigation.
Officers are not generally found "guilty" or "not guilty" of the
specifications, for it is fast becoming policy on many departments
to articulate a series of investigative findings which are more
descriptive of the actual outcome of the case. Following is a list of
findings in general use:

1. **No violation**—The allegation was true but it did not
   constitute a violation of law or policy.

2. **Not involved**—The officer charged with the offense was
   not involved in it (e.g. when a complainant jots down a
   wrong badge number).

3. **Unfounded**—The allegation was found to be baseless (e.g.
   the complainant lied or misrepresented).

4. **Not sustained**—There was evidence that the officer
   committed a violation of departmental policy, but not
   enough to convict him.

5. **Sustained**—The officer was either guilty as charged or
   guilty of a violation uncovered during the investigation.

Sound administrative practice holds that only "sustained"
complaints will be inserted in an officer's personnel record,
although a confidential card file may be kept on all departmental
complaints for record-keeping purposes.

Types of Internal Discipline

Officers found guilty of offenses are in some way disciplined. A good system of fair internal discipline is essential to the operation of any police department, regardless of its size. Discipline ought to be meted out according to a progressive scale of penalties—punishment commensurate with the offense—and the ramifications of improper conduct should be communicated to all personnel via departmental general orders. Following are types of internal discipline, progressing from the least to the most severe:

1. Oral reprimand.

2. Written reprimand (permanently inserted into the officer's personnel folder).

3. Transfer (to another, less-desirable assignment).

4. Extra duty.

5. Suspension.

6. Reduction in rank (for supervisory and command personnel).

7. Dismissal.

8. Criminal prosecution.

In some cases several categories of discipline may be instituted (e.g. suspension and rank reduction). Repeated violations of the same offense will of course result in progressively stringent discipline.

Personnel Selection

Because the reputation of the agency will to a large extent be determined by the efforts of those assigned to the internal affairs unit, extremely careful personnel selection must be maintained. Those chosen must have an extensive investigative background. Officers chosen must also demonstrate the ability of having a neutral or objective viewpoint concerning cases they may have to investigate. Personal friendships must take second place to the department's integrity. The officer must also be free from a feeling that all officers charged with an offense are guilty. The officers selected for this unit or detail must not be "the chief's men" or acknowledged "headhunters." Overconcentrated efforts to find the guilty of all department policy may result in a serious morale problem.

School children eagerly board a patrol car for an inspection tour. *(Courtesy of the Leavenworth Police Department)*

Chapter 29

COMMUNITY RELATIONS

When in 1957 the St. Louis Police Department operationalized the Nation's first formal community relations division, there was evidence that most policemen, especially rank-and-file officers, viewed the concept as a frivolous nonessential undertaking at best, and at worst a dangerous experimentation during a period of critical manpower shortages. Over the years, however, this rather myopic view has changed and prevailing police opinion on the subject, pointed up by a recent survey conducted by the International Association of Chiefs of Police, now accepts the need for better police-community relationships and the formation of specialized police components to work toward that end. There is also evidence to indicate that many citizens view the idea in a positive way, although similar opinion surveys show a great deal of distrust and hostility still exists regarding the police, especially in minority communities.

Although police-community relations programs are aimed at the entire community, certain problems are unique to culturally deprived areas—e.g. language barriers, high unemployment, inaccessibility to government, escalating crime rates—and special attention must be given to them. Furthermore, racial rioting has motivated many police administrators to implement extraordinary programs. Not all of these programs have been successful, but what is important is that there now exists in law enforcement a genuine desire to improve relations between police and the citizenry they have sworn to serve.

A SYSTEMS APPROACH TO COMMUNITY RELATIONS

Police departments that seek to promote respect for police goals and to improve their "image" will not be successful unless a systems approach is employed. Taking into consideration the nature of American social conditions, it is not unfair to state that

The police display—a way to bring the department closer to the community. *(Courtesy of the Leavenworth Police Department)*

most communities are not homogeneous groupings of like-minded persons, but areas in which divergent racial, ethnic, and social classes live, work, and recreate. Therefore, a multifaceted approach to the issue is necessary. This is not to say that a police department should not emphasize a particular problem area, but not to the exclusion of the rest of the community. It will not be sufficient to simply make officers available for speaking engagements, for this will create gaps in the overall program. Many individuals do not belong to civic associations and they will not be reached by policemen who respond only to requests to address these limited audiences. The Philadelphia Police Department has found that the formula, communication + courtesy + concern = good community relations, is a workable one, but it must be applied to all the diverse publics in a community in order to be successful.

TYPES OF COMMUNITY RELATIONS PROGRAMS

The International City Management Association (ICMA) has identified five broad types of police-community relations programs:

1. **Educational programs,** which are "issue related" in design and which have as their aim the bringing of community leaders together to discuss mutual problems and concerns.

2. **Police institutes on community relations,** in which participants are brought together in a controlled environment to discuss selected issues. Guest speakers and consultants, experts in their field, are brought in to address the assemblage.

3. **Police training,** a formulated course of study offered to both pre-service and in-service officers as either specialized study in community relations or as an addition to a more comprehensive curriculum.

4. **Metropolitan police-community relations programs,** which are decentralized programs found in precincts or neighborhood city halls. A favorite device is the formation of police advisory committees made up of officers and citizens working together. A newer technique is the "community relations trailer," a specially equipped house trailer which is towed to various neighborhoods and schools.

5. **Special theme programs,** which are essentially programs aimed at a specific area of interest—youth, blacks, Mexican-Americans, press relations. These types of programs are generally employed to lessen crisis situations, such as those that exist immediately following a massive civil disturbance.

OBSTACLES TO GOOD COMMUNITY RELATIONS

Law enforcement faces an uphill fight in its attempt to build a meaningful relationship with the community. Creating a favorable public attitude toward the police task is no easy undertaking, especially in light of the fact that many police-citizen contacts are punitive in nature. Harold Barney of the International Association of Chiefs of Police surveyed the field and found seven factors that consistently impede the development of community relations

More and more police departments are employing extraordinary devices
aimed at improving relations with the citizenry. The top photo is of a mobile
community relations trailer. The bottom photo is the inside view. *(Courtesy
of the Orlando Police Department)*

programs:

1. The traditional fear of the law and its agents, which is quite real and must be recognized.

2. Errors in judgment on the part of individual officers, a problem that will continue to occur.

3. Unpopular police actions in the form of enforcement of unpopular laws and ordinances.

4. Refusing special privileges to people who fill important posts.

5. Attacks in the press by columnists sympathetic with those who employ confrontationist tactics.

6. Political pressure.

7. The necessity of overcoming an unsavory police reputation.

Add to Barney's factors an additional element—contemporary police labor militancy—and it becomes immediately apparent that police administrators have their hands full in fighting the problem of police isolation.

A MODEL COMMUNITY RELATIONS POLICY:
THE CINCINNATI POLICE DEPARTMENT

The Police Community Relations Section of the Cincinnati Police Department was formally established in August, 1966, staffed initially by a police captain and two community relations specialists. The stated mission of this unit comprises the basic goals of all police community relations divisions:

> To provide a function of the police agency with defined goals and qualified staff and authority to provide adequate and meaningful programs within, as well as without, the division which will ultimately create a greater harmony between the police and all people of the community. These goals in their purest form promote efficiency of the police agency in terms of winning the hearts, minds, and confidence of the people to support the police in law enforcement responsibilities by, in turn, accepting citizen responsibilities.

Children receive Halloween candy from officer at district police station. *(Courtesy of the Metropolitan Police Department, City of St. Louis)*

According to written departmental policy, the functions of the unit are the following:

1. To develop positive programs to bring about a better understanding and improved cooperation with the community and to spearhead programs designed to gain greater public support and confidence with a goal of reducing crime.

2. To develop policies and procedures as related to the police-community relations activities of the division.

3. To actively engage in various community relations projects and programs with civic and fraternal organizations, as well as with schools; to develop and present programs which are material to greater respect for the law.

4. To participate directly in the development of the police district-community relations committee and to assist unit commander and co-chairman of each district committee in planning programs, meetings, and district-level community relations activities.

5. To coordinate activities of the police department in the area of public relations: speakers, tours, and develop special programs such as Law Enforcement Week and National Police Week.

6. To cooperate with all news media in presenting the police function to the public in its true perspective of maintenance of law and order, preservation of the peace, and protection of the public.

7. To develop programs for the presentation of police recruit and in-service training classes.

8. To develop a course in community relations for inclusion in the University of Cincinnati Police Science Program.

9. To act as liaison between the police and minority group organizations in the handling of grievances.

10. To cooperate with other human relations organizations in developing programs and seminars for presentation to the police and to other organizations.

11. To promote programs which will assist the ordinary citizen and the rank-and-file policeman in getting along.

12. To cooperate with all community agencies as a listening post; to stop "talking at" people and serve as an intelligence agency and a barometer of the pulse of the community.

A MODEL COMMUNITY RELATIONS PROGRAM: THE LOS ANGELES POLICE DEPARTMENT

A leader in the area of police community relations is the Los Angeles Police Department. The LAPD's community relations program is fast becoming a model for other departments to emulate, and one that is continually changing and expanding.

Although the initial efforts of the community relations program were directed toward the most troubled areas of the city, the current program includes a broad spectum of activities for the entire community. Those listed below are embraced in a concept which the department refers to as "total community involvement."

Crime Prevention

The crime prevention program makes available information that the general public can use for home, business, and car. An example of which, "lock your car," is designed to deter car thieves.

Youth-Oriented Programs

These programs afford opportunities for police officers and young people to engage in nonpunitive relationships while working and competing in sports, and numerous other positive educational character building activities. A few of the youth-oriented programs follow.

1. The Law Enforcement Explorer Program—intended to interest young men in a career in law enforcement and develop an awareness of civic responsibility.

2. The Housing Authority Police-Youth Program—designed to reach youth within the housing projects where concentrated population presents inordinate living conditions.

3. Summer Camping—consists of four one-week summer

The police department conducts an unarmed defense exhibition in a shopping center mall. *(Courtesy of the Orlando Police Department)*

sessions Monday through Friday, including swimming, archery, canoeing, and fishing.

4. The Athletic Unit—establishes and coordinates athletic leagues and events through the Youth Service Officers of the seventeen geographical patrol divisions.

Other areas in youth work include the LAPD Junior Band, Teen Post Incorporated, Special Events Unit, The Annual Student Leadership Symposium on Law and Order, and the Annual Boy's Day Safety Programs. The Department's school program is designed to establish contact between the police and students at all grade levels. The humanism and friendliness of police officers are imparted to approximately 8,000 students per week. Police and school officials agree that this program, presented in an atmosphere of learning, is invaluable in creating a sense of concern for orderly behavior and responsibility for the maintenance of law and order. Periodic workshops are held with top school board administrators to formulate curriculum and develop in-service education for teachers. Three devices are used in the school program are

1. **Policeman Bill**—Involves discussions of the history of policing and the role of the police in society.

2. **Junior Crime Prevention Program**—Four times yearly officers equipped with visual aids and handout material visit fourth grade classes throughout the city to impress on the students the consequences of criminal acts.

3. **"Lets Get Acquainted"**—A classroom question and answer session in which policemen discuss, among other subjects, drug abuse.

A MODEL MINORITY RELATIONS PROGRAM:
THE ST. LOUIS POLICE DEPARTMENT

The St. Louis Police Department operates one of the most comprehensive minority relations programs in the country. The department maintains numerous store-front centers, staffed by policemen, wherein complaints may be lodged by citizens who would otherwise have been isolated from their police department.

A police-community relations specialist and his young assistants—the Neighborhood Youth Corps. *(Courtesy of the Police Department, City of Baltimore)*

In addition, each police division coordinates a youth council which acts as a liaison between officers and schools in the districts. Officers are regularly assigned to visit Headstart Programs in the City to teach pedestrian safety. A special youth program has community relations officers working with the hardcore unemployed. An ongoing program to improve sanitation conditions is carried out in conjunction with a citizen's committee organized for that purpose.

Every policeman on the department is affected by the agency's commitment to better police-minority relations. During their

Officer discusses neighborhood problem with citizen in district "storefront" police-community relations center. *(Courtesy of the Metropolitan Police Department, City of St. Louis)*

many weeks of training in the police academy, all recruits take a three-hour credit-college course in human relations. Taught by sociologists and psychologists from local colleges and universities, the course includes instruction in human behavior, the nature of prejudice, American culture, and social disorganization. Field trips led by a social worker are conducted to acquaint new officers with the socioeconomic conditions of the city. All recruits are assigned to a tour of duty in one of the storefront centers prior to graduation. Refresher courses in human relations are given to officers at least once each year, and first-line supervisors are required to devote three days of their on-duty time working with district community relations officers.

THE PATROLMAN'S ROLE

Regardless of how comprehensive a police-community relations

The best community relations program is the beat officer who cares. *(Courtesy of the St. Petersburg Police Department)*

is, it will fail if the uniformed patrolmen are not sympathetic with it. Police-community relations is nothing more than the aggregate of relationships of each officer to each private citizen, so it logically follows that those officers who most often contact citizens—patrolmen—will have the most dramatic impact on the department's total program. In some cases the creation of a formal community relations unit has had a negative effect on patrol officers by giving the tacit impression that public relations, like burglary investigations, planning and research, and criminalistics, is an activity that should be undertaken by the specialized unit assigned to that function. It is essential that patrolmen be apprised that the community relations component is no more than an adjunct to the uniformed patrol officers—the department's real hope for improved relations with the citizenry.

(Courtesy of the Miami Police Department)

Chapter 30

RECORDS AND COMMUNICATIONS

RECORDS

$\mathbf{A}$ police records system is the "memory bank" of any law enforcement agency. There can be no dispute as to the importance of this vital police function. Police administrators, whether they are in command of small, medium, or large police organizations, must rely on the records division to collect, categorize, file, and be able to retrieve information. Of critical importance is the ability to have immediately available certain types of data. All the hours devoted to the collection, analization, and filing of reports are often of little value if the product cannot be relocated in a short period of time.

Many types of records are routine in nature. Minor complaints and simple noninjury accident reports fall into this category. There are, however, certain files and reports which must be available for immediate use. Information on local criminal personalities, citizens having mental problems, and those individuals who have demonstrated violence against police personnel must be arranged to insure quick location and dissemination to the field officer requesting a "record check."

The responsibilities of the records division are divided into three major categories:

1. Maintenance of booking data and other records concerning the identification of individuals, crimes, accidents, property, and evidence.
2. Public information or assistance.
3. Records control through audits.

Purposes Served

There are many uses or purposes that an effective records system serves, among which are

1. **Determining the extent and needs of police services.** This is

accomplished through the collection of statistics on incidents of crimes, disturbances, and traffic hazards and accidents. Through the use of these statistics a police administrator is able to plan for selective enforcement techniques and determine the amount of personnel needed for each shift, month, or season of the year.

2. **Giving a traffic profile.** By the use of traffic records (i.e. citations, written warnings, accident reports, and miscellaneous reports concerning street conditions, lighting conditions, traffic signal failures) the traffic commander is able to predict future traffic situations. He is also able to combat traffic violations and accidents by the deployment of personnel, and to assist the street department by suggesting needed repairs or improvements.

3. **Assisting in investigation of criminal cases.** The police records division is a useful tool by which the investigator can secure information concerning individuals, vehicles, and locations. The investigator is able to compare methods of operation used in previous cases with a current crime in an attempt to find similarities. Many criminals use the same method of operation (M.O. or *modus operandi*) for each crime they commit.

4. **Long-range planning for personnel.** By analyzing statistics concerning the percentage of crime rate increases and the projected growth of crime, the chief of police is in a position to plan for future manpower needs. Armed with these statistics, he is able to defend reasonable additional personnel requests.

5. **Long-range planning for police equipment.** The rate of growth for an organization will affect its needs for additional equipment. Police vehicles, weapons, communications, and building expansion must be planned prior to an immediate need.

The Master Card Index

The master card index is the heart of the records section. It is an alphabetically filed card index listing all individuals or business firms that were contacted by the police agency. Of interest to police personnel are those personalities or firms who fall into one

Records division. File cabinets containing pictures, fingerprints, and criminal histories of persons coming in official contact with the police department are maintained in the identification section. *(Courtesy of the Oakland Police Department)*

of the following categories:
1. Arrested and booked.
2. Wanted by police for questioning or arrest.
3. Complaining parties.
4. Victims of a crime or traffic accident.
5. Witnesses to a crime.
6. Persons contacted as suspects but not arrested.
7. Missing persons.
8. Traffic violators.
9. Individuals with gun permits.
10. Locally licensed individuals or firms.

A master index file card for an individual should contain the following information:
1. The full name of the individual.
2. His date of birth.
3. A basic description (male-white-30 years-6'0"-175-brn-brn).
4. Reason he was contacted (*suspect-victim-witness*).
5. The offense or circumstance.
6. The case number.
7. If arrested, the charge and booking number.

With this information readily available to police records personnel, an officer's request for information should have a quick and efficient response.

Classification of Cases

To insure proper administration, criminal and noncriminal cases should be classified. The FBI lists Part One offenses, which have been discussed in Chapter 12, as:

1. Criminal homicide.
2. Rape.
3. Robbery.
4. Aggravated assault.
5. Burglary—breaking or entering.
6. Larceny—theft.
7. Auto theft.

Part Two offenses are as follows:

8. Other assaults.
9. Forgery and counterfeiting.
10. Embezzlement and fraud.
11. Stolen property (buying, receiving, possessing).
12. Weapons (carrying, possessing).
13. Prostitution.
14. Sex offenses.
15. Offenses against family and children.
16. Narcotic drug laws.
17. Liquor laws.
18. Drunkenness.
19. Disorderly conduct.
20. Vagrancy.
21. Gambling.
22. Driving while intoxicated.
23. Violation of road and driving laws (endangering public safety).
24. Parking violations.
25. Other violations of traffic and motor vehicle laws.
26. Other offenses (not classified above).
    a. Arson.
    b. Blackmail.
    c. Burglary tools (possession, etc.).
    d. Escape from jail.
    e. Malicious mischief (damage to property).
    f. Obscene literature, pictures, etc. (possession, etc.).
    g. Parole violation.
    h. Public nuisances.

    i.   Subversive activities, criminal syndicalism, sabotage.

    j.   Trespass.

    k.   Miscellaneous (not otherwise classified).

  27. Suspicion.

Part Three cases are concerned with lost and found persons, animals, and property.

  28. Lost.

  29. Found.

Part Four cases involve injury or accident considerations.

  30. Fatal motor vehicle traffic accidents.

  31. Personal injury motor vehicle traffic accidents.

  32. Property damage motor vehicle traffic accidents.

  33. Other traffic accidents (except motor vehicle).

  34. Public accidents (except firearms and dog bite).

  35. Home accidents (except firearms and dog bite).

  36. Occupational accidents (except traffic and other public, firearms, and dog bite).

  37. Firearm accidents (not suicide).

  38. Dog Bites.

  39. Suicides.

  40. Suicide attempts.

  41. Sudden death and bodies found.

  42. Sick cared for.

  43. Mental cases.

Part Five cases:

  44. Miscellaneous officers.

  45. Miscellaneous public.

  46. Special orders.

  47. General orders.

  48. Rules and regulations.

The National Crime Information Center[1]

Computerized Index

Today law enforcement is facing criminals who have at their disposal sophisticated equipment, weapons, and other resources to abet their lawless activity. Even so, they are no match for highly

---

[1] Source: An information bulletin entitled *"NCIC"* disseminated by The Federal Bureau of Investigation.

One of the Nation's first police computer centers. *(Courtesy of the Metropolitan Police Department, City of St. Louis)*

trained members of law enforcement who are skilled in patrol and investigative techniques and who use scientific equipment to maintain law and order.

Computers are not new to law enforcement. They have been used over the years for administrative programs, statistics, payroll, etc. The FBI's computerized index of criminal information has been designed for the rapid interchange of information among law enforcement agencies. This dramatic new "instant information retrieval system" is the National Crime Information Center (NCIC).

The idea of NCIC was conceived as a result of law enforcement's growing need for vital information in a hurry. Scientific advances in computer technology appeared to offer a solution to these needs. What heretofore was either beyond comprehension for other than scientific minds or was not feasible economically, now appeared to fit into the police scheme of operations. The FBI, in conjunction with the Advisory Group to the Committee on Uniform Crime Records, International Association of Chiefs of Police (IACP), which group is made up of law enforcement representatives from local, state, and Federal agencies, recognized the value computers could be to law enforcement. After a series of meetings, policies and procedures were formulated which eventually led to the establishment of NCIC. On January 27, 1967, the computer center at FBI Headquarters in Washington,

D.C. commenced "on the air" operations and since that time the system has expanded at a rate far exceeding original estimates.

Success came to the NCIC through the close cooperation between local and state law enforcement authorities and the FBI. Both technical and human growing pains were and are still encountered as the system expands, and money for local operations is not always available. Recognizing this financial restraint, the Law Enforcement Assistance Administration, U.S. Department of Justice, has offered its support to local agencies in the form of special monetary grants for participation in NCIC.

Sharing of Police Information

Through the cooperative efforts of officers at all levels of law enforcement, local, state and Federal, a united front has now been established to fight crime. While law enforcement officers have always worked side by side to combat lawlessness in society, this most recent advance makes possible even greater cooperation. Participating police departments, sheriffs' offices, state police facilities, and Federal law enforcement agencies are now immediately sharing accessible data. Centralized computers

A local terminal through which inquiries and replies are made to and from the various computerized information systems, including the FBI's National Crime Information Center. The Inquiry is made by activating the keyboard, while replies are transmitted on the television-like screen. *(Courtesy of the Police Department, City of Baltimore)*

strengthen the cooperative relationship among law enforcement agencies.

Next to manpower, information is the most important asset to a police agency. The NCIC provides an immediate flow of pertinent data for the officer on the street. With information available immediately, police officers are in a better position to make an action decision. On the other hand, lengthy delay in communications and inaccessible information benefit the criminal. NCIC is one of the greatest innovations law enforcement has seen in decades and represents a unique investigative tool you can use in helping to maintain law and order. It assists the police in the discharge of responsibilities with dispatch and thoroughness, resulting in a higher risk of detection for the offender.

The NCIC Network

The NCIC's computer equipment is located at FBI headquarters in Washington, D.C. The present equipment includes rapid access storage units with a capability of accommodating nearly two million records representing criminal activities. In a matter of seconds stored information can be retrieved through equipment in the telecommunications network. Connecting terminals, placed near the radio dispatcher, are located throughout the country in police departments, sheriffs' offices, state police facilities, and Federal law enforcement agencies. Police dispatchers can respond quickly to requests from officers on the street. The NCIC, as well as operating statewide systems, furnishes computerized data in a matter of seconds to all agencies participating in the centralized state systems. The goal of NCIC is to serve as a national index to fifty statewide computer systems and heavily populated metropolitan area systems.

NCIC headquarters with its computerized system might be compared to a large automated "file cabinet" with each file having its own label or classification. Such a cabinet of data contains information concerning:

1. Stolen, missing, or recovered guns.
2. Stolen articles.
3. Wanted persons.
4. Stolen/wanted vehicles.
5. Stolen license plates.

6. Stolen/embezzled/missing securities—stocks, bonds, currency, etc.

These labels serve to describe the types of records available in the NCIC files.

STOLEN, MISSING, or RECOVERED GUNS. This valuable file contains a listing of stolen or missing guns identified by make, caliber, type, and serial number. To enter these guns in file, it is essential to have the date of theft, the identity of the agency holding the theft report, and that agency's case number, in addition to the identifying data. To search the gun file, the serial number and the make of the gun should be furnished the computer. If a gun has been recovered and an NCIC inquiry reveals there is no theft report, the weapon can still be entered into a file as a recovered gun. In the event a theft report is later made, a search will immediately reveal that the weapon has already been recovered.

STOLEN ARTICLES. A listing is contained in this file of items of property not designated under the other classifications. Articles are described in terms of types, brand names, serial numbers, and models. The date of theft, the identity of the police agency holding the theft report, and that agency's case number are also included in an article entry. Such a file is useful to the police because of the wide variety of stolen property listed. A value criterion exists for entering stolen property in this file; however, local discretion based on investigative experience and sound police judgment is the controlling factor in making entries of articles, regardless of the value. In making inquiries of this file, the computer should be furnished the serial number and the type of article.

WANTED PERSONS. Included in this file are the names of persons against whom charges or warrants have been filed for extraditable offenses. To make an inquiry, it is essential to furnish a person's name and date of birth or some other numerical descriptor peculiar to him. It is helpful to furnish his social security number, military serial number, or similar identification. Information such as height, weight, and hair color cannot be searched in this file, but in entering the record of a wanted person, these items must be set forth. In addition, it is essential to furnish the offense for which an individual is wanted, the date of the arrest warrant, the identity of the law enforcement agency holding the warrant for this person, and that agency's case number. If he owns a vehicle and is known to be using it while a fugitive, the identifying number of the vehicle and the license plate number should be entered into his record. In the event that inquiry is made concerning this vehicle, the wanted person's record will be revealed.

STOLEN WANTED VEHICLE and STOLEN LICENSE PLATE FILES. These two files are closely related to each other, the only difference being separate methods by which NCIC receives data to be placed in storage. For entry into the stolen vehicle file, the information needed is the automobile make and model, the vehicle identification number, the license plate number, the state of registration of the license number, the type of license plate where pertinent (truck-trailer-taxi-dealer), the color of the automobile, the car's date of theft, the identity of the agency holding the theft report, and that agency's case number. The license plate file requires the same information; however, no vehicle is involved. To search these files all that is required is the vehicle identification number or the license number and state of registration.

STOLEN/EMBEZZLED/MISSING SECURITIES. This file contains serially numbered, identifiable securities which have been stolen, embezzled, or are otherwise missing. Securities, for the purpose of this file, include currency (paper money—both real and counterfeit) and those documents which are of the types traded in securities exchanges—stock, bonds, etc. Also included in the file are warehouse receipts, traveler's checks, and money orders. Personal notes and checks, cashier's checks, officer's checks, and certified checks are not included in this file.

Securities are basically described in terms of type, serial number, denomination, issuer, and owner (and social security number if owner is a person). Other descriptive expressions which are helpful to identify securities are readily available from observation of the security and are termed "sinking fund," "series A," "collateral trust," "cumulative," "convertible," etc. The date of theft, the identity of the police agency holding the theft report, and that agency's case number are also included in a security entry.

This file is useful because of the mobility of security thieves and the speed with which NCIC can advise on the receipt of an inquiry, whether a questionable security has been entered in NCIC as having been stolen or embezzled or as missing. To make an inquiry, it is necessary to furnish type, serial number, and denomination. A special provision makes it possible to obtain information concerning securities taken from one person by inquiring by type and owner and/or social security number of the owner.

NCIC–THE INVESTIGATIVE TOOL. It is quickly recognized that all records in NCIC contain lead-type information. If a police officer receives a positive response to an inquiry, he will not terminate his investigation upon receipt of a given record but should immediately confirm with the agency which initially entered the record. This agency is called the originating agency. Data in file concern criminal activity and can be useful in guiding the officer to exercise caution and to remain extremely alert in any given situation. Cooperating agencies entering records into NCIC are responsible for maintaining the accuracy of their records, updating them whenever necessary, and removing them when no longer active. The value of the system is continually enhanced through cooperation of this sort, resulting in benefits to all law enforcement.

If a uniformed officer is on routine patrol and observes a speeder, he has a license number with which to make inquiry; an abandoned car will reveal a vehicle identification number. A disorderly conduct arrest could identify a badly wanted fugitive when the offender's name or alias and date of birth are furnished the computer. Guns which are confiscated from felons and rioters can be checked through NCIC and, if no theft record is found, they can be entered as recovered weapons—as long as they remain in police custody. Serial numbers on television sets, chain saws, musical instruments, stocks, bonds, traveler's checks, and currency found in possession of police "characters" and suspected procurers of stolen property might be on file in NCIC and could furnish valuable clues to the solving of a crime at a distant location. NCIC is a storehouse of a vast amount of vital information which continues to grow in volume and scope. Alert patrolmen and investigators are daily confronted with suspicious circumstances warranting a check of NCIC.

COMMUNICATIONS

Naturally the communications section works very closely with the records division. The mission of the police communications unit is to maintain a flow of information from the station to mobile police units. Thus, communication is the lifeline to the police officer, as it is his only method of requesting information, receiving calls, obtaining assistance, and receiving orders from his supervisor.

The Police Complaint Desk

The police complaint desk may be staffed by supervisory personnel, sworn police officers, or clerical personnel, or a combination of the three. Some police departments have found it

A small city's communications center—small, cluttered, and seemingly disorganized, yet compact and effective. *(Courtesy of the Wallace N. LaPeters Collection)*

profitable to assign policemen recovering from injuries to this type of duty. The basic functions of the complaint desk are the following:

1. Receive and evaluate requests for police services.
2. Relay information to and from dispatchers regarding requests for service and assistance for field units.
3. Summon wreckers or tow trucks, ambulances, and rescue units when required.
4. Maintain towing logs.
5. Maintain ambulance dispatch log.
6. Receive inquiries from the public and provide general information.
7. Maintain repossession reports to clarify unfounded stolen car complaints.
8. Monitor the NAWAS (National Warning System) for tests,

Complaint officers *(foreground)* take incoming calls and relay the information to the radio dispatchers *(in the booth)* via conveyer belt. *(Courtesy of the Oakland Police Department)*

participate in exercises, and maintain a log of all such participation.

Police Radio Dispatch Operators

Police dispatchers are usually females, and although their duties may vary from agency to agency, some of the most common tasks are

1. Assign calls to the field units.
2. Relay requests from field units to the complaint desk for action.
3. Communicate orders or information from field unit supervisors to their shift personnel.

A modern communications center with two channels operating simultaneously. *(Courtesy of the of the Wichita Police Department)*

The police dispatcher—a busy person. *(Courtesy of the Los Angeles County Sheriff's Department)*

4. Maintain a card file or other methods to indicate the status of each unit (i.e. in service or out of service)
5. Utilize "wanted" vehicle file to provide information to the field units.
6. Monitor and report radio equipment malfunctions.

Teletype Operations

A breakthrough for the exchange of information from agency to agency has been the Teletype: *LETS*—Law Enforcement Teletype System. To receive full value from this useful police tool, records and communication personnel have the following duties:

1. Transmit case numbers by Teletype and maintain a log of numbers issued.
2. Maintain a file of messages originated by the department and other agencies and cancel messages when advised.
3. Obtain and relay information on drivers' licenses and vehicle license tags.
4. Send and receive telegrams.
5. Receive and disseminate weather information.
6. Operate Teletype machines on department, local agencies, state and national networks.

The Teletype machine, the only means of direct long-range communications that many small police departments have to connect them with other agencies.

Operating Procedures

In many areas of the country, police and radio frequencies are overtaxed. It is therefore mandatory that courtesy be extended and that a priority of use be established. The assignment of priority must be scheduled on a need-to-use basis. Naturally, the patrol units will be assigned top priority, followed by traffic units, uniformed sergents, uniformed lieutenants, and detective units.

The messages must be spoken clearly and must take as little time as possible. Radio transmissions are not representative of an officer's actual speaking voice, so certain devices are employed to insure accuracy. One device, a phonetic alphabet, is used to convert letters into words:

A —Alfa	G —Golf
B —Bravo	H —Hotel
C —Charlie	I —India
D —Delta	J —Juliet
E —Echo	K —Kilo
F —Foxtrot	L —Lima

City of Detroit map is being prepared for the communications department—only one of the many functions performed by the police department's graphic arts section. *(Courtesy of the Detroit Police Department)*

N—November	U—Uniform
O—Oscar	V—Victor
P—Papa	W—Whiskey
Q—Quebec	X—X-ray
R—Romeo	Y—Yankee
S—Sierra	Z—Zulu

By utilizing this method, an officer can unmistakably convert easily misunderstood letters on a license plate into words and transmit them to the police dispatcher, who will change them back to letters for the computer.

Another device, the APCO 10 Code, is found in Appendix D.

APPENDICES

Appendix A

WRITING RESEARCH PAPERS

Students often approach with trepidation the writing of a research paper, for a number of reasons. First, many junior college in-service police students enroll in coursework within their major without having taken a college-level English or composition course. Second, there is no real way of knowing how well one is doing in the writing of a paper until after it is graded, lending an air of uncertainty to the undertaking. Third, the system of criminal justice is so vast that a multiplicity of prospective research topics are available, making it difficult to arrive at a final choice. Courses in composition and instructions from individual professors will go a long way toward clearing up these and other problems, as will practice at writing. It is not the intent of this rather brief guide to replace English courses or professorial advice but to supplement those sources of information.

SELECTING THE TOPIC

Professors will occasionally either assign paper topics to students or post a list of suggested topics. However, most college teachers like to give their charges a good deal of operating independence in this regard, and often it is the student himself who will have to choose and develop a topic, a task that requires clear thinking and a systematic approach. One of the most commonly made mistakes is selecting too broad a topic, one that volumes of books have been written about—e.g. juvenile delinquency, crime, law, patrol, traffic, investigation. If a student is interested in a broad subject, say correctional institutions, he should review different components of the general subject and narrow his topic to one of them. A good device to use is this: turn to the chapter in this (or any other) introductory text that relates to the subject matter of interest. Look at the subtitles in the chapter and choose the one that best suits the course in question.

For example, Chapter 17 of this book is titled "Correctional Institutions and Jails" and it contains certain subgroupings which, if outlined, would look like this:

I. Introduction
II. Historical Summary
   A.   The Ancient Experience
   B.   Post-Revolutionary America
       1. Solitary confinement
       2. The congregate system
   C.   The Post-Civil War Period
       1. The reformatory idea
       2. The three-step grading system
   D.   The Twentieth-Century American Experience
       1. Conditions in the Twenties
       2. The creation of the Federal Bureau of Prisons (1930)
       3. The effect of the New Deal upon corrections
III. Types of Confinement Institutions
   A.   Lockups and City Jails
   B.   County Jails
   C.   Juvenile Institutions
   D.   State Prisons
   E.   Federal Prisons
IV. Basic Functions of Contemporary Correctional Institution
   A.   The Protective Function
   B.   The Punitive Function
   C.   The Rehabilitative Function
V. Classification of Offenders
   A.   The Prosocial Offender
   B.   The Antisocial Offender
   C.   The Asocial Offender
VI. Treatment of Offenders
   A.   Clinical Services
   B.   Religious Programs
   C.   Educational and Vocational Programs
VII. The Collaborative Institution
VIII. Conclusion

Most of these subgroupings are prospective term projects and the farther down the outline one goes, the narrower the topic. The outline can also be lengthened, thus yielding other subgroupings, and other prospective topics. The recommendations of the Presidents Commission on Law Enforcement (Appendix C) also contains prospective topics.

BACKGROUND READING

Once the topic is chosen, general reading should be undertaken in the subject area. The library's card catalog section and the various reference indexes are a good place to start. An encyclopedia may also be helpful in giving a general overview. Either during or after the background reading, a tentative bibliography (a selected list of readings, books, periodicals, etc.) should be completed in order to compile material for the paper. The bibliography in this text is rather comprehensive and should also be consulted.

THE PRELIMINARY OUTLINE

When the major features of the topic have been fixed in the student's mind, a preliminary outline should be prepared, using the materials collected in the background reading. Each aspect of the topic should be titled and listed, being careful to insure that all the important elements are covered. When the list is complete, each aspect should be arranged in some logical way, preferably in the order that it will be used in the paper.

COLLECTING MATERIAL

Once the preliminary steps are out of the way, it is time to begin collecting reference material for the paper. The tentative bibliography is a first step in this direction. When the appropriate reference books are found, the practice of "skimming" should be employed to conserve reading time. This may be done by reading only the introduction and conclusion of each chapter, along with the subheadings. When a relevant passage is found, it should be read in its entirety. The information may be retained in three ways:

1. By reducing it to note form on 3″ x 5″ cards or on notebook paper.

2. By photocopying the appropriate material (this can be expensive, but photocopies may also be included in the appendix of the finished paper).

3. By checking the reference material out of the library.

THE PAPER

The manuscript should be done on white, unlined paper 8½" x 11" in size. It should be either printed or typed, with a left margin of approximately one inch and a right margin of at least one-half inch. The typing should be double-spaced.

The following is generally conceded to be an acceptable arrangement of a research paper:

1. **Title Page** (title of paper, student's name, the date, the name of the class and the professor, and the academic term).
2. **Table of Contents**
3. **The Text**
4. **Bibliography**
5. **Appendix**

The following is a sample Table of Contents for a research paper entitled "Police Review Boards":

TABLE OF CONTENTS

Footnotes

Footnotes are necessary to identify material quoted or paraphrased. Footnotes should be numbered consecutively and placed either at the bottom of the page or in a section entitled "Notes," which is placed immediately before the bibliography. If footnotes are placed at the bottom of the page, they should be separated from the text by a space of approximately one-half inch and a line about one-and-one-half inches in length. The first line of the footnote is indented. The following are examples of the most commonly documented references:

Single-Volume Works

1. William J. Bopp, *The Police Rebellion: A Quest for Blue Power* (Springfield: Charles C Thomas, Publisher, 1971), p. 161.

Multivolumed Works

2. Ralph R. Judson, *Criminal Law,* 6th ed. (Boston: Randolph Publishing Corp. 1961), V.1, pp. 6-11.

Periodicals

3. William J. Mathias, "Perceptions of Police Relationships with Ghetto Citizens," *The Police Chief,* V. XXXVIII, March, 1971, p. 44.

Anthologies

4. Jacob Jackson, "Police in Politics," in *Issues in Law Enforcement,* by Winston Petry (New York: Randall Press), 1968, pp. 16-21.

Bibliography

Bibliographic entries vary slightly from footnotes in that page numbers are eliminated, the authors' last names are placed first, and the entries are placed in alphabetical order. An example:

Bopp, William J., *The Police Rebellion: A Quest for Blue Power,* Springfield, Charles C Thomas, Publisher, 1971.

THE CORRECTED PAPER

When the professor corrects the term paper he may make use of certain symbols to save time and space. Marks used in correcting papers are found in the following listing of proofreaders' marks:

∧	Correct as margin indicates	≡	Under word means caps
stet	Let it stand	=	Under word small caps
✗	Battered letter	—	Under word means Italic
≡	Straighten lines	*rom*	Change to Roman
///	Unevenly spaced-line up	*ital*	Change to Italic
No ¶	No paragraph	*bf*	Bold face
out see copy	Omission here	⋏	Comma
¶	Paragraph	;/	Semicolon
tr	Transpose	⊙	Colon
	Delete as indicated	⊙	Period
	Delete—close up	?/	Interrogation mark
⊖	Upside down	//	Exclamation mark
⌣	Close up	/=	Hyphen
#	Insert space		Apostrophe
	Push down this space		Quotation marks
□	Indent one em		Superior letter or figure
	Move to left/or right		Inferior letter or figure
	Raise/or lower		Brackets
////	Hair space letters	(|)	Parenthesis
wf	Wrong font		One-em dash
Sc	Small capitals		Two-em dash
Caps	Capitals	*lc*	Lower case
C + Sc	Caps—small caps	OK?	Is this right?

Proofreaders' marks.

A LIBRARY GUIDE

The college library will have a direct and measurable effect on a student's academic achievements. To some a library represents a world wherein one can go for knowledge, entertainment, seclusion, and contemplation; while to others a library is a cold, ominous structure that should be entered with great reluctance. In many instances the college library by its very nature is a foreboding facility. It is often large, crowded, seemingly disorganized, and understaffed. Yet the key to success is knowledge, thus making it not only desirable for students to understand the workings of a library, but absolutely essential. It is the purpose of this brief guide to give beginning students an introduction to the use of a college library. Although libraries in the various institutions of higher learning differ, certain universal principles are the same. These principles will remain identical regardless of the institution's size, location, or purpose.

THE LIBRARY COLLECTION

Most libraries have a vast collection of materials which are available for use by students and members of the academic community. Much of the general collection is on open shelves so that students may locate with ease the material which they are seeking; however, some works are not within plain view and must be brought to the student from storage facilities in the library. Libraries generally contain the following materials.

The General Book Collection
The book collection is contained on open shelves, except where space prohibits full displays or in the case of rare or noncirculating books. Tens of thousands of volumes are often available to library users. While the ultimate decision to order a book rests with the acquisitions staff, many volumes are purchased on request of students and faculty.

Periodicals
Thousands of periodicals representing scores of fields are received and displayed by the college library. Current issues are

located in the periodical section and are arranged on stacks alphabetically according to title. Most of these journals are indexed in the various indexing services located in the reference department.

Government Documents

Most major libraries are depositories for Federal and state publications. These documents are frequently the original source of information found in commercial publications. For statistical information they are often the most current source. The *Monthly Catalog of Government Publications,* and the *Monthly Checklist of State Publications,* located in the reference department, should be consulted for this type of information.

Microfilms

Because of the storage problem created by keeping on file large numbers of newspapers and periodicals, libraries often reduce to microfilm back editions of certain publications. The most commonly preserved documents are editions of local newspapers, the *Wall Street Journal,* and *The New York Times.* Microfilmed copies of *The New York Times,* an historical newspaper, may date back beyond the turn of the century, affording students an opportunity to conduct in-depth research from a source once removed from an actual incident of occurrence. For a minimal fee, photocopies may be made of the film.

Recordings

Collections of recordings, generally 33 1/3 stereo music records, are available in most libraries, though they generally must be utilized in a special section equipped with phonographs. In addition to musical recordings, instructional materials may also be found in this medium.

Curriculum Material

In cooperation with academic departments of the institution, the library may maintain special sections of material—textbooks, magazines, documents, speeches, etc.—to be utilized by student majors. The material will be assigned to the section for use in the library, but may not be circulated.

Browsing Collection

The browsing collection contains fiction and nonfiction

material of current interest. It is constantly being updated by library personnel.

Special Collections

One section of the library, often referred to as the Readers' Services Office, will house the rare books collection. These volumes may be used only in the office.

Vertical File

The vertical file is a collection of pamphlets, brochures, clippings, etc., arranged alphabetically by subject. A subject index is kept in the reference collection, where the file is located. Materials may generally be borrowed for two weeks.

HOW TO BORROW BOOKS

When admitted to a college, students are automatically granted the privilege to use its library. As some type of control is necessary, identification is issued which students must present when checking out books. Although some institutions issue library cards, many let student body cards serve as library charge cards. Materials may be borrowed for a specific period of time, generally two weeks, with renewal periods of an additional two weeks common. Books selected from open shelves should be taken to the circulation desk, located at the entrance of the library, to be checked out. Library personnel are there to assist students, so when a volume cannot be found on the shelf, assistance may be obtained at the circulation desk.

CLASSIFICATION SYSTEMS

All books contain markings which allow them to be classified by subject and placed in specific sections of the library. Libraries utilize one of two systems to classify books: the Library of Congress Classification System, or the Dewey Decimal Classification System. On the spine of each book is an identification number which assigns the book a place among books of the same or similar subjects.

Library of Congress Classification System

In the Library of Congress System, the first part of the

identification number denotes a particular subject, while the last part gives it an individual place on the shelves. Following is an outline of the Library of Congress Classification System:

A	General works, Indexes, Yearbooks, etc.	LA	History of Education
AE	Encyclopedias	LB	Teaching; Administration
B	Philosophy	LC	Special Education Topics
BF	Psychology	LD	Colleges and Universities
BL	Religion; Mythology	M	Music
C	General History; Biography; Genealogy	N	Art
		P	Philology, Linguistics
		PA	Classical Languages and Literature
D	World History	PB	Modern European Languages and Literature
E	U.S. History, General		
F	Local History and History of the Americas	PN	Literary History
G	Geography; Anthropology	PQ	Romance Literatures
		PR	English Literature
H	Social Sciences	PS	American Literature
HA	Statistics	PT	Germanic Literature
HB	Economics	PZ	Juvenile Literature
HC	Economic History	Q	Science
HD	Agriculture; Industry	QA	Mathematics
HE	Transportation	QC	Physics
HF	Commerce	QD	Chemistry
HG	Finance	QH	Natural History
HJ	Public Finance	QK	Botany
HM	Sociology	QL	Zoology
HQ	Family; Marriage	R	Medicine
HT	Communities; Races	S	Agriculture
HV	Social Welfare; Criminology	T	Technology
		U-V	Military and Naval Science
HX	Socialism; Communism		
J	Political Science	Z	Books, Libraries, and Subject Bibliography
K	Law		
L	Education		

Most police science, criminal justice, law enforcement, and criminology books will be found in the HV section; however, because of the diversity of the field, related volumes will also be located in sections HM, HT, J, K, and Q. For example, a book on specialized police procedures may be numbered HV7899, while a volume on the criminal law may be numbered K2656.

Dewey Decimal Classification System

The Dewey Decimal System divides subjects into ten general categories and assigns a numerical designation to each:

000 General Works
100 Philosophy and Related Disciplines
200 Religion
300 Social Sciences
400 Language
500 Pure Science
600 Technology
700 Arts
800 Literature and Rhetoric
900 History, etc.

Police science, criminal justice, law enforcement, and criminology books are grouped in the Social Science class (300). The subgroupings within this class are

342   Constitutional Law
343   Criminal Law
352   Local Units of Governments
363.2 Police Services
363.3 Services in Support of Order and Security
363.4 Services for Control of Public Morals
364   Criminology
365   Penology

Additional numbers in the classification designate further subgroupings and shelf designations. For example, a book on police patrol procedures will be numbered: 363.232.

HOW TO LOCATE MATERIAL

Library materials may be located by browsing through the book stacks, but this is a rather haphazard method, although necessary at times. A more systematic technique is to use the card catalog.

Card Catalog

The card catalog is the key to much of the information contained in the library. It is generally located near the reference desk and is divided into three parts:

1. **By Author**—If you know the author of a book, look in the author catalog under his last name.

2. **By Title**—If you know the title of a book but not the author, look in the title catalog under the first word of the title, disregarding "a," "an," and "the."
3. **By Subject**—If you know neither the name of a book nor its author, look under the specific subject in the subject catalog.

The card catalog holds cards which contain the call number in the upper left-hand corner along with the title of the book, its author, the date and place of publication, the publisher, the number of pages, and a brief descriptive comment.

SERVICES TO STUDENTS

Reference

The chief function of the reference department is to assist students in making more effective use of the library's resources. Highly trained reference librarians are on duty to aid patrons in the use of reference books, the card catalog, periodicals, or in compiling bibliographies on a specific subject. The library's microfilm resources are also serviced through this department.

Reserve Books

Books placed on reserve are located behind the circulation desk. These are assigned by professors for specific courses and may be identified by a certain color tape (often red) on the spine. All reserve books are serviced from the circulation desk. They often may not be removed from the library and must be returned to the desk within a specified time period, generally two hours. On occasion, some reserve books can be checked out overnight.

Duplicating Service

Library materials, notes, or other personal documents may be reproduced at a nominal cost. Students are occasionally offered a choice of dry or wet copying.

Interlibrary Loan Service

Most libraries belong to a nationwide interlibrary loan service, which is a cooperative effort created to share resources. If a student's library is a participant and a book he needs is not con-

Appendix C

A SAMPLE APPLICATION FORM FOR POLICE EMPLOYMENT

APPLICATION FOR EMPLOYMENT WITH ARLINGTON COUNTY, VIRGINIA

INSTRUCTIONS: Read the Announcement relating to this position and be sure you have the requirements stated. Type or print your answers in ink. Answer every question clearly and completely. All statements are subject to investigation and verification. Where a question does not apply, answer "None." Attach blank continuation sheets where necessary and sign each sheet. Do not send original manuscripts; attach copies only. Unless you are employed by Arlington County, your application will not be retained for longer than one year.

RETURN TO PERSONNEL DEPARTMENT, ARLINGTON COUNTY, COURT HOUSE, ARLINGTON, VIRGINIA

1. Title of position for which you are applying

(COPY FULL TITLE FROM ANNOUNCEMENT)

Titles of other positions you are applying for:
2. ....
3. ....
4. ....

5a. Your Name

(LAST NAME) (FIRST) (MIDDLE)

5b. Name of Husband or Wife

(LAST NAME) (FIRST) (MIDDLE)

6. Your Street Address

(NUMBER) (STREET)

7. Your City and State

(CITY) (POSTAL ZONE) (STATE)

8. Your Telephone:
(HOME)
(OFFICE)

9. Sex (check)
☐ Male
☐ Female

11. Place of Birth
(CITY)
(STATE)

12. Date of Birth
(MONTH) (DAY) (YEAR)

13. Height and Weight
Height .... Ft. .... In.
Weight .... Pounds

14. What is your Social Security Number?

15. Marital Status (Check one which applies)
☐ Single   ☐ Widowed
☐ Divorced ☐ Married
☐ Separated

16. Not counting yourself, how many dependents do you have?

17. Do you now have full U.S. citizenship?
☐ Yes ☐ No

18. Do you have a driver's license?
☐ Yes ☐ No

19. What is your present status under the Selective Service Act?

20. How many days' notice will you need to begin work?

21. What is the lowest starting salary you will accept?
(SEE ANNOUNCEMENT)

22. May we ask your present employer about you?
☐ Yes ☐ No

23. List any occupational license, registration certificate, or journeyman's card which you hold:

24. List names of any County employees who are relatives of yours:

25. If you have worked for the County, give date you left:
(MONTH) (YEAR)

26. List two previous addresses and time of residency:
(a) ....
(b) ....

27. Are you receiving any disability compensation?
☐ Yes ☐ No

28. Have you any physical defect or disease whatsoever?
☐ Yes ☐ No

29. Have you ever had epilepsy or any nervous ailment or been a patient in an institution for treatment of such ailment?
☐ Yes ☐ No

30. Except for parking violations, were you
(a) ever arrested for any violation of law? Yes ☐ (a) ☐ No
(b) ever indicted for any violation of law, or have you been a defendant in any criminal action? ☐ (b) ☐
(c) ever convicted of any violation of law? ☐ (c) ☐

31. Were you ever dismissed or asked to resign from any employment?
☐ Yes ☐ No

NOTE: If you answered "yes" to any of the items numbered 27 through 31, give particulars and disposition in item number 34.

DO NOT WRITE IN THIS BLOCK
For Personnel Department Use Only
Date Application form received in Personnel:

Expires	Perf.	Exp. & Training	Interview	Written	Exam		Rejected	Accepted	Name
					Raw Score		☐	☐	
Rank					Conv. Score				
					Wgt.				
					Grade				

Notification

Date: By: Fingerprints   Date: Classif.: Medical

IMPORTANT: On back of this sheet you are to list information on training and experience. This information may be rated as a part of your examination and thus affect your final grade. Answer in detail. If more space is needed, attach additional sheets.

1-1070 – 1

32. Circle highest school grade you completed:	Give name and location of grammar school or high school you last attended:		Did you gr~ uate?	did you hool?
Grammar school — 1 2 3 4 5 6 7 8	School		☐ Yes	....
High school* — 9 10 11 12	Location		☐ No	ı ∽∪ı ....

Complete this item if you have taken courses at business, trade, armed services, correspondence, or night school:					
Name of school	Subject	No. of weeks	No. hours weekly	Did you finish?	Date you left
....	....	....	....	☐ Yes	Month ....
....	....	....	....	☐ No	Year ....

Name of college or university	Major subjects studied and semester hours credit in each	Dates attended		Total semester hours credit	What degree did you receive?
		From	To		
....	....	....	....	....	....
....	....	....	——	....	....

Name of graduate school	Major subjects studied and semester hours credit in each	Dates attended		Total semester hours credit	What degree did you receive?
		From	To		
....	....	....	....	....	....
....	....	....	....	....	....

* If you have a high school equivalency diploma, give State and year of issue:

33. EXPERIENCE: In block **A** below, list the required information concerning your present position and then work back, using a separate block for each previous position. If you are not now employed, enter the word "Unemployed" after "Position" in block **A**. If you have had military service, enter it below in its proper sequence. All periods of time unaccounted for in the blocks below or on blank continuation sheets will be considered periods of unemployment.

A	Position	Date Hired	Date Left	Starting Salary	Last Salary
	Employer	Address			Number hours you worked per week
B	Position	Date Hired	Date Left	Starting Salary	Last Salary
	Employer	Address			Number hours you worked per week
C	Position	Date Hired	Date Left	Starting Salary	Last Salary
	Employer	Address			Number hours you worked per week
D	Position	Date Hired	Date Left	Starting Salary	Last Salary
	Employer	Address			Number hours you worked per week
E	Position	Date Hired	Date Left	Starting Salary	Last Salary
	Employer	Address			Number hours you worked per week

34. Use this space to explain an answer of "Yes" to questions 27 through 31; also, to give any special qualifications not covered elsewhere in your application (such as publications, honors, fellowships, or memberships in professional or scientific societies).

35. I hereby certify that every statement I have made in this application is true and complete to the best of my knowledge and belief, and I understand that any false or incomplete statement I have made may result in my forfeiting all rights of employment with Arlington County.

Date ....   Signature of Applicant ....

(**NOTE**: UNSIGNED APPLICATIONS MAY BE REJECTED WITHOUT FURTHER NOTICE)

WORK EXPERIENCE SUMMARY – SUPPLEMENT TO APPLICATION FOR EMPLOYMENT		
You are to use this supplemental sheet to provide additional information concerning the positions you listed in item 33 of the application. For example, in item 33A–Supplemental on this sheet you are to provide additional information concerning the position you listed in 33A of the application. It is important for you to furnish all information requested below in sufficient detail to enable the Personnel Department to give you full credit in evaluating your qualifications.		
(33A– Supplemental)	Employer:	No. of employees you supervised:
Name and title of your immediate supervisor	Your reason for changing employment:	
Describe your work:		
(33B– Supplemental)	Employer:	No. of employees you supervised:
Name and title of your immediate supervisor:	Your reason for changing employment:	
Describe your work:		

I hereby certify that every statement I have made in this application is true and complete to the best of my knowledge and belief, and I understand that any false or incomplete statement I have made may result in my forfeiting all rights of employment with Arlington County.

Date ....   Signature of Applicant ....

1.1070 – 1 A   (NOTE: UNSIGNED APPLICATIONS MAY BE REJECTED WITHOUT FURTHER NOTICE)

(33C–Supplemental)	Employer:		No. of Employees you supervised:
Name and title of your immediate supervisor:		Your reason for changing employment:	
Describe your work:			

(33D–Supplemental)	Employer:		No. of Employees you supervised:
Name and title of your immediate supervisor:		Your reason for changing employment:	
Describe your work:			

(33E–Supplemental)	Employer:		Number of Employees you supervised:
Name and title of your immediate supervisor:		Your reason for changing employment:	
Describe your work:			

Appendix D

THE LAW ENFORCEMENT EDUCATION PROGRAM (LEEP): STUDENT ELIGIBILITY AND RESPONSIBILITY

STUDENT ELIGIBILITY

From Law Enforcement Assistance Administration (LEAA), United States Department of Justice

LEEP is a program intended to develop professional law enforcement officers through higher education. LEEP provides educational opportunity through financial aid and is directed to students having the ability and desire to provide professional performance in the criminal justice system.

LEEP provides two types of financial aid to students enrolled in colleges and universities:

1. A loan not to exceed $1,800 per academic year for full-time study toward a certificate, associate or higher degree in areas (directly) related to and required in law enforcement.

2. Grants not to exceed $300 per semester or $2000 per quarter for part-time study of degree-creditable courses related and useful in law enforcement.

Grants are limited to law enforcement officers, as defined in the Manual. An eligible officer may also qualify for a loan if he is both a full-time student and a full-time employee. Loans are available to full-time students, pre-service or in-service.

Individual pre-service students should be carefully selected, taking into consideration their sincerity and willingness to pursue careers in the field of criminal justice.

A. General Conditions of Eligibility for Loans or Grants

1. Citizen Status

The applicant must be a citizen or national of the United States or a person who is in the United States, its possessions, or its territories, for other than a temporary purpose and is or intends to become a permanent resident thereof.

Puerto Rico and the District of Columbia are considered as

states under the Act; the Virgin Islands, Guam, and American Samoa are defined as territories or possessions of the United States. Residents of the Trust Territory of the Pacific Islands are eligible for LEEP awards through schools located in "states", the Virgin Islands, Guam, or American Samoa if the residents are in those areas for other than temporary purposes.

2. Social Security Number

An applicant must have a social security number before his request for funds can be approved. The Student Application and Note form will not be accepted by the Office of Academic Assistance without a proper social security number.

3. Student Enrollment

An applicant must be accepted for admission by a LEEP participating college or university. He may be a degree candidate or a nondegree student who meets current requirements to petition for acceptance into a degree program. An applicant is considered eligible for LEEP if admitted, even though he may be required to take remedial courses. A student who is studying outside of the United States or its territories, as defined by the Act, cannot receive LEEP funds.

4. Age and Physical Limitations

There is no age or physical requirement in determining LEEP eligibility; however, the student should acquaint himself with employment requirements of various criminal justice agencies and should be counseled regarding general employment qualifications for law enforcement positions.

5. Concurrent Federal Assistance

A student receiving LEEP assistance under this Act is not precluded by the Office of Academic Assistance from receiving funds for which he qualifies under other Federal student-assistance programs, including veterans and social security benefits. Either LEEP grants or loans are eligible as matching funds for Educational Opportunity Grants authorized by the Higher Education Act of 1965 (P.L. 89-329) and administered by the U.S. Office of Education.

6. Exclusions

Public Law 91-472, the 1971 appropriations Act for the Departments of State, Justice, and Commerce, the Judiciary, and Related Agencies, contains certain restrictions with respect to the funding of students engaged in activities detrimental to the operation of educational institutions. It reads:

> SEC. 705. No part of the funds appropriated under this Act shall be used to provide a loan, guarantee of a loan, a grant, the salary of, or any remuneration whatever to any individual applying for admission, attending, employed by, teaching at (or doing research at an institution of higher education who has engaged in conduct on or after August 1, 1969, which involves the use of or the assistance to others in the use of) force or threat of force or the seizure of property under the control of an institution of higher education, to require or prevent the availability of certain curriculum, or to prevent the faculty, administrative officials, or students in such institution from engaging in their duties or pursuing their studies at such institution.

It is the responsibility of the institution and the Student Financial Aid officer to take reasonable and prudent action to insure dissemination and enforcement of this provision. Fair notice shall be given to an affected individual of any proposed cessation of payments. Opportunity shall be given to him to be heard as to whether he has engaged in conduct included under the above provision of the appropriations Act.

With regard to Fiscal Year 1970 funds, the 1970 appropriations Act (P.L. 90-153) includes the provisions of Section 705 above plus the following additional stipulations:

> **Provided**, that such limitation upon the use of money appropriated in this Act shall not apply to a particular individual until the appropriate institution of higher education at which such conduct occurred shall have had an opportunity to initiate or has completed such proceedings as it deems appropriate but which are not dilatory in order to determine whether the provisions of this limitation upon the use of appropriated funds shall apply: **Provided further**, that such institution shall certify to the Secretary of Health, Education, and Welfare at quarterly semester intervals that it is in compliance with the provision.

The Department of Justice has interpreted this provision as requiring quarterly or semester reports only if incidents occur which require the institution to withhold funds under this provision during that period. Reports should be in narrative form, setting forth those instances in which the provision required the withholding of funds. The provision and the reporting requirement apply only to grants and loans made with funds awarded an institution in Fiscal Year 1970.

All certifications of compliance should be sent to:

Records Unit
Accreditation and Institutional Eligibility Staff
Bureau of Higher Education
U.S. Office of Education
Washington, D.C. 20202

7. Priorities

The Act makes it clear that Congress feels that "crime is essentially a local problem." This mandates that funds are to be made available first to local and state officers, with secondary emphasis upon the Federal law enforcement officer and the pre-service student preparing for a career in police, corrections, or a court system. The order of priority for assigning available LEEP funds is as follows:

a.   All returning LEEP recipients, in-service and pre-service, including transfers.
b.   Local or state law enforcement officers on academic leave, with or without pay, enrolled as full-time students.
c.   Local or state law enforcement officers working full-time, enrolled as full-time students.
d.   Local or state law enforcement officers working full-time, enrolled as part-time students.
e.   Eligible teachers (see Part B, Section 5, below).
f.   Eligible Federal law enforcement officers enrolled as full-time students.
g.   Eligible Federal law enforcement officers enrolled as part-time students.
h.   Pre-service students enrolled full-time in eligible programs.
i.   Eligible local or state law enforcement officers working toward a law degree (see Part B, Section 6, below).

The term "law enforcement" as used above and throughout this Manual includes not only police but also corrections, probation, parole, and courts. Consequently, applications from personnel in corrections, probation, parole, and courts must be given equal treatment with applications from police officers. The number of awards approved should be proportionate to the number of eligible applicants from each area.

Part-time law enforcement employees are not eligible for LEEP grants and part-time pre-service students are not eligible for LEEP loans.

Students, other than those working toward a law degree, who participated in LEEP during the previous academic year have priority over any student applying for LEEP aid for the first time. Thus, a pre-service student who received a LEEP loan during the previous academic year has priority for funds over local or state law enforcement officers applying for assistance for the first time. In-service students working toward a law degree are to be funded only after all other demands are met.

In order to accommodate the above priorities, institutions should establish a schedule for students to follow in applying for LEEP assistance. While it may be reasonable to expect pre-service students to apply for financial aid at a relatively early date, it would be unrealistic to impose this restriction on in-service officers because of the nature of their employment schedules. Therefore, institutions must notify their local law enforcement communities of registration deadlines. All applications received prior to four weeks before registration begins must be considered in relation to the priorities indicated above. Applicants received after the deadline may be considered on a first-come, first-served basis.

The full eligibility of all applicants must be met in descending order of priorities as listed above. Should the funds available be inadequate for meeting the maximum eligibility of all applicants in any given priority group, an institution has the option of reducing the amount of the LEEP award to less than the maximum eligibility. The method used must be applied uniformly to all applicants in the priority group affected. Procedures for adjusting awards might be (1) limiting the award to a predetermined number of credit hours per person or (2) assigning each eligible applicant a set percentage of his maximum entitlement.

STUDENT RESPONSIBILITY

The role of the practicing law enforcement officer is a rapidly changing one. In addition to the pressures to keep pace in an era of marked social change, the demands placed on those in the criminal justice system require an ever-increasing knowledge of social behavior and management techniques. The criminal justice system encompasses a number of professional fields of major importance open to men and women with appropriate education and training.

By participating in LEEP, qualified men and women benefit themselves as well as the nation. Those already in law enforcement can receive funds to finance college studies—and thus to enhance their career opportunities—while simultaneously adding to the reservoir of skills in their criminal justice agencies. Students who seek to enter the criminal justice system can also receive financial aid while preparing themselves for a variety of meaningful, rewarding careers in public service.

The student must accept the responsibilities associated with the opportunity to acquire higher education under the Law Enforcement Education Program.

A. General Responsibilities

1. The student should apply for LEEP assistance at the Student Financial Aid Office (SFAO) at the time he applies for admission to an institution of higher education.

2. Pre-service students should apply early so that the institution can have a firm idea of how many pre-service students are requesting aid. Many schools establish deadlines for application, often as early as six months before opening fall enrollment. However, the institution should observe the priority for in-service officers up to four weeks before registration.

3. It is incumbent upon the student to accurately complete the appropriate parts of the Student Application and Note (SAN).

4. The student must sign the SAN, verifying receipt of financial aid at the time cash or credit is disbursed to him.

5. The student must promptly notify the Office of Academic Assistance (OAA) through the SFAO, of all changes in name, address, student status, including change in institution, and employment if a grantee.

6. The student must respond promptly to correspondence from the Office of Academic Assistance.

B. In-Service Student

1. The in-service student must discuss each term's program of

study with the official authorized by his employing agency to approve and certify on the SAN that the program of study undertaken is relevant to his job or related to law enforcement. He should also discuss his program of study with the program director of the institution.

2. The in-service student must maintain full-time employe status (as minimum of thirty hours per week) as a law enforcement officer of a publicly funded agency who meets the eligibility requirements stated in the previous section.

3. The student who is in an officially organized cadet program is considered a full-time in-service employee if he works a sufficient number of hours to be so classified by the employing agency.

4. Grant funds shall be advanced only to an applicant who enters into an agreement with the Law Enforcement Assistance Administration to remain in the service of his employing law enforcement agency for a period of two years following completion of any course for which grant funds are advanced to the applicant.

5. It is advisable that the in-service student apply for an academic leave of absence from his employing agency for full-time study before he applies for admission to the educational institution.

6. If an in-service student receives a grant and a loan simultaneously, he must maintain full-time employment status with his law enforcement agency as well as full-time student status.

C. Pre-Service Student

1. The pre-service student must commit himself to a career in law enforcement to qualify for loan assistance. Through counseling on the campus and contact with potential employers, the pre-service student should obtain guidance regarding courses needed to satisfy future initial employment qualifications.

2. The pre-service student must take at least fifteen semester credit hours, or their equivalent, in courses directly related to law enforcement.

3. The pre-service student must maintain full-time student status, defined as a minimum of twelve credit hours for an undergraduate student in a fifteen-hour system and as nine credit hours

for a graduate student in a twelve-hour system. If the student needs less than a full-time course load to complete the degree requirements, he is considered a full-time student for his last school session.

4. The pre-service student is obligated to seek and obtain full-time employment with a publicly funded law enforcement agency after completion or termination of his education, or else must repay his LEEP awards within the terms of the SAN.

D. Loan Repayment Provisions

A LEEP loan enters the repayment phase when a borrower ceases to be a full-time student. Loan repayment is required if a borrower is not employed by a law enforcement agency. A LEEP borrower agrees to repay the principal amount of his loan plus simple interest within ten years after the repayment period begins, or within a shorter period if indicated. Interest accrues at the rate of seven percent per annum on the unpaid balance, but only during the period of repayment. Repayment must be not less than $50 per month, paid in regular quarterly installments of $150. The first payment is due nine months after a student ceases to be a full-time student.

1. Grace Period

The period of time between which the borrower terminates full-time student status and the repayment period begins is called the "grace period." During this time, no payment is required and no interest accrues. The LEEP grace period is of six months' duration and applies only to the loan.

2. Cancellation

a. **Forgiveness of indebtedness** for full-time law enforcement service is provided in the Act:

> "the total amount of any. . .loan, plus interest, shall be cancelled for service as a full-time officer or employee of a (public) law enforcement agency at the rate of twenty-five percent of the total amount of such loans plus interest for each complete year of such service or its equivalent. . ."

Loan cancellation on previous borrowing cannot be earned during periods of full-time student status.

Included in the category of employment eligible for twenty-five percent loan cancellation is full-time service as a teacher of subjects directly related to criminal justice within an organized program of law enforcement education at any institution of higher education which participates in LEEP, provided;

(1) The program is offered by and administered as a separate college, school, or department which offers a certificate or associate, baccalaureate, or graduate degree (as opposed to the fifteen credit-hour concentration for loans) in one or more of the three disciplines: police, corrections, or courts.

(2) The separate college, school, or department is headed by a chairman or program coordinator who devotes the majority of his time to this activity.

Cancellation benefits will be limited to teachers who submit to the Law Enforcement Assistance Administration certification' from the chief administrative office of the organized law enforcement program to the following conditions:

(1) Name of college, school, or department and name of the organized program of criminal justice.

(2) Proportion of time chairman or coordinator functions in such capacity.

(3) Teacher is a full-time employee.

(4) Teaching service covers a complete academic year (or its equivalent).

(5) Service is devoted primarily to teaching criminal justice subjects.

(6) The teacher is not a full-time student (loan cancellation cannot be earned concurrently with student status).

A complete academic year of teaching service shall be comprised of any two complete and successive half-years, not including a summer session. Teaching full-time during the second half of one academic year and the first half of the following academic year shall be considered as a complete academic year of teaching.

b. Disability. A borrower's loan(s) may be canceled for permanent and total disability. Such disability normally is construed to mean inability to engage in any substantial gainful activity because of a medically determinable impairment which is expected to continue for a long and indefinite period of time or to result in death.

Determination as to whether or not a student is entitled to

cancellation on a disability basis shall be made by the Office of Academic Assistance, based on medical evidence supplied by the borrower.

c. **Death**. A borrower's loan(s) may be canceled upon his death if a certificate of death or other official proof is filed with the Office of Academic Assistance.

d. **Bankruptcy**. Official notice of adjudication must be filed with the Office of Academic Assistance. OAA reserves the right to determine the actual amount of the loan, plus interest, which may be canceled.

A LEEP recipient's indebtedness may be canceled in the event the recipient is duly adjudicated as bankrupt if the indebtedness is due and payable at the time of the adjudication. However, if the recipient is earning annual loan cancellation or service credit on any grant at the time of filing for bankruptcy, his LEEP liability is considered to be contingent and unliquidated, and, therefore, an adjudication of bankruptcy will not affect his LEEP responsibilities. A previous LEEP recipient who is adjudicated as bankrupt is not eligible for further LEEP grants and loans.

3. Deferment

a. **Armed Forces Service**. Interest shall not accrue and installments need not be paid on any loan during any period, not in excess of four (4) years, in which the borrower is a member of the Armed Forces of the United States. A copy of DD-214 (Armed Forces of the United States Report of Transfer or Discharge) must be submitted to the Office of Academic Assistance at such time as the borrower terminates his tour of duty in the Armed Forces.

b. **Continuing Student Status**. As long as a borrower is a full-time student, even though he may transfer to another institution, no loan repayment is required and no interest accrues.

c. **Undue Hardship**. In the event that a borrower is unable, due to extraordinary circumstances, to comply with his obligation to repay his indebtedness, he may make application to the Office of Academic Assistance for deferment of repayment. Interest will continue to accrue even though repayment may be deferred.

4. Loss of Full-time Student Status

If a borrower fails to complete or withdraws from the degree or certificate program of the fifteen-hour criminal justice concentration in which he is enrolled, or if he becomes a part-time student, his loan enters the repayment phase.

Should a borrower whose loan has entered the repayment phase resume full-time study after the grace period has expired, and again borrow under LEEP, the new obligation shall be added to the remaining outstanding balance.

E. Grant Repayment Provisions

A grant must be repaid whenever a recipient does not fulfill his service obligation following completion of a course for which a grant was awarded. Disability, death, and bankruptcy provisions applicable to loan cancellation also apply to defaulted LEEP grants.

F. Student Unrest Provisions

Current legislation stipulates that Federal student-assistance funds shall not be awarded to students who forcefully obstruct the operations of educational institutions.

BIBLIOGRAPHY

BOOKS

American Bar Association, *Law and Courts in the News* (Chicago: ABA, 1960).

American Correctional Association, *Manual of Correctional Standards* (Washington: American Correctional Association, 1968).

Barnes, Halrry Elmer, and Teeters, Negley K., *New Horizons in Criminology,* 3rd ed. (Englewood Cliffs, N.J.: Prentice-Hall, Inc., 1959).

Black, Algernon, *The People and the Police* (New York: McGraw-Hill Book Co., 1968).

Blum, Richard H., *Police Selection* (Springfield: Charles C Thomas, Publisher, 1964).

Bopp, William J., *The Police Rebellion* (Springfield: Charles C Thomas, Publisher, 1971).

Breihan, Carl W., *Jesse James* (New York: Frederick Fell, Inc. 1953).

Bristow, Allen P., *Field Interrogation,* 2nd ed. (Springfield: Charles C Thomas, Publisher, 1970).

Bruce, Robert V., *1887: Year of Violence* (New York: Bobbs-Merrill, 1959).

Cavan, Ruth Shonle, *Criminology,* 3rd ed. (New York: Thomas Y. Crowell Co., 1962).

Chapman, Samuel G., and St. John, Eric T., *The Police Heritage in England in America* (East Lansing, Mich.: Michigan State University, 1962).

Cherrington, Ernest H., *The Evolution of Prohibition in the United States of America* (Montclair, N.J.: Patterson Smith Publishing Corp. Originally published in 1920, reprinted in 1969).

Clark, Norman H., *The Dry Years and After: Prohibition and Social Change in Washington* Seattle: University of Washington Press, 1965).

Clinard, Marshall B., *The Black Market* (Montclair, N.J.: Patterson Smith Publishing Corp. Originally published in 1952, reprinted in 1969).

Coleman, Walter J., *Labor Disturbances in Pennsylvania 1850-1880* (New York: Arno Press. Originally published in 1936, reprinted in 1969).

Current, Richard T., Williams, T. Harry, and Friedel, Frank, *American History: a Survey* (New York: Alfred A. Knopf, 1964).

Curry, J.E., and King, Glen D., *Race Tensions and the Police* (Springfield: Charles C Thomas, Publisher, 1962).

Dressler, David, *Practice and Theory in Probation and Parole* (New York: Columbia University Press, 1959).

Earle, Alice Morse, *Curious Punishments of Bygone Days* (Montclair, N.J.: Patterson Smith Publishing Corp. Originally published in 1896, reprinted in 1969).

549

Earle, Howard H., *Police-Community Relations,* 2nd ed. (Springfield: Charles C Thomas, Publisher, 1970).

Eldefonso, Edward, Coffey, Richard, and Grace, Richard C., *Principles of Law Enforcement* (New York: John Wiley and Sons Inc., 1968).

Ferguson, Wallace K., and Bruun, Geoffrey, *A Survey of European Civilization: Ancient Times to 1520,* 4th ed. (Boston: Houghton Mifflin Co., 1969).

Fishman, Joseph F., *Crucibles of Crime* (Montclair, N.J.: Patterson Smith Publishing Corp. Originally published in 1923, reprinted in 1969).

Flynn, John J., and Wilkie, John E., *History of the Chicago Police* (New York: Arno Press. Originally published in 1924, reprinted in 1971).

Foess, Claude M., *Calvin Coolidge* (Boston: Little Brown and Co., 1940).

Fosdick, Raymond B., *American Police Systems* (New York: The Century Co., 1921).

Gammage, Allan Z., *Police Training in The United States* (Springfield: Charles C Thomas, Publisher, 1963).

Germann, A.C., Day, Frank D., and Gallati, Robert, R.J., *Introduction to Law Enforcement and Criminal Justice* (Springfield: Charles C Thomas, Publisher, 1970).

Gilmore, N. Ray, and Gilmore, Gladys, *Readings in California History* (New York: Thomas Y. Crowell Co., 1966).

Goebel, Julius, Jr., and Naughton, T. Raymond, *Law Enforcement In Colonial New York* (Montclair, N.J.: Patterson Smith Publishing Corp. Originally published in 1944, reprinted in 1970).

Graper, Elmer D., *American Police Administration* (New York: The Macmillan Co., 1921).

Grob, Gerald, N., and Beck, Robert N. *American Ideas,* Vol. 1 (New York: The Free Press, 1963).

Hafen, Leroy R., and Rister, Carl Coke, *Western America,* 2nd ed. (Englewood Cliffs, N.J.: Prentice Hall, Inc. 1950).

Hanna, Donald G., and Kleberg, John R., *A Police Records System for the Small Department* (Springfield: Charles C Thomas, Publisher, 1969).

Harrison, Leonard V., *Police Administration in Boston* (Cambridge: Harvard Law School, 1934).

Haskell, Martin R., and Yablonsky, Lewis, *Crime and Delinquency* (Chicago: Rand McNally and Co., 1970).

Hawke, David, *The Colonial Experience* (New York: The Bobbs-Merrill Company, 1966).

Hichborn, Franklin, *The System* (Montclair, N.J.: Patterson Smith Publishing Corp. Originally published in 1915, reprinted in 1969).

Holcolmb, Richard L., *Police Patrol* (Springfield: Charles C Thomas, Publisher, 1968).

Iannone, Nathan F., *Supervision of Police Personnel* (Englewood Cliffs, N.J.: Prentice Hall, Inc., 1970).

International City Managers Association, *Municipal Police Administration,* 5th ed. (Washington: ICMA, 1961).

Johnson, Elmer Hubert, *Crime, Corrections, and Society* (Homewood, Ill.: The Dorsey Press, 1968).

Karlen, Delmar, et al. *Anglo American Criminal Justice* (New York: Oxford University Press, 1968).

Kefauver, Estes, *Crime in America* (New York: Greenwood Press Publishers, 1968).

Kirk, Paul L., and Bradford, Lowell W., *The Crime Laboratory: Organization and Operation* (Springfield: Charles C Thomas, Publisher, 1965).

Kooken, Don L., *Ethics in Police Service* (Springfield: Charles C Thomas, Publisher, 1957).

Lane, Roger, *Policing the City—Boston: 1822-1855* (Cambridge: Harvard University Press, 1967).

Lane, Winthrop, D., *Civil War in West Virginia* (New York: Arno Press. Originally published in 1921, reprinted in 1969).

Leonard, V.A., *The Police Communications System* (Springfield: Charles C Thomas, Publisher, 1970).

Leonard, V.A., *The Police Enterprise* (Springfield: Charles C Thomas, Publisher, 1969).

Leonard, V.A., *Police Organization and Management* (Brooklyn: The Foundation Press, 1951).

Leonard, V.A., *Police Patrol Organization* (Springfield: Charles C Thomas, Publisher, 1970).

Leonard, V.A., and More, Harry W., *Police Organization and Management* (Mineola, N.Y.: The Foundation Press, 1971).

Leuchtenburg, William E., *Franklin D. Roosevelt and The New Deal* (New York: Harper and Row, Publishers, Inc., 1963).

Levinson, Edward, *I Break Strikes!* (New York: Arno Press. Originally published in 1935, reprinted in 1969).

Liversidge, John, *Britain in the Roman Empire* (New York: Frederick Praeger, Publisher, 1968).

Lofton, John, *Justice and the Press* (Boston: Beacon Press, 1966).

Mayo, Katherine, *Justice to All: The Story of the Pennsylvania State Police* (New York: Arno Press. Originally published in 1917, reprinted in 1971).

McAdoo, William, *Guarding a Great City* (New York: Arno Press. Originally published in 1906, reprinted in 1971).

Merz, Charles, *A Dry Decade* (Seattle: University of Washington Press, 1969).

Mott, Frank Luther, *The News in America* (Cambridge: Harvard University Press, 1952).

Osgood, Herbert, L., *The American Colonies in the Seventeenth Century* (Gloucester: Peter Smith, 1957).

Overstreet, Harry, and Overstreet, Bonaro, *The FBI in Our Open Society* (New York: W.W. Norton and Co., Inc., 1969).

Owings, Chloe, *Women Police* (Montclair, N.J.: Patterson Smith Publishing Corp. Originally published in 1925, reprinted in 1969).

Pell, Arthur R., *Police Leadership* (Springfield: Charles C Thomas, Publisher, 1967).

Reckless, Walter C., *Vice in Chicago* (Montclair, N.J.: Patterson Smith Publishing Corp. Originally published in 1933, reprinted in 1969).

Reith, Charles, *A New Study of Police History* (London: Oliver and Boyd, 1956).

Reith, Charles, *A Short History of the British Police* (London: Oxford University Press, 1948).

Richardson, James F., *The New York Police* (New York: Oxford University Press, 1970).

Romier, Lucien, *A History of France* (New York: St. Martins Press, 1966).

Saklatvala, Beram · *The Origins of the English People* (New York: Taplinger Publishing Co., 1969).

Savage, Edward, H., *Police Records and Recollections* (Boston: John P. Dale & Company, 1873).

Schultz, Donald O., *Special Problems in Law Enforcement* (Springfield: Charles C Thomas, Publisher, 1971).

Schultz, Donald O., and Norton, Loran A., *Police Operational Intelligence* (Springfield: Charles C Thomas, Publisher, 1968).

Semmes, Raphael, *Crime And Punishment in Early Maryland* (Montclair, N.J.: Patterson Smith Publishing Corp. Originally published in 1938, reprinted in 1970).

Shay, Frank, *Judge Lynch: His First Hundred Years* (Montclair, N.J.: Patterson Smith Publishing Corp. Originally published in 1938, reprinted in 1969).

Smith, Bruce, *The State Police* (New York: The Macmillan Co., 1925).

Smith, Ralph Lee, *The Tarnished Badge* (New York: Thomas Y. Crowell Co., 1965).

Socialist Publishing Society, *The Accused and The Accusers* (New York: Arno Press. Originally published in 1887, reprinted in 1969).

Sprogle, Howard O., *The Philadelphia Police: Past and Present* (Philadelphia, 1887).

Stein, Leon, and Taft, Phillip, Eds., *The Pullman Strike* (New York: Arno Press. Originally published in 1914, reprinted in 1969).

Sullivan, John L., *Introduction to Police Science* (New York: McGraw Hill, Inc., 1966).

Sutherland, Edwin H., and Cressey, Donald R., *Principles of Criminology,* 6th ed. (New York: J.B. Lippincott Co., 1960).

Sutherland, Edwin H., and Cressey, Donald R., *Principles of Criminology,* 8th ed. (New York: J.B. Lippincott Co., 1970).

Vollmer, August, *The Police and Modern Society* (Berkeley: University of California Press, 1936).

Walling, George W., *Recollections of a New York Police Chief* (New York: 1887).

Weston, Paul B., and Wells, Kenneth M., *The Administration of Justice* (Englewood Cliffs, N.J.: Prentice-Hall, Inc., 1967).

Weston, Paul B., and Wells, Kenneth M., *Criminal Investigation* (Englewood Cliffs, N.J.: Prentice-Hall, Inc., 1970).

Whisenand, Paul M., and Cline, James L., *Patrol Operations* (Englewood Cliffs, N.J.: Prentice-Hall, Inc., 1971).

Whitlock, Brand, *On the Enforcement of Law In Cities* (Montclair, N.J.: Patterson Smith Publishing Corp. Originally published in 1913, reprinted in 1969).

Wilson, James Q., *Varieties of Police Behavior* (Cambridge, Mass.: Harvard University Press, 1969).

Wilson, O.W., *Parker on Police* (Springfield: Charles C Thomas, Publisher, 1957).

Winsor, Justin, *The Memorial History of Boston*, vol. 3 (Boston, 1881).

Woods, Arthur, *Policewoman and Public* (New York: Arno Press. Originally published in 1919, reprinted in 1971).

Wright, R. Gene, and Marlo, John A., *The Police Officer and Criminal Justice* (New York: McGraw-Hill Book Co., 1970).

GOVERNMENTAL AND QUASI GOVERNMENTAL DOCUMENTS

Chamber of Commerce of the State of New York, *Papers and Proceedings of Committee on the Police Problem, City of New York* (1905).

Citizens Police Committee, *Chicago Police Problems* (Montclair, N.J.: Patterson Smith Publishing Corp. Originally published in 1931, reprinted in 1969).

The Cleveland Foundation, *Criminal Justice in Cleveland* (Montclair, N.J.: Patterson Smith Publishing Corp. Originally published in 1922, reprinted in 1969).

Federal Bureau of Investigation, *Uniform Crime Reports 1969* (Washington: U.S. Government Printing Office, 1970).

Illinois Association for Criminal Justice, *The Illinois Crime Survey* (Montclair, N.J.: Patterson Smith Publishing Corp. Originally published in 1929, reprinted in 1969).

Missouri Association for Criminal Justice, *The Missouri Crime Survey* (St. Louis, Mo., Association for Criminal Justice, 1926).

National Commission on the Causes and Prevention of Violence, *Violence in America* (New York: Signet Books, 1969).

National Commission on Law Observance and Enforcement, George Wickersham, Chairman, (1931).
Report No. 1, *Preliminary Report on Prohibition.*
Report No. 2, *Enforcement of the Prohibition Laws of the United States.*
Report No. 11, *Lawlessness in Law Enforcement.*
Report No. 14, *Police.*

National Police Convention, *Official Proceedings of the National Police Convention* (New York: Arno Press. Originally published in 1871, reprinted in 1971).

National Popular Government League, *Report Upon the Illegal Practices of the U.S. Department of Justice* (New York: Arno Press. Originally published in 1920, reprinted in 1969).

New York Police Department, *Semi-Annual Report of the Police Commissioner of New York* (New York: New York Police Department, 1918).

President's Commission on Law Enforcement and Administration of Justice, *Task Force Report: Corrections* (Washington: U.S. Government Printing Office, 1967).

President's Commission on Law Enforcement and Administration of Justice, *Task Force Report: The Courts* (Washington: U.S. Government Printing Office, 1967).

President's Commission on Law Enforcement and Administration of Justice, *Task Force Report: Crime and Its Impact—An Assessment* (Washington: U.S. Government Printing Office, 1967).

President's Commission on Law Enforcement and Administration of Justice, *Task Force Report: Organized Crime* (Washington: U.S. Government Printing Office, 1967).

President's Commission on Law Enforcement and Administration of Justice, *Task Force Report: The Police* (Washington: U.S. Government Printing Office, 1967).

United Nations Department of Social Affairs, *Probation and Related Measures* (New York: United Nations, 1951).

U.S. Census Bureau, *General Statistics of Cities* (1915) (Washington: U.S. Census Bureau, 1915).

United States Courts, Division of Probation, *The Presentence Investigation Report* (Washington: U.S. Government Printing Office).

United States Department of Health, Education, and Welfare, *Annual Report of Federal Activities in Juvenile Delinquency, Youth Development, and Related Fields* (1971).

DEPARTMENTAL HISTORIES

Albuquerque Police Department
Baltimore Police Department
Berkeley Police Department
California Highway Patrol
Chicago Police Department
Cincinnati Police Department
Detroit Police Department
Fitchburg, Massachusetts, Police Department
Flint, Michigan, Police Department
International Association of Chiefs of Police
Kansas City Police Department
Los Angeles County Sheriff's Department
Los Angeles Police Department
Maryland State Police
New Orleans Police Department
New York Police Department
New York State Police
Pennsylvania State Police
Philadelphia Police Department
St. Louis Police Department
San Antonio Police Department
San Francisco Police Department
Texas Department of Public Safety
Tucson Police Department

United States Department of Justice
United States Department of Treasury
Wichita Police Department

GLOSSARY OF LEGAL TERMS

A

accumulative sentence—A sentence, additional to others, imposed at the same time for several distinct offenses; one sentence to begin at the expiration of another.

adjudication—Giving or pronouncing a judgment or decree; also the judgment given.

adversary system—The system of trial practice in the United States and some other countries in which each of the opposing, or adversary parties, has full opportunity to present and establish his opposing contentions before the court.

allegation—The assertion, declaration, or statement of a party to an action, made in a pleading, setting out what he expects to prove.

amicus curiae—(a-mi′ kus kū′ ri-ē) A friend of the court; one who interposes and volunteers information upon some matter of law.

appearance—The formal proceeding by which a defendant submits himself to the jurisdiction of the court.

appellant—(a-pel′ant) The party appealing a decision or judgment to a higher court.

appellate court—A court having jurisdiction of appeal and review; not a "trial court."

appelle—(ap-e-le′) The party against whom an appeal is taken.

arraignment—In criminal practice, to bring a prisoner to the bar of the court to answer to a criminal charge.

arrest of judgment—The act of staying the effect of a judgment already entered.

attorney of record—Attorney whose name appears in the permanent records or files of a case.

B

bail—To set at liberty a person arrested or imprisoned, on security being taken, for his appearance on a specified day and place.

bail bond—An obligation signed by the accused, with sureties, to secure his presence in court.

bailiff—A court attendant whose duties are to keep order in the courtroom and to have custody of the jury.

banc—(bangk) Bench; the place where a court permanently or regularly sits. A "sitting **in banc**" is a meeting of all the judges of a court, as distinguished from the sitting of a single judge.

bench warrant—Process issued by the court itself, or "from the bench," for the attachment or arrest of a person.

best evidence—Primary evidence, as distinguished from secondary; the best and highest evidence of which the nature of the case is susceptible.

binding instruction—One in which jury is told if they find certain conditions to be true they must find for plaintiff, or defendant, as case might be.

bind over—To hold on bail for trial.

brief—A written or printed document prepared by counsel to file in court, usually setting forth both facts and law in support of his case.

burden of proof—In the law of evidence, the necessity or duty of affirmatively proving a fact or facts in dispute.

C

calling the docket—The public calling of the docket or list ·of causes at commencement of term of court, for setting a time for trial or entering orders.

cause—A suit, litigation or action, civil or criminal.

certiorari—(sér′shi-ō-rā′rī) An original writ commanding judges or officers of inferior courts to certify or to return records of proceedings in a cause for judicial review.

challenge to the array—Questioning the qualifications of an entire jury panel, usually on the grounds of partiality or some fault in the process of summoning the panel.

chambers—Private office or room of a judge.

change of venue—The removal of a suit begun in one county or district, to another, for trial, or from one court to another in the same county or district.

circuit courts—Originally, courts whose jurisdiction extended over several counties or districts, and whose sessions were held in such counties or districts alternately; today, a circuit court may hold all its sessions in one county.

circumstantial evidence All evidence of indirect nature: the process of decision by which court or jury may reason from circumstances known or proved to establish by inference the principal fact.

code—A collection, compendium or revision of laws systematically arranged into chapters, table of contents and index and promulgated by legislative authority.

commit—To send a person to prison, to an asylum, workhouse, or reformatory by lawful authority.

commom law—Law which derives its authority solely from usages and customs of immemorial antiquity, or from the judgments and decrees of courts. Also called "case law."

commutation—The change of a punishment from a greater degree to a lesser degree, as from death to life imprisonment.

competency—In the law of evidence, the presence of those characteristics which render a witness legally fit and qualified to give testimony.

complainant—Synonymous with "plaintiff."

complaint—The first or initiatory pleading on the part of the complainant, or plaintiff, in a civil action.

concurrent sentence—Sentences for more than one crime in which the time of each is to be served concurrently, rather than successively.

contempt of court—Any act calculated to embarrass, hinder, or obstruct a court in the administration of justice, or calculated to lessen its authority or dignity. Contempts are of two kinds: direct and indirect. Direct contempts are those committed in the immediate presence of the court; indirect is the term chiefly used with reference to the failure or refusal to obey a lawful order.

corpus delicti—(kor'pus dē-lik'tī) The body (material substance) upon which a crime has been committed, e.g. the corpse of a murdered man, the charred remains of a burned house.

corroborating evidence—Evidence supplementary to that already given and tending to strengthen or confirm it.

court reporter—A person who transcribes by shorthand or stenographically takes down testimony during court proceedings.

courts of record—Those whose proceedings are permanently recorded, and which have the power to fine or imprison for contempt. Courts not of record are those of lessor authority whose proceedings are not permanently recorded.

criminal insanity—Lack of mental capacity to do or abstain from doing a particular act; inability to distinguish right from wrong.

cross-examination—The questioning of a witness in a trial, or in the taking of a deposition, by the party opposed to the one who produced the witness.

cumulative sentence—Separate sentences (each additional to the others) imposed against a person convicted upon an indictment containing several counts, each charging a different offense. (Same as accumulative sentence.)

D

damages—Pecuniary compensation which may be recovered in the courts by any person who has suffered loss, detriment, or injury to his person, property, or rights, through the unlawful act or negligence of another.

de novo—(dē nō'vō) Anew, afresh. A "trial de novo" is the retrial of a case.

default—A "default" in an action of law occurs when a defendant omits to plead within the time allowed or fails to appear at the trial.

demur—(dē-mér') To file a pleading (called "a demurrer"), admitting the truth of the facts in the complaint, or answer, but contending they are legally insufficient.

deposition—The testimony of a witness not taken in open court, but in pursuance of authority given by statute or rule of court to take testimony elsewhere.

direct evidence—Proof of facts by witnesses who saw acts done or heard words spoken as distinguished from circumstantial evidence, which is called indirect.

direct examination—The first interrogation of a witness by the party on whose behalf he is called.

directed verdict—An instruction by the judge to the jury to return a specific verdict.

discovery—A proceeding whereby one party to an action may be informed as to facts known by other parties or witnesses.

dismissal without prejudice—Permits the complainant to sue again on the same cause of action, while dismissal "with prejudice" bars the right to bring or maintain an action on the same claim or cause.

dissent—A term commonly used to denote the disagreement of one or more judges of a court with the decision of the majority.

domicile—That place where a person has his true and permanent home. A person may have several residences, but only one domicile.

double jeopardy—Common-law and constitutional prohibition against more than one prosecution for the same crime, transaction, or omission.

due process—Law in its regular course of administration through the courts of justice. The guarantee of due process requires that every man have the protection of a fair trial.

E

embezzlement—The fraudulent appropriation by a person to his own use or benefit of property or money intrusted to him by another.

eminent domain—The power to take private property for public use by condemnation.

enjoin—To require a person, by writ of injunction from a court of equity, to perform, or to abstain or desist from, some act.

entrapment—The act of officers or agents of a government in inducing a person to commit a crime not contemplated by him, for the purpose of instituting a criminal prosecution against him.

equity, courts of—Courts which administer remedial justice according to the system of equity as distinguished from courts of common law. Equity courts are sometimes called courts of chancery.

estoppel—(es-top' el) A person's own act, or acceptance of facts, which preclude his later making claims to the contrary.

et al.—An abbreviation of **et alii,** meaning "and others."

et seq.—An abbreviation for **et sequentes,** or **et sequentia,** "and the following."

ex contractu—(ex kon-trak' tu) In both civil and common law, rights and causes of action are divided into two classes: those arising ex contractu (from a contract) and ex delicto (from a wrong or tort).

ex delicto—(ex de-lik' tō) Rights and causes of action arising from a wrong or "tort."

ex parte—(ex par' te) By or for one party; done for, in behalf of, or on the application of, one party only.

ex post facto—(eks pōst fak' to) After the fact; an act or fact occurring after some previous act or fact, and relating thereto.

exception—A formal objection to an action of the court, during the trial of a cause, in refusing a request or overruling an objection; implying that the party excepting does not acquiesce in the decision of the court, but will seek to procure its reversal.

exhibit—A paper, document, or other article produced and exhibited to a court during a trial or hearing.

expert evidence—Testimony given in relation to some scientific, technical, or professional matter by experts, i.e. persons qualified to speak authoritatively by reason of their special training, skill, or familiarity with the subject.

extenuating circumstances—Circumstances which render a crime less aggravated, heinous, or reprehensible than it would otherwise be.

extradition—The surrender by one state to another of an individual accused or convicted of an offense outside its own territory, and within the territorial jurisdiction of the other.

F

fair comment—A term used in the law of libel, applying to statements made by a writer in an honest belief of their truth, relating to official act, even though the statements are not true in fact.

fair preponderance—Evidence sufficient to create in the minds of the triers of fact the conviction that the party upon whom is the burden has established its case.

false arrest—Any unlawful physical restraint of another's liberty, whether in prison or elsewhere.

felony—A crime of a graver nature than a misdemeanor. Generally, an offense punishable by death or imprisonment in a penitentiary.

fiduciary—(fi-dū' shi-ā-ri) A term derived from the Roman law, meaning a person holding the character of a trustee, in respect to the trust and confidence involved in it and the scrupulous good faith and candor which it requires.

forcible entry and detainer—A summary proceeding for restoring possession of land to one who has been wrongfully deprived of possession.

forgery—The false making or material altering, with intent to defraud, of any writing which, if genuine, might be the foundation of a legal liability.

fraud—An intentional perversion of truth; deceitful practice or device resorted to with intent to deprive another of property or other right, or in some manner to do him injury.

G

garnishment—A proceeding whereby property, money, or credits of a debtor, in possession of another (the garnishee) are applied to the debts of the debtor.

garnishee—(noun) The person upon whom a garnishment is served, usually a debtor of the defendant in the action; (verb) to institute garnishment proceedings.

general demurrer—A demurrer which raises the question whether the pleading against which it is directed lacks the definite allegations essential to a cause of action, or defense.

gratuitous guest—In automobile law, a person riding at the invitation of the owner of a vehicle, or his authorized agent, without payment of a consideration or a fare.

H

habeas corpus—(ha'be-as kor'pus)(Lat.) "You have the body." The name given a variety of writs whose object is to bring a person before a court or judge. In most common usage, it is directed to the official or person detaining another, commanding him to produce the body of the prisoner or person detained so the court may determine if such person has been denied his liberty without due process of law.

harmless error—In appellate practice, an error committed by a lower court during a trial, but not prejudicial to the rights of the party and for which the court will not reverse the judgment.

hearsay—Evidence not proceeding from the personal knowledge of the witness.

hostile witness—A witness who is subject to cross-examination by the party who called him to testify, because of his evident antagonism toward that party as exhibited in his direct examination.

hypothetical question—A combination of facts and circumstances, assumed or proved, stated in such a form as to constitute a coherent state of facts upon which the opinion of an expert can be asked by way of evidence in a trial.

I

impeachment of witness—An attack on the credibility of a witness by the testimony of other witnesses.

inadmissible—That which, under the established rules of evidence, cannot be admitted or received.

in banc—On the bench; all judges of the court sitting together to hear a cause.

in camera—(in kam'e-ra) In chambers; in private.

incompetent evidence—Evidence which is not admissible under the established rules of evidence.

indeterminate sentence—An indefinite sentence of "not less than" and "not more than" so many years, the exact term to be served being afterwards determined by parole authorities within the minimum and maximum limits set by the court or by statute.

indictment—An accusation in writing found and presented by a grand jury, charging that a person therein named has done some act, or been guilty of some omission, which, by law, is a crime.

inferior court—Any court subordinate to the chief appellate tribunal in a particular judicial system.

information—An accusation for some criminal offense, in the nature of an indictment, from which it differs only in being presented by a competent public officer instead of a grand jury.

injunction—A mandatory or prohibitive writ issued by a court.

inns of court—Societies of barristers in England.

instruction—A direction given by the judge to the jury concerning the law of the case.

inter alia—(in ter a'li-a) Among other things or matters.

inter alios—(in'ter a'li-os) Among other persons; between others.

interlocutory—Provisional; temporary; not final. Refers to orders and decrees of a court.

interrogatories—Written questions propounded by one party and served on adversary, who must provide written answers thereto under oath.

irrelevant—Evidence not relating or applicable to the matter in issue; not supporting the issue.

J

jurisprudence—The philosophy of law, or the science which treats of the principles of positive law and legal relations.

jury—A certain number of men, selected according to law, and sworn to inquire of certain matters of fact, and declare the truth upon evidence laid before them.

> **grand jury**—A jury of inquiry whose duty is to receive complaints and accusations in criminal cases, hear the evidence and find bills of

indictment in cases where they are satisfied a trial ought to be had.

petit jury—The ordinary jury of twelve (or fewer) persons for the trial of a civil or criminal case. So called to distinguish it from the grand jury.

jury commissioner—An officer charged with the duty of selecting the names to be put into a jury wheel, or of drawing the panel of jurors for a particular term of court.

L

leading question—One which instructs a witness how to answer or puts into his mouth words to be echoed back; one which suggests to the witness the answer desired. Prohibited on direct examination.

letters rogatory—(rog′a-tō-ri) A request by one court of another court in an independent jurisdiction, that a witness be examined upon interrogatories sent with the request.

libel—A method of defamation expressed by print, writing, pictures, or signs. In its most general sense any publication that is injurious to the reputation of another.

levy—A seizure; the obtaining of money by legal process through seizure and sale of property. The raising of the money for which an execution has been issued.

limitation—A certain time allowed by statute in which litigation must be brought.

lis pendens—(līs pen′denz) A pending suit.

locus delicti—(lō′kus de-lik′tī) The place of the offense.

M

malfeasance—(mal-fē′zans) Evil doing; ill conduct; the commission of some act which is positively prohibited by law.

malicious prosecution—An action instituted with intention of injuring defendant and without probable cause, and which terminates in favor or the person prosecuted.

mandamus—(man-dā-′mus) The name of a writ which issues from a court of superior jurisdiction, directed to an inferior court, commanding the performance of a particular act.

mandate—A judicial command or precept proceeding from a court or judicial officer, directing the proper officer to enforce a judgment, sentence, or decree.

manslaughter—The unlawful killing of another without malice; may be either voluntary, upon a sudden impulse, or involuntary, in the commission of some unlawful act.

master in chancery—An officer of a court of chancery who acts as an assistant to the judge.

material evidence—Such as is relevant and goes to the substantial issues in dispute.

mesne—(mēn) Internediate; intervening.

misdemeanor—Offenses less than felonies; generally those punishable by fine or imprisonment otherwise than in penitentiaries.

misfeasance—A misdeed or trespass. The improper performance of some act which a person may lawfully do.

mistrial—An erroneous or invalid trial; a trial which cannot stand in law because of lack of jurisdiction, wrong drawing of jurors, or disregard of some other fundamental requisite.

mitigating circumstance—One which does not constitute a justification or excuse of an offense, but which may be considered as reducing the degree of moral culpability.

moot—Unsettled; undecided. A moot point is one not settled by judicial decisions.

moral turpitude—Conduct contrary to honesty, modesty, or good morals.

municipal courts—In the judicial organization of some states, courts whose territorial authority is confined to the city or community.

murder—The unlawful killing of a human being by another with malice aforethought, either express or implied.

N

ne exeat—(nē ek′sē-at) A writ which forbids the person to whom it is addressed to leave the country, the state, or the jurisdiction of the court.

negligence—The omission to do something which a reasonable man, guided by ordinary considerations, would do; or the doing of something which a reasonable and prudent man would not do.

nisi prius—(nī′ sī prī′ us) Courts for the initial trial of issues of fact, as distinguished from appellate courts.

no bill—This phrase, indorsed by a grand jury on an indictment, is equivalent to "not found" or "not a true bill." It means that, in the opinion of the jury, evidence was insufficient to warrant the return of a formal charge.

nolle prosequi—(nol′ e pros′ e-kwī) A formal entry upon the record by the plaintiff in a civil suit, or the prosecuting officer in a criminal case, by which he declares that he "will no further prosecute" the case.

nolo contendere—(nō′lō kon-ten′de-rē) A pleading usually used by defendants in criminal cases, which literally means **I will not contest it.**

nominal party—One who is joined as a party or defendant merely because the technical rules of pleading require his presence in the record.

non compos mentis—(non kom′pos) Not sound or mind; insane.

non obstante veredicto—(non ob-stan′tē ve-re-dik′to) Notwithstanding the verdict. A judgment entered by order of court for one party, although there has been a jury verdict against him.

notice to produce—In practice, a notice in writing requiring the opposite party to produce a certain described paper or document at the trial.

O

objection—The act of taking exception to some statement or procedure in trial. Used to call the court's attention to improper evidence or procedure.

of counsel—A phrase commonly applied to counsel employed to assist in the preparation or management of the case, or its presentation on appeal, but who is not the principal attorney of record.

opinion evidence—Evidence of what the witness thinks, believes, or infers in regard to fact in dispute, as distinguished from his personal knowledge of the facts; not admissible except (under certain limitations) in the case of experts.

ordinary—A judicial officer, in several of the states, clothed by statute with powers in regard to wills, probate, administration, guardianship.

out of court—One who has no legal status in court is said to be "out of court," i.e. he is not before the court. For example, when a plaintiff, by some act of omission or commission, shows that he is unable to maintain his action, he is frequently said to have put himself "out of court."

P

panel—A list of jurors to serve in a particular court, or for the trial of a particular action; denotes either the whole body of persons summoned as jurors for a particular term of court or those selected by the clerk by lot.

parties—The persons who are actively concerned in the prosecution or defense of legal proceeding.

peremptory challenge—The challenge which the prosecution or defense may use to reject a certain number of prospective jurors without assigning any cause.

plaintiff—A person who brings an action; the party who complains or sues in a personal action and is so named on the record.

polling the jury—A practice whereby the jurors are asked individually whether they assented, and still assent, to the verdict.

power of attorney—An instrument authorizing another to act as one's agent or attorney.

praecipe—(prē´si-pe) An original writ commanding the defendant to do the thing required; also, an order addressed to the clerk of a court, requesting him to issue a particular writ.

prejudicial error—Synonymous with "reversible error"; an error which warrants the appellate court in reversing the judgment before it.

preliminary hearing—Synonymous with "preliminary examination"; the hearing given a person charged with crime by a magistrate or judge to determine whether he should be held for trial.

preponderance of evidence—Greater weight of evidence, or evidence which is more credible and convincing to the mind, not neccessarily the greater number of witnesses.

presentment—An informal statement in writing by a grand jury to the court that a public offense has been committed, from their own knowledge or observation, without any bill of indictment laid before them.

presumption of fact—An inference as to the truth or falsity of any proposition or fact, drawn by a process of reasoning in the absence of actual certainty of its truth or falsity, or until such certainty can be ascertained.

presumption of law—A rule of law that courts and judges shall draw a particular inference from a particular fact, or from particular evidence.

probation—In modern criminal administration, allowing a person convicted of some minor offense (particularly juvenile offenders) to go at large, under a suspension of sentence, during good behavior, and generally under the supervision or guardianship of a probation officer.

prosecutor—One who instigates the prosecution upon which an accused is arrested or who prefers an accusation against the party whom he suspects to be guilty; also, one who takes charge of a case and performs function of trial lawyer for the people.

prosecutrix—A female prosecutor.

Q

quaere—(kwē′rē) A query; question; doubt.

quash—To overthrow; vacate; to annul or void a summons or indictment.

quasi judicial—(kwā′sī) Authority or discretion vested in an officer wherein his acts partake of a judicial character.

quid pro quo—What for what, a fair return or consideration.

quo warranto—(kwō wo-ran′tō) A writ issuable by the state, through which it demands an individual to show by what right he exercises an authority which can only be exercised through grant or franchise emanating from the state.

R

reasonable doubt—An accused person is entitled to acquittal if, in the minds of the jury, his guilt has not been proved beyond a "reasonable doubt"; that state of the minds of jurors in which they cannot say they feel an abiding conviction as to the truth of the charge.

rebuttal—The introduction of rebutting evidence; the showing that statements of witnesses as to what occurred is not true; the stage of a trial at which such evidence may be introduced.

redirect examination—Follows cross-examination, and is had by the party who first examined the witness.

referee—A person to whom a cause pending in a court is referred by the court to take testimony, hear the parties, and report thereon to the court. He is an officer exercising judicial powers and is an arm of the court for a specific purpose.

removal, order of—An order by a court directing the transfer of a cause to another court.

reply—When a case is tried or argued in court, the argument of the plaintiff in answer to that of the defendant. A pleading in response to an answer.

rest—A party is said to "rest" or "rest his case" when he has presented all the evidence he intends to offer.

retainer—Act of the client in employing his attorney or counsel, and also denotes the fee which the client pays when he retains the attorney to act for him.

rule of court—An order made by a court having competent jurisdiction. Rules of court are either general or special; the former are the regulations by which the practice of the court is governed; the latter are special orders made in particular cases.

rule nisi, or rule to show cause—(nī′ sī) A court order obtained on motion by either party to show cause why the particular relief sought should not be granted.

S

search and seizure, unreasonable—In general, an examination without authority of law of one's premises or person with a view to discovering stolen contraband or illicit property or some evidence of guilt to be used in prosecuting a crime.

search warrant—An order in writing, issued by a justice or magistrate, in the name of the state, directing an officer to search a specified house or other premises for stolen property. Usually required as a conditon precedent to a legal search and seizure.

self-defense—The protection of one's person or property against some injury attempted by another. The law of "self defense" justifies an act done in the reasonable belief of immediate danger. When acting in justifiable self-defense, a person may not be punished criminally nor held responsible for civil damages.

separation of witnesses—An order of the court requiring all witnesses to remain outside the courtroom until each is called to testify, except the plaintiff or defendant.

sheriff—An officer of a county, chosen by popular election, whose principal duties are aid of criminal and civil courts; chief preserver of the peace. He serves processes, summons juries, executes judgments, and holds judicial sales.

sine qua non—(sī´ ne kwā non) An indispensable requisite.

slander—Base and defamatory spoken words tending to prejudice another in his reputation, business, or means of livelihood. "Libel" and "slander" both are methods of defamation, the former being expressed by print, writings, pictures, or signs; the latter orally.

stare decisis—(sta´re de-si´sis) The doctrine that, when a court has once laid down a principle of law as applicable to a certain set of facts, it will adhere to that principle and apply it to future cases where the facts are substantially the same.

state's evidence—Testimony given by an accomplice or participant in a crime, tending to convict others.

statute—The written law in contradistinction to the unwritten law.

stay—A stopping or arresting of a judicial proceeding by order of the court.

stipulation—An agreement by attorneys on opposite sides of a case as to any matter pertaining to the proceedings or trial. It is not binding unless assented to by the parties, and most stipulations must be in writing.

subpoena—(su-pē´na) A process to cause a witness to appear and give testimony before a court or magistrate.

subpoena duces tecum—(su-pē´na dū´sēz tē´kum) A process by which the court commands a witness to produce certain documents or records in a trial.

substantive law—The law dealing with rights, duties, and liabilities, as distinguished from adjective law, which is the law regulating procedure.

summons—A writ directing the sheriff or other officer to notify the named person that an action has been commenced against him in court and that he is required to appear, on the day named, and answer the complaint in such action.

supersedeas—(sū-pér-sē´dē-as) A writ containing a command to stay proceedings at law, such as the enforcement of a judgment pending an appeal.

T

talesman—(tālz´man) A person summoned to act as a juror from among the by-standers in a court.

testimony—Evidence given by a competent witness, under oath; as distinguished from evidence derived from writings and other sources.

tort—An injury or wrong committed, either with or without force, to the person or property of another.

transcript—The official record of proceedings in a trial or hearing.

transitory—Actions are "transitory" when they might have taken place anywhere, and are "local" when they could occur only in some particular place.

trial de novo—(dē nō'vō) A new trial or retrial had in an appellate court in which the whole case is gone into as if no trial had been had in a lower court.

true bill—In criminal practice, the indorsement made by a grand jury upon a bill of indictment when they find it sufficient evidence to warrant a criminal charge.

U

undue influence—Whatever destroys free will and causes a person to do something he would not do if left to himself.

unlawful detainer—A detention of real estate without the consent of the owner or other person entitled to its possession.

usury—The taking of more for the use of money than the law allows.

V

venire—(vē-nī'rē) Technically, a writ summoning persons to court to act as jurors; popularly used as meaning the body of names thus summoned.

venire facias de novo—(fā'she-as dē nō'vō) A fresh or new venire, which the court grants when there has been some impropriety or irregularity in returning the jury, or where the verdict is so imperfect or ambiguous that no judgment can be given upon it.

veniremen—(vē-nī 'rē-men) Members of a panel of jurors.

venure—(ven ū) The particular county, city, or geographical area in which a court with jurisdiction mayy hear and determine a case.

verdict—In practice, the formal and unanimous decision or finding made by a jury, reported to the court and accepted by it.

voir dire—(vwor dēr) To speak the truth. The phrase denotes the preliminary examination which the court may make of one presented as a witness or juror, as to his qualifications.

W

waiver of immunity—A means authorized by statutes by which a witness, in advance of giving testimony or producing evidence, may renounce the fundamental right guaranteed by the constitutions that no person shall be compelled to be a witness against himself.

warrant of arrest—A writ issued by a magistrate, justice, or other competent authority, to a sheriff, or other officer, requiring him to arrest the body of a person therein named and bring him before the magistrate or court to answer to a specified charge.

weight of evidence—The balance of preponderance of evidence; the inclination of the greater amount of credible evidence, offered in a trial, to support one side of the issue rather than the other.

willful—A "willful" act is one done intentionally, without justifiable cause, as distinguished from an act done carelessly or inadvertently.

with prejudice—The term, as applied to judgment of dismissal, is as conclusive of rights of parties as if action had been prosecuted to final adjudication adverse to the plaintiff.

without prejudice—A dismissal "without prejudice" allows a new suit to be brought on the same cause of action.

witness—One who testifies to what he has seen, heard, or otherwise observed.

writ—An order issuing from a court of justice and requiring the performance of a specified act, or giving authority and commission to have it done.

writ of error coram nobis—(ko'ram no'bis) A common-law writ, the purpose of which is to correct a judgment in the same court in which it was rendered, on the ground of error of fact.

NAME INDEX

Accardo, Anthony, 125
Adonis, Joe, 125
Ahern, Frank, 474-475
Alexander the Great, 473
Alfred, King, 9
Ames, Fisher, 29
Ashworth, Ray, 111
Augustus, John, 257-258
Austin, Stephen, 52

Baldwin, Lola, 81
Ballard, John, 26
Barnes, Harry E., 262, 270, 300
Barney, Harold, 489
Bass, Sam, 53
Bates, Sanford, 263
Beck, Robert N., 13
Bertillion, Alphonse, 68-69
Beccaria, Cesare, 176
Billings, William, 26
Bopp, William J., 138
Breihan, Carl, 56
Bristow, Allen, 129
Brockway, Zebulon, 271, 299-300
Brostron, Curtis, 159
Bruun, Geofrey, 6
Bugbee, James M., 36
Burger, Warren, 254-255, 339
Butler, Smedley, 103

Capone, Al, 96, 97, 107
Cavan, Ruth Shonle, 167
Chapman, George S., 64
Chapman, Samuel G., 206
Charlemagne, 9
Charles II, King, 22
Charmichael, Stokely, 142
Chesebrough, William, 17
Clarke, Christopher, 26
Clark, Tom C., 255
Clinard, Marshall, 120
Coffey, Alan, 81
Coleman, Walter, 70

Coleman, William T., 50
Colquhoun, Patrick, 23, 29, 30, 83
Comstock, Anthony, 330
Coolidge, Calvin, 75-76
Costello, Augustine, 84
Costello, Frank, 125
Cotton, John, 13
Covell, Howard V., 119
Cressey, Donald, 173, 260, 275, 299
Current, Richard, 27, 59, 113
Curtis, Edwin U., 73-76

Dale, Thomas, 15
Davis, E.J., 45
Day, Frank D., 5, 30, 213
De Bore, Etienne, 28
De Reimer, Issac, 19
Diana, Lewis, 258
Dillinger, John, 114
Donovan, William, 474
Dressler, David, 262
Duryea, Charles, 78
Duryea, Frank, 78

Earle, Alice M., 21
Earp, Wyatt, 53, 54
Edward I, King, 10
Edward II, King, 10
Eldefonso, Edward, 81
Eliot, Samuel A., 36
Engles, Frederick, 176
Evers, Medgar, 139

Fayol, Henri, 360
Ferguson, Wallace K., 6
Fielding, Henry, 23, 29
Fisher, King, 53
Fishman, Joseph, 271-272
Floyd, Pretty Boy, 115
Foess, Claude, 75
Fosdick, Raymond, 35, 61, 84
Fouche, Henry, 474
Frankfurter, Felix, 100

573

SUBJECT INDEX

A

Acts
  Judiciary Act of 1789, 27
  Juvenile Delinquency Prevention and
  Control Act of 1968, 190-196
  Omnibus Crime Control and Safe
  Streets Act of 1968, 153-154
  Pendleton Act of 1883, 65-66
  Postal Act (1829), 27
  Volstead Act, 89-91
Administration, Police, 342-363
  bi-partisan administrative boards, 62
  communications, 362-363
  commission government plan, 62
  leadership, 343-347
    top managers, 344-345
    middle managers, 345-346
    first line supervisors, 346-347
  partisan administrative boards, 42-43
  processes of, 355-361
  single executive control, 62-63
  state control, 43-44, 60-61
  organization, 347-355
    principles, 347-350
    clarification, 350-355
      organization Charting, 350
      position Descriptions, 350-355
  policymaking, 361-362
American Civil Liberties Union, 80
American Federation of Labor, 73
American Revolution, 25-26
Anglo-Saxons, 7-9
  churl, prototype of yeoman farmer, 8
  tribal police system, 8
    combat, trial by, 8
    compurgation, trial by, 8
    ordeal, trial by, 8
Arizona Rangers, 78
Armed Robbery, see Crime
Athens, 6
Auto Theft, see Crime

B

Baltimore Police Department, 44
Berkeley Police Department, 58, 84,
87-88, 104, 110, 115
Bilboes, 20-21
Black Panthers, 142-143
Border Patrol, 215-216, 393-395
Boston Police Department, 17-18, 26,
27, 32, 36-38, 64, 73-76, 138
  bill creating a day force, 36
  Broad Street Riot, 36
  harbor police, 37
  inspectors of police, 26
  police strike of 1919, 73-76
  town watch, 17-18, 37
"Bowery Boys", see Gangs
Bow Street Runners and Patrol, 23, 29
Bureau of Internal Revenue, 94

C

Cadets, 112, 322-324
California Highway Patrol, 129, 445
"Canvas Town", 26
Carnegie Steel Strike, 72
Charlemagne, capitularies of, 9
Chicago Police Department, 44, 66-67,
71, 72, 81, 96-97, 103, 138
Cincinnati, 28, 42, 63, 85, 105, 109-110,
115, 159, 491-493
Civil disobedience, see Crime
Civil War, American
  affect on policing, 37, 41
  draft riots, 37, 45-46
  military police, 44
Cleveland, 44, 100
Coast Guard, 94
Colorado Rangers, 78
Commissions